All Tomorrow's Parties

The Velvet Underground Story

Koren Shadmi

Life Drawn
by Humanoids

Koren Shadmi
Writer & Artist

Jake Thomas
Editor

AndWorld Design
Letterer

Sandy Tanaka
Senior Designer

Jerry Frissen
Senior Art Director

Fabrice Giger
Publisher

Esther Kim - Marketing Director
Holly Aitchison - Sales Director
Amanda Lucido - Operations Director

Rights and Licensing
licensing@humanoids.com

Press and Social Media
pr@humanoids.com

Sales
sales@humanoids.com

ALL TOMORROW'S PARTIES: THE VELVET UNDERGROUND STORY. First Printing, 2023. This book is a publication of Humanoids, Inc. 8033 Sunset Blvd. #628, Los Angeles, CA 90046.

Library of Congress Control Number:
2023935623

Life Drawn is an imprint of Humanoids, Inc.

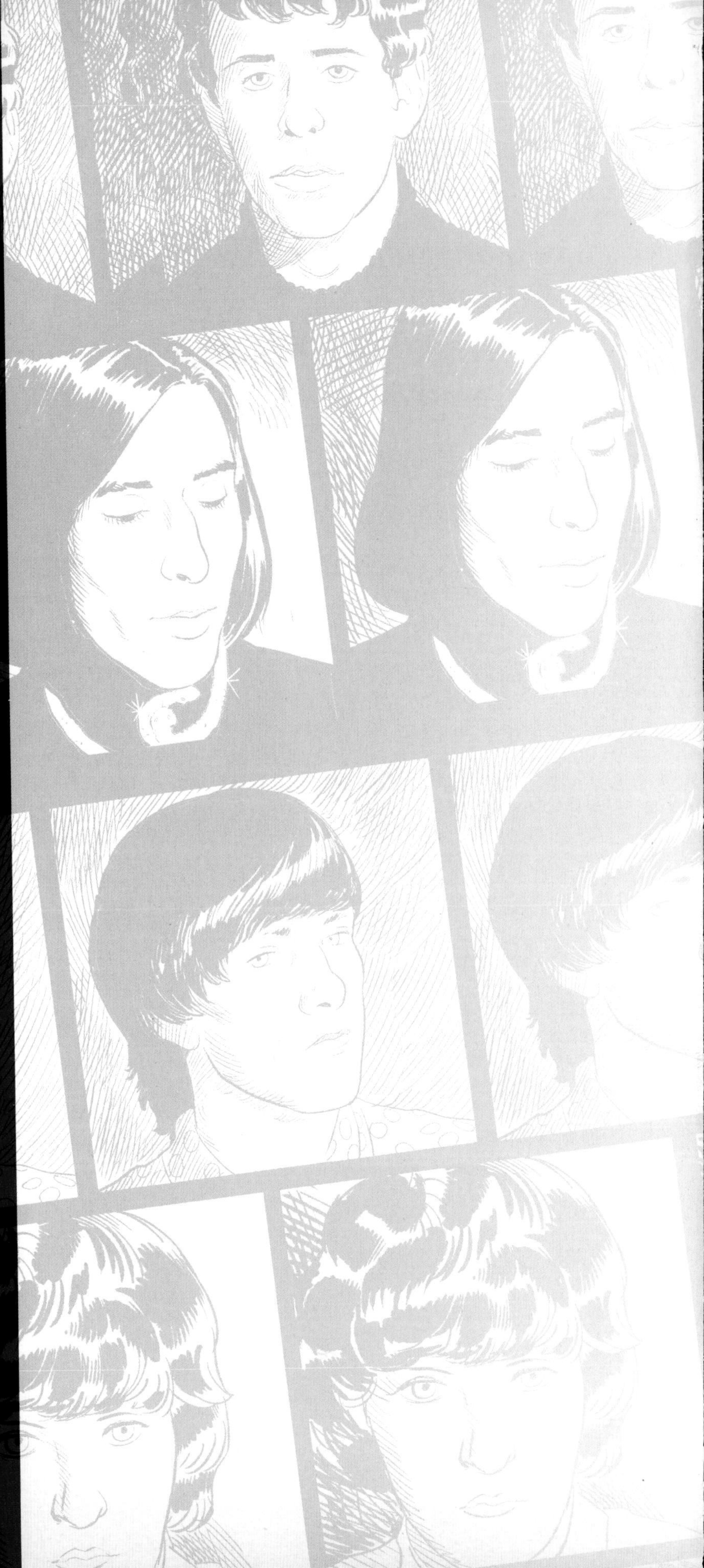

NOTES ON THE UNDERGROUND
By Jon King

1970. Boring commuter town in Kent. I'm 15.

A friend is playing me an LP he's filched from his dad, a music & film reviewer for a Sunday paper who thinks the record is shite.

The sleeve art's by Andy Warhol, a peel off banana skin, super cool. *The Velvet Underground and Nico*.

The needle drops and I'm blown away. Dissonance, angst, poisonous lyrics from a dark, chthonic reality. I'd discovered American music and gorged on *Highway 61 Revisited* & *Blonde on Blonde*, *The Band*, *Electric Ladyland*, MC5, Motown, and James Brown, but this music is awesome. New York tales that reek of reality: a junkie's *Seven Brides for Seven Brothers*; a love letter to Chinese rocks; and a disengaged chanteuse force-marched through hymns to a pointless spectacle, her voice as flat as a kipper's dick; the plinky pop of "Sunday Morning;" a hymn to anomie… It's beautiful, inspiring the teenage me, two thousand miles away, with its outsider ambition, truth, and not giving a fuckery. I long-term borrow/steal the vinyl from my mate, listening to it over & over, writing out the lyrics, as I do with every record I love, my notebooks filled with words from an elsewhere.

1971. *Andy Warhol's Velvet Underground featuring Nico* drops in the UK, a double album sampler of the band's first 3 albums. I hear "Sister Ray" for the first time, an unimprovable 17-minute racket that twirls and swirls and growls from a shardlike amped up vamp to a tsunami of noise grinding under Reed's deadpan narrative about a louche demimonde that had blossomed under the threat of nuclear Armageddon, far-right repression, and social collapse. I play it as loud as my mono deck can bear. John Cale's conservatoire genius sparkles and his aggressive one-two with Reed thrills, two heavyweights fighting for a TKO. It's as good as music gets where the marketplace isn't front-of-mind. I think on this track, 5 years on, when writing the words to "Anthrax."

1972. *Live At Max's Kansas City* fills my sky. A brilliant recording from a disordered, thrilling milieu a kid from a dull English town can only fantasize about. By the time I get to go to the US at 18, in '73, the Velvet Underground is toast. I never see them play.

But years later, I meet Lou, or rather am stood tongue-tied in the presence; and elsewhere bump into Nico, a beautiful ruin crashing at our manager's flat; best of all, I'm asked to sing a couple of Nico tunes, "Mutterlein" & "Fearfully in Danger" (in German!), with John Cale and his band at Wrozlaw's Capitol Theatre, one of John's tribute shows to Nico. *Ich habe genug.*

What Koren Shadmi has done in this book is take all the angst, hubris, ego, paranoia, and brilliance that made Reed and Cale create one of the greatest bands in rock history—and nearly kill each other in the process—and translated it beautifully onto paper. None of us can actually go back to New York in the late '60s and experience the Velvets in ascendance, but reading this book may be the next best thing.

No-one who loves outsider music can fail to fall for the Velvets, even at such distance. Their struggles are ours, their work a proof that integrity grows strong in failure. Their music still inspires. Listen again. Change the world.

Jonathan Michael King is an English musician, songwriter, and Grammy-nominated art director in the post-punk band Gang of Four.

NEW YORK

1987

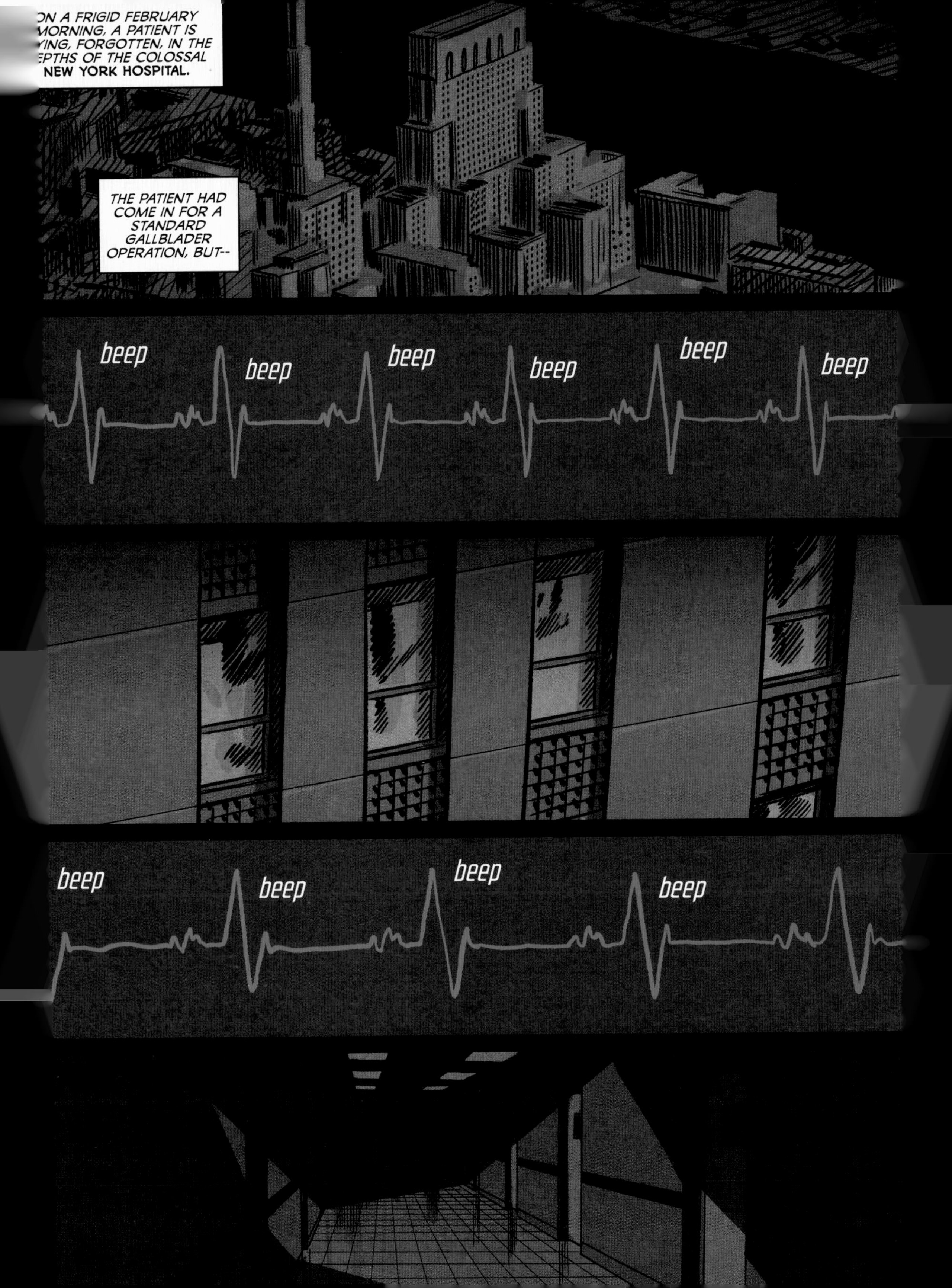
ON A FRIGID FEBRUARY MORNING, A PATIENT IS YING, FORGOTTEN, IN THE EPTHS OF THE COLOSSAL NEW YORK HOSPITAL.
THE PATIENT HAD COME IN FOR A STANDARD GALLBLADER OPERATION, BUT--
beep
beep
beep
beep
beep
beep
beep
beep
beep
beep

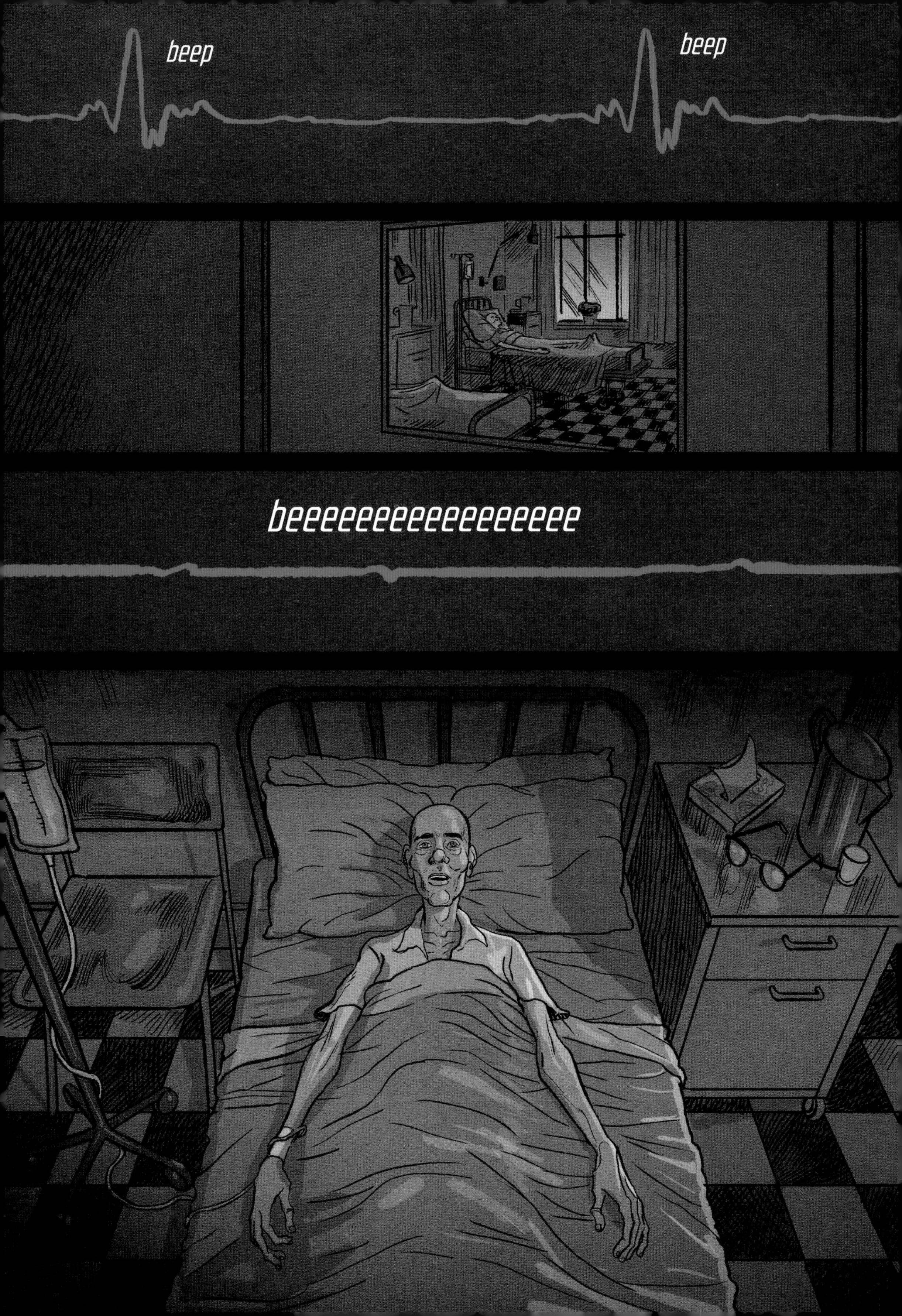
beep
beep
beeeeeeeeeeeeeeeeee

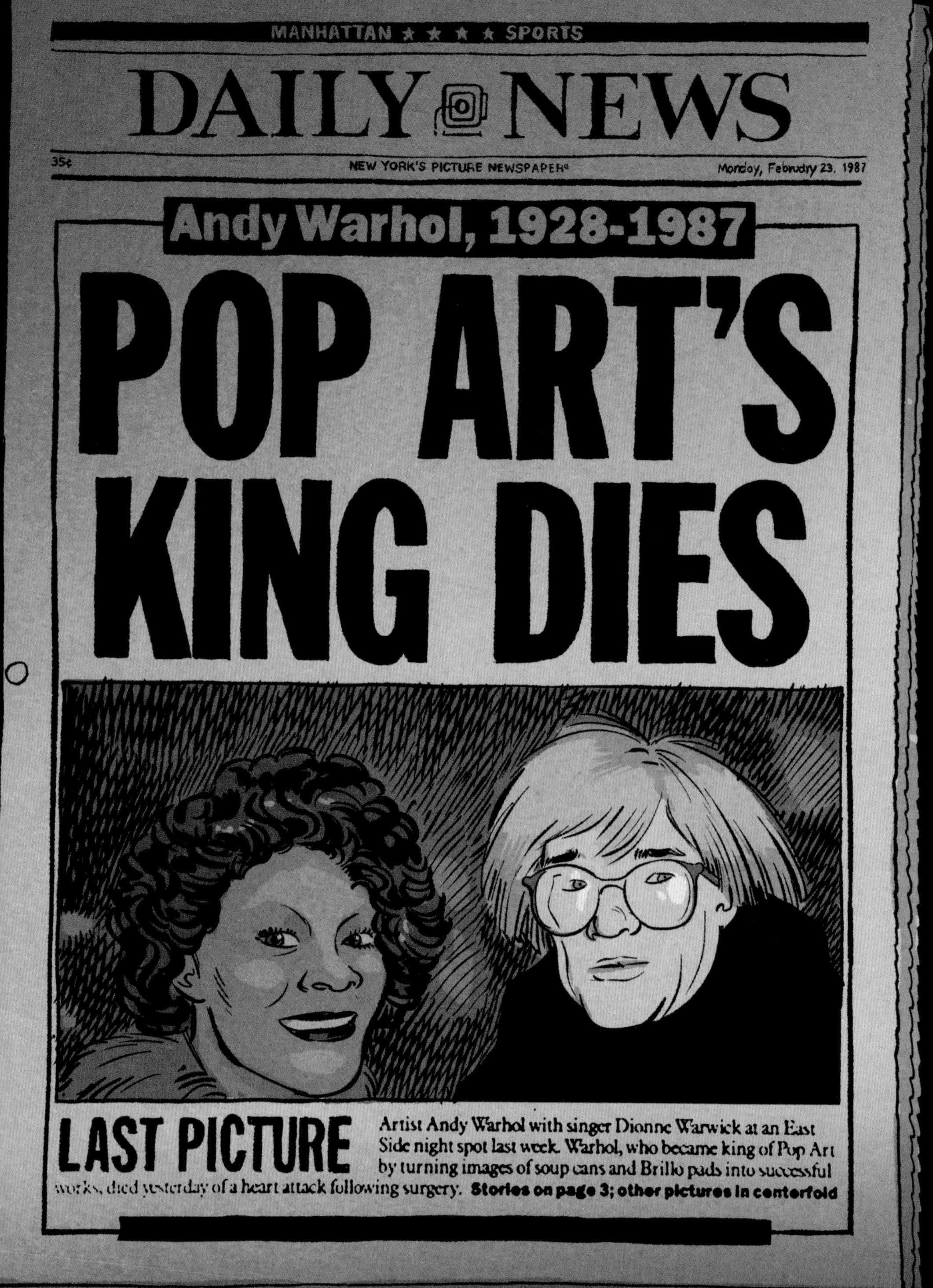
MANHATTAN ★ ★ ★ ★ SPORTS

DAILY NEWS

35¢ NEW YORK'S PICTURE NEWSPAPER® Monday, February 23, 1987

Andy Warhol, 1928-1987

POP ART'S KING DIES

LAST PICTURE Artist Andy Warhol with singer Dionne Warwick at an East Side night spot last week. Warhol, who became king of Pop Art by turning images of soup cans and Brillo pads into successful works, died yesterday of a heart attack following surgery. **Stories on page 3; other pictures in centerfold**

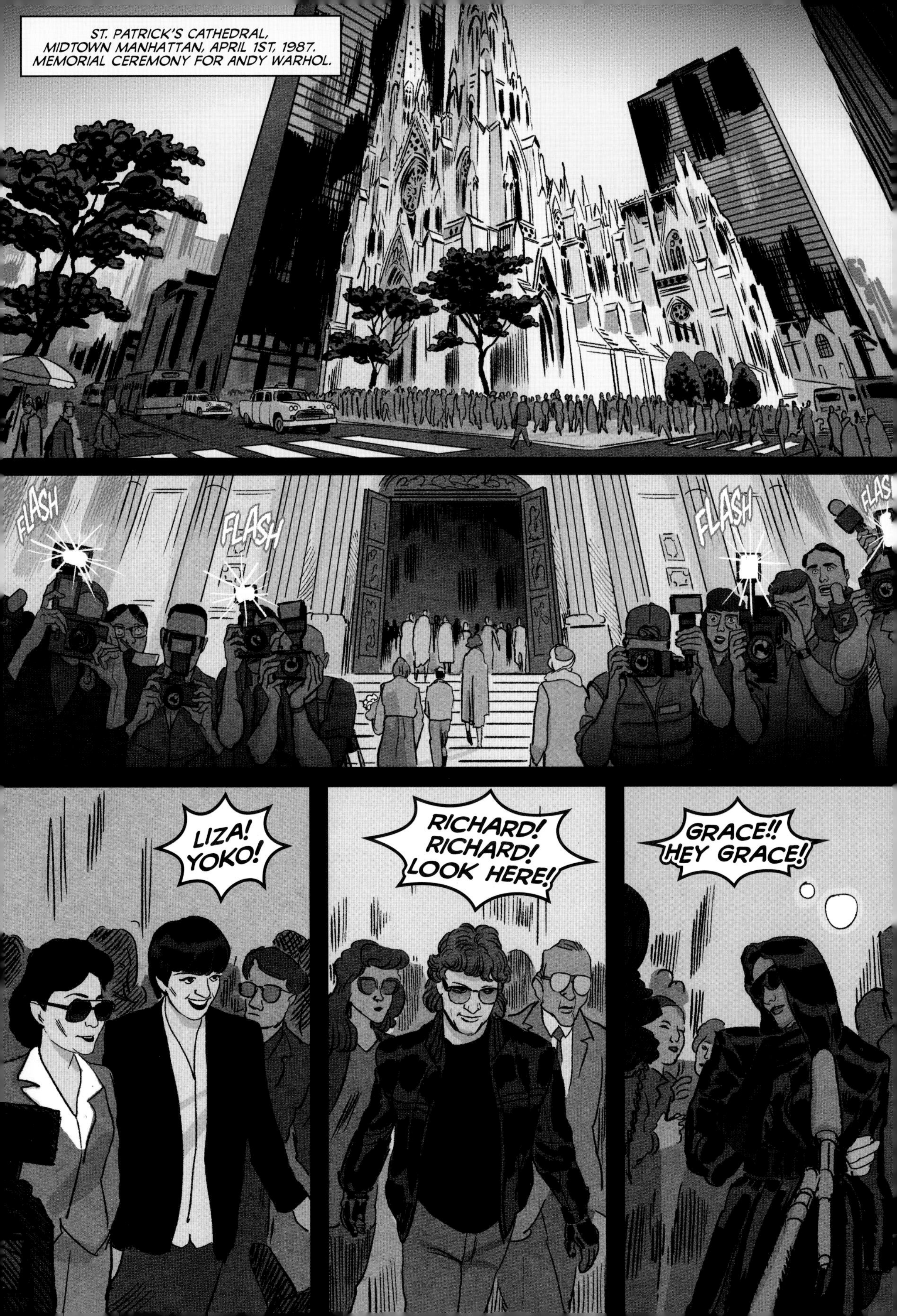
ST. PATRICK'S CATHEDRAL, MIDTOWN MANHATTAN, APRIL 1ST, 1987. MEMORIAL CEREMONY FOR ANDY WARHOL.
FLASH
FLASH
FLASH
FLASH
LIZA! YOKO!
RICHARD! RICHARD! LOOK HERE!
GRACE!! HEY GRACE!

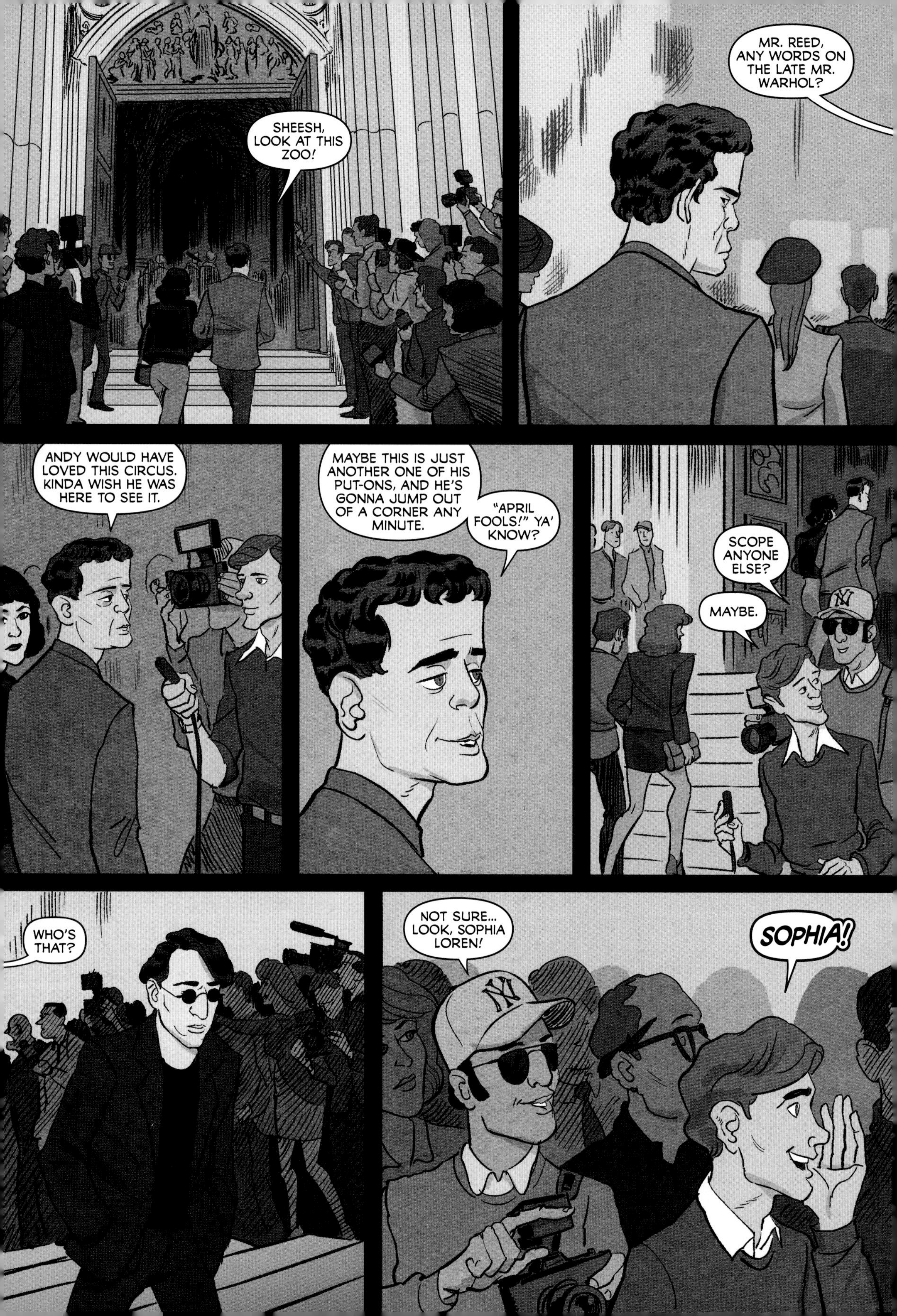
SHEESH, LOOK AT THIS ZOO!
MR. REED, ANY WORDS ON THE LATE MR. WARHOL?
ANDY WOULD HAVE LOVED THIS CIRCUS. KINDA WISH HE WAS HERE TO SEE IT.
MAYBE THIS IS JUST ANOTHER ONE OF HIS PUT-ONS, AND HE'S GONNA JUMP OUT OF A CORNER ANY MINUTE.
"APRIL FOOLS!" YA' KNOW?
SCOPE ANYONE ELSE?
MAYBE.
WHO'S THAT?
NOT SURE... LOOK, SOPHIA LOREN!
SOPHIA!

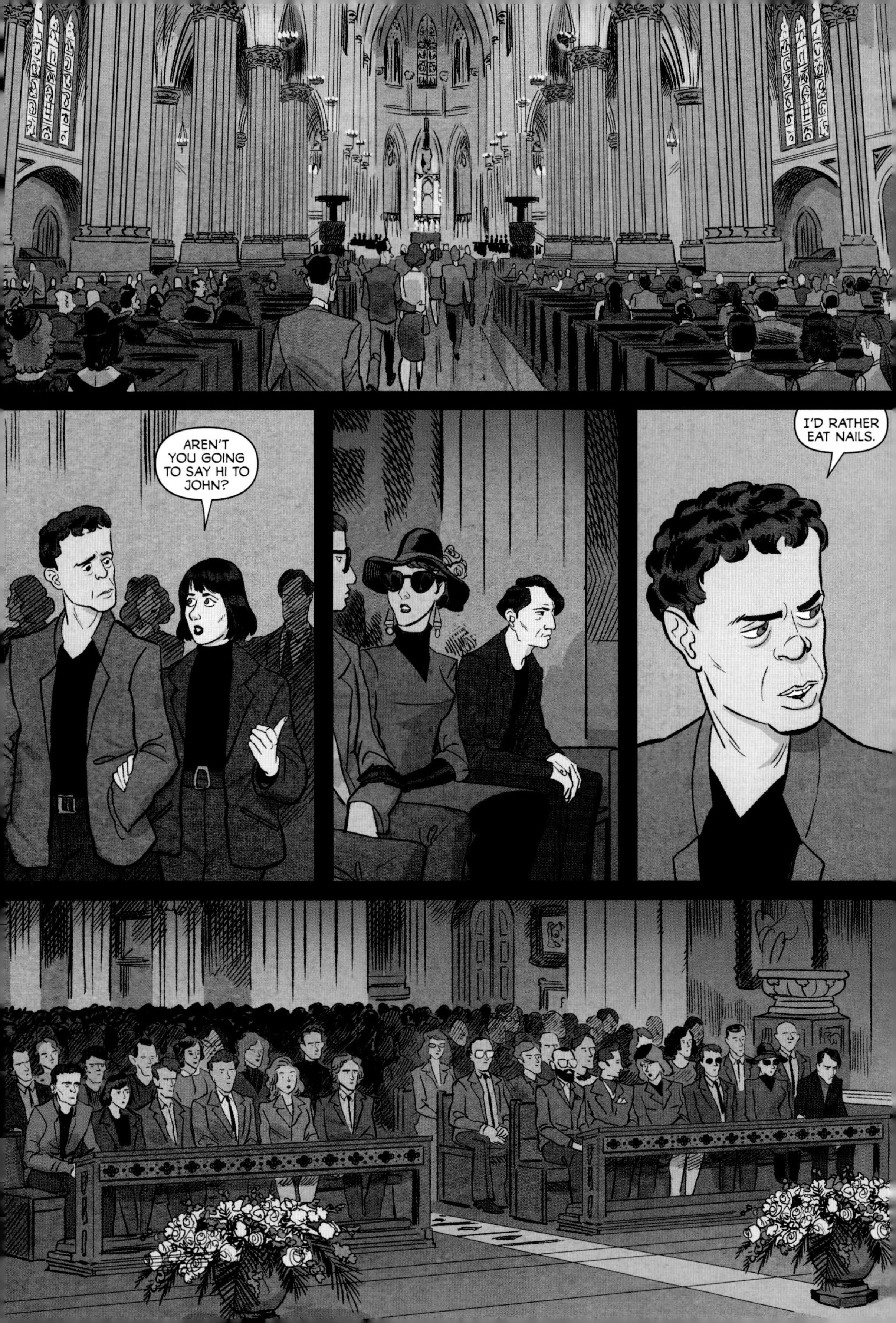
AREN'T YOU GOING TO SAY HI TO JOHN?
I'D RATHER EAT NAILS.

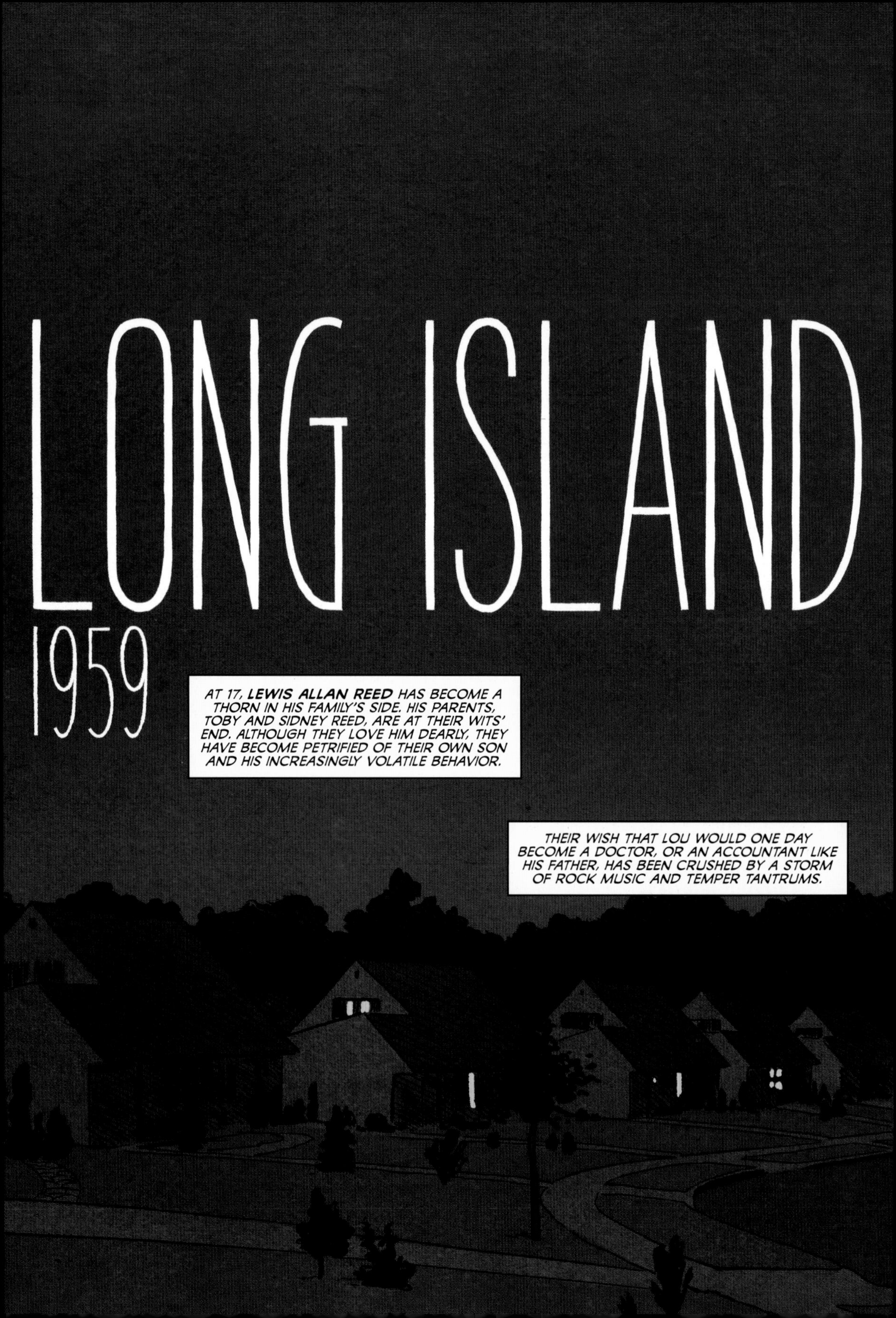
LONG ISLAND
1959
AT 17, LEWIS ALLAN REED HAS BECOME A THORN IN HIS FAMILY'S SIDE. HIS PARENTS, TOBY AND SIDNEY REED, ARE AT THEIR WITS' END. ALTHOUGH THEY LOVE HIM DEARLY, THEY HAVE BECOME PETRIFIED OF THEIR OWN SON AND HIS INCREASINGLY VOLATILE BEHAVIOR.
THEIR WISH THAT LOU WOULD ONE DAY BECOME A DOCTOR, OR AN ACCOUNTANT LIKE HIS FATHER, HAS BEEN CRUSHED BY A STORM OF ROCK MUSIC AND TEMPER TANTRUMS.

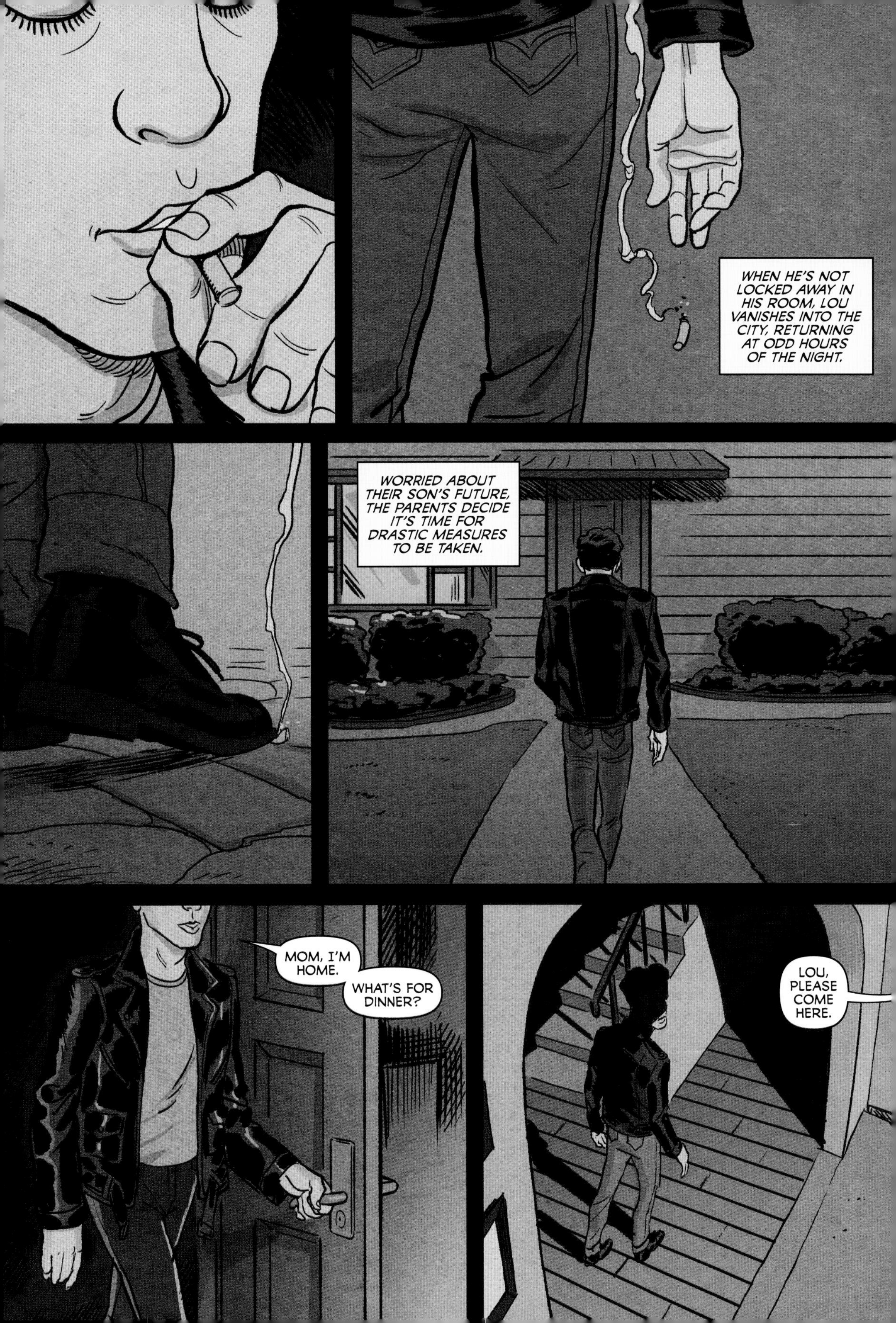
WHEN HE'S NOT LOCKED AWAY IN HIS ROOM, LOU VANISHES INTO THE CITY, RETURNING AT ODD HOURS OF THE NIGHT.
WORRIED ABOUT THEIR SON'S FUTURE, THE PARENTS DECIDE IT'S TIME FOR DRASTIC MEASURES TO BE TAKEN.
MOM, I'M HOME.
WHAT'S FOR DINNER?
LOU, PLEASE COME HERE.

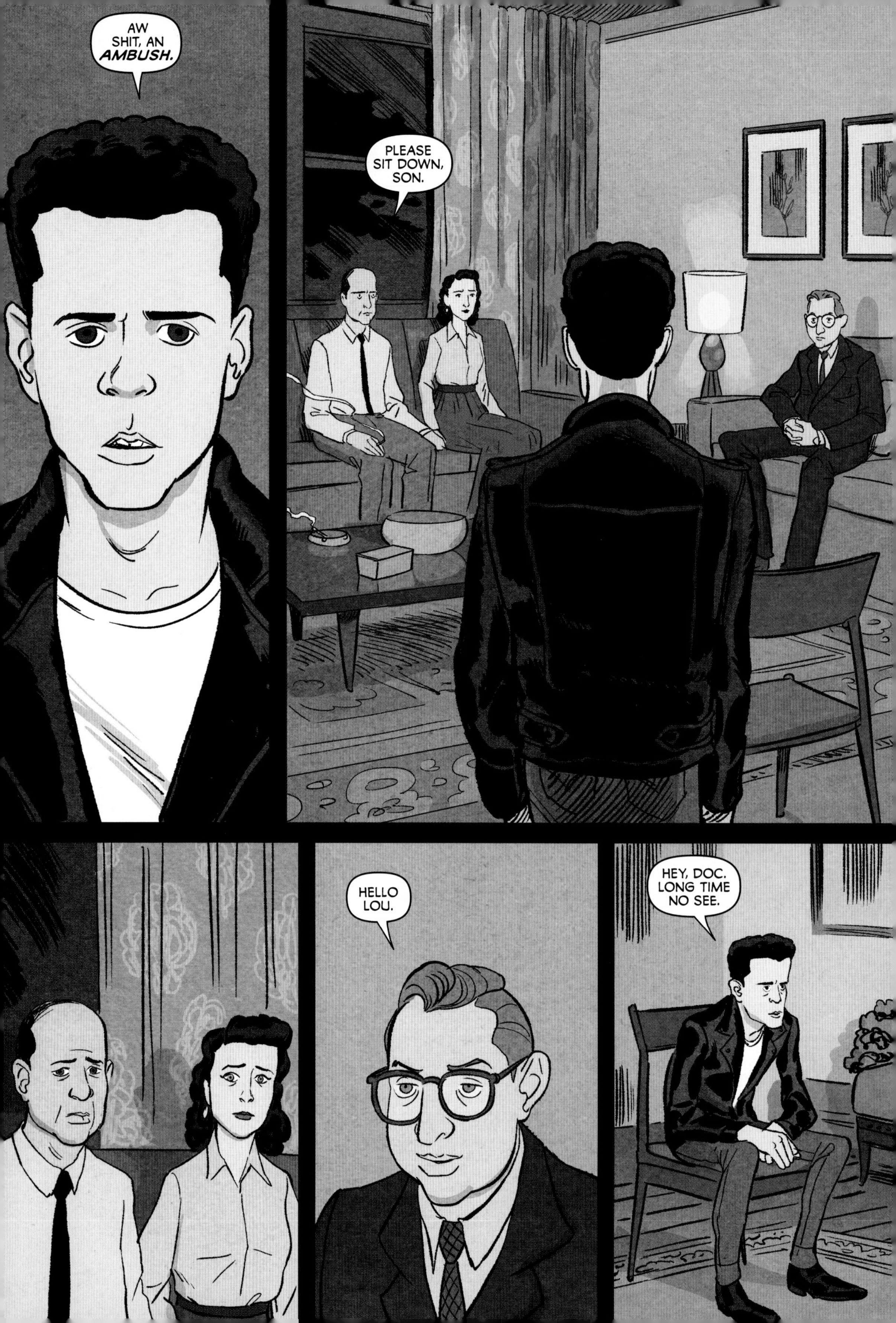
AW SHIT, AN *AMBUSH.*
PLEASE SIT DOWN, SON.
HELLO LOU.
HEY, DOC. LONG TIME NO SEE.

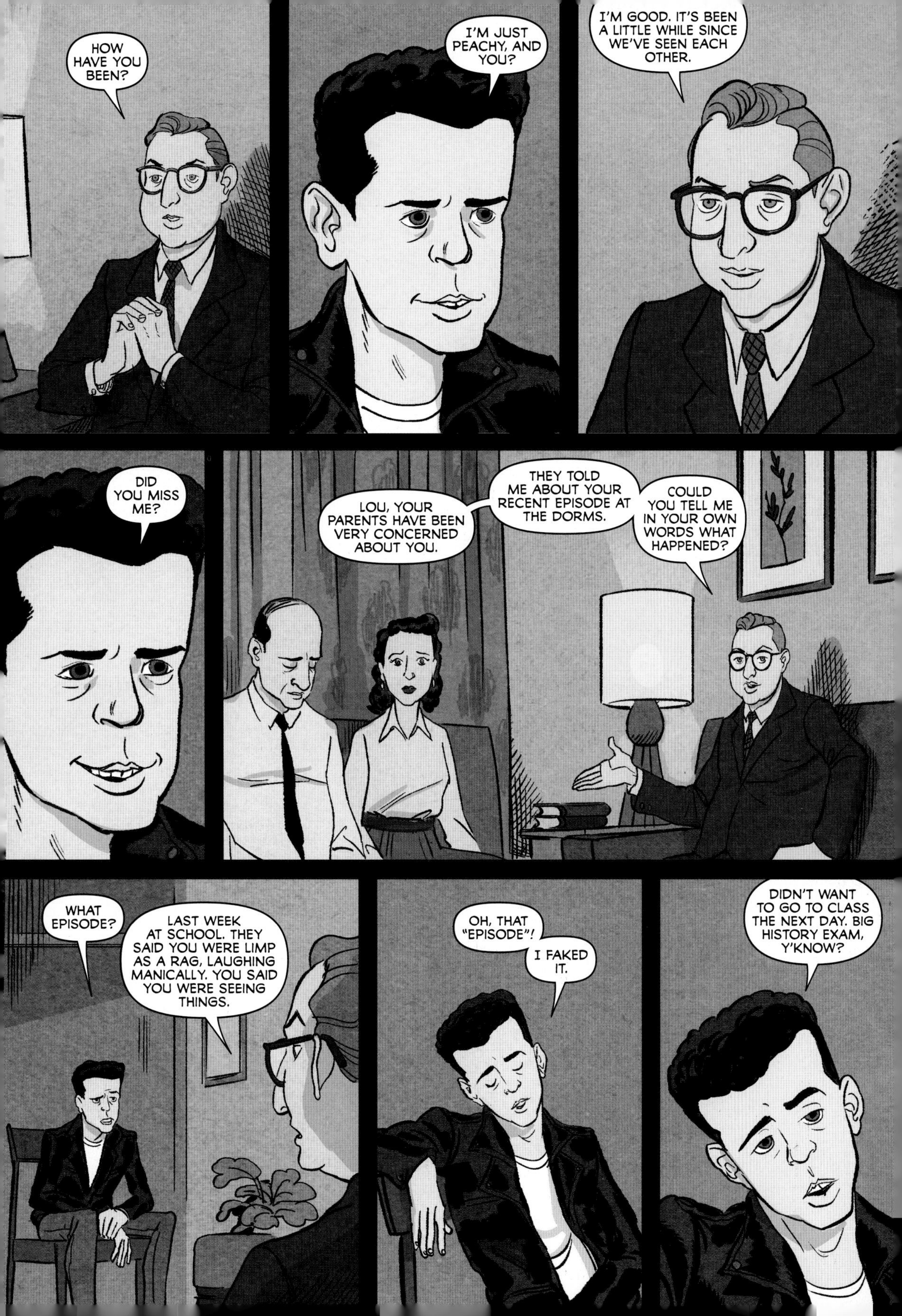
HOW HAVE YOU BEEN?
I'M JUST PEACHY, AND YOU?
I'M GOOD. IT'S BEEN A LITTLE WHILE SINCE WE'VE SEEN EACH OTHER.
DID YOU MISS ME?
LOU, YOUR PARENTS HAVE BEEN VERY CONCERNED ABOUT YOU.
THEY TOLD ME ABOUT YOUR RECENT EPISODE AT THE DORMS.
COULD YOU TELL ME IN YOUR OWN WORDS WHAT HAPPENED?
WHAT EPISODE?
LAST WEEK AT SCHOOL. THEY SAID YOU WERE LIMP AS A RAG, LAUGHING MANICALLY. YOU SAID YOU WERE SEEING THINGS.
OH, THAT "EPISODE"!
I FAKED IT.
DIDN'T WANT TO GO TO CLASS THE NEXT DAY. BIG HISTORY EXAM, Y'KNOW?

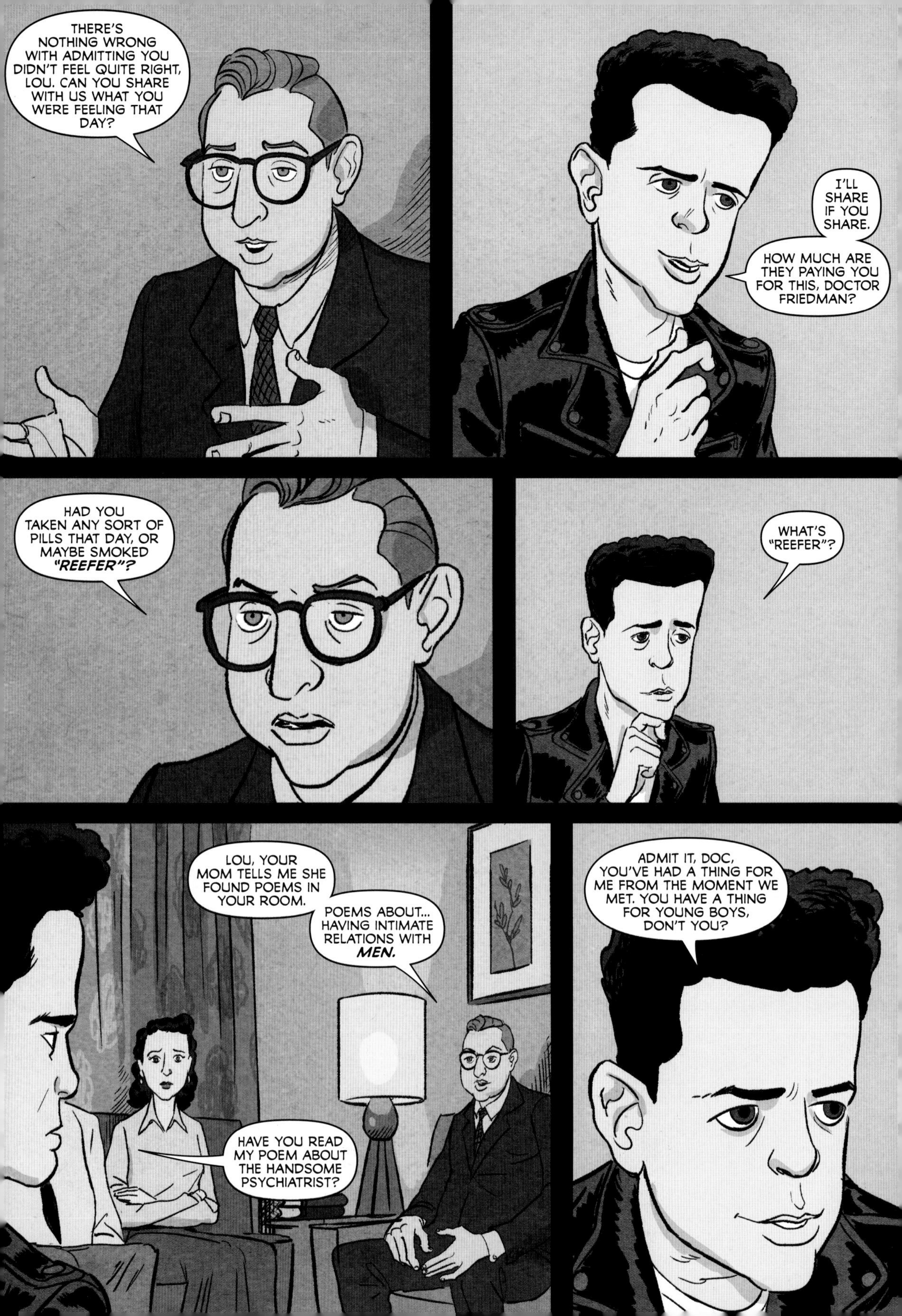
THERE'S NOTHING WRONG WITH ADMITTING YOU DIDN'T FEEL QUITE RIGHT, LOU. CAN YOU SHARE WITH US WHAT YOU WERE FEELING THAT DAY?
I'LL SHARE IF YOU SHARE.
HOW MUCH ARE THEY PAYING YOU FOR THIS, DOCTOR FRIEDMAN?
HAD YOU TAKEN ANY SORT OF PILLS THAT DAY, OR MAYBE SMOKED *"REEFER"?*
WHAT'S "REEFER"?
LOU, YOUR MOM TELLS ME SHE FOUND POEMS IN YOUR ROOM.
POEMS ABOUT... HAVING INTIMATE RELATIONS WITH *MEN.*
HAVE YOU READ MY POEM ABOUT THE HANDSOME PSYCHIATRIST?
ADMIT IT, DOC, YOU'VE HAD A THING FOR ME FROM THE MOMENT WE MET. YOU HAVE A THING FOR YOUNG BOYS, DON'T YOU?

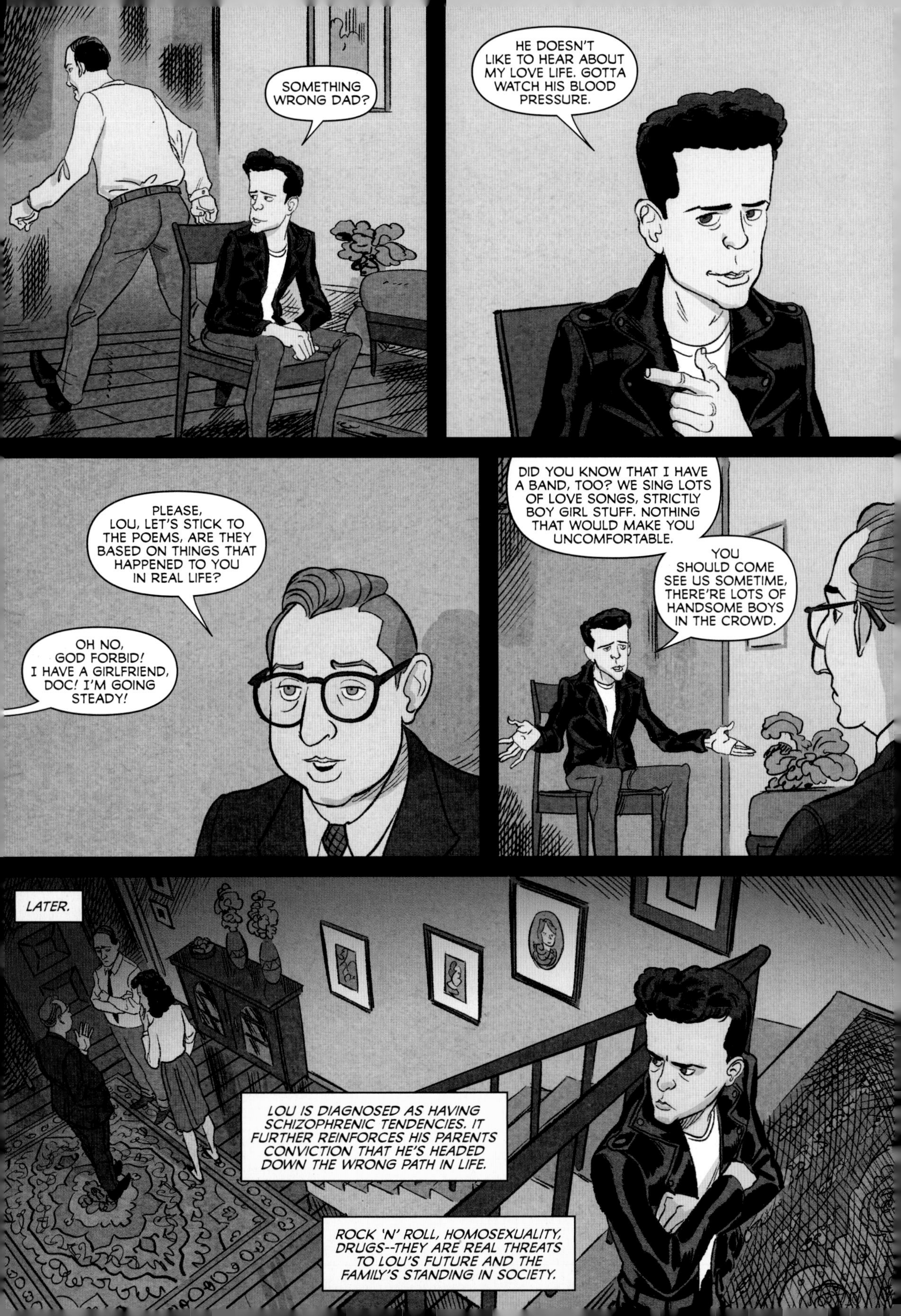
SOMETHING WRONG DAD?
HE DOESN'T LIKE TO HEAR ABOUT MY LOVE LIFE. GOTTA WATCH HIS BLOOD PRESSURE.
PLEASE, LOU, LET'S STICK TO THE POEMS, ARE THEY BASED ON THINGS THAT HAPPENED TO YOU IN REAL LIFE?
OH NO, GOD FORBID! I HAVE A GIRLFRIEND, DOC! I'M GOING STEADY!
DID YOU KNOW THAT I HAVE A BAND, TOO? WE SING LOTS OF LOVE SONGS, STRICTLY BOY GIRL STUFF. NOTHING THAT WOULD MAKE YOU UNCOMFORTABLE.
YOU SHOULD COME SEE US SOMETIME, THERE'RE LOTS OF HANDSOME BOYS IN THE CROWD.
LATER.
LOU IS DIAGNOSED AS HAVING SCHIZOPHRENIC TENDENCIES. IT FURTHER REINFORCES HIS PARENTS CONVICTION THAT HE'S HEADED DOWN THE WRONG PATH IN LIFE.
ROCK 'N' ROLL, HOMOSEXUALITY, DRUGS--THEY ARE REAL THREATS TO LOU'S FUTURE AND THE FAMILY'S STANDING IN SOCIETY.

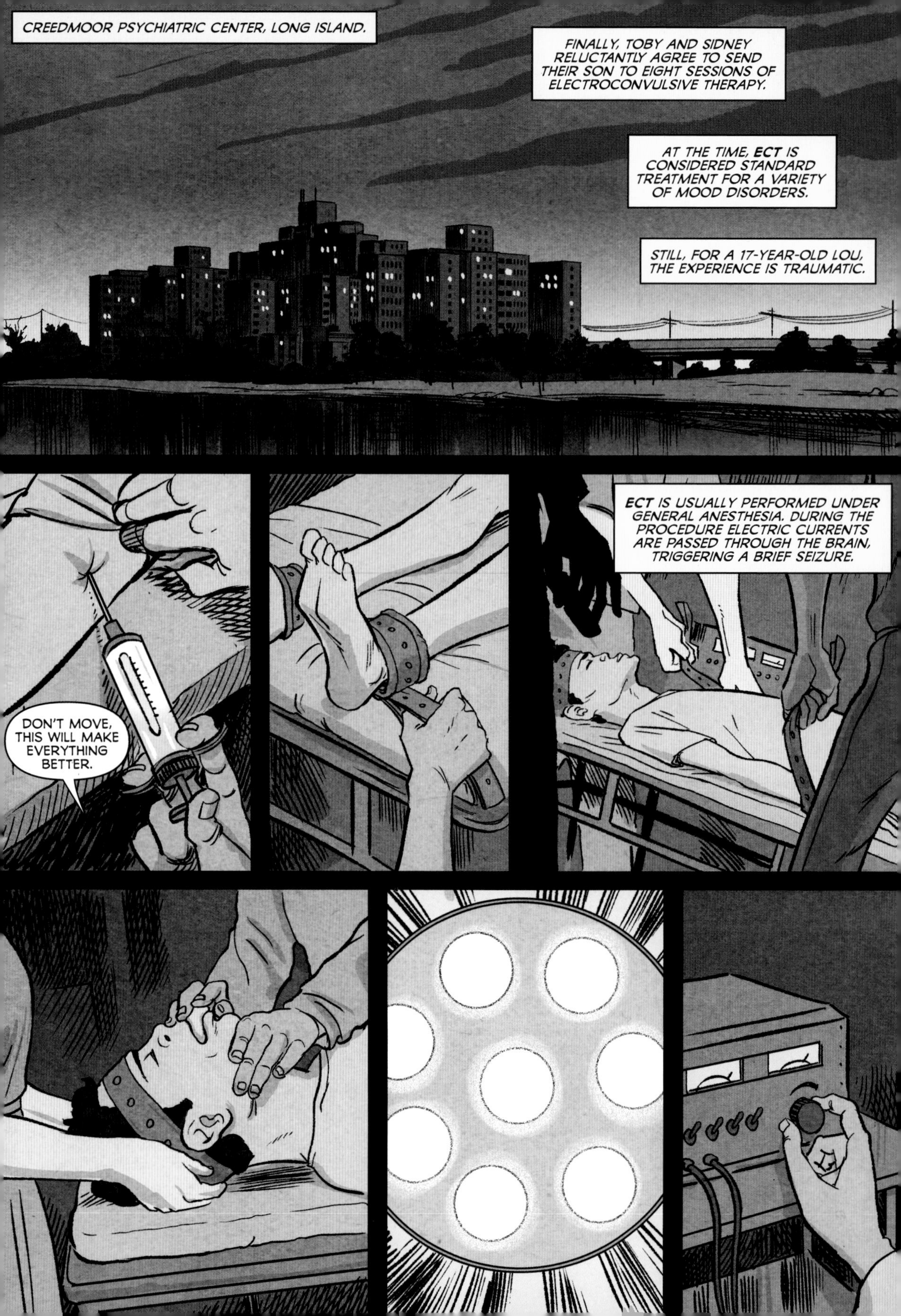
CREEDMOOR PSYCHIATRIC CENTER, LONG ISLAND.
FINALLY, TOBY AND SIDNEY RELUCTANTLY AGREE TO SEND THEIR SON TO EIGHT SESSIONS OF ELECTROCONVULSIVE THERAPY.
AT THE TIME, ECT IS CONSIDERED STANDARD TREATMENT FOR A VARIETY OF MOOD DISORDERS.
STILL, FOR A 17-YEAR-OLD LOU, THE EXPERIENCE IS TRAUMATIC.
DON'T MOVE, THIS WILL MAKE EVERYTHING BETTER.
ECT IS USUALLY PERFORMED UNDER GENERAL ANESTHESIA. DURING THE PROCEDURE ELECTRIC CURRENTS ARE PASSED THROUGH THE BRAIN, TRIGGERING A BRIEF SEIZURE.

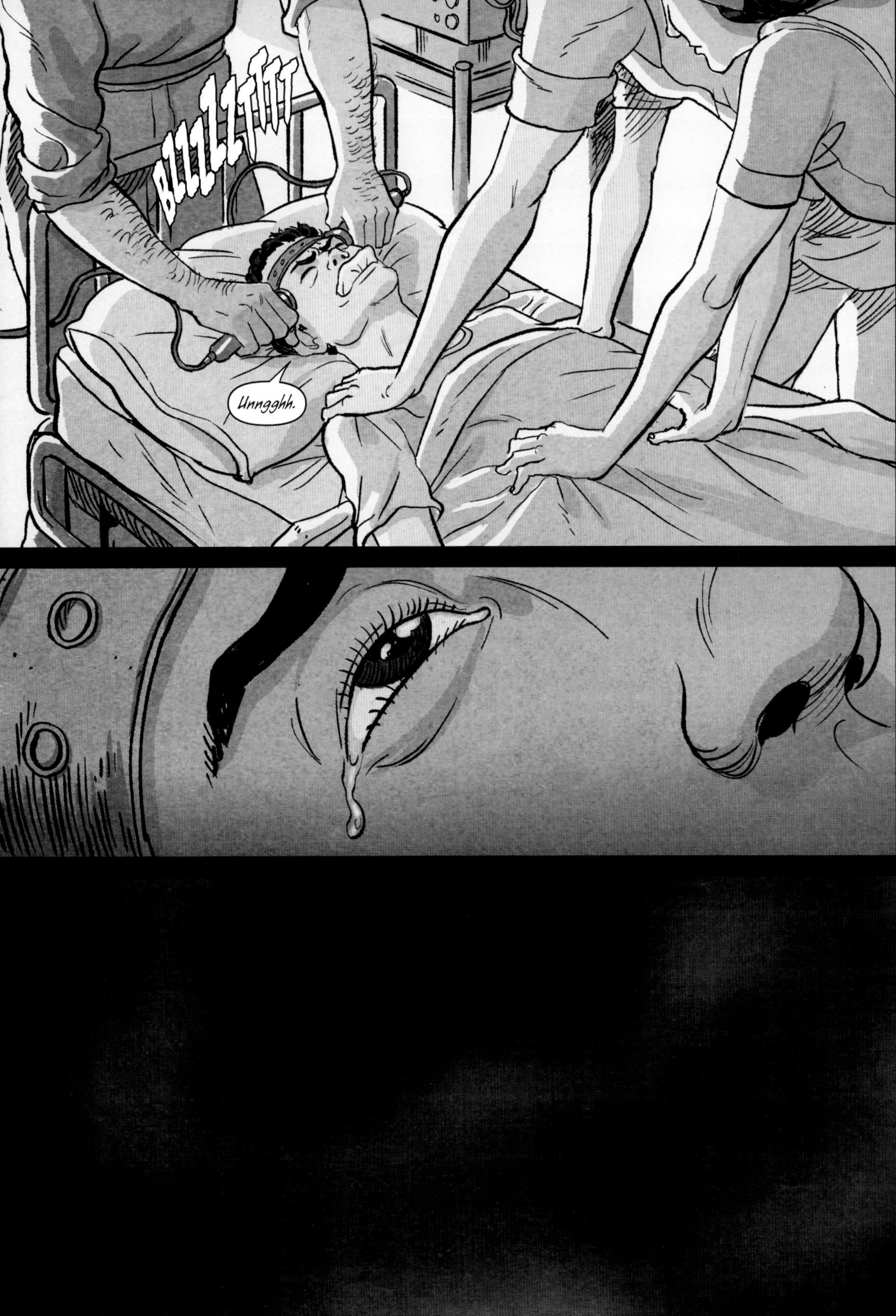
BZZZZZTTTT
Unngghh.

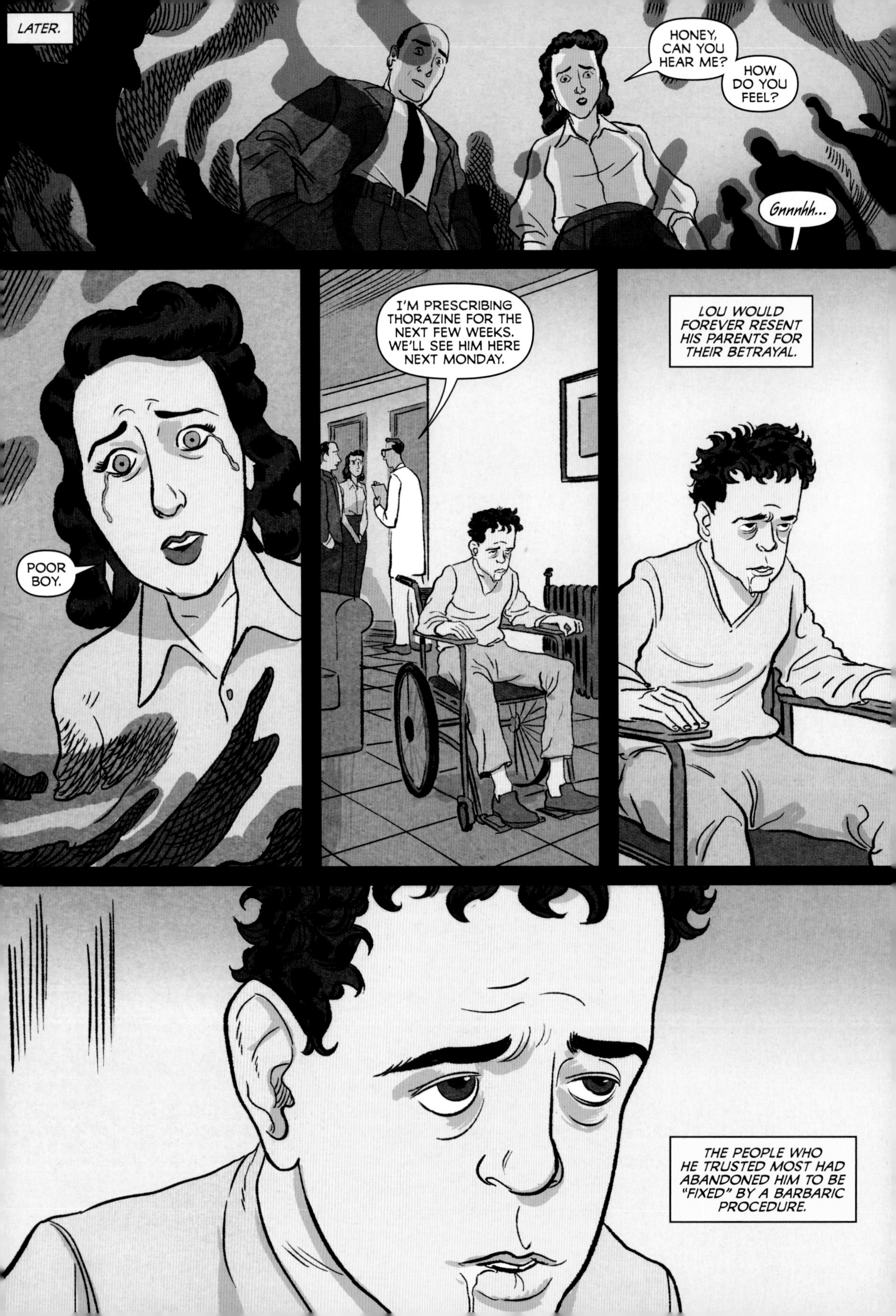
LATER.
HONEY, CAN YOU HEAR ME?
HOW DO YOU FEEL?
Gnnnhh...
POOR BOY.
I'M PRESCRIBING THORAZINE FOR THE NEXT FEW WEEKS. WE'LL SEE HIM HERE NEXT MONDAY.
LOU WOULD FOREVER RESENT HIS PARENTS FOR THEIR BETRAYAL.
THE PEOPLE WHO HE TRUSTED MOST HAD ABANDONED HIM TO BE "FIXED" BY A BARBARIC PROCEDURE.

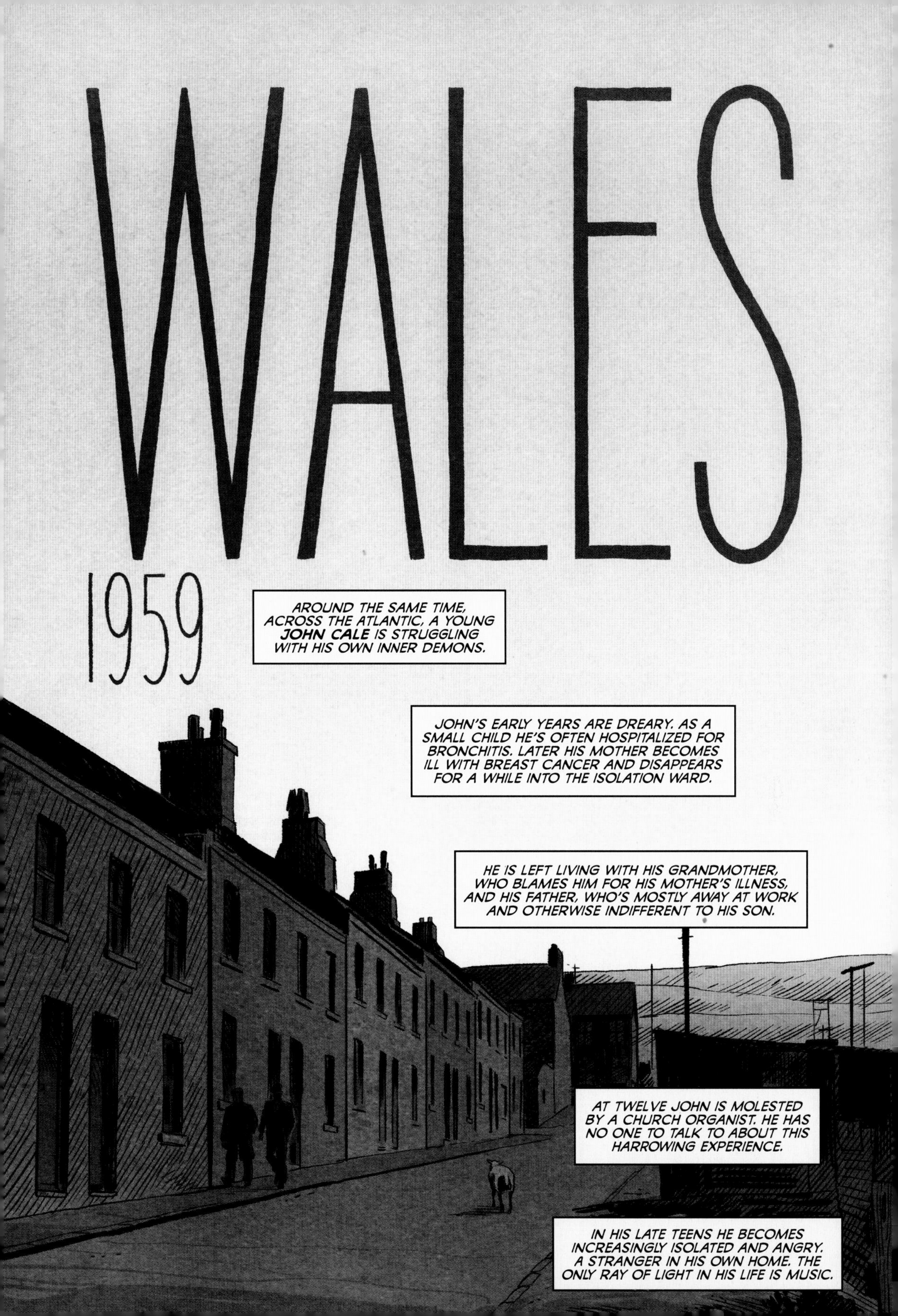
WALES
1959
AROUND THE SAME TIME, ACROSS THE ATLANTIC, A YOUNG JOHN CALE IS STRUGGLING WITH HIS OWN INNER DEMONS.
JOHN'S EARLY YEARS ARE DREARY. AS A SMALL CHILD HE'S OFTEN HOSPITALIZED FOR BRONCHITIS. LATER HIS MOTHER BECOMES ILL WITH BREAST CANCER AND DISAPPEARS FOR A WHILE INTO THE ISOLATION WARD.
HE IS LEFT LIVING WITH HIS GRANDMOTHER, WHO BLAMES HIM FOR HIS MOTHER'S ILLNESS, AND HIS FATHER, WHO'S MOSTLY AWAY AT WORK AND OTHERWISE INDIFFERENT TO HIS SON.
AT TWELVE JOHN IS MOLESTED BY A CHURCH ORGANIST. HE HAS NO ONE TO TALK TO ABOUT THIS HARROWING EXPERIENCE.
IN HIS LATE TEENS HE BECOMES INCREASINGLY ISOLATED AND ANGRY. A STRANGER IN HIS OWN HOME. THE ONLY RAY OF LIGHT IN HIS LIFE IS MUSIC.

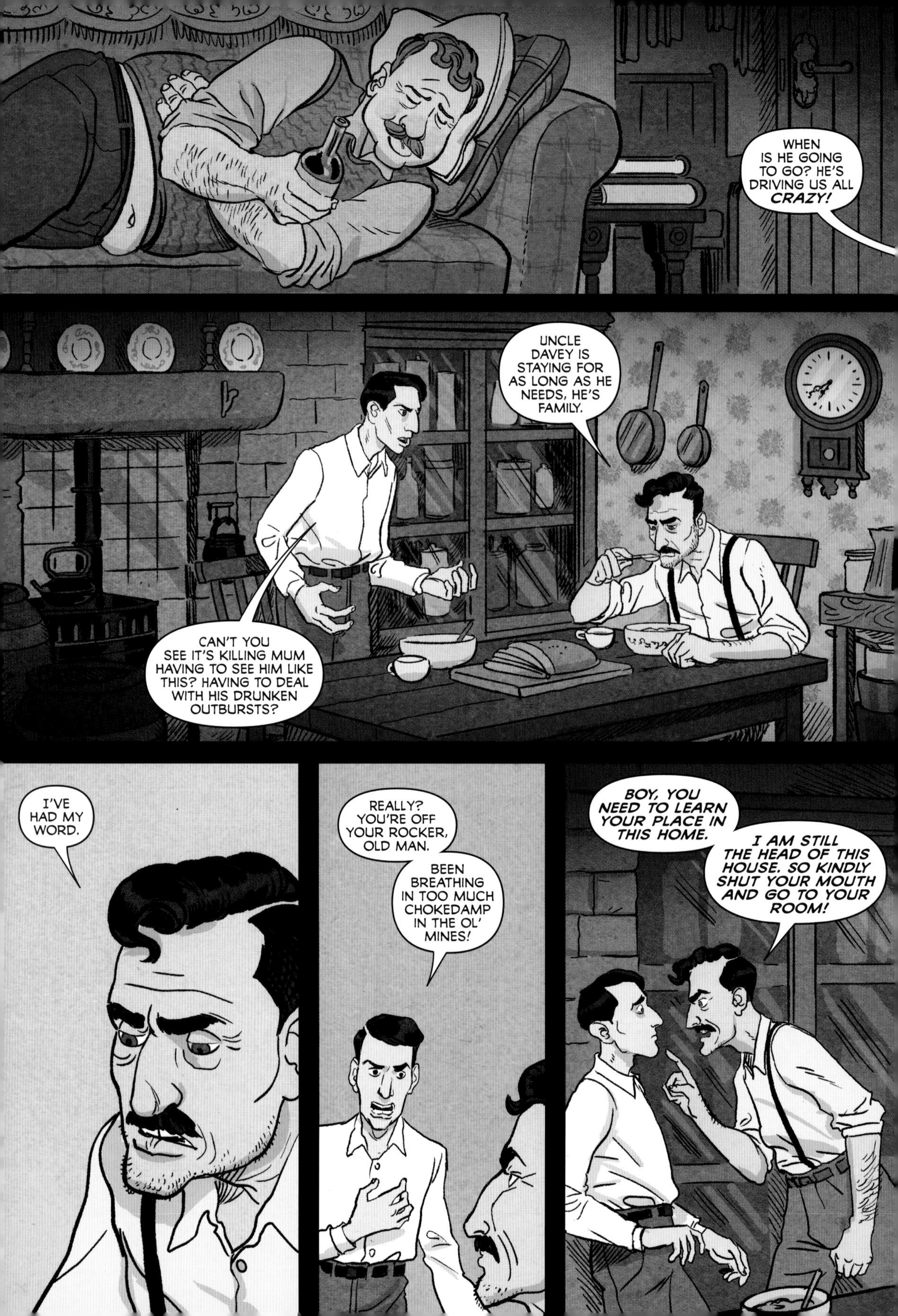
WHEN IS HE GOING TO GO? HE'S DRIVING US ALL *CRAZY!*
UNCLE DAVEY IS STAYING FOR AS LONG AS HE NEEDS, HE'S FAMILY.
CAN'T YOU SEE IT'S KILLING MUM HAVING TO SEE HIM LIKE THIS? HAVING TO DEAL WITH HIS DRUNKEN OUTBURSTS?
I'VE HAD MY WORD.
REALLY? YOU'RE OFF YOUR ROCKER, OLD MAN.
BEEN BREATHING IN TOO MUCH CHOKEDAMP IN THE OL' MINES!
BOY, YOU NEED TO LEARN YOUR PLACE IN THIS HOME.
I AM STILL THE HEAD OF THIS HOUSE. SO KINDLY SHUT YOUR MOUTH AND GO TO YOUR ROOM!

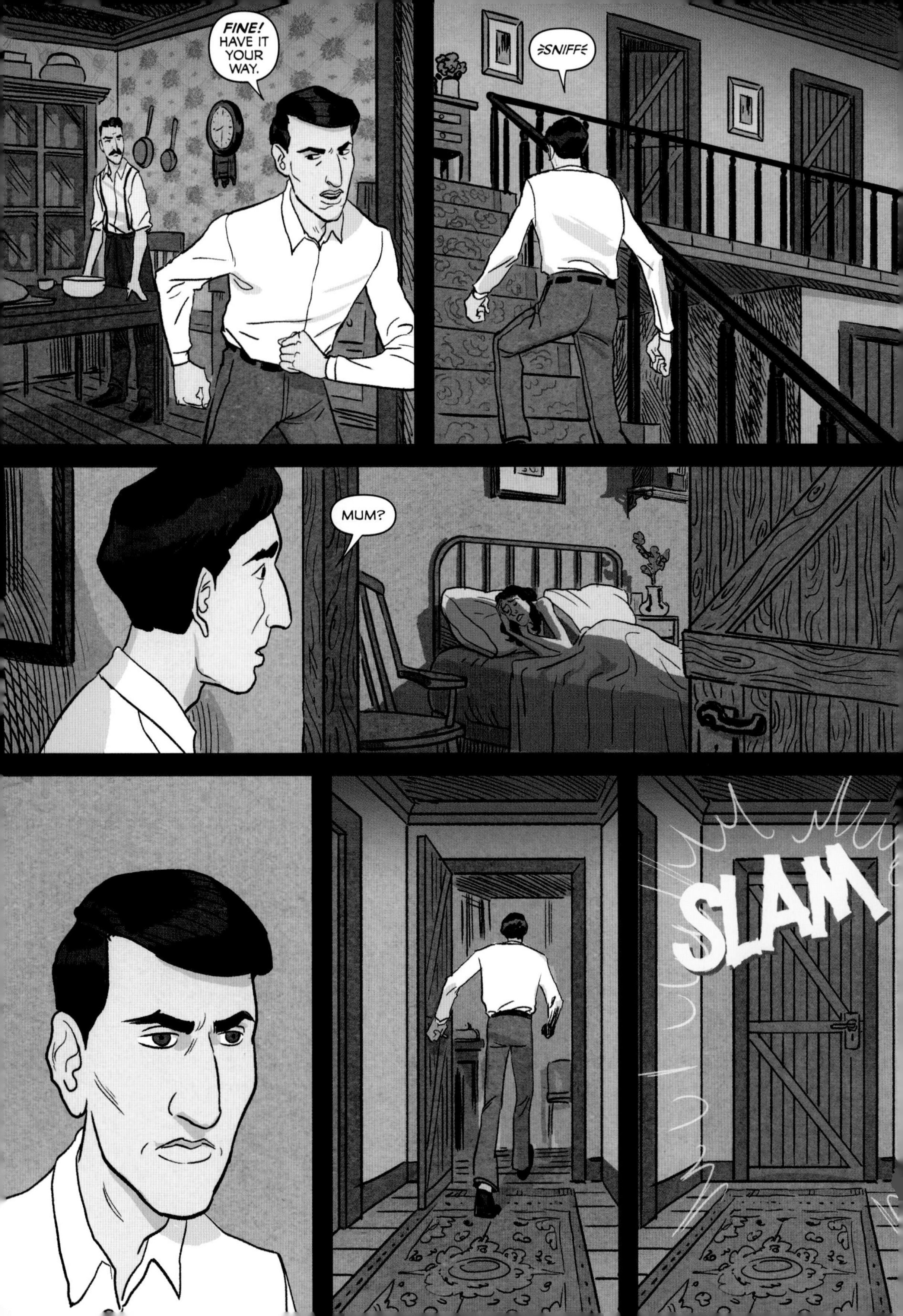
FINE! HAVE IT YOUR WAY.
SNIFF
MUM?
SLAM

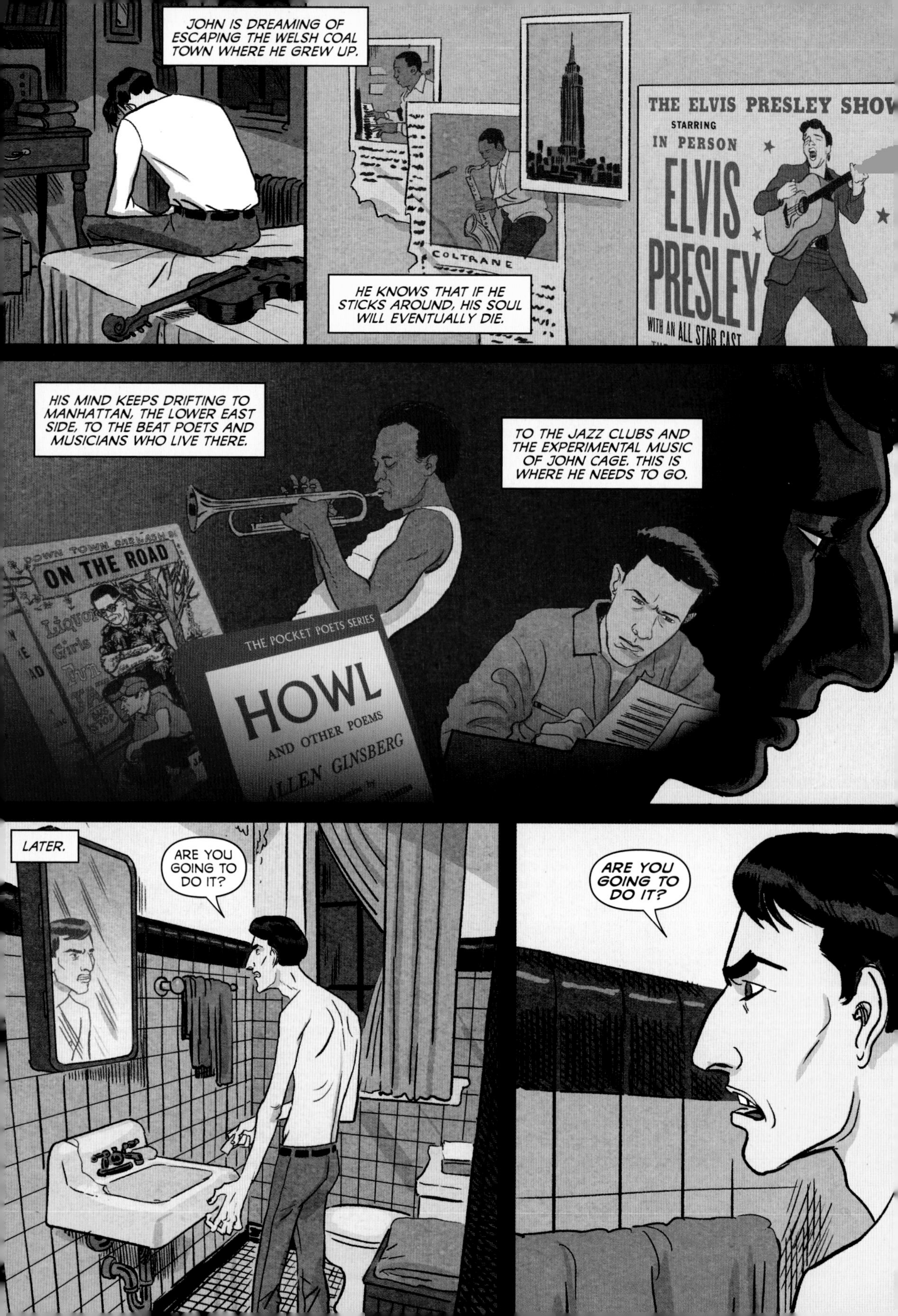
JOHN IS DREAMING OF ESCAPING THE WELSH COAL TOWN WHERE HE GREW UP.
COLTRANE
THE ELVIS PRESLEY SHOW
STARRING
IN PERSON
ELVIS PRESLEY
WITH AN ALL STAR CAST
HE KNOWS THAT IF HE STICKS AROUND, HIS SOUL WILL EVENTUALLY DIE.
HIS MIND KEEPS DRIFTING TO MANHATTAN, THE LOWER EAST SIDE, TO THE BEAT POETS AND MUSICIANS WHO LIVE THERE.
TO THE JAZZ CLUBS AND THE EXPERIMENTAL MUSIC OF JOHN CAGE. THIS IS WHERE HE NEEDS TO GO.
ON THE ROAD
THE POCKET POETS SERIES
HOWL
AND OTHER POEMS
ALLEN GINSBERG
LATER.
ARE YOU GOING TO DO IT?
ARE YOU GOING TO DO IT?

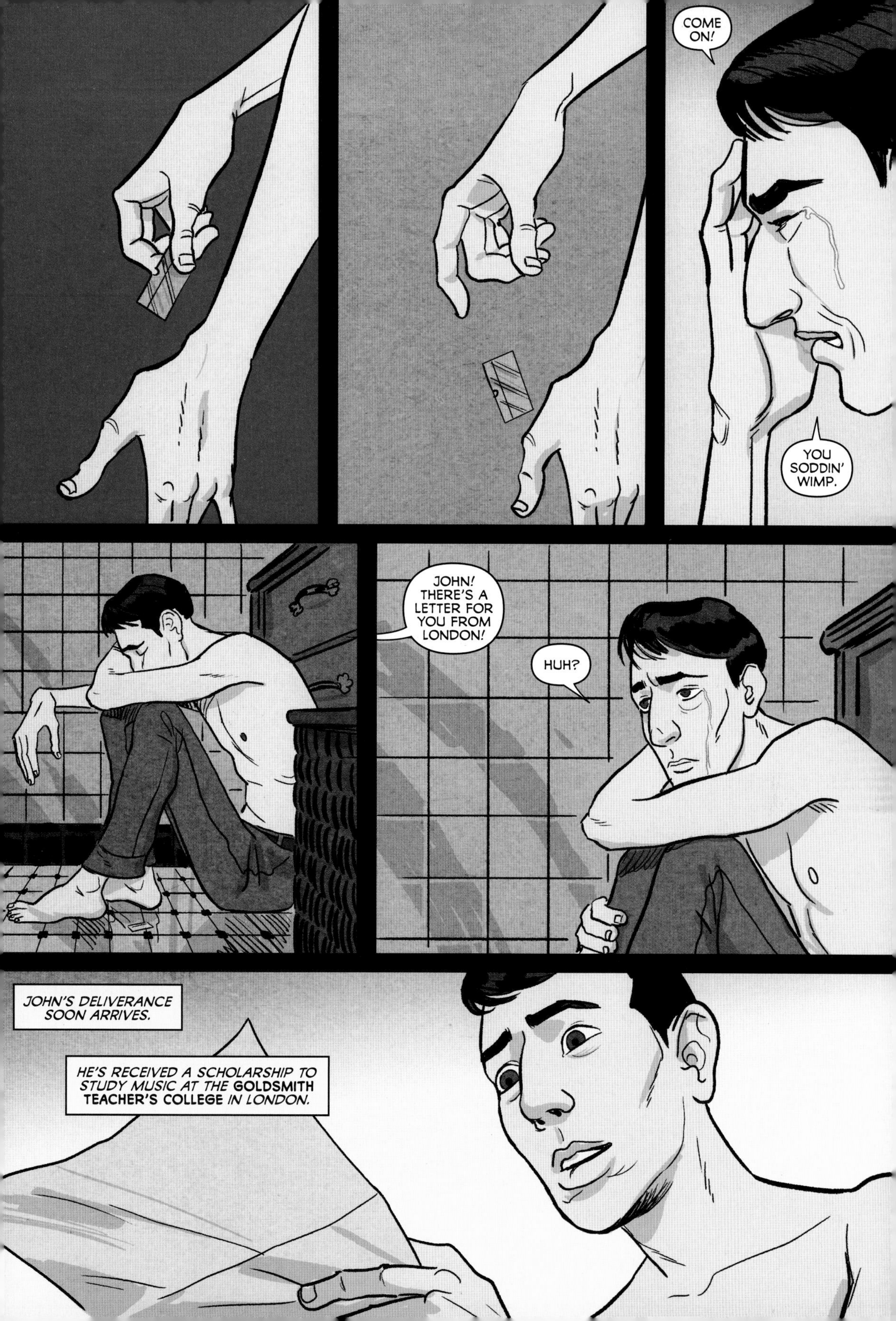
COME ON!
YOU SODDIN' WIMP.
JOHN! THERE'S A LETTER FOR YOU FROM LONDON!
HUH?
JOHN'S DELIVERANCE SOON ARRIVES.
HE'S RECEIVED A SCHOLARSHIP TO STUDY MUSIC AT THE GOLDSMITH TEACHER'S COLLEGE IN LONDON.

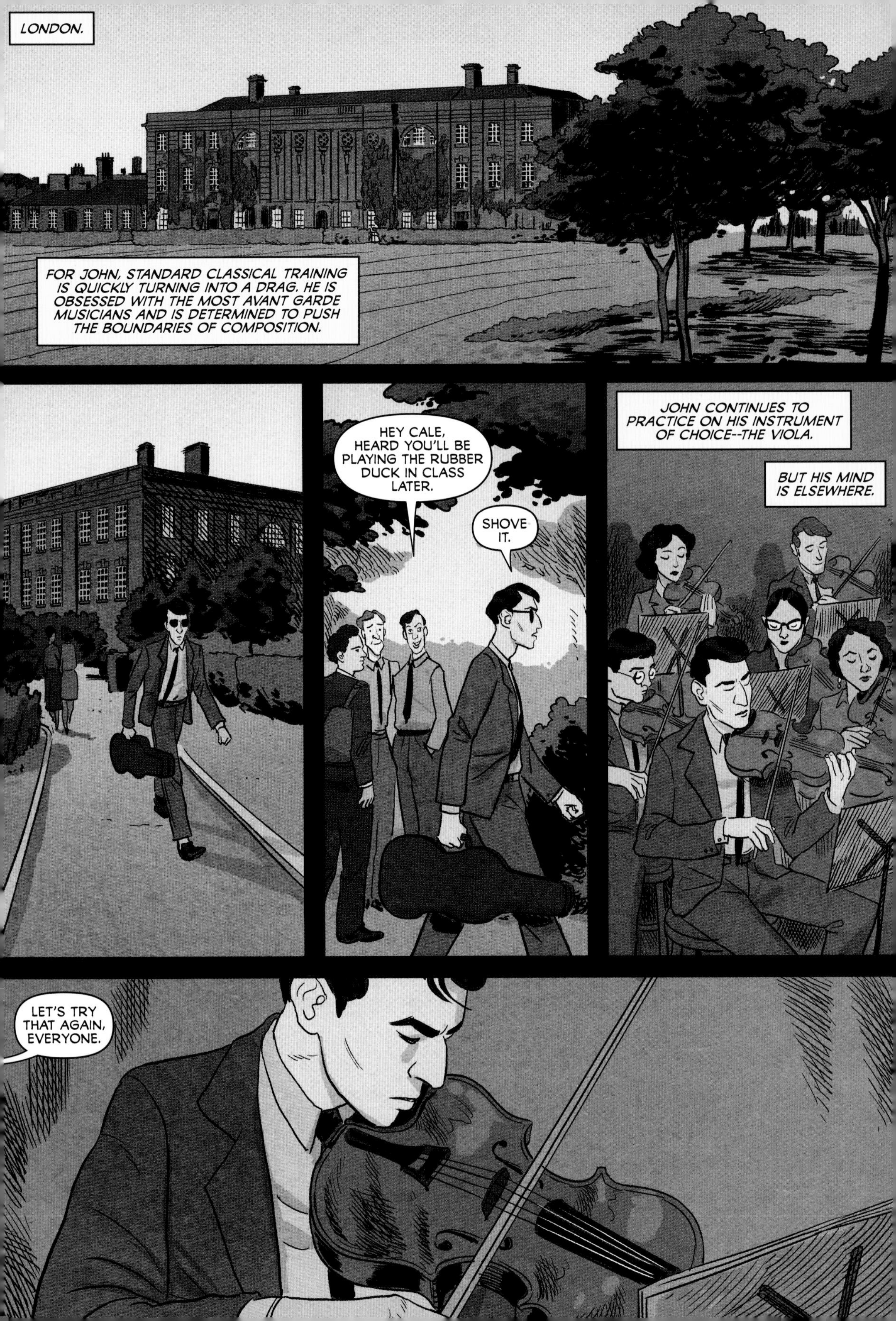
LONDON.
FOR JOHN, STANDARD CLASSICAL TRAINING IS QUICKLY TURNING INTO A DRAG. HE IS OBSESSED WITH THE MOST AVANT GARDE MUSICIANS AND IS DETERMINED TO PUSH THE BOUNDARIES OF COMPOSITION.
HEY CALE, HEARD YOU'LL BE PLAYING THE RUBBER DUCK IN CLASS LATER.
SHOVE IT.
JOHN CONTINUES TO PRACTICE ON HIS INSTRUMENT OF CHOICE--THE VIOLA.
BUT HIS MIND IS ELSEWHERE.
LET'S TRY THAT AGAIN, EVERYONE.

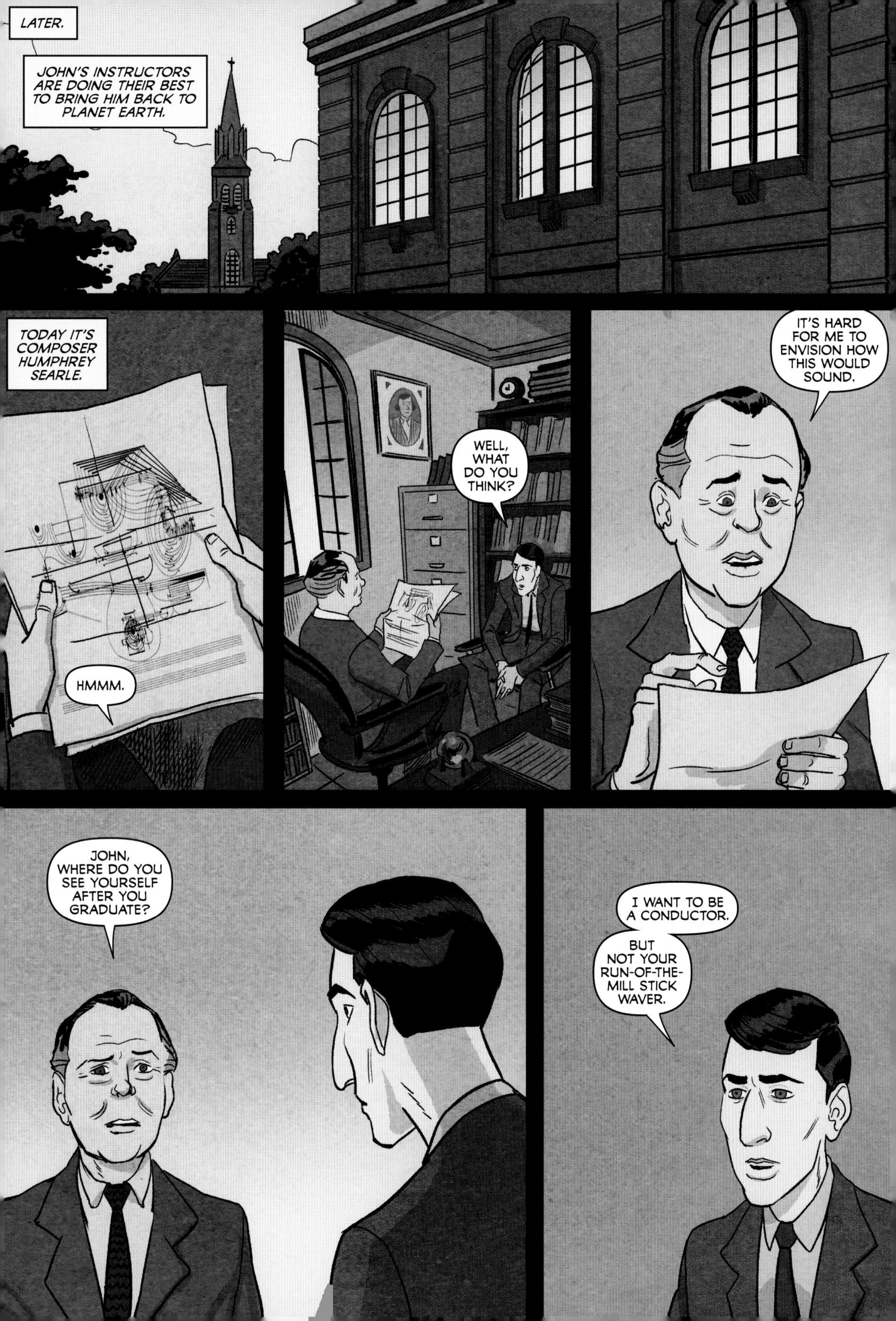
LATER.
JOHN'S INSTRUCTORS ARE DOING THEIR BEST TO BRING HIM BACK TO PLANET EARTH.
TODAY IT'S COMPOSER HUMPHREY SEARLE.
HMMM.
WELL, WHAT DO YOU THINK?
IT'S HARD FOR ME TO ENVISION HOW THIS WOULD SOUND.
JOHN, WHERE DO YOU SEE YOURSELF AFTER YOU GRADUATE?
I WANT TO BE A CONDUCTOR.
BUT NOT YOUR RUN-OF-THE-MILL STICK WAVER.

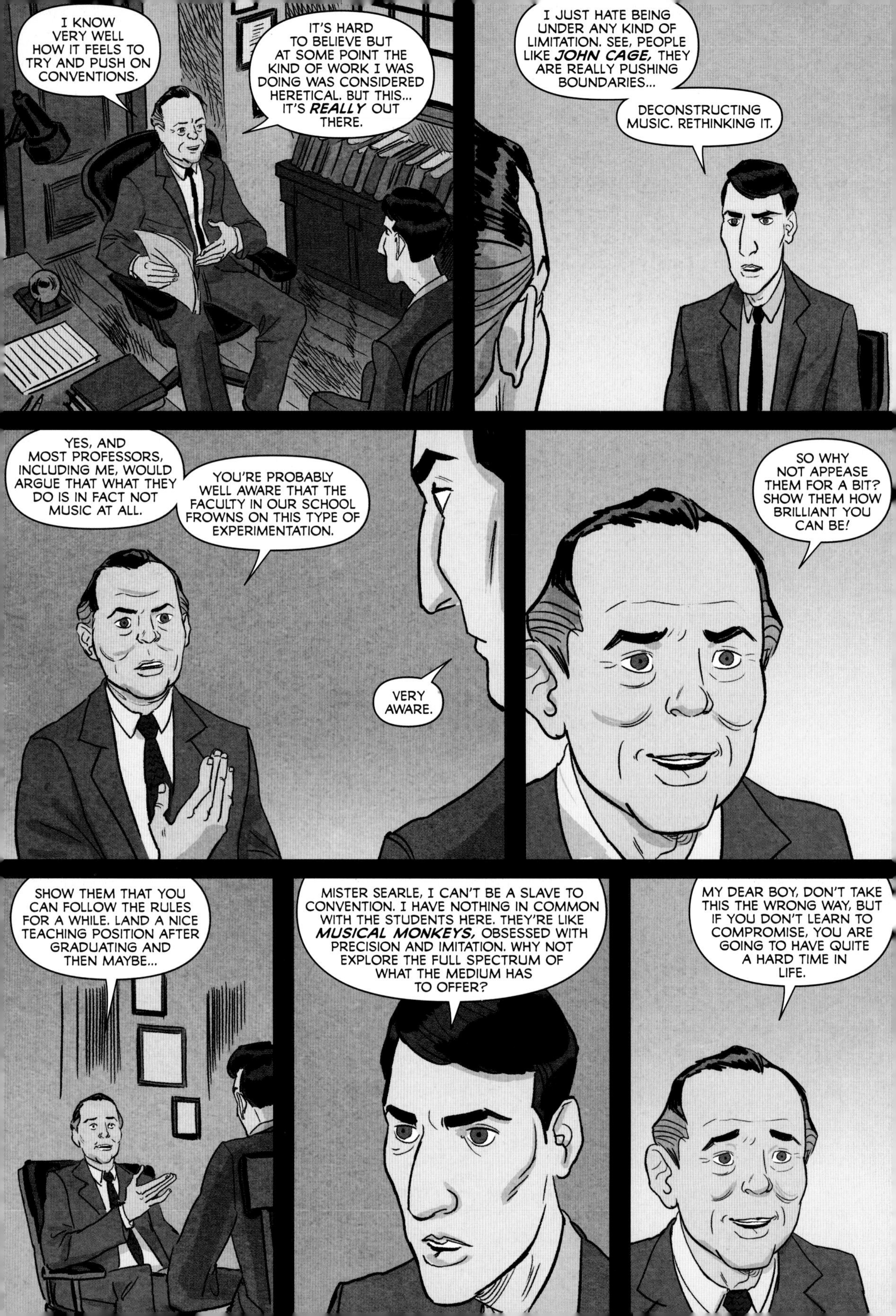
I KNOW VERY WELL HOW IT FEELS TO TRY AND PUSH ON CONVENTIONS.
IT'S HARD TO BELIEVE BUT AT SOME POINT THE KIND OF WORK I WAS DOING WAS CONSIDERED HERETICAL. BUT THIS... IT'S ***REALLY*** OUT THERE.
I JUST HATE BEING UNDER ANY KIND OF LIMITATION. SEE, PEOPLE LIKE ***JOHN CAGE,*** THEY ARE REALLY PUSHING BOUNDARIES...
DECONSTRUCTING MUSIC. RETHINKING IT.
YES, AND MOST PROFESSORS, INCLUDING ME, WOULD ARGUE THAT WHAT THEY DO IS IN FACT NOT MUSIC AT ALL.
YOU'RE PROBABLY WELL AWARE THAT THE FACULTY IN OUR SCHOOL FROWNS ON THIS TYPE OF EXPERIMENTATION.
VERY AWARE.
SO WHY NOT APPEASE THEM FOR A BIT? SHOW THEM HOW BRILLIANT YOU CAN BE!
SHOW THEM THAT YOU CAN FOLLOW THE RULES FOR A WHILE. LAND A NICE TEACHING POSITION AFTER GRADUATING AND THEN MAYBE...
MISTER SEARLE, I CAN'T BE A SLAVE TO CONVENTION. I HAVE NOTHING IN COMMON WITH THE STUDENTS HERE. THEY'RE LIKE ***MUSICAL MONKEYS,*** OBSESSED WITH PRECISION AND IMITATION. WHY NOT EXPLORE THE FULL SPECTRUM OF WHAT THE MEDIUM HAS TO OFFER?
MY DEAR BOY, DON'T TAKE THIS THE WRONG WAY, BUT IF YOU DON'T LEARN TO COMPROMISE, YOU ARE GOING TO HAVE QUITE A HARD TIME IN LIFE.

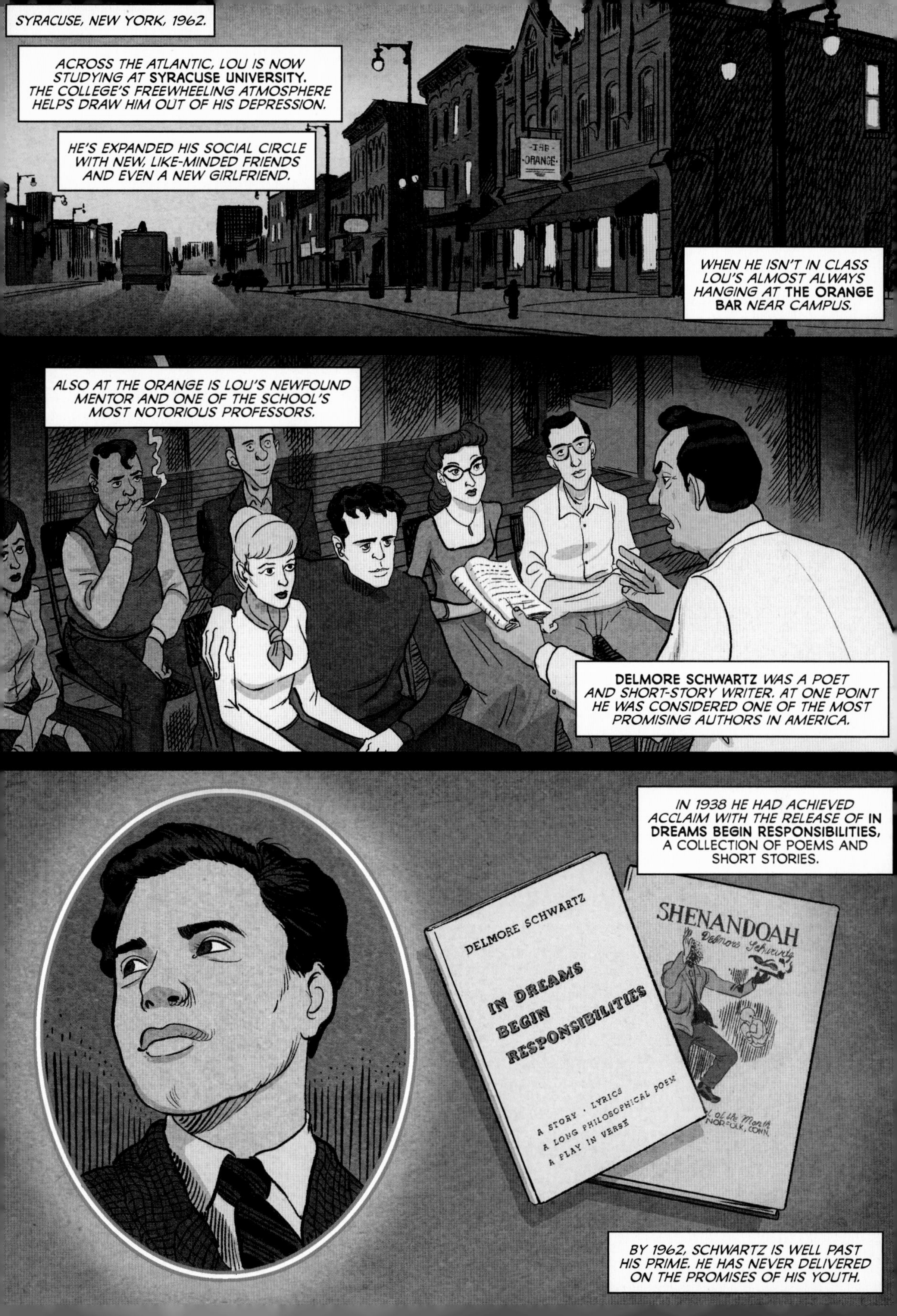
SYRACUSE, NEW YORK, 1962.
ACROSS THE ATLANTIC, LOU IS NOW STUDYING AT SYRACUSE UNIVERSITY. THE COLLEGE'S FREEWHEELING ATMOSPHERE HELPS DRAW HIM OUT OF HIS DEPRESSION.
HE'S EXPANDED HIS SOCIAL CIRCLE WITH NEW, LIKE-MINDED FRIENDS AND EVEN A NEW GIRLFRIEND.
THE ORANGE
WHEN HE ISN'T IN CLASS LOU'S ALMOST ALWAYS HANGING AT THE ORANGE BAR NEAR CAMPUS.
ALSO AT THE ORANGE IS LOU'S NEWFOUND MENTOR AND ONE OF THE SCHOOL'S MOST NOTORIOUS PROFESSORS.
DELMORE SCHWARTZ WAS A POET AND SHORT-STORY WRITER. AT ONE POINT HE WAS CONSIDERED ONE OF THE MOST PROMISING AUTHORS IN AMERICA.
IN 1938 HE HAD ACHIEVED ACCLAIM WITH THE RELEASE OF IN DREAMS BEGIN RESPONSIBILITIES, A COLLECTION OF POEMS AND SHORT STORIES.
DELMORE SCHWARTZ
IN DREAMS BEGIN RESPONSIBILITIES
A STORY · LYRICS
A LONG PHILOSOPHICAL POEM
A PLAY IN VERSE
SHENANDOAH
Delmore Schwartz
NORFOLK, CONN.
BY 1962, SCHWARTZ IS WELL PAST HIS PRIME. HE HAS NEVER DELIVERED ON THE PROMISES OF HIS YOUTH.

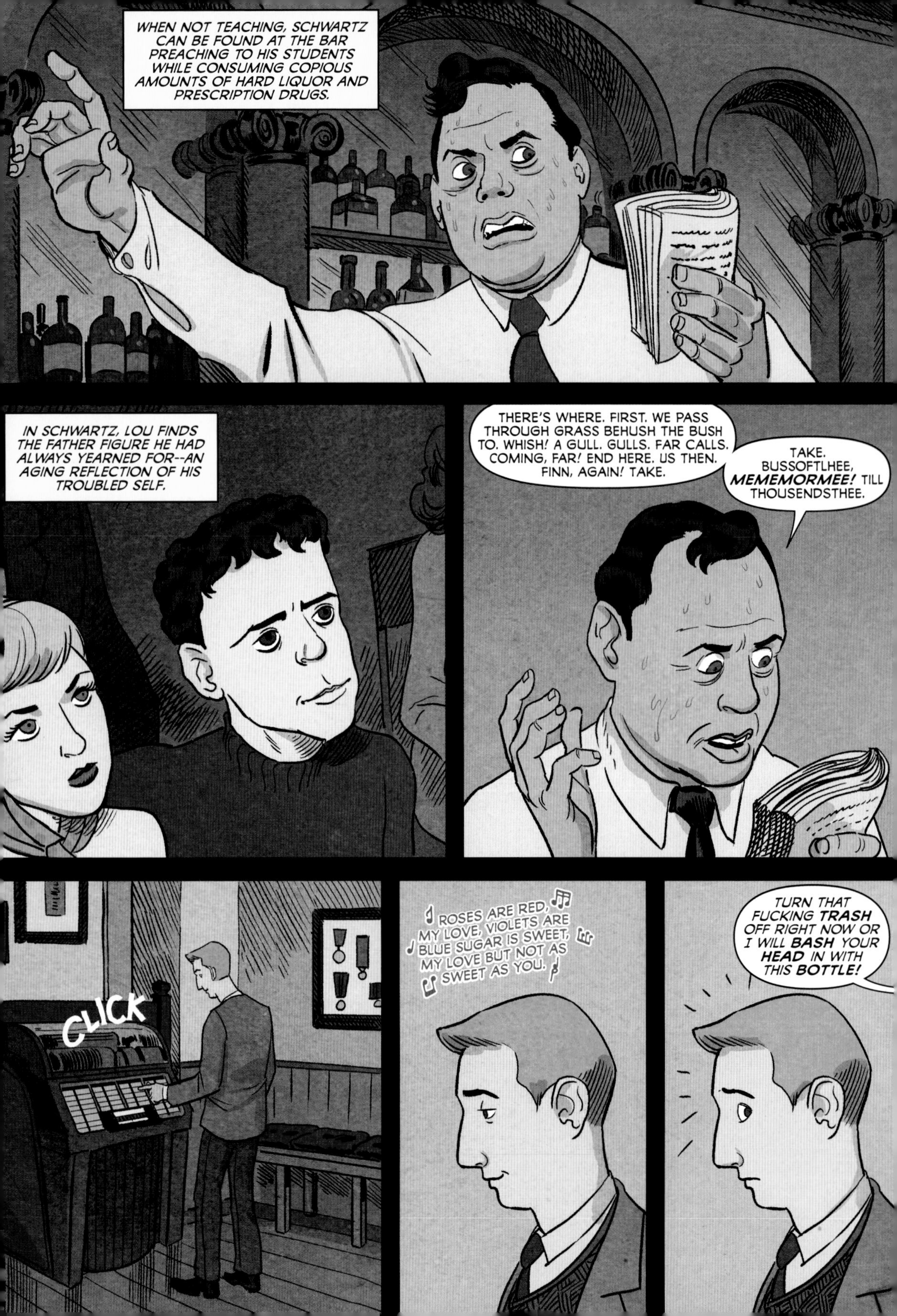

WHEN NOT TEACHING, SCHWARTZ CAN BE FOUND AT THE BAR PREACHING TO HIS STUDENTS WHILE CONSUMING COPIOUS AMOUNTS OF HARD LIQUOR AND PRESCRIPTION DRUGS.
IN SCHWARTZ, LOU FINDS THE FATHER FIGURE HE HAD ALWAYS YEARNED FOR--AN AGING REFLECTION OF HIS TROUBLED SELF.
THERE'S WHERE. FIRST. WE PASS THROUGH GRASS BEHUSH THE BUSH TO. WHISH! A GULL. GULLS. FAR CALLS. COMING, FAR! END HERE. US THEN. FINN, AGAIN! TAKE.
TAKE. BUSSOFTLHEE, **MEMEMORMEE!** TILL THOUSENDSTHEE.
CLICK
ROSES ARE RED, MY LOVE, VIOLETS ARE BLUE SUGAR IS SWEET, MY LOVE BUT NOT AS SWEET AS YOU.
TURN THAT FUCKING **TRASH** OFF RIGHT NOW OR I WILL **BASH** YOUR **HEAD** IN WITH THIS **BOTTLE!**

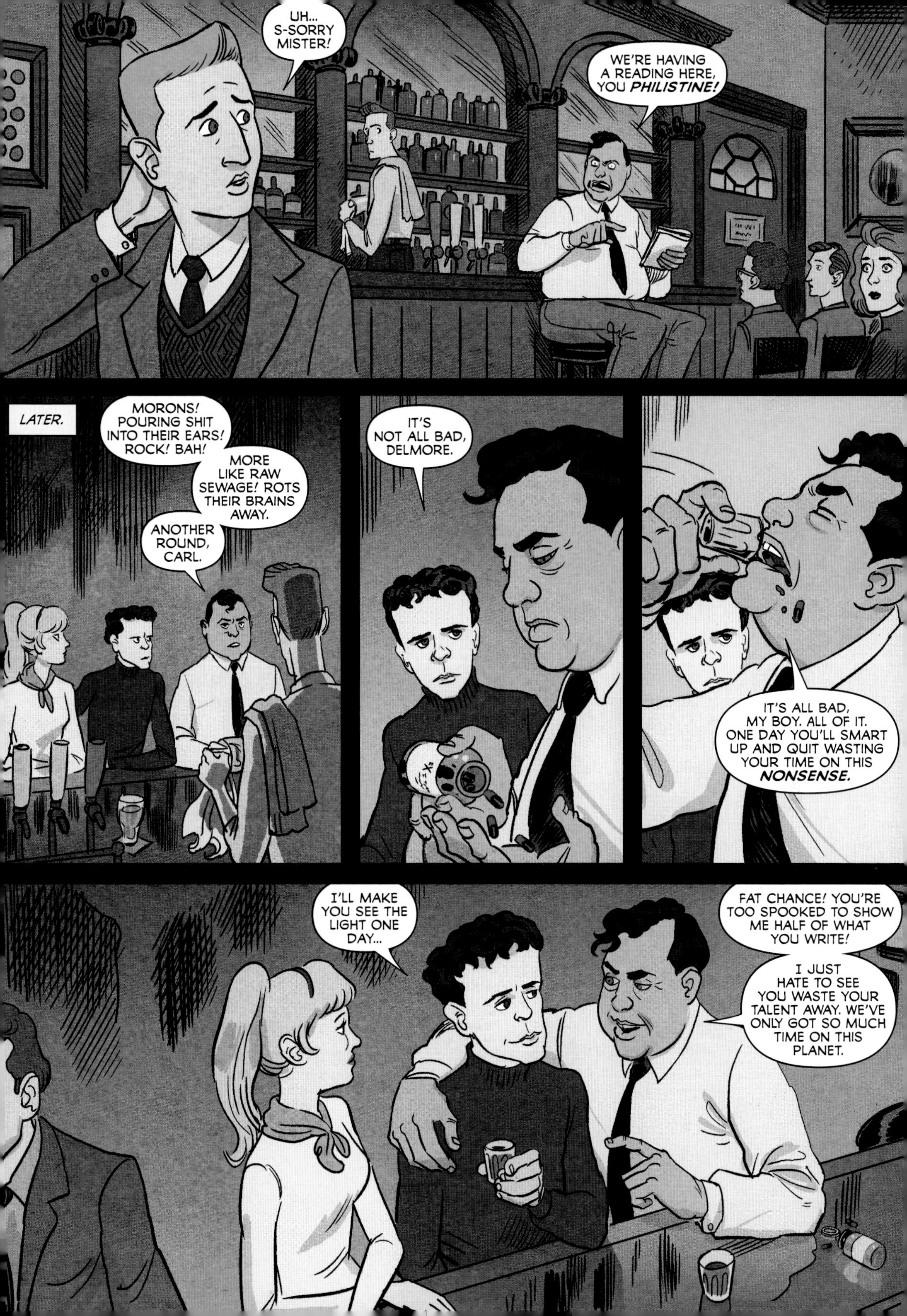

UH... S-SORRY MISTER!
WE'RE HAVING A READING HERE, YOU *PHILISTINE!*
LATER.
MORONS! POURING SHIT INTO THEIR EARS! ROCK! BAH!
MORE LIKE RAW SEWAGE! ROTS THEIR BRAINS AWAY.
ANOTHER ROUND, CARL.
IT'S NOT ALL BAD, DELMORE.
IT'S ALL BAD, MY BOY. ALL OF IT. ONE DAY YOU'LL SMART UP AND QUIT WASTING YOUR TIME ON THIS *NONSENSE.*
I'LL MAKE YOU SEE THE LIGHT ONE DAY...
FAT CHANCE! YOU'RE TOO SPOOKED TO SHOW ME HALF OF WHAT YOU WRITE!
I JUST HATE TO SEE YOU WASTE YOUR TALENT AWAY. WE'VE ONLY GOT SO MUCH TIME ON THIS PLANET.

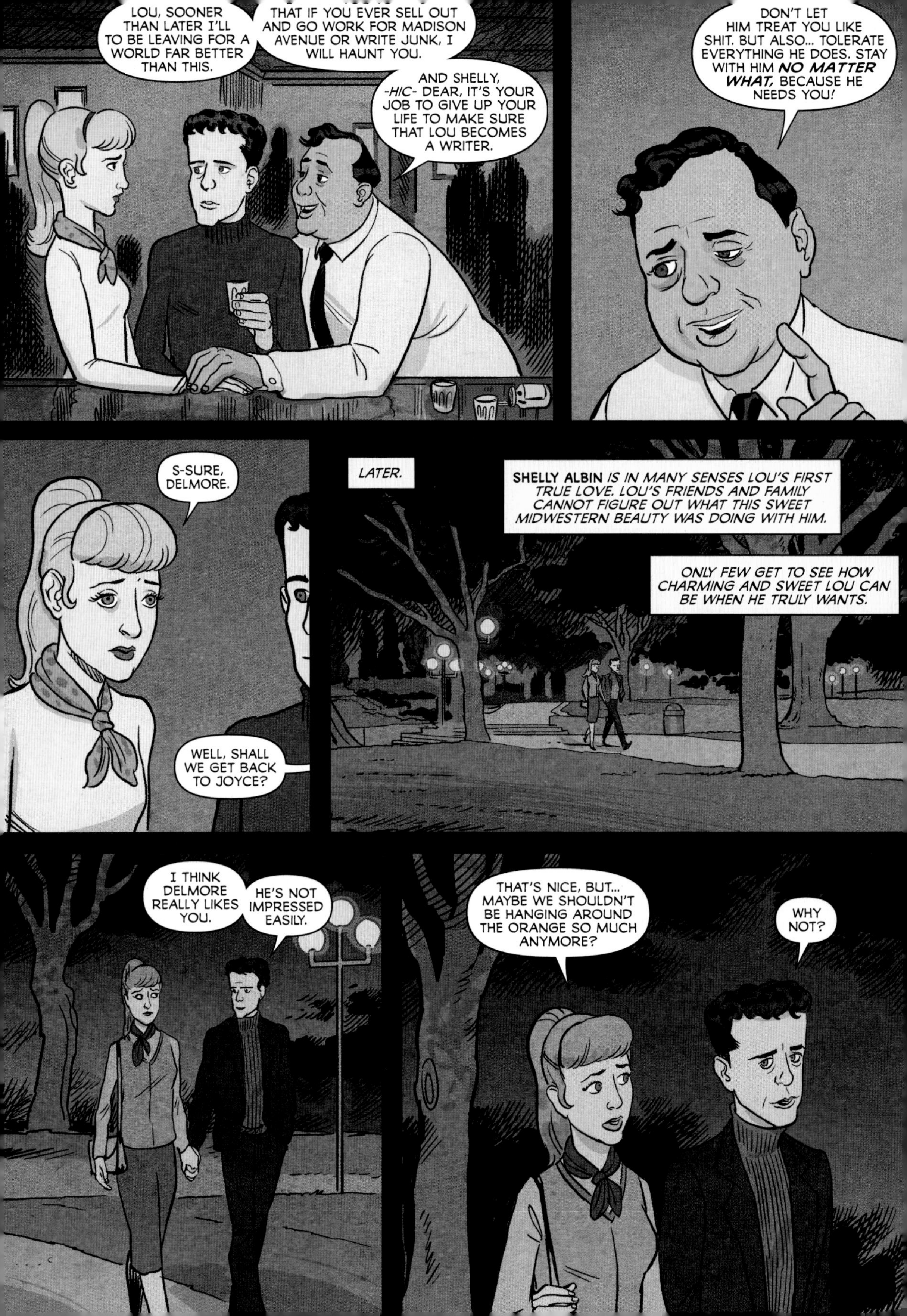
LOU, SOONER THAN LATER I'LL TO BE LEAVING FOR A WORLD FAR BETTER THAN THIS.
THAT IF YOU EVER SELL OUT AND GO WORK FOR MADISON AVENUE OR WRITE JUNK, I WILL HAUNT YOU.
AND SHELLY, -HIC- DEAR, IT'S YOUR JOB TO GIVE UP YOUR LIFE TO MAKE SURE THAT LOU BECOMES A WRITER.
DON'T LET HIM TREAT YOU LIKE SHIT. BUT ALSO... TOLERATE EVERYTHING HE DOES. STAY WITH HIM NO MATTER WHAT, BECAUSE HE NEEDS YOU!
S-SURE, DELMORE.
WELL, SHALL WE GET BACK TO JOYCE?
LATER.
SHELLY ALBIN IS IN MANY SENSES LOU'S FIRST TRUE LOVE. LOU'S FRIENDS AND FAMILY CANNOT FIGURE OUT WHAT THIS SWEET MIDWESTERN BEAUTY WAS DOING WITH HIM.
ONLY FEW GET TO SEE HOW CHARMING AND SWEET LOU CAN BE WHEN HE TRULY WANTS.
I THINK DELMORE REALLY LIKES YOU.
HE'S NOT IMPRESSED EASILY.
THAT'S NICE, BUT... MAYBE WE SHOULDN'T BE HANGING AROUND THE ORANGE SO MUCH ANYMORE?
WHY NOT?

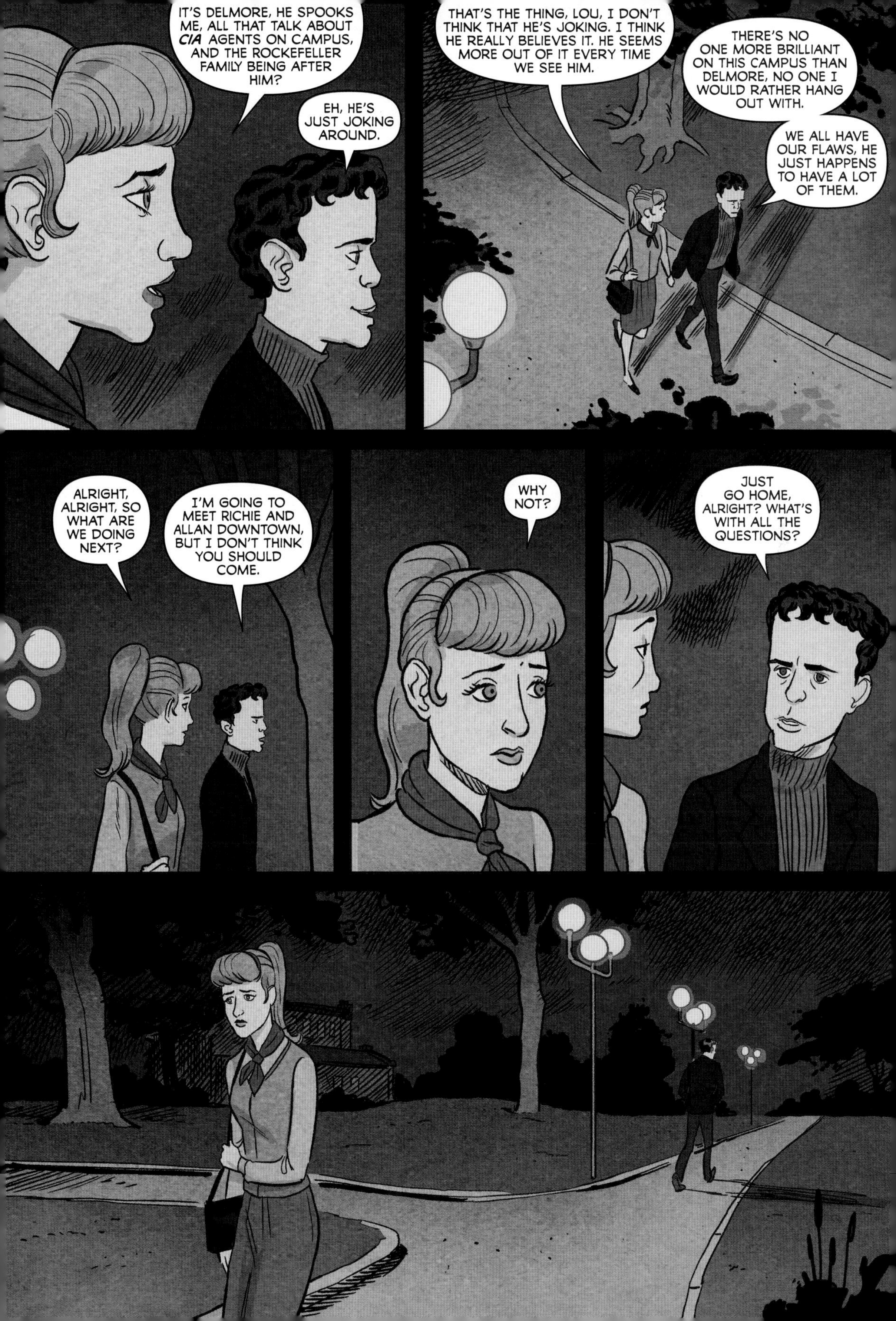
IT'S DELMORE, HE SPOOKS ME, ALL THAT TALK ABOUT *CIA* AGENTS ON CAMPUS, AND THE ROCKEFELLER FAMILY BEING AFTER HIM?
EH, HE'S JUST JOKING AROUND.
THAT'S THE THING, LOU, I DON'T THINK THAT HE'S JOKING. I THINK HE REALLY BELIEVES IT. HE SEEMS MORE OUT OF IT EVERY TIME WE SEE HIM.
THERE'S NO ONE MORE BRILLIANT ON THIS CAMPUS THAN DELMORE, NO ONE I WOULD RATHER HANG OUT WITH.
WE ALL HAVE OUR FLAWS, HE JUST HAPPENS TO HAVE A LOT OF THEM.
ALRIGHT, ALRIGHT, SO WHAT ARE WE DOING NEXT?
I'M GOING TO MEET RICHIE AND ALLAN DOWNTOWN, BUT I DON'T THINK YOU SHOULD COME.
WHY NOT?
JUST GO HOME, ALRIGHT? WHAT'S WITH ALL THE QUESTIONS?

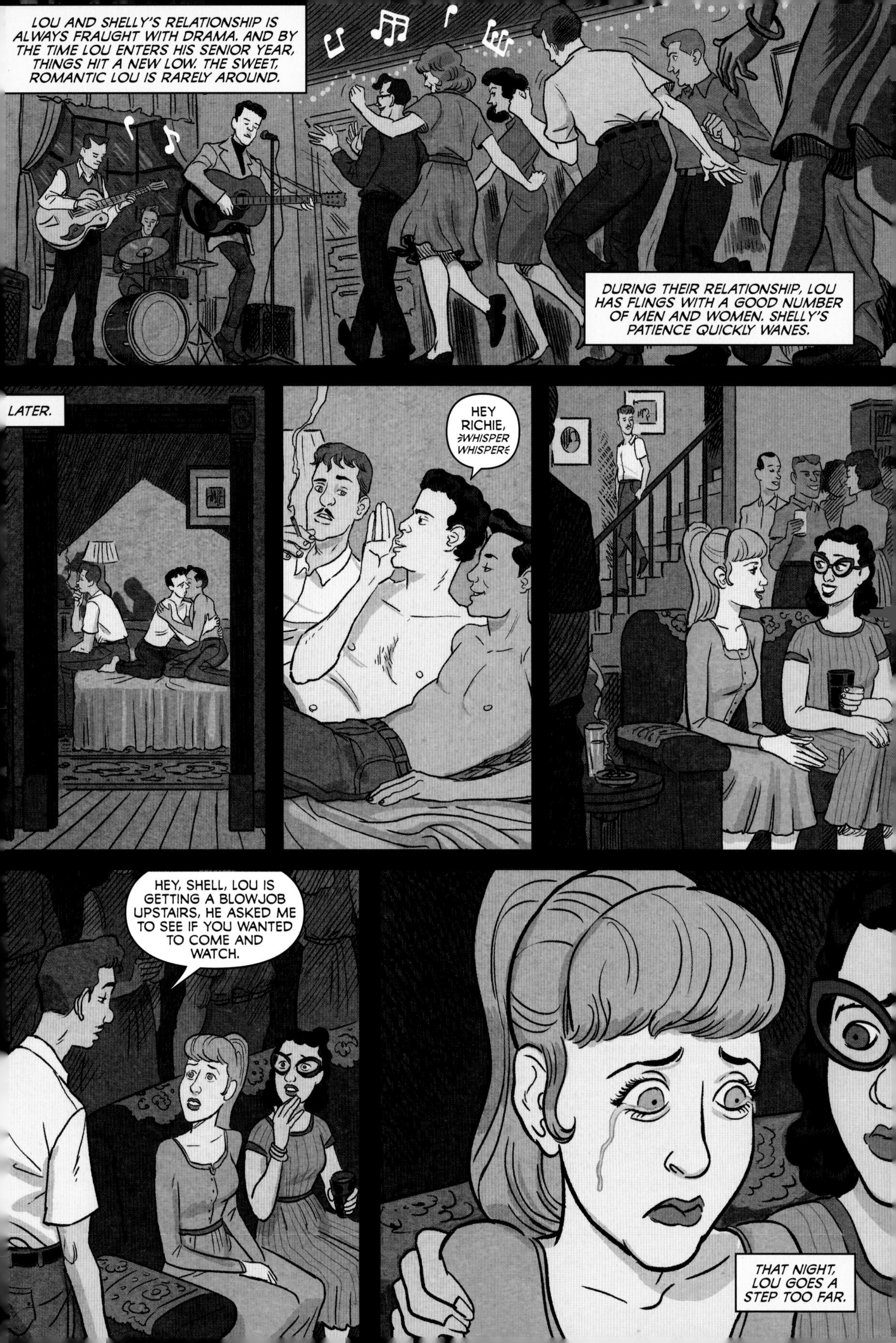

LOU AND SHELLY'S RELATIONSHIP IS ALWAYS FRAUGHT WITH DRAMA. AND BY THE TIME LOU ENTERS HIS SENIOR YEAR, THINGS HIT A NEW LOW. THE SWEET, ROMANTIC LOU IS RARELY AROUND.
DURING THEIR RELATIONSHIP, LOU HAS FLINGS WITH A GOOD NUMBER OF MEN AND WOMEN. SHELLY'S PATIENCE QUICKLY WANES.
LATER.
HEY RICHIE, WHISPER WHISPER
HEY, SHELL, LOU IS GETTING A BLOWJOB UPSTAIRS, HE ASKED ME TO SEE IF YOU WANTED TO COME AND WATCH.
THAT NIGHT, LOU GOES A STEP TOO FAR.

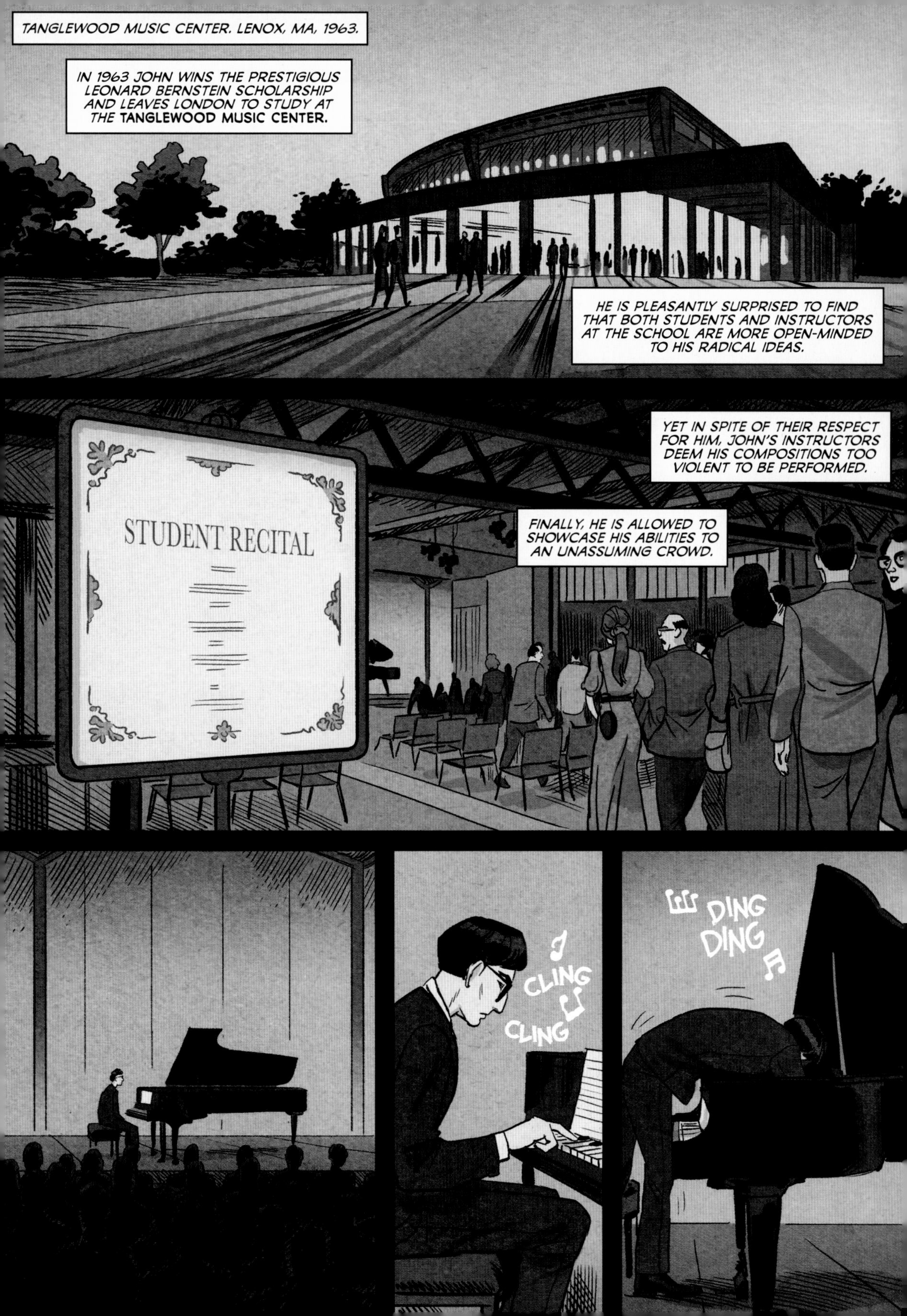

TANGLEWOOD MUSIC CENTER. LENOX, MA, 1963.
IN 1963 JOHN WINS THE PRESTIGIOUS LEONARD BERNSTEIN SCHOLARSHIP AND LEAVES LONDON TO STUDY AT THE TANGLEWOOD MUSIC CENTER.
HE IS PLEASANTLY SURPRISED TO FIND THAT BOTH STUDENTS AND INSTRUCTORS AT THE SCHOOL ARE MORE OPEN-MINDED TO HIS RADICAL IDEAS.
STUDENT RECITAL
YET IN SPITE OF THEIR RESPECT FOR HIM, JOHN'S INSTRUCTORS DEEM HIS COMPOSITIONS TOO VIOLENT TO BE PERFORMED.
FINALLY, HE IS ALLOWED TO SHOWCASE HIS ABILITIES TO AN UNASSUMING CROWD.
CLING
CLING
DING
DING

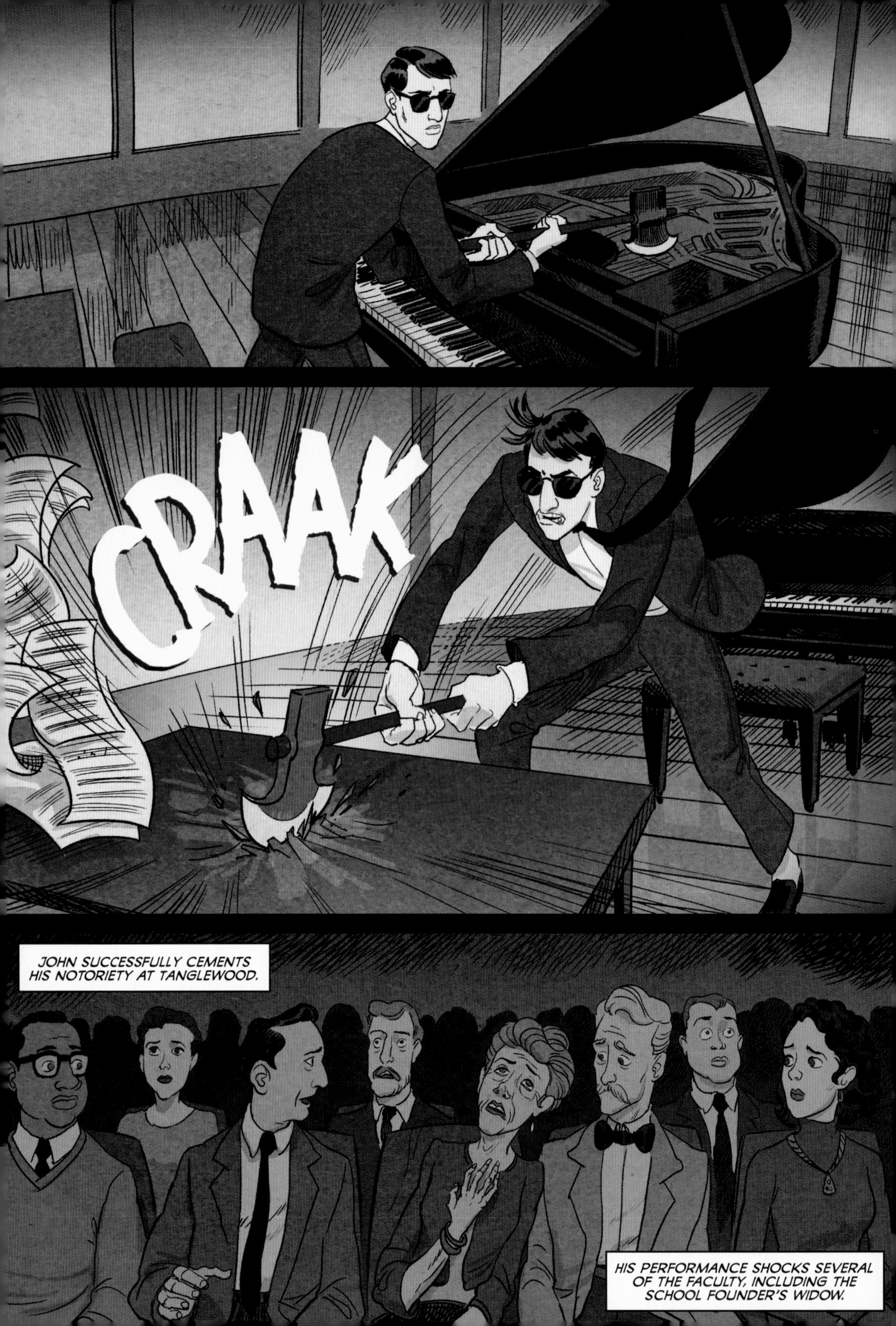
CRAAK
JOHN SUCCESSFULLY CEMENTS HIS NOTORIETY AT TANGLEWOOD.
HIS PERFORMANCE SHOCKS SEVERAL OF THE FACULTY, INCLUDING THE SCHOOL FOUNDER'S WIDOW.

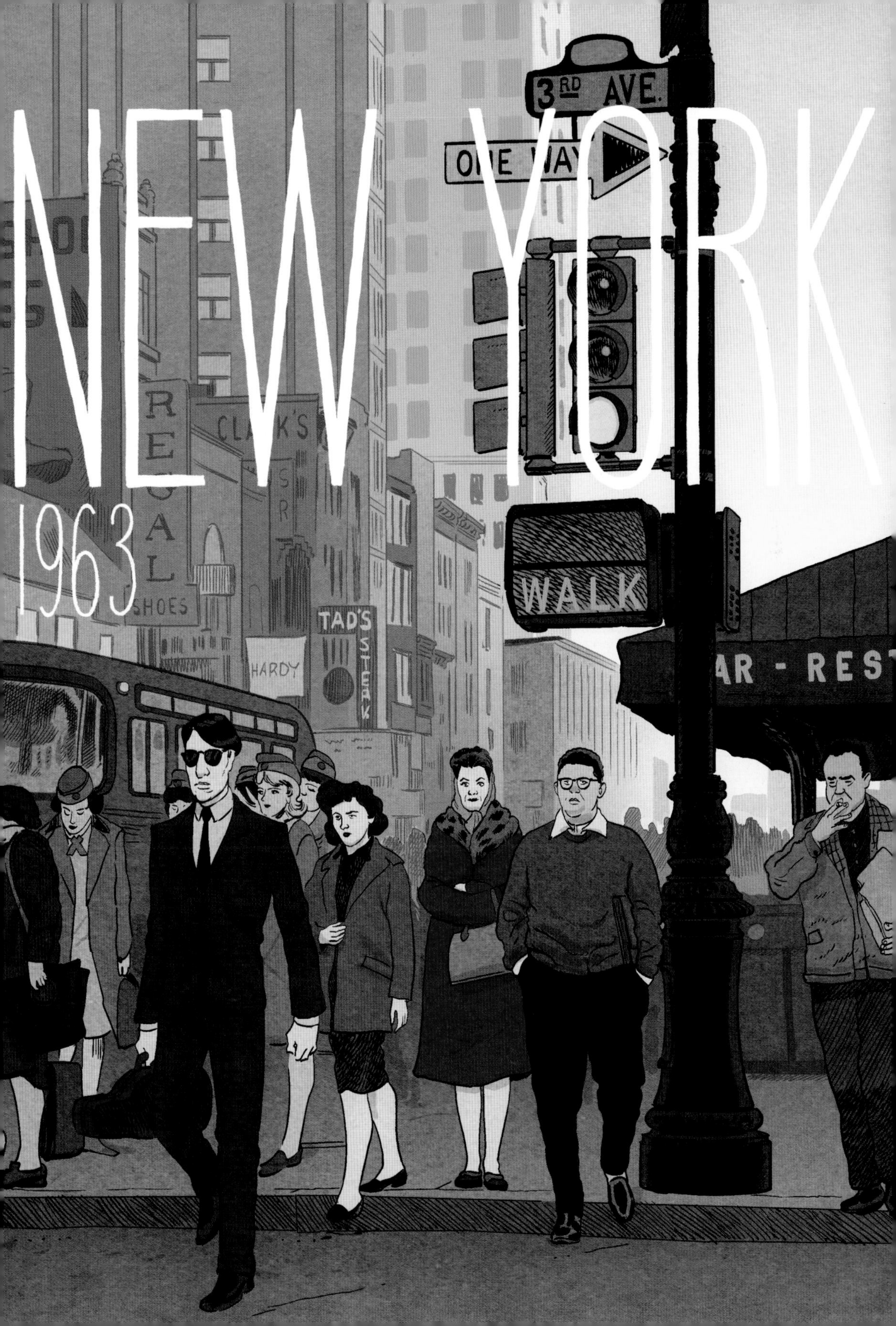
NEW YORK
1963
3RD AVE.
ONE WAY
WALK
REGAL
SHOES
CLARK'S
TAD'S
STEAK
HARDY
AR - REST

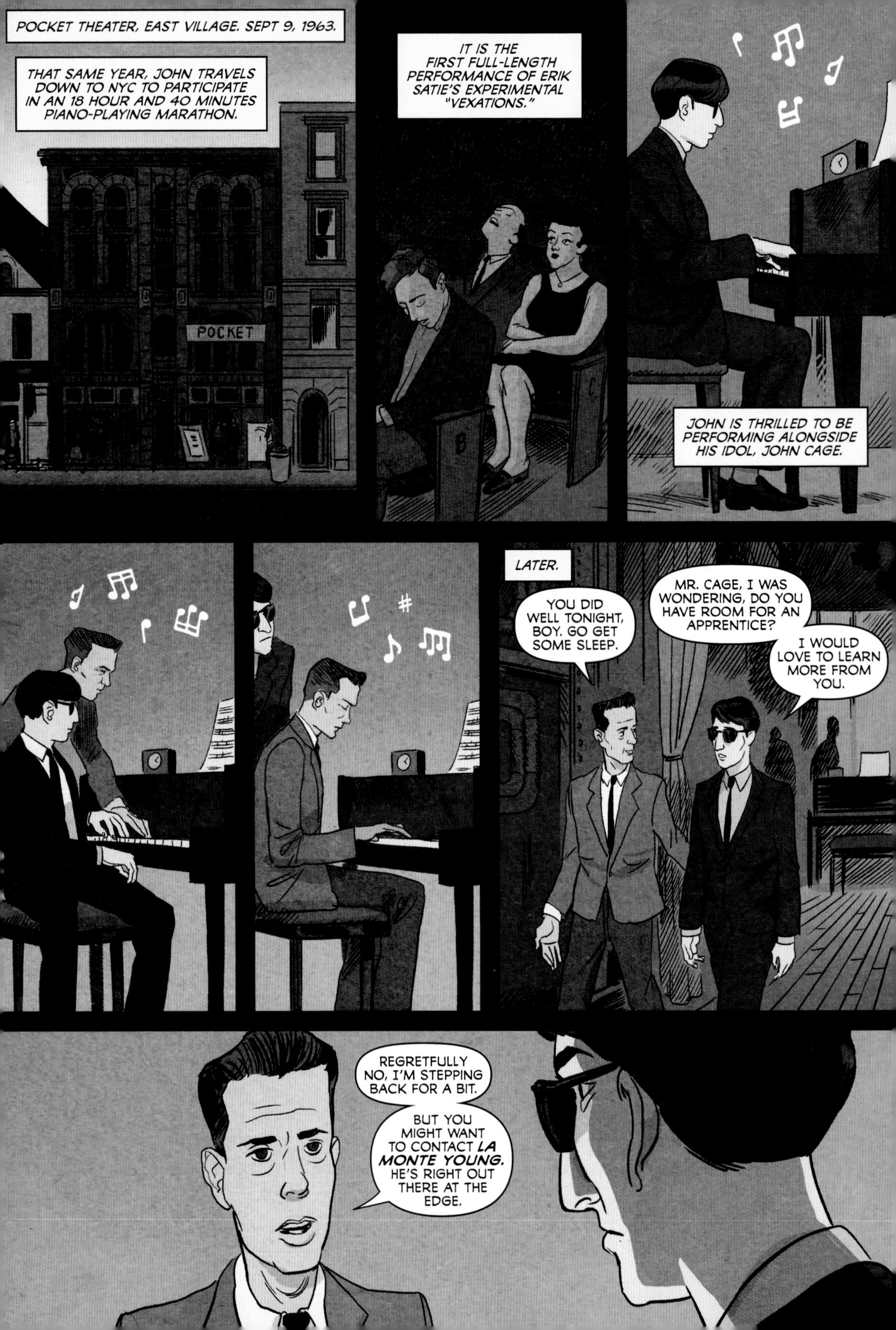
POCKET THEATER, EAST VILLAGE. SEPT 9, 1963.
THAT SAME YEAR, JOHN TRAVELS DOWN TO NYC TO PARTICIPATE IN AN 18 HOUR AND 40 MINUTES PIANO-PLAYING MARATHON.
POCKET
IT IS THE FIRST FULL-LENGTH PERFORMANCE OF ERIK SATIE'S EXPERIMENTAL "VEXATIONS."
JOHN IS THRILLED TO BE PERFORMING ALONGSIDE HIS IDOL, JOHN CAGE.
LATER.
YOU DID WELL TONIGHT, BOY. GO GET SOME SLEEP.
MR. CAGE, I WAS WONDERING, DO YOU HAVE ROOM FOR AN APPRENTICE?
I WOULD LOVE TO LEARN MORE FROM YOU.
REGRETFULLY NO, I'M STEPPING BACK FOR A BIT.
BUT YOU MIGHT WANT TO CONTACT *LA MONTE YOUNG.* HE'S RIGHT OUT THERE AT THE EDGE.

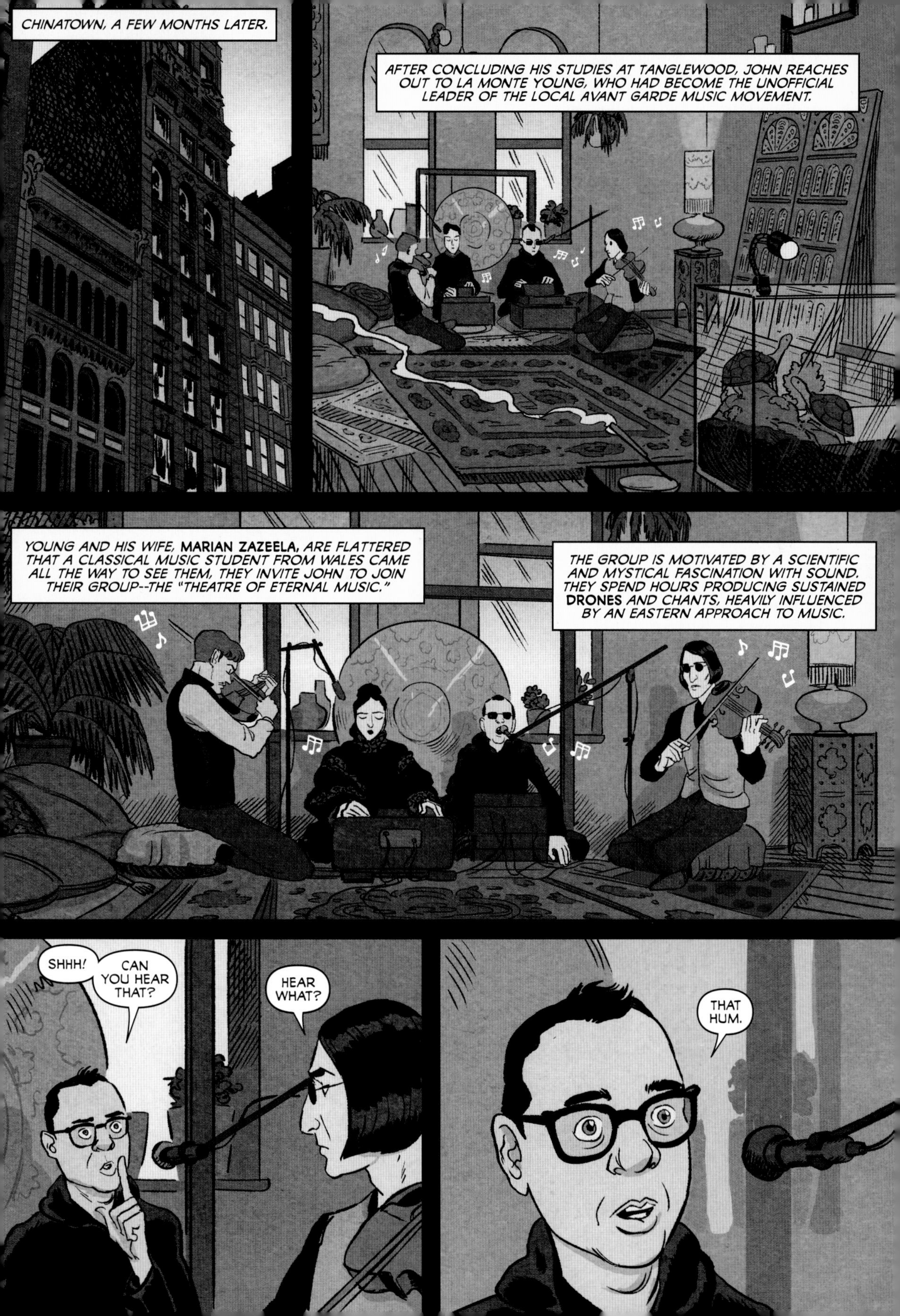
CHINATOWN, A FEW MONTHS LATER.
AFTER CONCLUDING HIS STUDIES AT TANGLEWOOD, JOHN REACHES OUT TO LA MONTE YOUNG, WHO HAD BECOME THE UNOFFICIAL LEADER OF THE LOCAL AVANT GARDE MUSIC MOVEMENT.
YOUNG AND HIS WIFE, MARIAN ZAZEELA, ARE FLATTERED THAT A CLASSICAL MUSIC STUDENT FROM WALES CAME ALL THE WAY TO SEE THEM, THEY INVITE JOHN TO JOIN THEIR GROUP--THE "THEATRE OF ETERNAL MUSIC."
THE GROUP IS MOTIVATED BY A SCIENTIFIC AND MYSTICAL FASCINATION WITH SOUND. THEY SPEND HOURS PRODUCING SUSTAINED DRONES AND CHANTS, HEAVILY INFLUENCED BY AN EASTERN APPROACH TO MUSIC.
SHHH!
CAN YOU HEAR THAT?
HEAR WHAT?
THAT HUM.

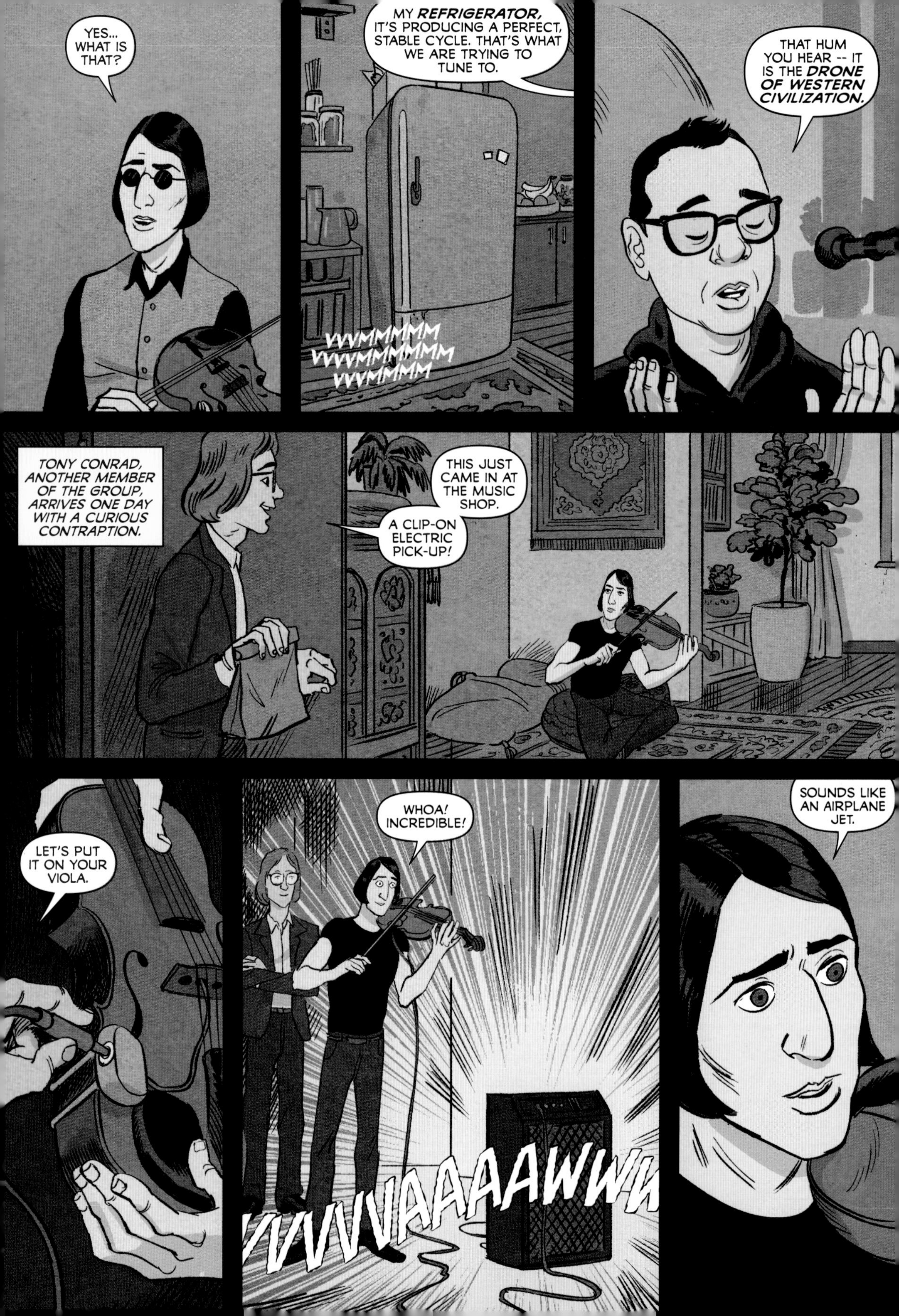
YES... WHAT IS THAT?
MY REFRIGERATOR, IT'S PRODUCING A PERFECT, STABLE CYCLE. THAT'S WHAT WE ARE TRYING TO TUNE TO.
VVVMMMMM VVVVMMMMMM VVVMMMM
THAT HUM YOU HEAR -- IT IS THE DRONE OF WESTERN CIVILIZATION.
TONY CONRAD, ANOTHER MEMBER OF THE GROUP, ARRIVES ONE DAY WITH A CURIOUS CONTRAPTION.
THIS JUST CAME IN AT THE MUSIC SHOP.
A CLIP-ON ELECTRIC PICK-UP!
LET'S PUT IT ON YOUR VIOLA.
WHOA! INCREDIBLE!
VVVVVAAAAAWWW
SOUNDS LIKE AN AIRPLANE JET.

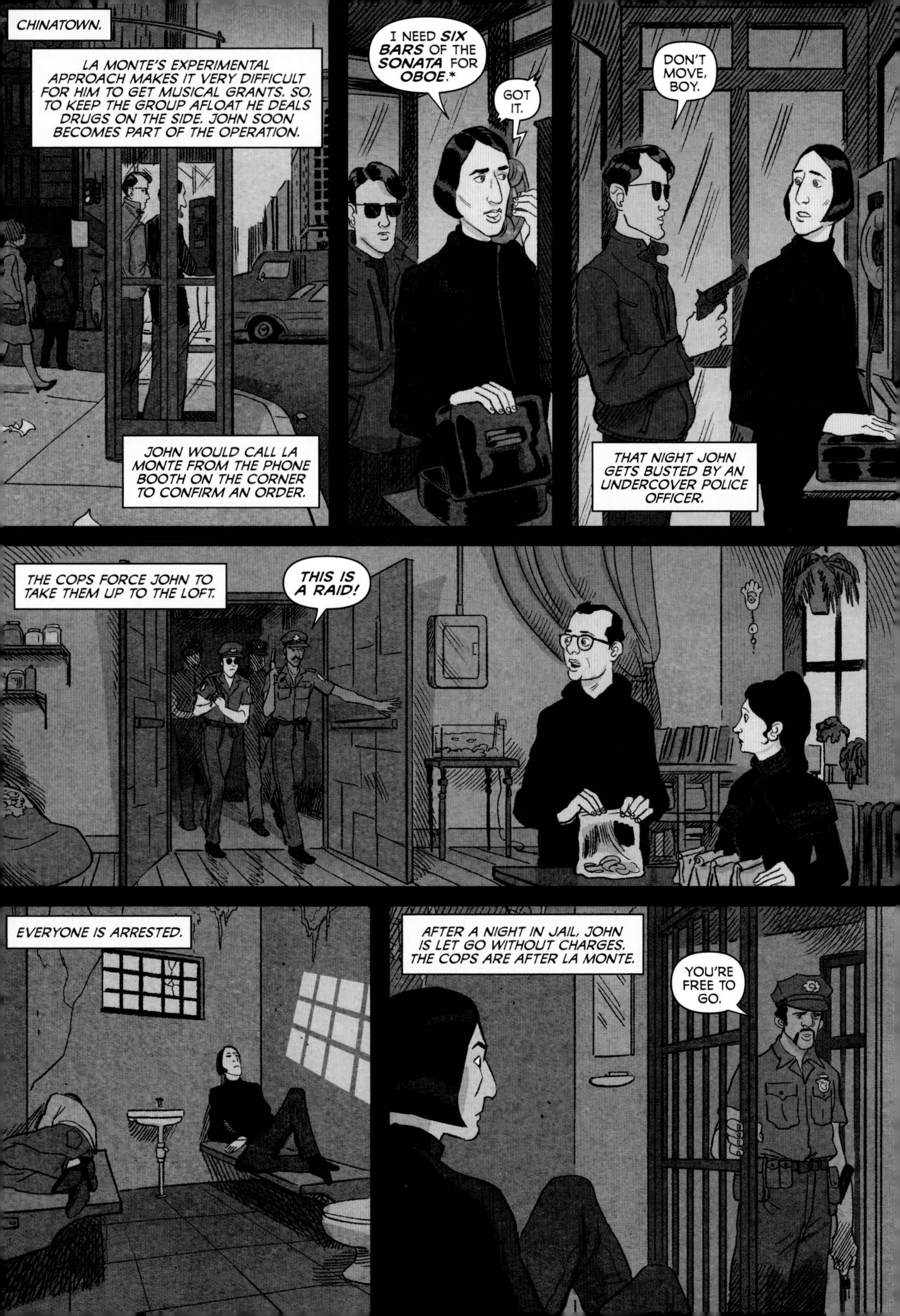
CHINATOWN.
LA MONTE'S EXPERIMENTAL APPROACH MAKES IT VERY DIFFICULT FOR HIM TO GET MUSICAL GRANTS. SO, TO KEEP THE GROUP AFLOAT HE DEALS DRUGS ON THE SIDE. JOHN SOON BECOMES PART OF THE OPERATION.
JOHN WOULD CALL LA MONTE FROM THE PHONE BOOTH ON THE CORNER TO CONFIRM AN ORDER.
I NEED SIX BARS OF THE SONATA FOR OBOE.*
GOT IT.
DON'T MOVE, BOY.
THAT NIGHT JOHN GETS BUSTED BY AN UNDERCOVER POLICE OFFICER.
THE COPS FORCE JOHN TO TAKE THEM UP TO THE LOFT.
THIS IS A RAID!
EVERYONE IS ARRESTED.
AFTER A NIGHT IN JAIL, JOHN IS LET GO WITHOUT CHARGES. THE COPS ARE AFTER LA MONTE.
YOU'RE FREE TO GO.

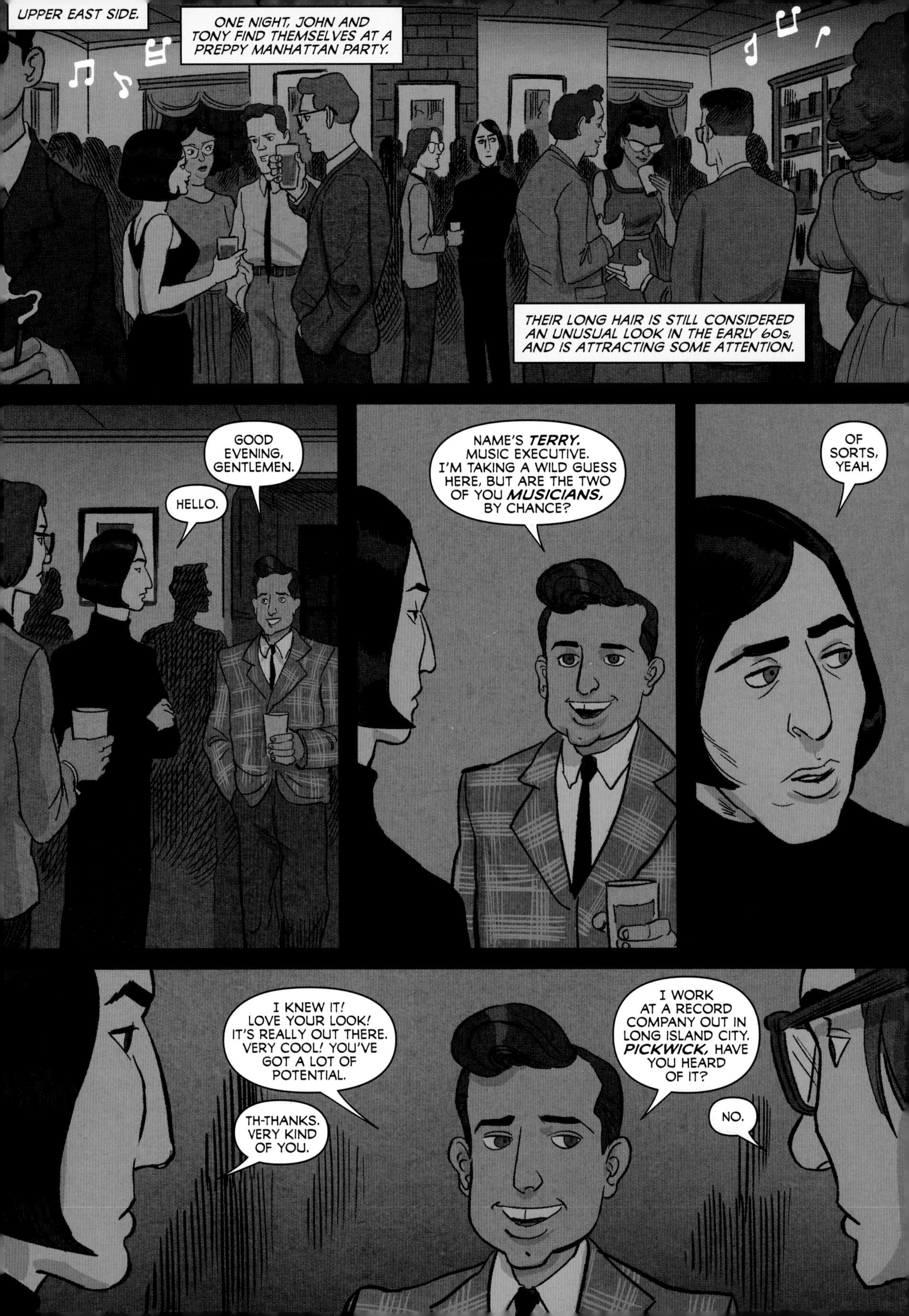
UPPER EAST SIDE.
ONE NIGHT, JOHN AND TONY FIND THEMSELVES AT A PREPPY MANHATTAN PARTY.
THEIR LONG HAIR IS STILL CONSIDERED AN UNUSUAL LOOK IN THE EARLY 60s, AND IS ATTRACTING SOME ATTENTION.
GOOD EVENING, GENTLEMEN.
HELLO.
NAME'S **TERRY.** MUSIC EXECUTIVE. I'M TAKING A WILD GUESS HERE, BUT ARE THE TWO OF YOU **MUSICIANS,** BY CHANCE?
OF SORTS, YEAH.
I KNEW IT! LOVE YOUR LOOK! IT'S REALLY OUT THERE. VERY COOL! YOU'VE GOT A LOT OF POTENTIAL.
TH-THANKS. VERY KIND OF YOU.
I WORK AT A RECORD COMPANY OUT IN LONG ISLAND CITY. **PICKWICK,** HAVE YOU HEARD OF IT?
NO.

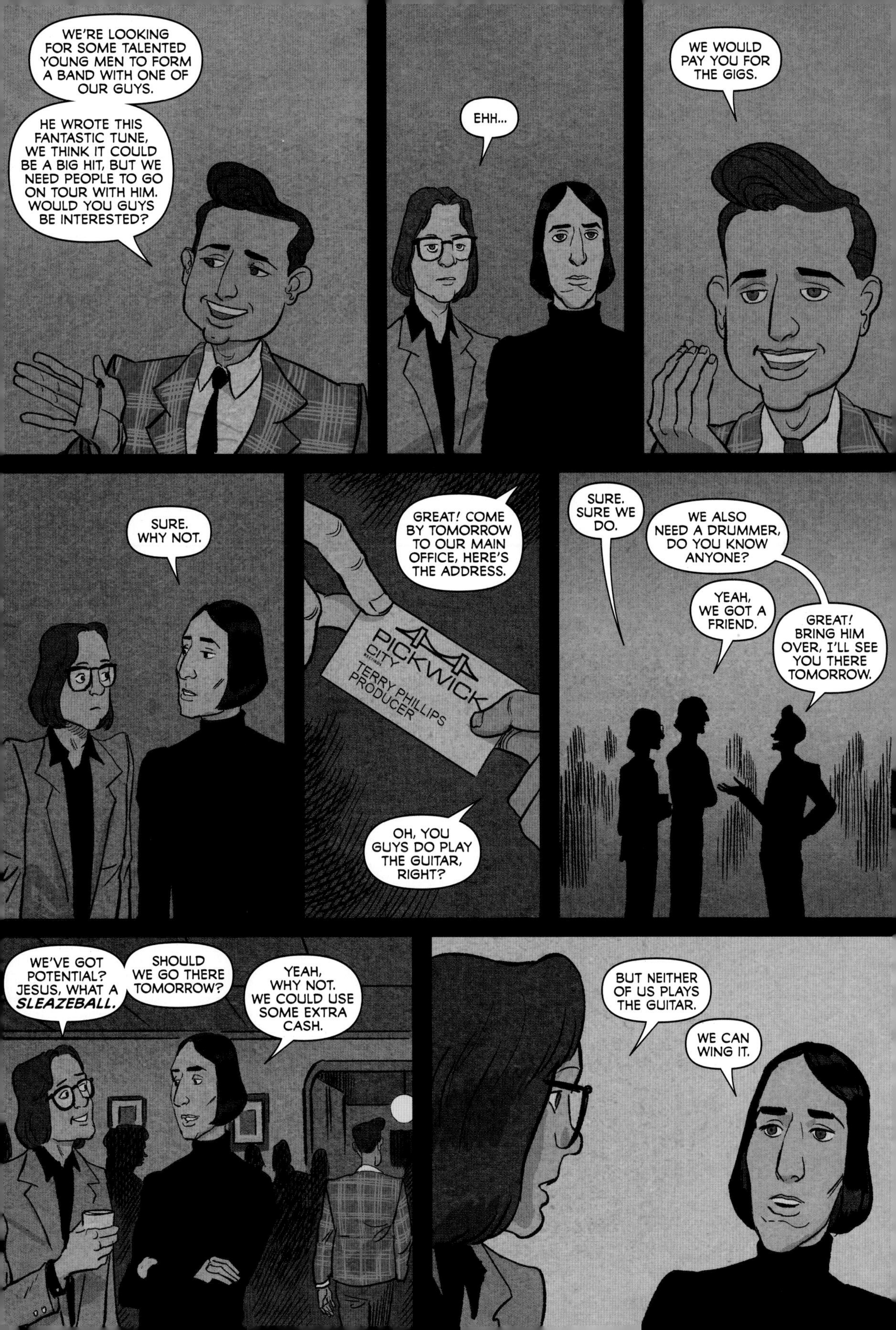

WE'RE LOOKING FOR SOME TALENTED YOUNG MEN TO FORM A BAND WITH ONE OF OUR GUYS.
HE WROTE THIS FANTASTIC TUNE, WE THINK IT COULD BE A BIG HIT, BUT WE NEED PEOPLE TO GO ON TOUR WITH HIM. WOULD YOU GUYS BE INTERESTED?
EHH...
WE WOULD PAY YOU FOR THE GIGS.
SURE. WHY NOT.
GREAT! COME BY TOMORROW TO OUR MAIN OFFICE, HERE'S THE ADDRESS.
PICKWICK
CITY
TERRY PHILLIPS
PRODUCER
OH, YOU GUYS DO PLAY THE GUITAR, RIGHT?
SURE. SURE WE DO.
WE ALSO NEED A DRUMMER, DO YOU KNOW ANYONE?
YEAH, WE GOT A FRIEND.
GREAT! BRING HIM OVER, I'LL SEE YOU THERE TOMORROW.
WE'VE GOT POTENTIAL? JESUS, WHAT A ***SLEAZEBALL.***
SHOULD WE GO THERE TOMORROW?
YEAH, WHY NOT. WE COULD USE SOME EXTRA CASH.
BUT NEITHER OF US PLAYS THE GUITAR.
WE CAN WING IT.

THE FOLLOWING DAY, JOHN, TONY AND THEIR "DRUMMER" FRIEND WALTER DE MARIA TAKE THE SUBWAY TO LONG ISLAND CITY. THE GROUP FINDS THE SCENE AT PICKWICK AMUSING.

WELCOME!

pickwick records

THE COMPANY SPECIALIZED IN HASTILY PRODUCED RECORDS CAPITALIZING ON WHATEVER MUSICAL TREND WAS BIG AT THE TIME.

PICKWICK ALBUMS WOULD BE RECORDED AND RELEASED AT A DIZZYING RATE, THE COVER WOULD BOAST NAMES OF MADE-UP BANDS. YOUNG BUYERS WOULD PURCHASE THESE RECORDS BELIEVING THEY WERE PERFORMED BY ESTABLISHED BANDS.

SHINDIG!

STEREO THE TWIST

Teddy Reynolds and the Twisters

HULLA BALOO!
Maxine Brown
Roy Orbison   Lloyd Price
Roger Miller   Garnet Mimm
Bobby Freeman   rook Be
Betty Everett   The Cl
Gene Pitney

ROCK 'N' ROLL at the SUGAR BOWL

HERE YOU GO, GUYS, BEFORE WE GET STARTED IF YOU DON'T MIND SIGNING THESE WORK AGREEMENT CONTRACTS.

THESE CONTRACTS ARE A RACKET.

SURE, MAN, WE'LL TAKE A LOOK AT THESE LATER.

OK, OK, NO RUSH, LET'S GO OVER TO MY OFFICE. THERE'S SOMEONE I'D LIKE YOU TO MEET.

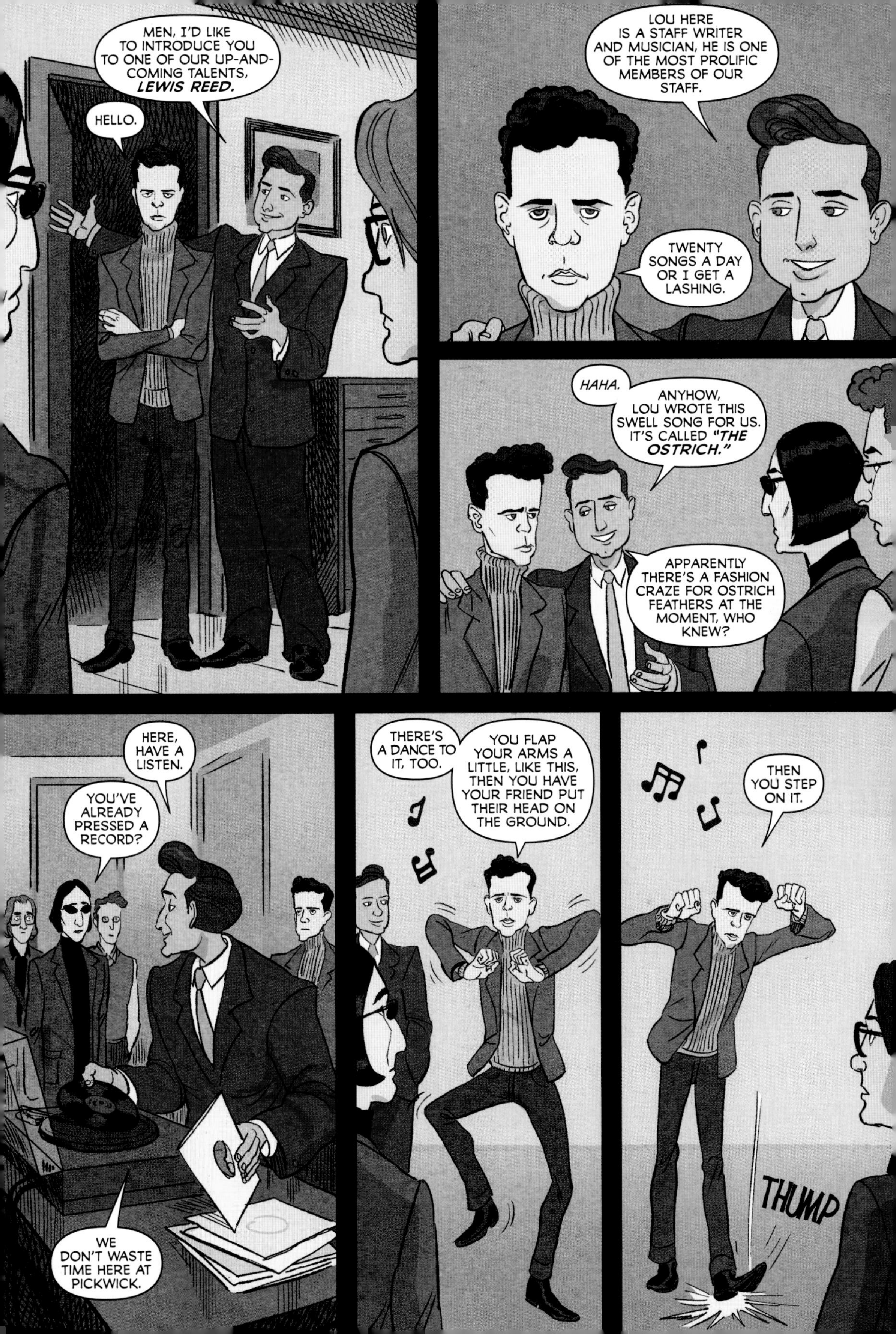
MEN, I'D LIKE TO INTRODUCE YOU TO ONE OF OUR UP-AND-COMING TALENTS, ***LEWIS REED.***
HELLO.
LOU HERE IS A STAFF WRITER AND MUSICIAN, HE IS ONE OF THE MOST PROLIFIC MEMBERS OF OUR STAFF.
TWENTY SONGS A DAY OR I GET A LASHING.
HAHA.
ANYHOW, LOU WROTE THIS SWELL SONG FOR US. IT'S CALLED ***"THE OSTRICH."***
APPARENTLY THERE'S A FASHION CRAZE FOR OSTRICH FEATHERS AT THE MOMENT, WHO KNEW?
HERE, HAVE A LISTEN.
YOU'VE ALREADY PRESSED A RECORD?
WE DON'T WASTE TIME HERE AT PICKWICK.
THERE'S A DANCE TO IT, TOO.
YOU FLAP YOUR ARMS A LITTLE, LIKE THIS, THEN YOU HAVE YOUR FRIEND PUT THEIR HEAD ON THE GROUND.
THEN YOU STEP ON IT.
THUMP

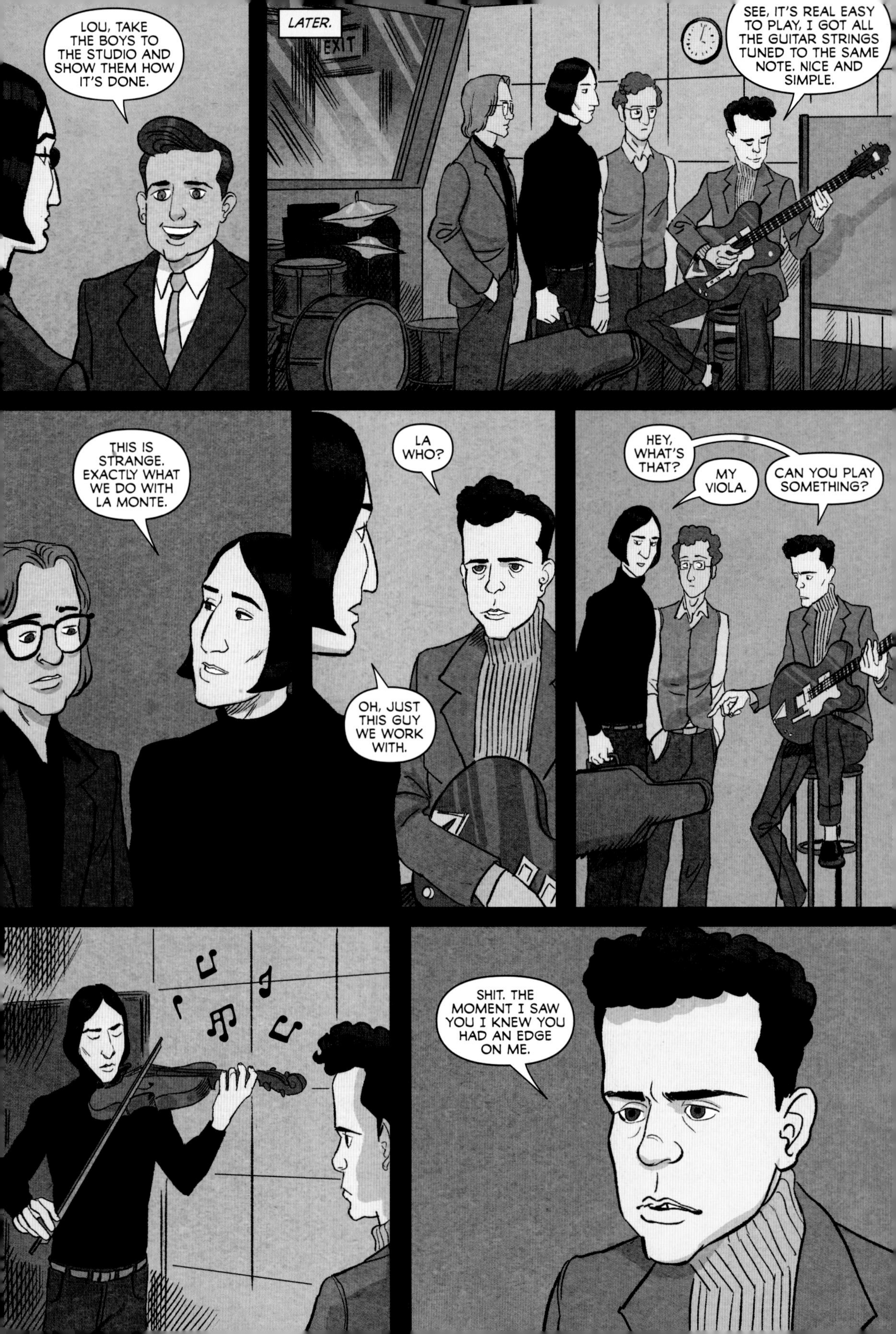
LOU, TAKE THE BOYS TO THE STUDIO AND SHOW THEM HOW IT'S DONE.
LATER.
EXIT
SEE, IT'S REAL EASY TO PLAY, I GOT ALL THE GUITAR STRINGS TUNED TO THE SAME NOTE. NICE AND SIMPLE.
THIS IS STRANGE. EXACTLY WHAT WE DO WITH LA MONTE.
LA WHO?
OH, JUST THIS GUY WE WORK WITH.
HEY, WHAT'S THAT?
MY VIOLA.
CAN YOU PLAY SOMETHING?
SHIT. THE MOMENT I SAW YOU I KNEW YOU HAD AN EDGE ON ME.

AND SO, PICKWICK'S RAGTAG BAND IS ASSEMBLED AND QUICKLY SENT TO APPEAR ON THE AMERICAN BANDSTAND SHOW.

LADIES AND GENTLEMEN, I'M PLEASED TO INTRODUCE YOU TO OUR VERY SPECIAL PERFORMERS TODAY: PLEASE WELCOME, THE PRIMITIVES.

YOU TAKE IT FORWARD, PUT YOUR HEAD BETWEEN YOUR KNEES.

AMERICAN BANDSTAND

DO THE OSTRICH, DO THE OSTRICH! DO JUST ABOUT ANYTHING YOU PLEASE.

NOW COME ON, GET READY, BABY, HERE WE GO!

THE TV APPEARANCE IS FOLLOWED BY A SHORT EAST COAST TOUR.

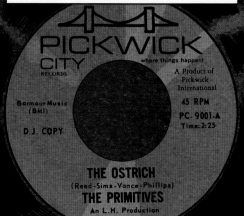

IN SPITE OF ALL THE PROMISES, THE PRIMITIVES' CLUMSY EFFORTS AREN'T ENOUGH TO PUSH "THE OSTRICH" INTO THE CHARTS.

PICKWICK CITY RECORDS
where things happen!
A Product of Pickwick International

Barmour Music (BMI)

D.J. COPY

45 RPM
PC-9001-A
Time: 2:25

THE OSTRICH
(Reed-Sims-Vance-Phillips)
THE PRIMITIVES
An L.H. Production

PICKWICK'S EXECUTIVES DON'T WASTE TIME AND PULL THE PLUG ON THEIR SLAPDASH EXPERIMENT.

SORRY LOU, BETTER LUCK NEXT TIME?

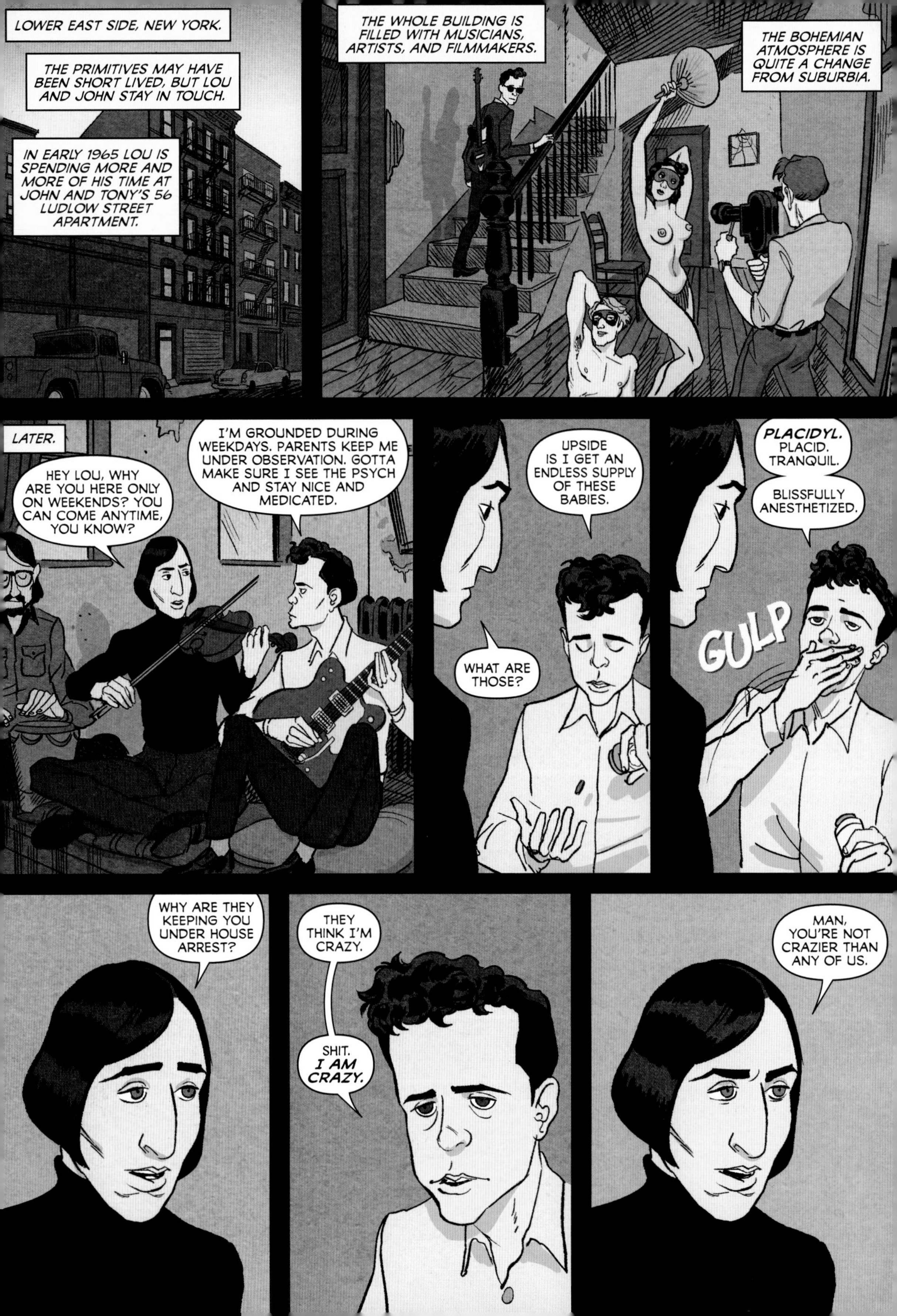
LOWER EAST SIDE, NEW YORK.
THE PRIMITIVES MAY HAVE BEEN SHORT LIVED, BUT LOU AND JOHN STAY IN TOUCH.
IN EARLY 1965 LOU IS SPENDING MORE AND MORE OF HIS TIME AT JOHN AND TONY'S 56 LUDLOW STREET APARTMENT.
THE WHOLE BUILDING IS FILLED WITH MUSICIANS, ARTISTS, AND FILMMAKERS.
THE BOHEMIAN ATMOSPHERE IS QUITE A CHANGE FROM SUBURBIA.
LATER.
HEY LOU, WHY ARE YOU HERE ONLY ON WEEKENDS? YOU CAN COME ANYTIME, YOU KNOW?
I'M GROUNDED DURING WEEKDAYS. PARENTS KEEP ME UNDER OBSERVATION. GOTTA MAKE SURE I SEE THE PSYCH AND STAY NICE AND MEDICATED.
UPSIDE IS I GET AN ENDLESS SUPPLY OF THESE BABIES.
WHAT ARE THOSE?
PLACIDYL. PLACID. TRANQUIL.
BLISSFULLY ANESTHETIZED.
GULP
WHY ARE THEY KEEPING YOU UNDER HOUSE ARREST?
THEY THINK I'M CRAZY.
SHIT. I AM CRAZY.
MAN, YOU'RE NOT CRAZIER THAN ANY OF US.

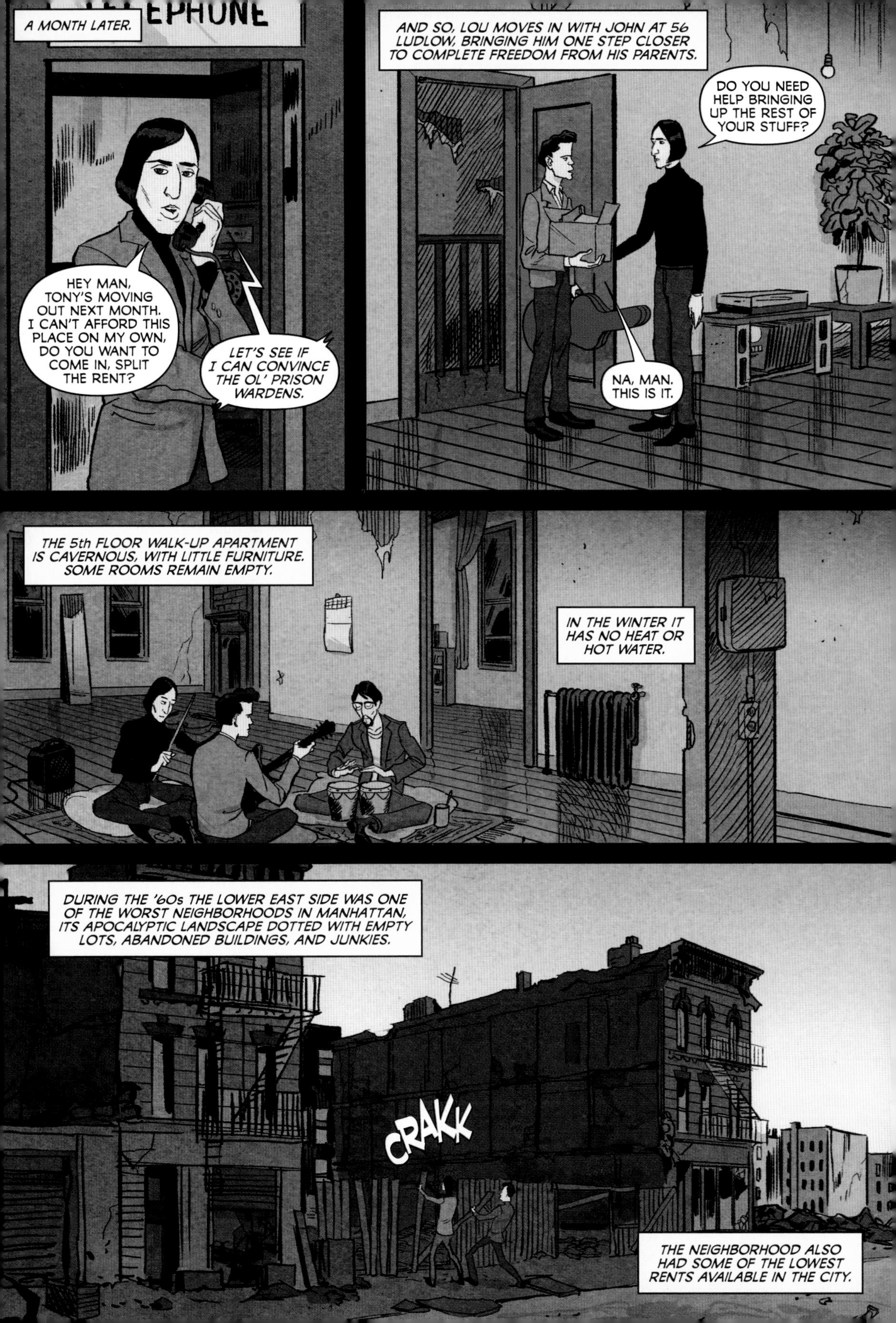

EPHONE
A MONTH LATER.
HEY MAN, TONY'S MOVING OUT NEXT MONTH. I CAN'T AFFORD THIS PLACE ON MY OWN, DO YOU WANT TO COME IN, SPLIT THE RENT?
LET'S SEE IF I CAN CONVINCE THE OL' PRISON WARDENS.
AND SO, LOU MOVES IN WITH JOHN AT 56 LUDLOW, BRINGING HIM ONE STEP CLOSER TO COMPLETE FREEDOM FROM HIS PARENTS.
DO YOU NEED HELP BRINGING UP THE REST OF YOUR STUFF?
NA, MAN. THIS IS IT.
THE 5th FLOOR WALK-UP APARTMENT IS CAVERNOUS, WITH LITTLE FURNITURE. SOME ROOMS REMAIN EMPTY.
IN THE WINTER IT HAS NO HEAT OR HOT WATER.
DURING THE '60s THE LOWER EAST SIDE WAS ONE OF THE WORST NEIGHBORHOODS IN MANHATTAN, ITS APOCALYPTIC LANDSCAPE DOTTED WITH EMPTY LOTS, ABANDONED BUILDINGS, AND JUNKIES.
CRAKK
THE NEIGHBORHOOD ALSO HAD SOME OF THE LOWEST RENTS AVAILABLE IN THE CITY.

SHIT, IT'S THOSE KIDS AGAIN.

HEY!

GET OFF OUR TURF, YOU FAGS!

CLONK

JOHN AND LOU LIVE THE TRUE STARVING ARTIST LIFE. SOME WEEKS THEY SUBSIDED ON NOTHING BUT OATMEAL.

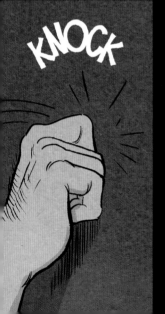

KNOCK

IT'S THAT TIME OF THE MONTH, BOYS, PAY OR PAIN.

GULP GULP

WE'RE GOOD FOR IT THIS TIME. GOT YOUR $25 RIGHT HERE, MR. RIVIERA.

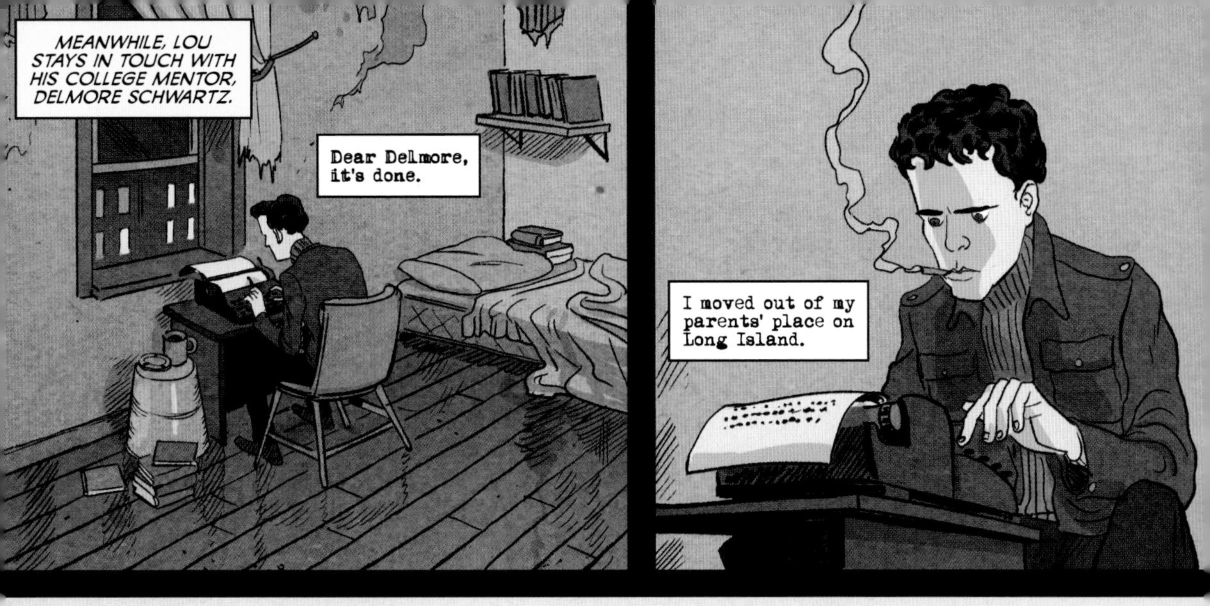
MEANWHILE, LOU STAYS IN TOUCH WITH HIS COLLEGE MENTOR, DELMORE SCHWARTZ.
Dear Delmore, it's done.
I moved out of my parents' place on Long Island.

I'm living in an apartment on the Lower East Side.

There are lots of artists and musicians here. Nobody's got any money, but they seem happier than anyone back in the 'burbs.

My roommate is a classically trained musician from Wales named John Cale, I think I've mentioned him before. He's very talented, he works with La Monte Young, who you may have heard of.

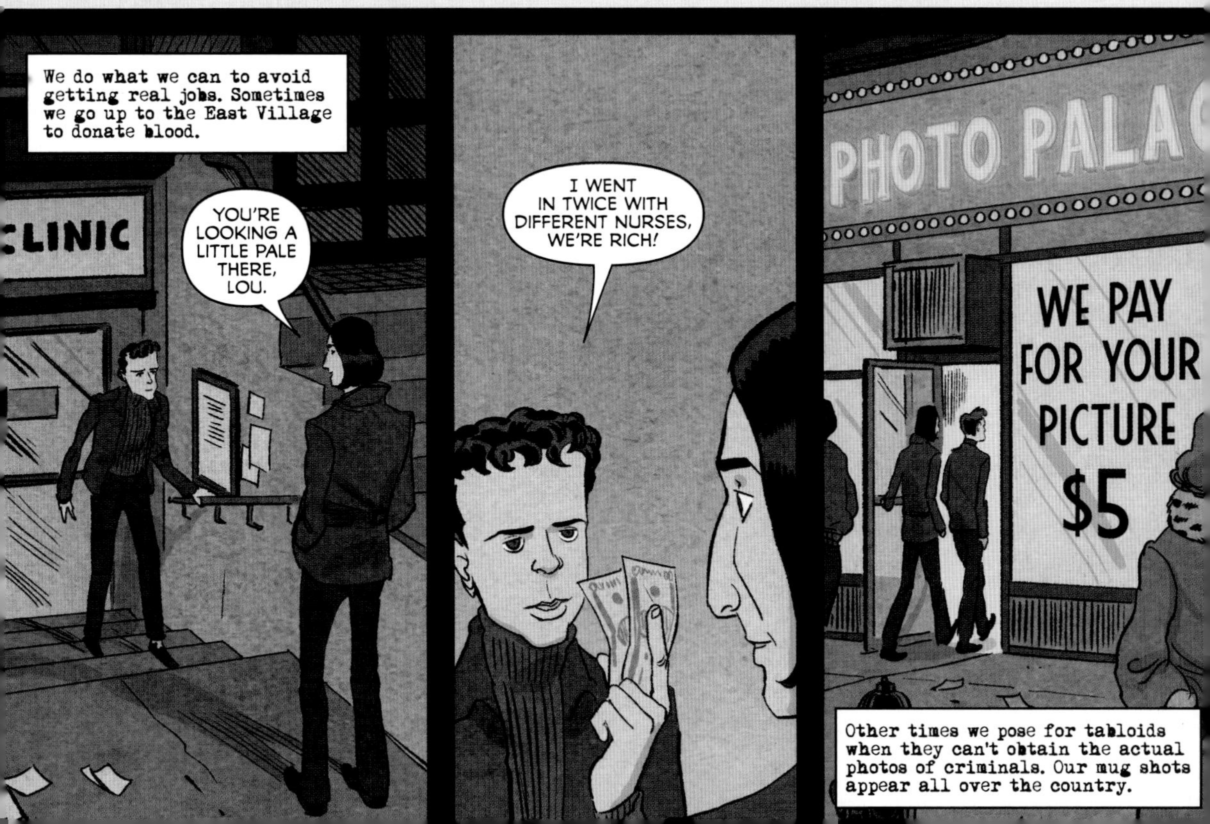
We do what we can to avoid getting real jobs. Sometimes we go up to the East Village to donate blood.
CLINIC
YOU'RE LOOKING A LITTLE PALE THERE, LOU.
I WENT IN TWICE WITH DIFFERENT NURSES, WE'RE RICH!
PHOTO PALAC
WE PAY FOR YOUR PICTURE $5
Other times we pose for tabloids when they can't obtain the actual photos of criminals. Our mug shots appear all over the country.

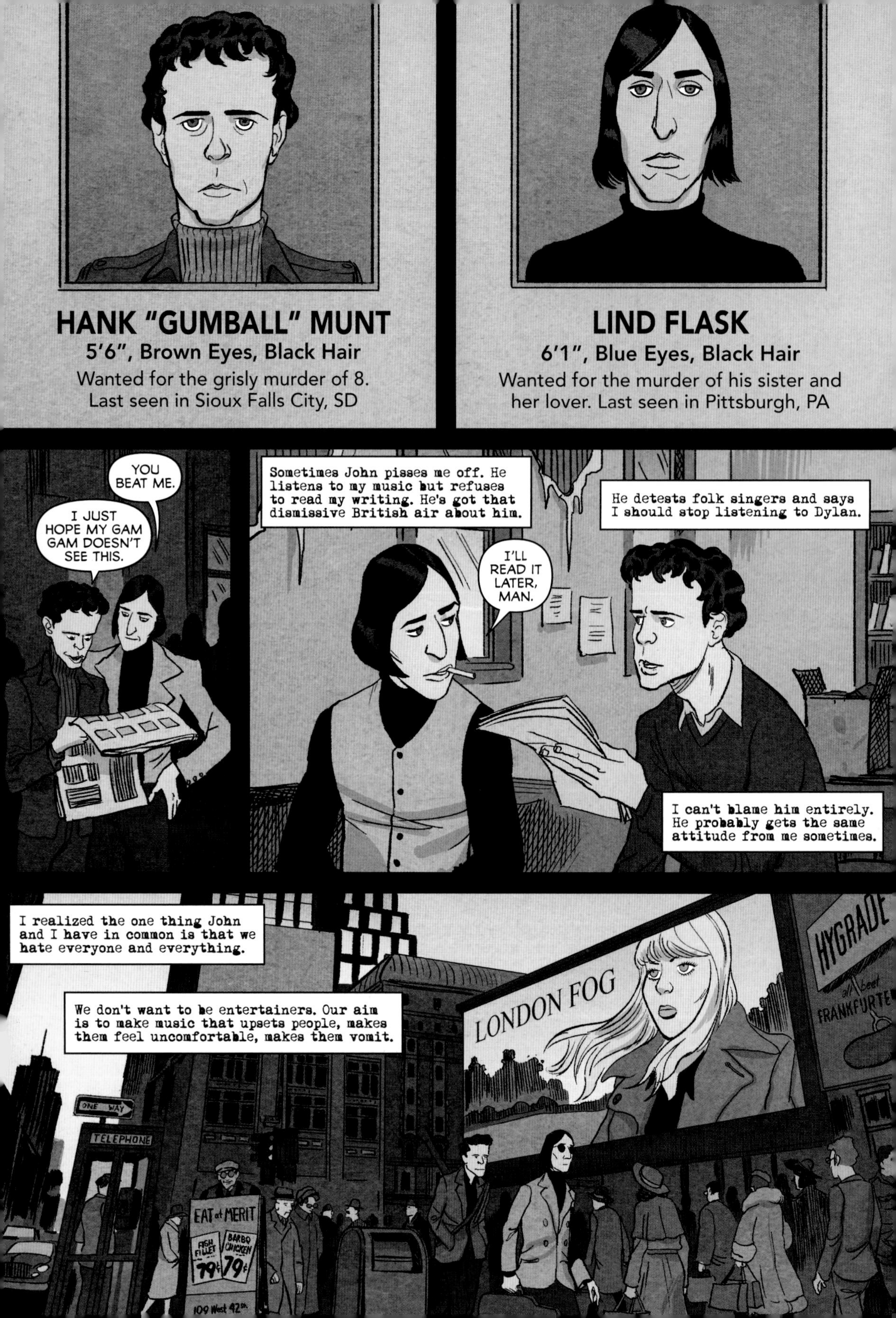

HANK "GUMBALL" MUNT
5'6", Brown Eyes, Black Hair
Wanted for the grisly murder of 8. Last seen in Sioux Falls City, SD
LIND FLASK
6'1", Blue Eyes, Black Hair
Wanted for the murder of his sister and her lover. Last seen in Pittsburgh, PA
I JUST HOPE MY GAM GAM DOESN'T SEE THIS.
YOU BEAT ME.
Sometimes John pisses me off. He listens to my music but refuses to read my writing. He's got that dismissive British air about him.
I'LL READ IT LATER, MAN.
He detests folk singers and says I should stop listening to Dylan.
I can't blame him entirely. He probably gets the same attitude from me sometimes.
I realized the one thing John and I have in common is that we hate everyone and everything.
We don't want to be entertainers. Our aim is to make music that upsets people, makes them feel uncomfortable, makes them vomit.
LONDON FOG
HYGRADE
ONE WAY
TELEPHONE
EAT at MERIT
FISH FILLET 79¢
BARBQ CHICKEN 79¢

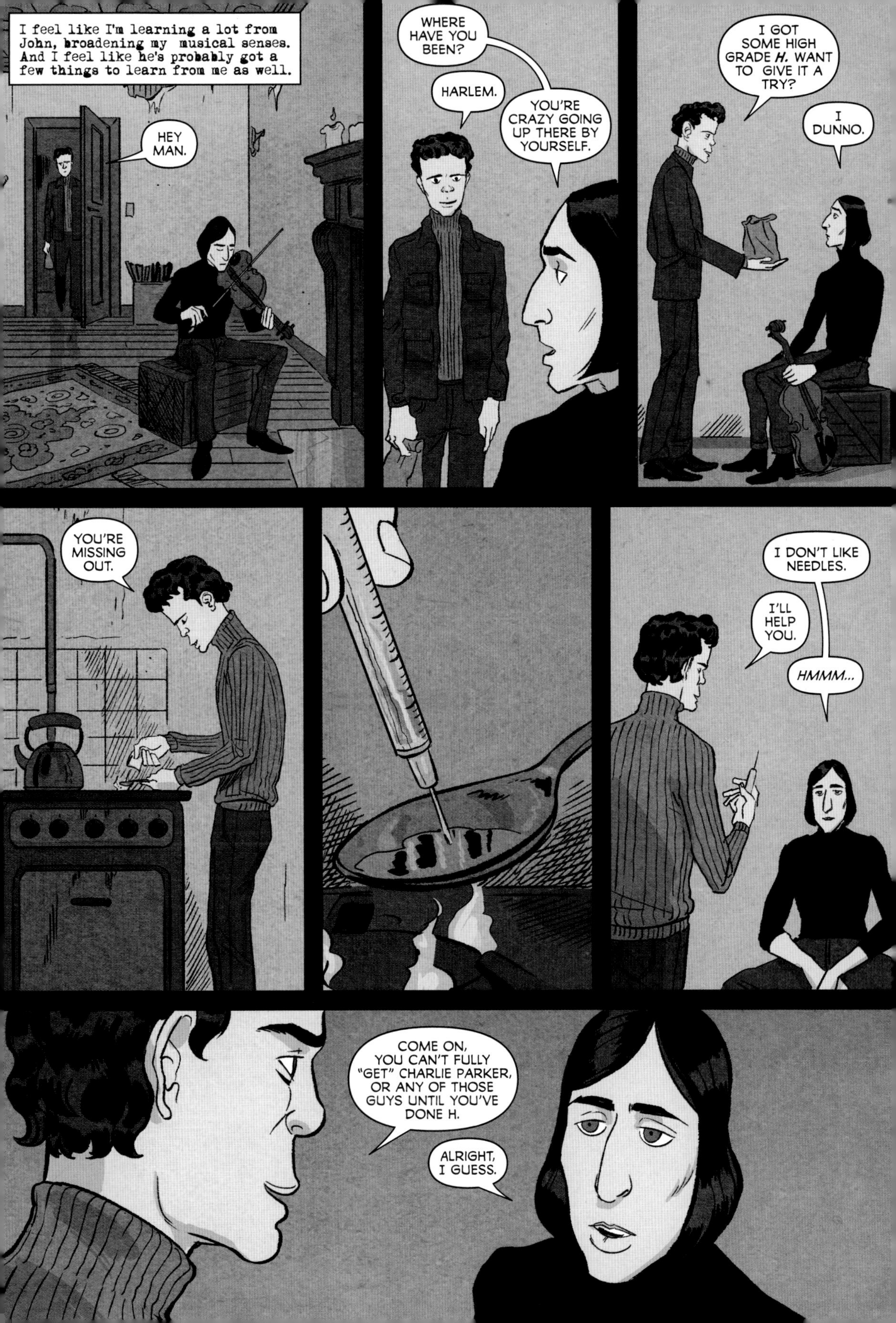
I feel like I'm learning a lot from John, broadening my musical senses. And I feel like he's probably got a few things to learn from me as well.
HEY MAN.
WHERE HAVE YOU BEEN?
HARLEM.
YOU'RE CRAZY GOING UP THERE BY YOURSELF.
I GOT SOME HIGH GRADE *H.* WANT TO GIVE IT A TRY?
I DUNNO.
YOU'RE MISSING OUT.
I DON'T LIKE NEEDLES.
I'LL HELP YOU.
HMMM...
COME ON, YOU CAN'T FULLY "GET" CHARLIE PARKER, OR ANY OF THOSE GUYS UNTIL YOU'VE DONE H.
ALRIGHT, I GUESS.

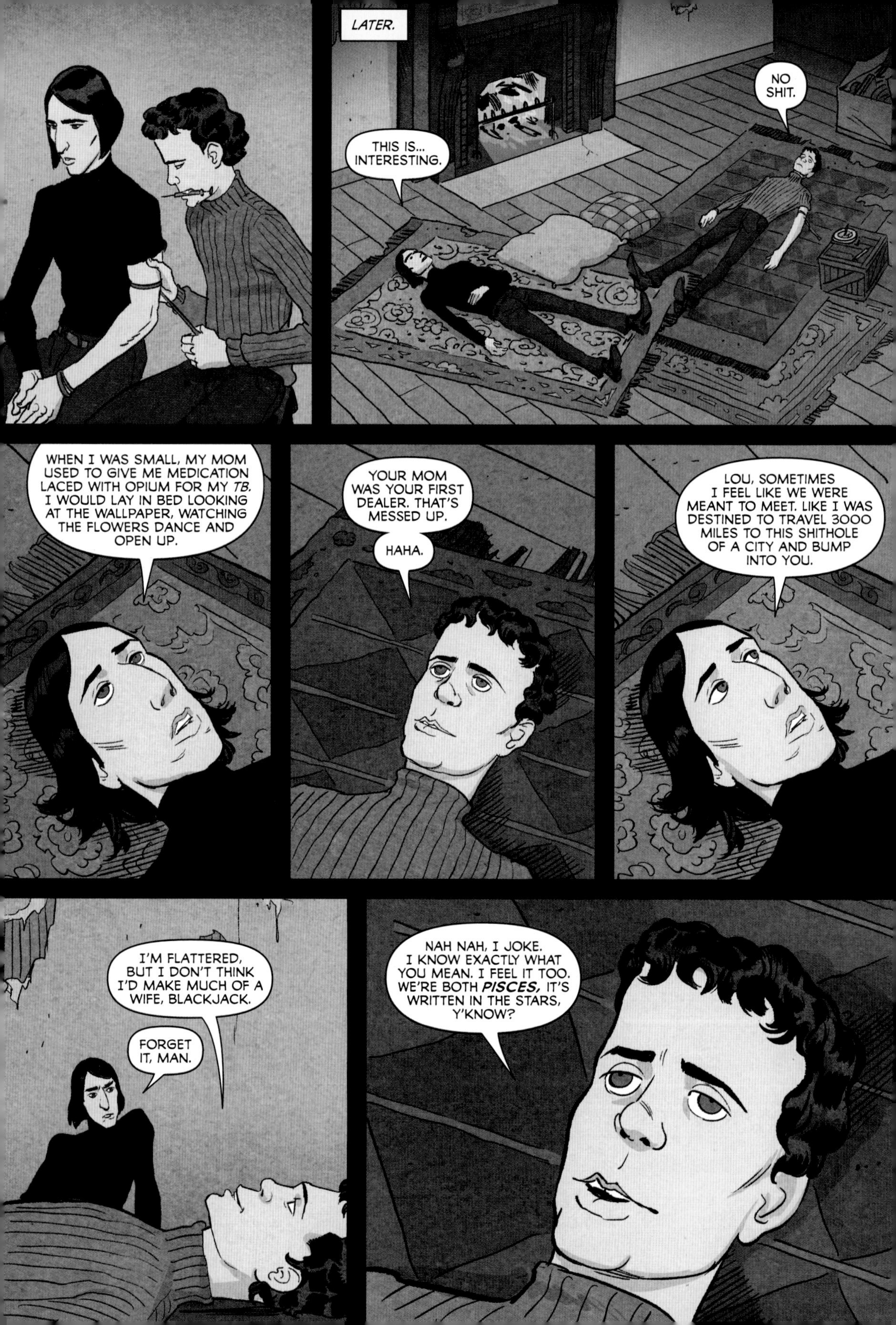
LATER.
THIS IS... INTERESTING.
NO SHIT.
WHEN I WAS SMALL, MY MOM USED TO GIVE ME MEDICATION LACED WITH OPIUM FOR MY *TB.* I WOULD LAY IN BED LOOKING AT THE WALLPAPER, WATCHING THE FLOWERS DANCE AND OPEN UP.
YOUR MOM WAS YOUR FIRST DEALER. THAT'S MESSED UP.
HAHA.
LOU, SOMETIMES I FEEL LIKE WE WERE MEANT TO MEET. LIKE I WAS DESTINED TO TRAVEL 3000 MILES TO THIS SHITHOLE OF A CITY AND BUMP INTO YOU.
I'M FLATTERED, BUT I DON'T THINK I'D MAKE MUCH OF A WIFE, BLACKJACK.
FORGET IT, MAN.
NAH NAH, I JOKE. I KNOW EXACTLY WHAT YOU MEAN. I FEEL IT TOO. WE'RE BOTH ***PISCES,*** IT'S WRITTEN IN THE STARS, Y'KNOW?

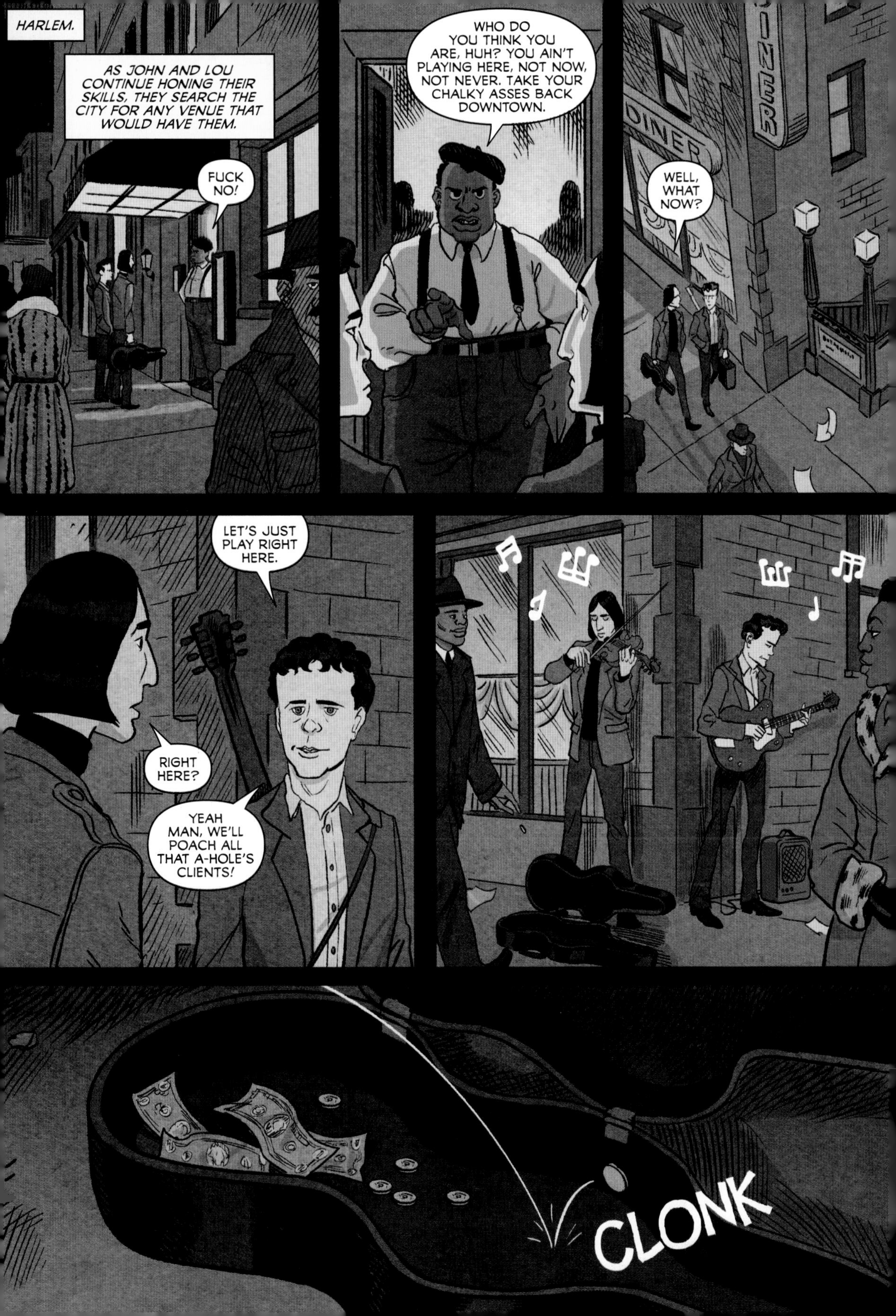
HARLEM.
AS JOHN AND LOU CONTINUE HONING THEIR SKILLS, THEY SEARCH THE CITY FOR ANY VENUE THAT WOULD HAVE THEM.
FUCK NO!
WHO DO YOU THINK YOU ARE, HUH? YOU AIN'T PLAYING HERE, NOT NOW, NOT NEVER. TAKE YOUR CHALKY ASSES BACK DOWNTOWN.
DINER
DINER
WELL, WHAT NOW?
LET'S JUST PLAY RIGHT HERE.
RIGHT HERE?
YEAH MAN, WE'LL POACH ALL THAT A-HOLE'S CLIENTS!
CLONK

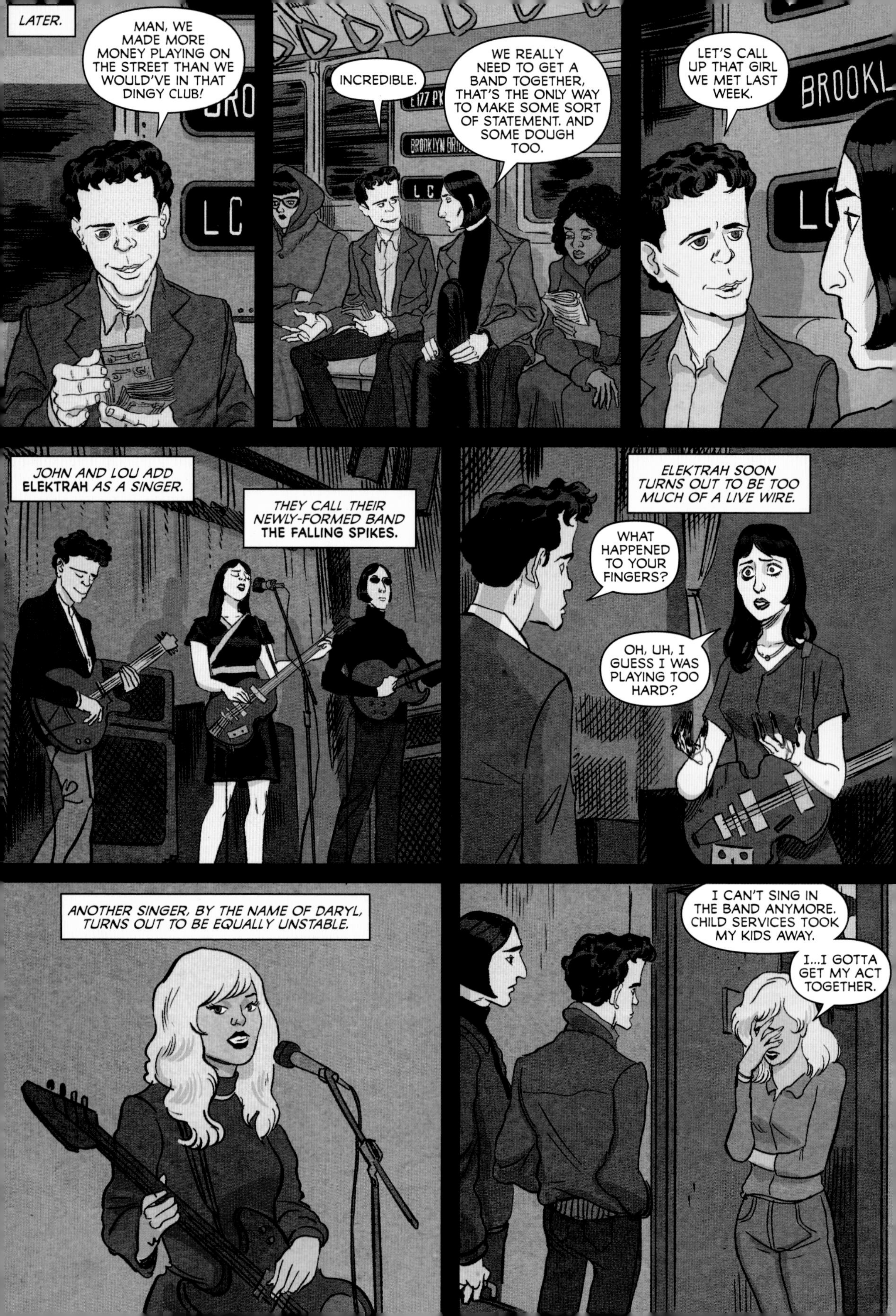
LATER.
MAN, WE MADE MORE MONEY PLAYING ON THE STREET THAN WE WOULD'VE IN THAT DINGY CLUB!
INCREDIBLE.
WE REALLY NEED TO GET A BAND TOGETHER, THAT'S THE ONLY WAY TO MAKE SOME SORT OF STATEMENT. AND SOME DOUGH TOO.
LET'S CALL UP THAT GIRL WE MET LAST WEEK.
BROOKL
JOHN AND LOU ADD ELEKTRAH AS A SINGER.
THEY CALL THEIR NEWLY-FORMED BAND THE FALLING SPIKES.
ELEKTRAH SOON TURNS OUT TO BE TOO MUCH OF A LIVE WIRE.
WHAT HAPPENED TO YOUR FINGERS?
OH, UH, I GUESS I WAS PLAYING TOO HARD?
ANOTHER SINGER, BY THE NAME OF DARYL, TURNS OUT TO BE EQUALLY UNSTABLE.
I CAN'T SING IN THE BAND ANYMORE. CHILD SERVICES TOOK MY KIDS AWAY.
I...I GOTTA GET MY ACT TOGETHER.

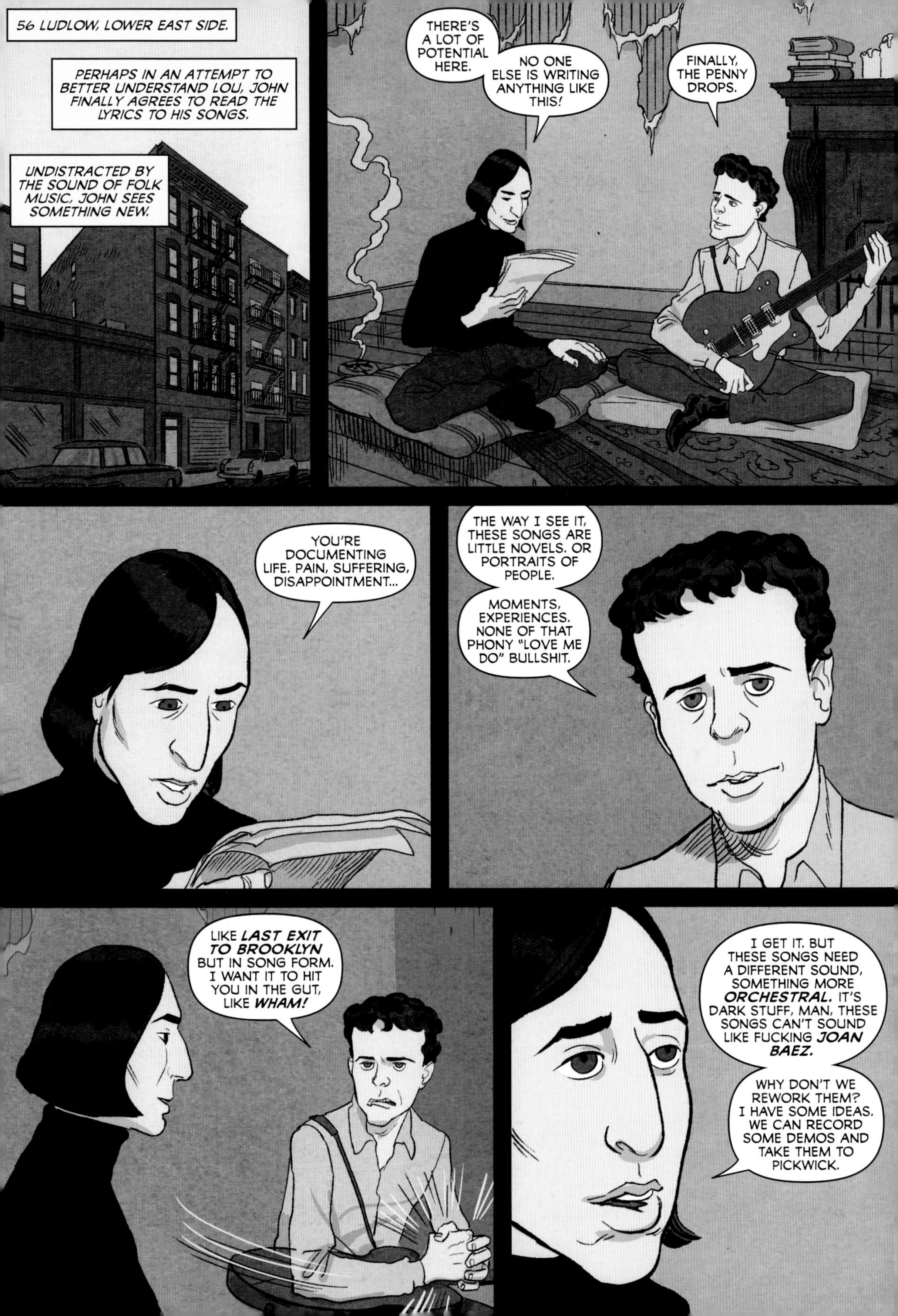
56 LUDLOW, LOWER EAST SIDE.
PERHAPS IN AN ATTEMPT TO BETTER UNDERSTAND LOU, JOHN FINALLY AGREES TO READ THE LYRICS TO HIS SONGS.
UNDISTRACTED BY THE SOUND OF FOLK MUSIC, JOHN SEES SOMETHING NEW.
THERE'S A LOT OF POTENTIAL HERE.
NO ONE ELSE IS WRITING ANYTHING LIKE THIS!
FINALLY, THE PENNY DROPS.
YOU'RE DOCUMENTING LIFE. PAIN, SUFFERING, DISAPPOINTMENT...
THE WAY I SEE IT, THESE SONGS ARE LITTLE NOVELS. OR PORTRAITS OF PEOPLE.
MOMENTS, EXPERIENCES. NONE OF THAT PHONY "LOVE ME DO" BULLSHIT.
LIKE ***LAST EXIT TO BROOKLYN*** BUT IN SONG FORM. I WANT IT TO HIT YOU IN THE GUT, LIKE ***WHAM!***
I GET IT. BUT THESE SONGS NEED A DIFFERENT SOUND, SOMETHING MORE ***ORCHESTRAL.*** IT'S DARK STUFF, MAN, THESE SONGS CAN'T SOUND LIKE FUCKING ***JOAN BAEZ.***
WHY DON'T WE REWORK THEM? I HAVE SOME IDEAS. WE CAN RECORD SOME DEMOS AND TAKE THEM TO PICKWICK.

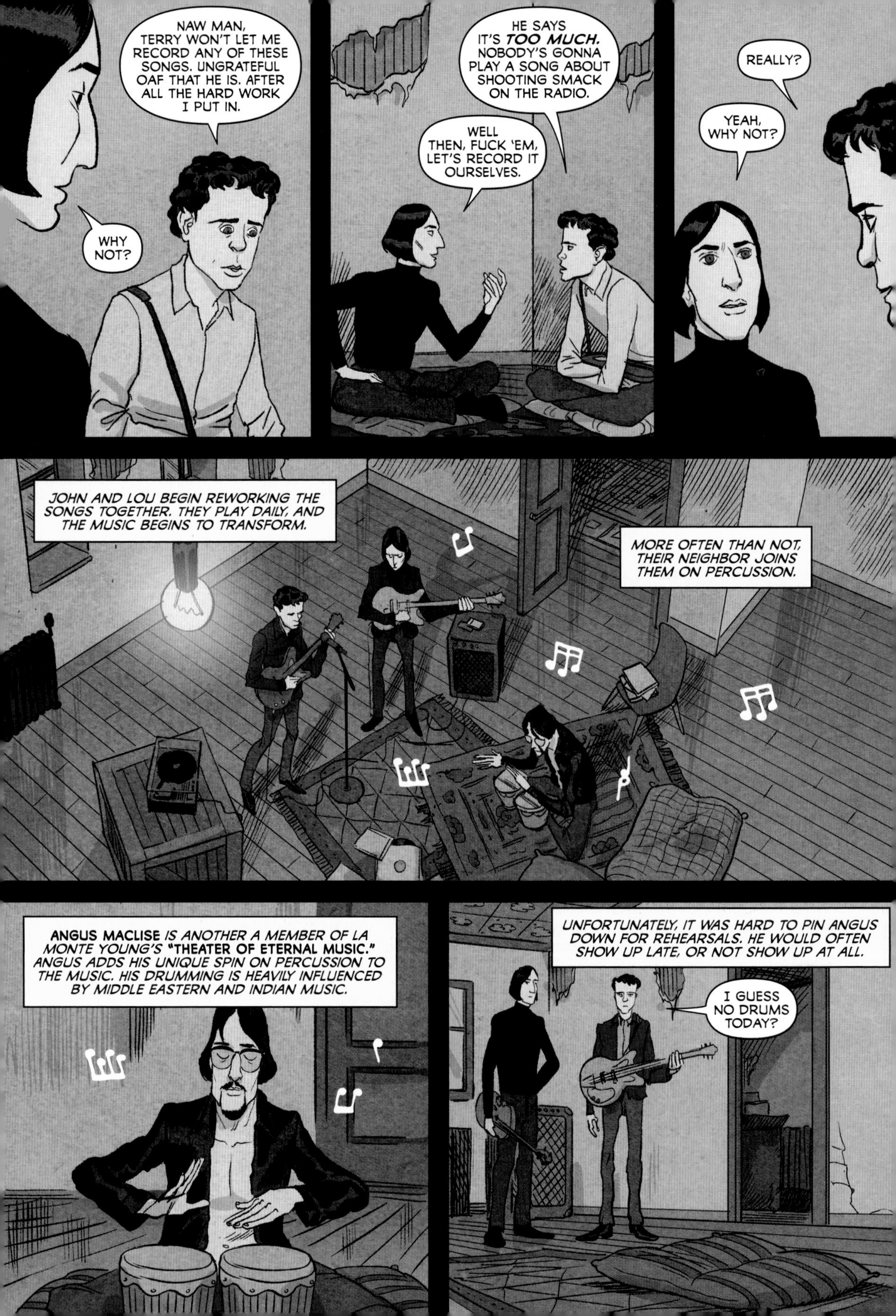
NAW MAN, TERRY WON'T LET ME RECORD ANY OF THESE SONGS. UNGRATEFUL OAF THAT HE IS. AFTER ALL THE HARD WORK I PUT IN.
WHY NOT?
HE SAYS IT'S *TOO MUCH.* NOBODY'S GONNA PLAY A SONG ABOUT SHOOTING SMACK ON THE RADIO.
WELL THEN, FUCK 'EM, LET'S RECORD IT OURSELVES.
REALLY?
YEAH, WHY NOT?
JOHN AND LOU BEGIN REWORKING THE SONGS TOGETHER. THEY PLAY DAILY, AND THE MUSIC BEGINS TO TRANSFORM.
MORE OFTEN THAN NOT, THEIR NEIGHBOR JOINS THEM ON PERCUSSION.
ANGUS MACLISE IS ANOTHER A MEMBER OF LA MONTE YOUNG'S **"THEATER OF ETERNAL MUSIC."** ANGUS ADDS HIS UNIQUE SPIN ON PERCUSSION TO THE MUSIC. HIS DRUMMING IS HEAVILY INFLUENCED BY MIDDLE EASTERN AND INDIAN MUSIC.
UNFORTUNATELY, IT WAS HARD TO PIN ANGUS DOWN FOR REHEARSALS. HE WOULD OFTEN SHOW UP LATE, OR NOT SHOW UP AT ALL.
I GUESS NO DRUMS TODAY?

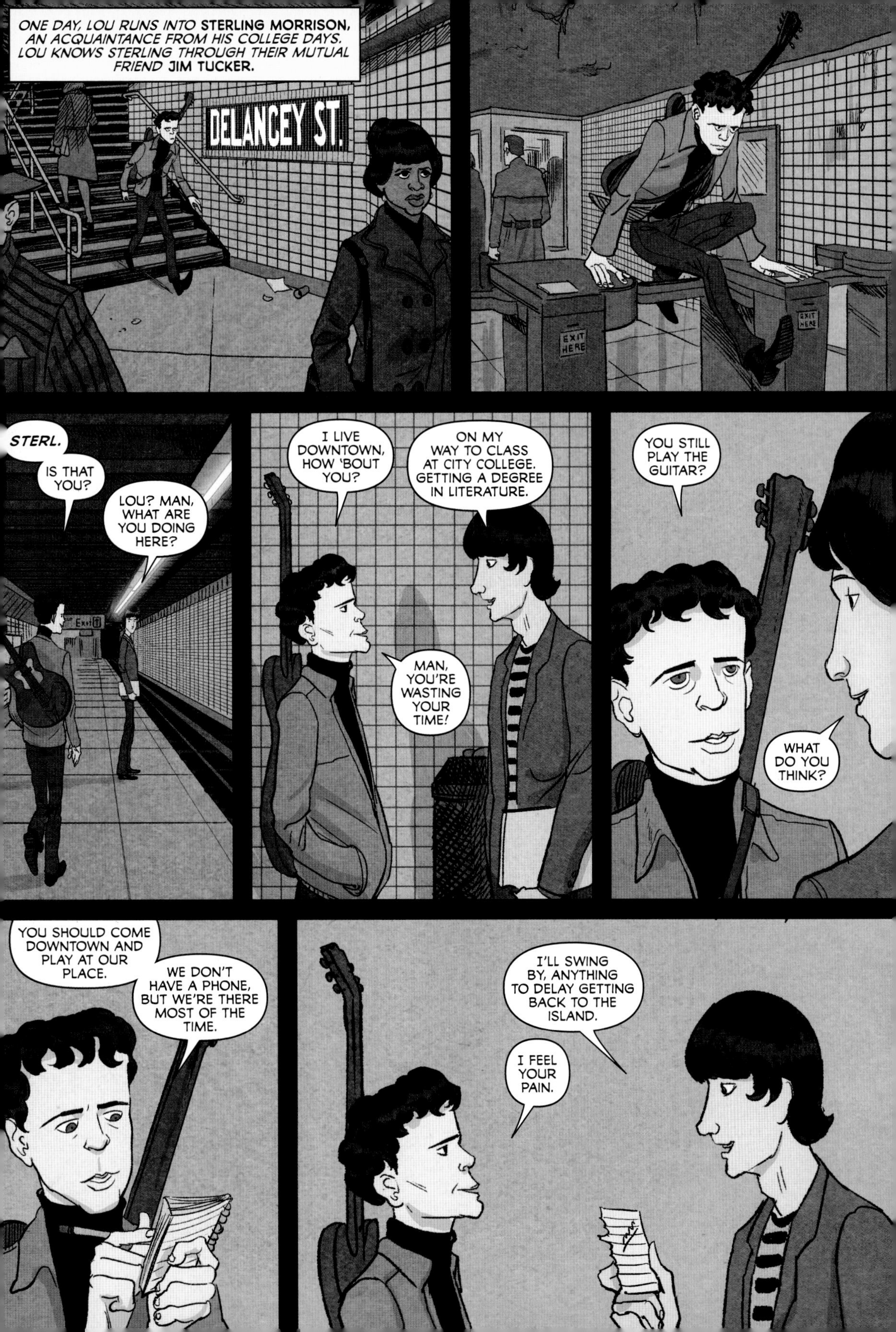
ONE DAY, LOU RUNS INTO STERLING MORRISON, AN ACQUAINTANCE FROM HIS COLLEGE DAYS. LOU KNOWS STERLING THROUGH THEIR MUTUAL FRIEND JIM TUCKER.
DELANCEY ST.
EXIT HERE
EXIT HERE
STERL.
IS THAT YOU?
LOU? MAN, WHAT ARE YOU DOING HERE?
I LIVE DOWNTOWN, HOW 'BOUT YOU?
ON MY WAY TO CLASS AT CITY COLLEGE. GETTING A DEGREE IN LITERATURE.
MAN, YOU'RE WASTING YOUR TIME!
YOU STILL PLAY THE GUITAR?
WHAT DO YOU THINK?
YOU SHOULD COME DOWNTOWN AND PLAY AT OUR PLACE.
WE DON'T HAVE A PHONE, BUT WE'RE THERE MOST OF THE TIME.
I'LL SWING BY, ANYTHING TO DELAY GETTING BACK TO THE ISLAND.
I FEEL YOUR PAIN.

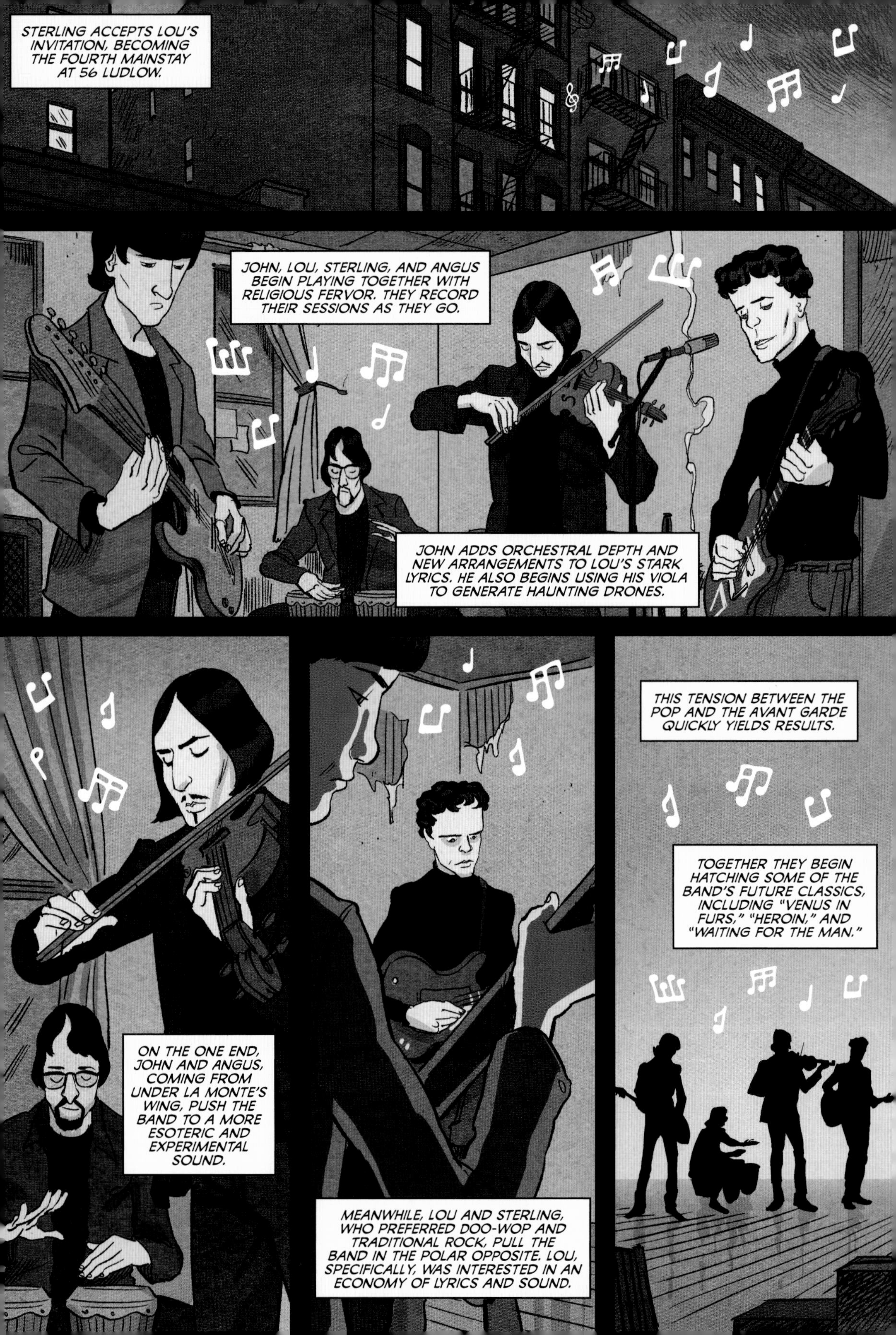
STERLING ACCEPTS LOU'S INVITATION, BECOMING THE FOURTH MAINSTAY AT 56 LUDLOW.
JOHN, LOU, STERLING, AND ANGUS BEGIN PLAYING TOGETHER WITH RELIGIOUS FERVOR. THEY RECORD THEIR SESSIONS AS THEY GO.
JOHN ADDS ORCHESTRAL DEPTH AND NEW ARRANGEMENTS TO LOU'S STARK LYRICS. HE ALSO BEGINS USING HIS VIOLA TO GENERATE HAUNTING DRONES.
ON THE ONE END, JOHN AND ANGUS, COMING FROM UNDER LA MONTE'S WING, PUSH THE BAND TO A MORE ESOTERIC AND EXPERIMENTAL SOUND.
MEANWHILE, LOU AND STERLING, WHO PREFERRED DOO-WOP AND TRADITIONAL ROCK, PULL THE BAND IN THE POLAR OPPOSITE. LOU, SPECIFICALLY, WAS INTERESTED IN AN ECONOMY OF LYRICS AND SOUND.
THIS TENSION BETWEEN THE POP AND THE AVANT GARDE QUICKLY YIELDS RESULTS.
TOGETHER THEY BEGIN HATCHING SOME OF THE BAND'S FUTURE CLASSICS, INCLUDING "VENUS IN FURS," "HEROIN," AND "WAITING FOR THE MAN."

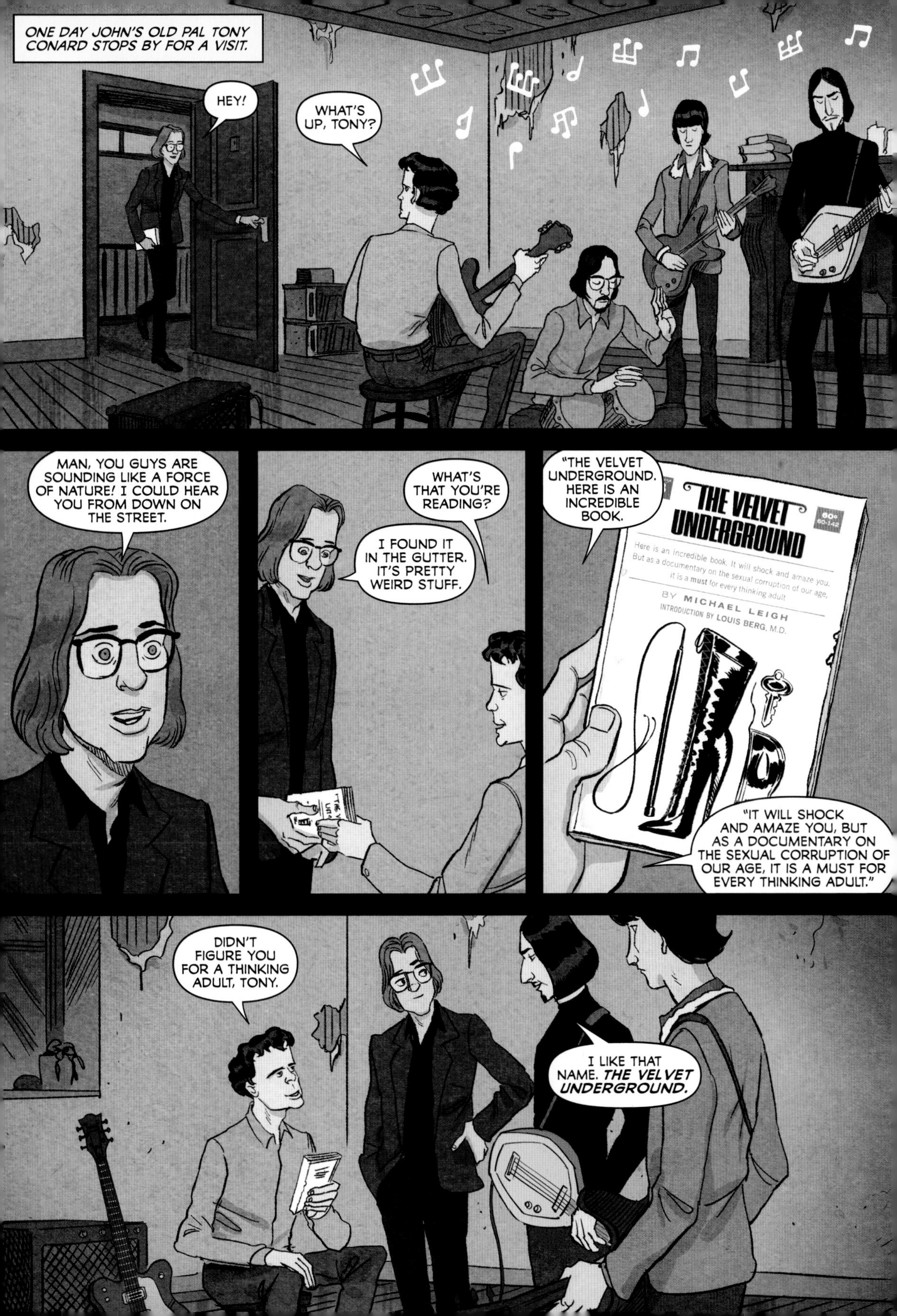
ONE DAY JOHN'S OLD PAL TONY CONARD STOPS BY FOR A VISIT.
HEY!
WHAT'S UP, TONY?
MAN, YOU GUYS ARE SOUNDING LIKE A FORCE OF NATURE! I COULD HEAR YOU FROM DOWN ON THE STREET.
WHAT'S THAT YOU'RE READING?
I FOUND IT IN THE GUTTER. IT'S PRETTY WEIRD STUFF.
"THE VELVET UNDERGROUND. HERE IS AN INCREDIBLE BOOK.
THE VELVET UNDERGROUND
60¢
60-142
Here is an incredible book. It will shock and amaze you. But as a documentary on the sexual corruption of our age, it is a must for every thinking adult
BY MICHAEL LEIGH
INTRODUCTION BY LOUIS BERG, M.D.
"IT WILL SHOCK AND AMAZE YOU, BUT AS A DOCUMENTARY ON THE SEXUAL CORRUPTION OF OUR AGE, IT IS A MUST FOR EVERY THINKING ADULT."
DIDN'T FIGURE YOU FOR A THINKING ADULT, TONY.
I LIKE THAT NAME. THE VELVET UNDERGROUND.

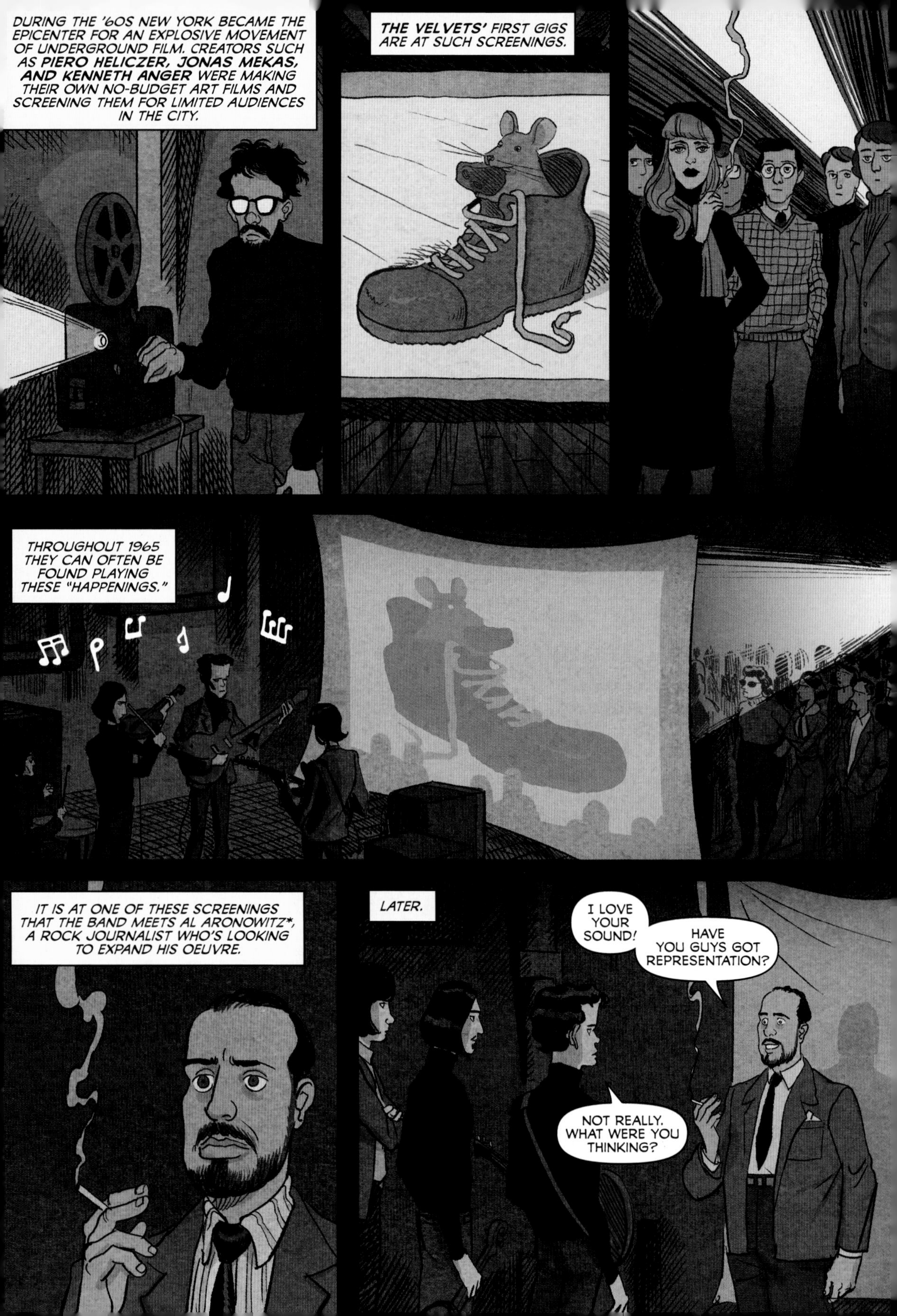
DURING THE '60S NEW YORK BECAME THE EPICENTER FOR AN EXPLOSIVE MOVEMENT OF UNDERGROUND FILM. CREATORS SUCH AS **PIERO HELICZER, JONAS MEKAS, AND KENNETH ANGER** WERE MAKING THEIR OWN NO-BUDGET ART FILMS AND SCREENING THEM FOR LIMITED AUDIENCES IN THE CITY.
THE VELVETS' FIRST GIGS ARE AT SUCH SCREENINGS.
THROUGHOUT 1965 THEY CAN OFTEN BE FOUND PLAYING THESE "HAPPENINGS."
IT IS AT ONE OF THESE SCREENINGS THAT THE BAND MEETS AL ARONOWITZ*, A ROCK JOURNALIST WHO'S LOOKING TO EXPAND HIS OEUVRE.
LATER.
I LOVE YOUR SOUND!
HAVE YOU GUYS GOT REPRESENTATION?
NOT REALLY. WHAT WERE YOU THINKING?

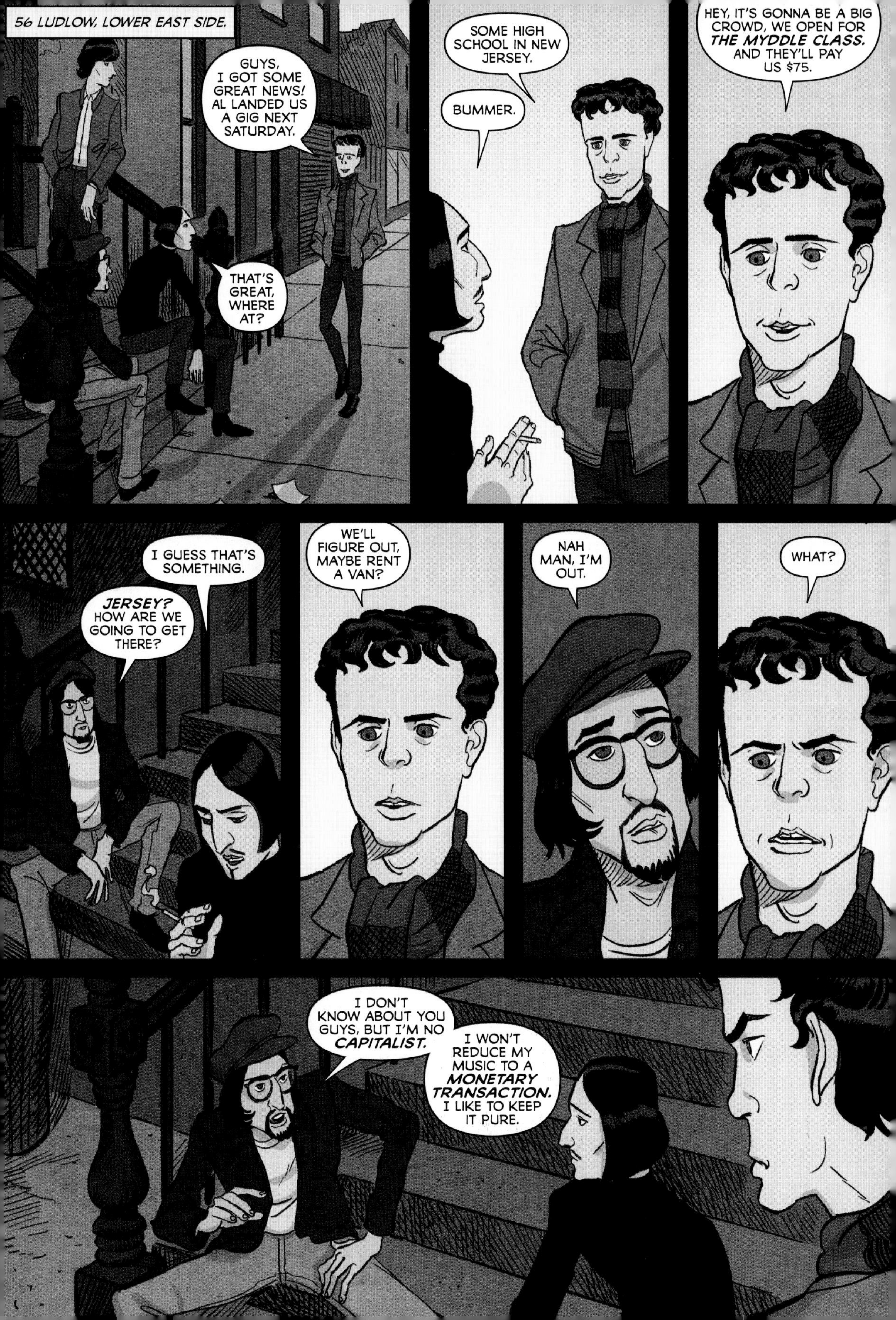
56 LUDLOW, LOWER EAST SIDE.
GUYS, I GOT SOME GREAT NEWS! AL LANDED US A GIG NEXT SATURDAY.
THAT'S GREAT, WHERE AT?
SOME HIGH SCHOOL IN NEW JERSEY.
BUMMER.
HEY, IT'S GONNA BE A BIG CROWD, WE OPEN FOR *THE MYDDLE CLASS.* AND THEY'LL PAY US $75.
I GUESS THAT'S SOMETHING.
JERSEY? HOW ARE WE GOING TO GET THERE?
WE'LL FIGURE OUT, MAYBE RENT A VAN?
NAH MAN, I'M OUT.
WHAT?
I DON'T KNOW ABOUT YOU GUYS, BUT I'M NO *CAPITALIST.*
I WON'T REDUCE MY MUSIC TO A *MONETARY TRANSACTION.* I LIKE TO KEEP IT PURE.

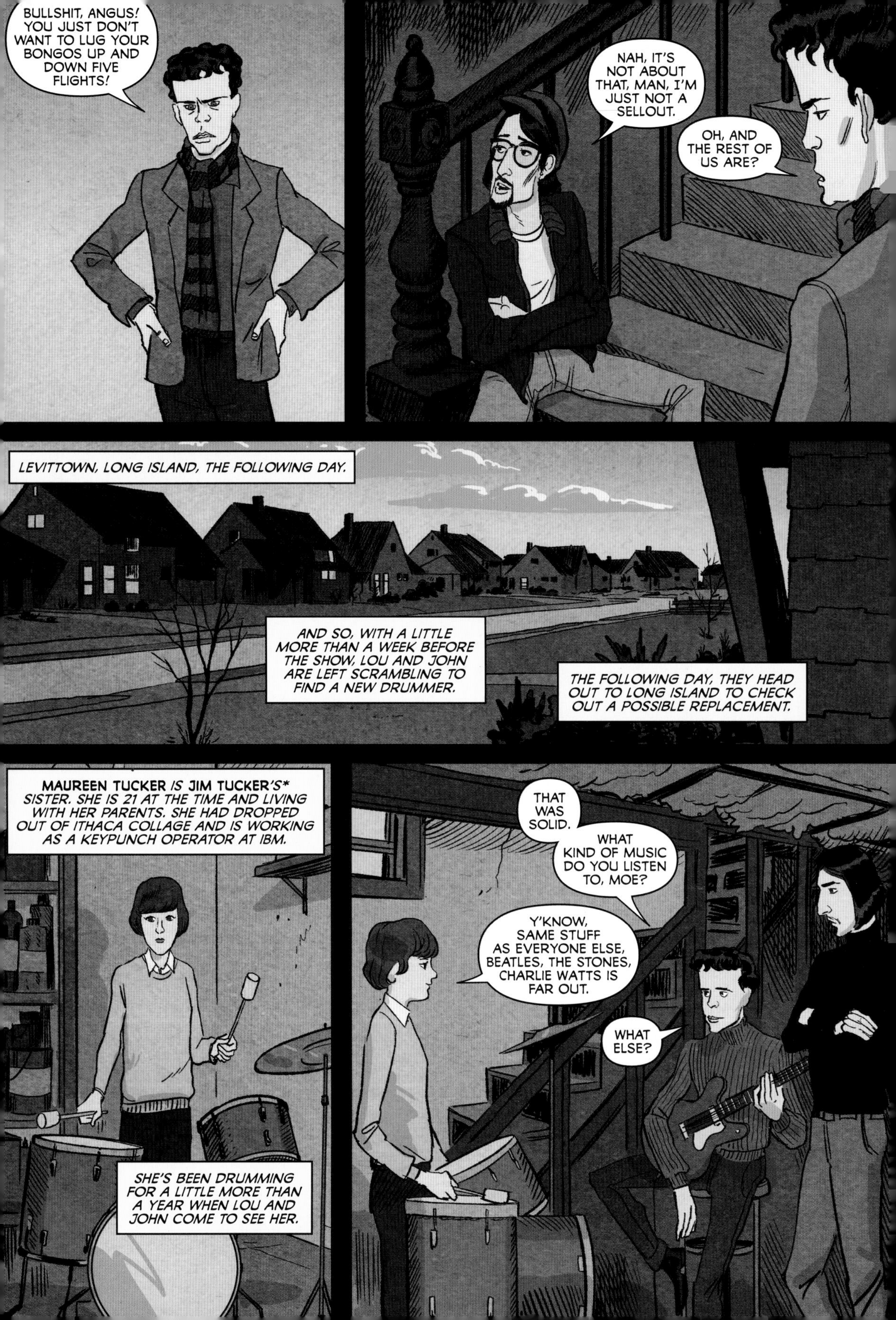
BULLSHIT, ANGUS! YOU JUST DON'T WANT TO LUG YOUR BONGOS UP AND DOWN FIVE FLIGHTS!
NAH, IT'S NOT ABOUT THAT, MAN, I'M JUST NOT A SELLOUT.
OH, AND THE REST OF US ARE?
LEVITTOWN, LONG ISLAND, THE FOLLOWING DAY.
AND SO, WITH A LITTLE MORE THAN A WEEK BEFORE THE SHOW, LOU AND JOHN ARE LEFT SCRAMBLING TO FIND A NEW DRUMMER.
THE FOLLOWING DAY, THEY HEAD OUT TO LONG ISLAND TO CHECK OUT A POSSIBLE REPLACEMENT.
MAUREEN TUCKER IS JIM TUCKER'S* SISTER. SHE IS 21 AT THE TIME AND LIVING WITH HER PARENTS. SHE HAD DROPPED OUT OF ITHACA COLLAGE AND IS WORKING AS A KEYPUNCH OPERATOR AT IBM.
SHE'S BEEN DRUMMING FOR A LITTLE MORE THAN A YEAR WHEN LOU AND JOHN COME TO SEE HER.
THAT WAS SOLID.
WHAT KIND OF MUSIC DO YOU LISTEN TO, MOE?
Y'KNOW, SAME STUFF AS EVERYONE ELSE, BEATLES, THE STONES, CHARLIE WATTS IS FAR OUT.
WHAT ELSE?

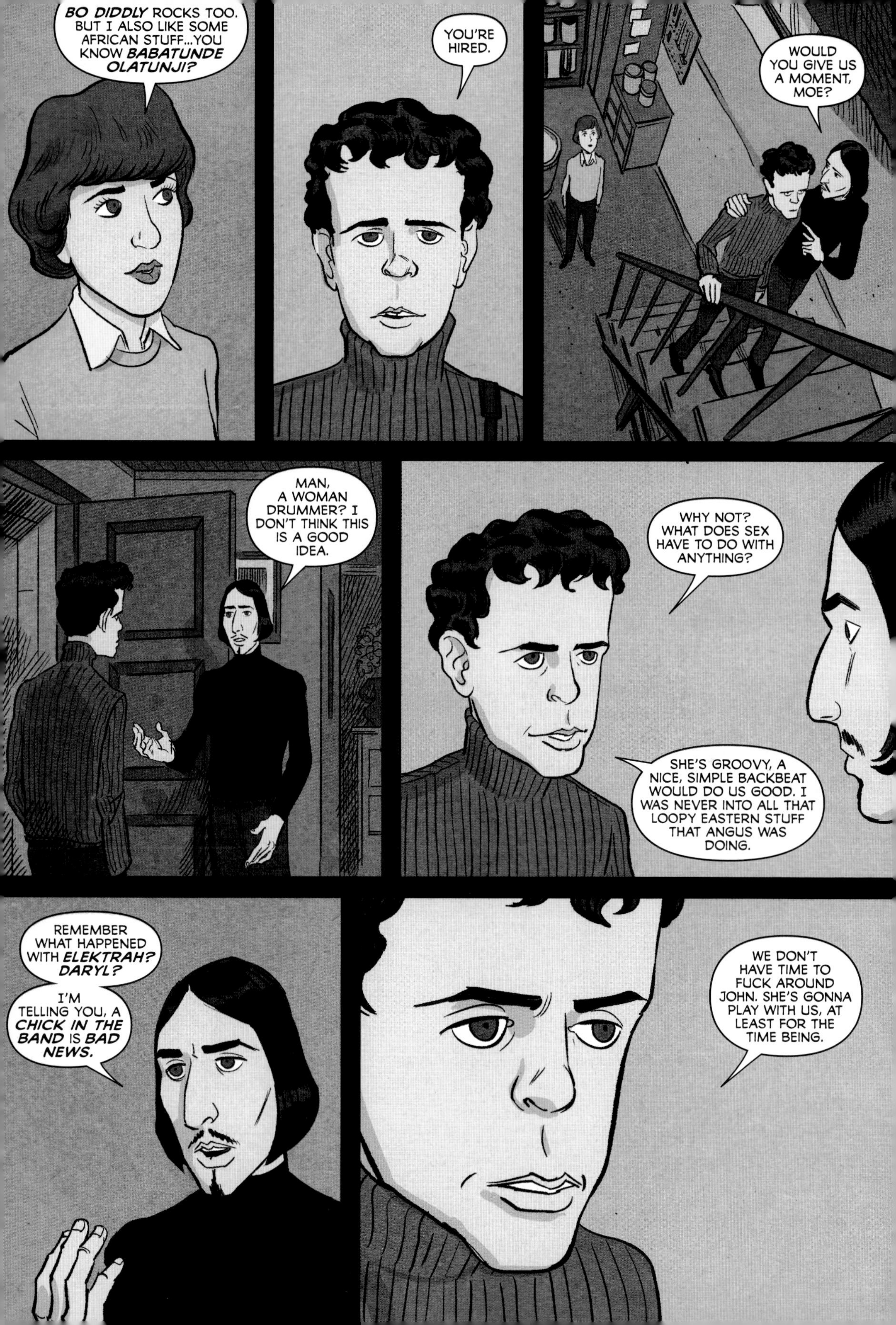
BO DIDDLY ROCKS TOO. BUT I ALSO LIKE SOME AFRICAN STUFF...YOU KNOW BABATUNDE OLATUNJI?
YOU'RE HIRED.
WOULD YOU GIVE US A MOMENT, MOE?
MAN, A WOMAN DRUMMER? I DON'T THINK THIS IS A GOOD IDEA.
WHY NOT? WHAT DOES SEX HAVE TO DO WITH ANYTHING?
SHE'S GROOVY, A NICE, SIMPLE BACKBEAT WOULD DO US GOOD. I WAS NEVER INTO ALL THAT LOOPY EASTERN STUFF THAT ANGUS WAS DOING.
REMEMBER WHAT HAPPENED WITH ELEKTRAH? DARYL?
I'M TELLING YOU, A CHICK IN THE BAND IS BAD NEWS.
WE DON'T HAVE TIME TO FUCK AROUND JOHN. SHE'S GONNA PLAY WITH US, AT LEAST FOR THE TIME BEING.

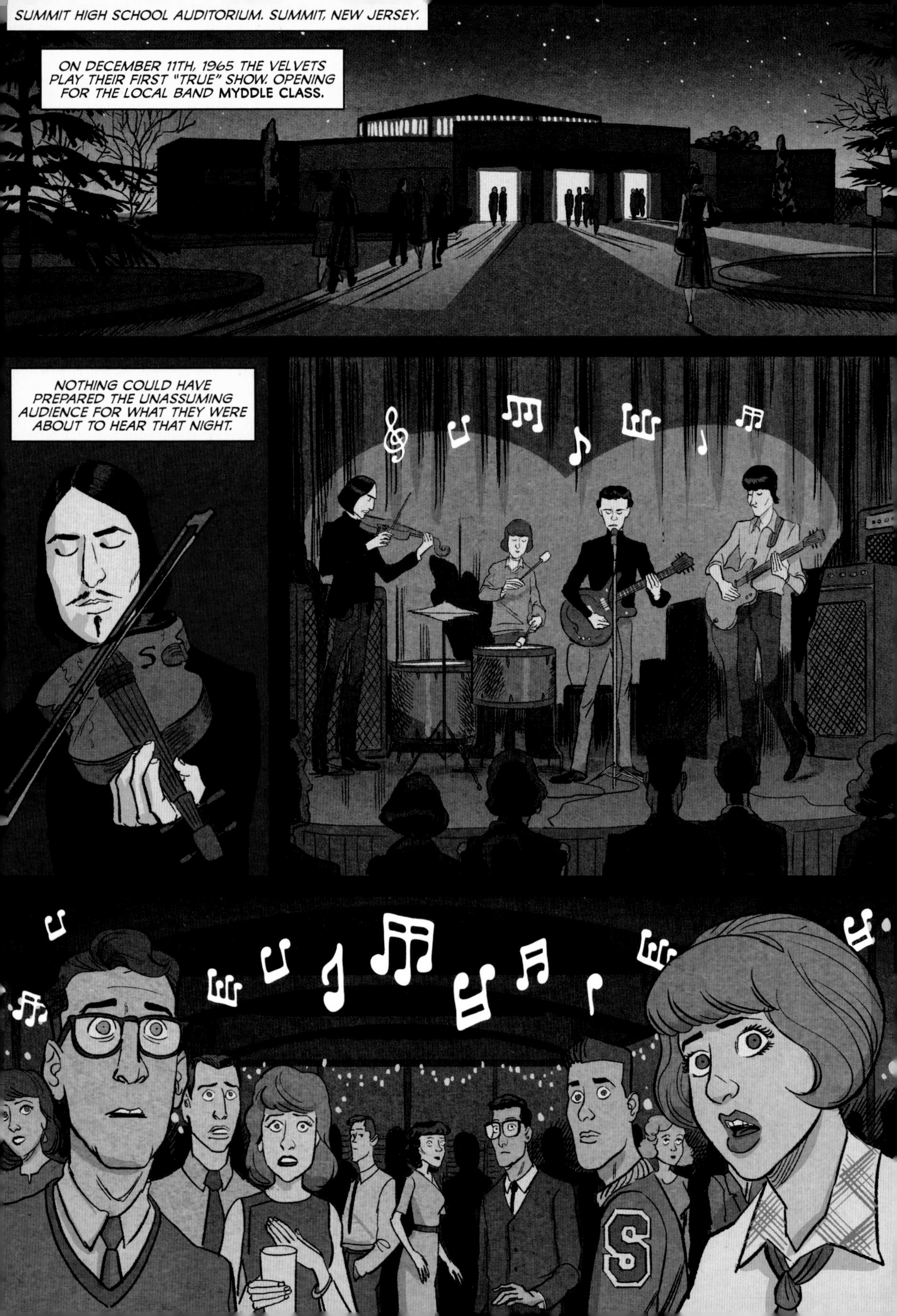
SUMMIT HIGH SCHOOL AUDITORIUM. SUMMIT, NEW JERSEY.
ON DECEMBER 11TH, 1965 THE VELVETS PLAY THEIR FIRST "TRUE" SHOW. OPENING FOR THE LOCAL BAND MYDDLE CLASS.
NOTHING COULD HAVE PREPARED THE UNASSUMING AUDIENCE FOR WHAT THEY WERE ABOUT TO HEAR THAT NIGHT.

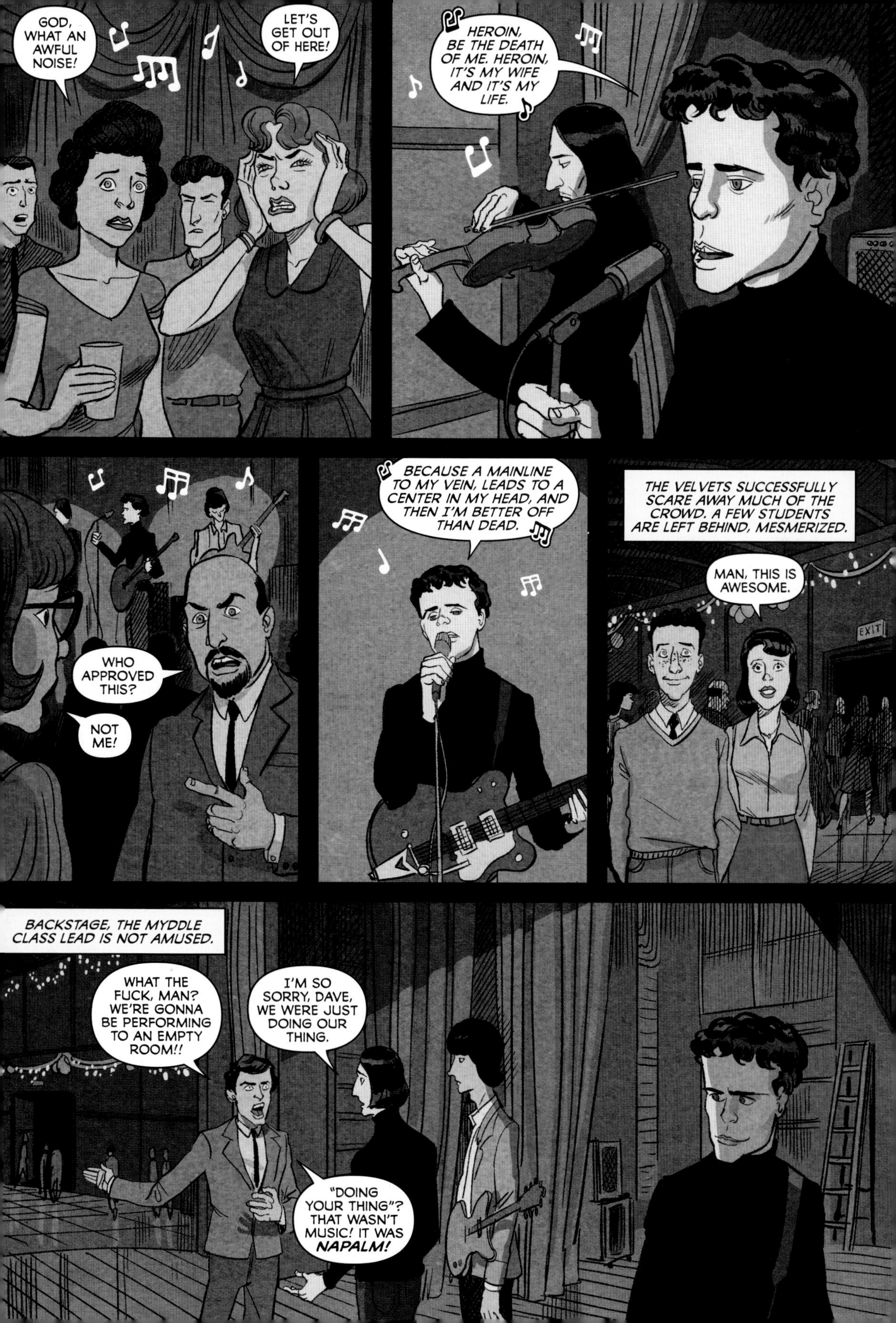
GOD, WHAT AN AWFUL NOISE!
LET'S GET OUT OF HERE!
HEROIN, BE THE DEATH OF ME. HEROIN, IT'S MY WIFE AND IT'S MY LIFE.
WHO APPROVED THIS?
NOT ME!
BECAUSE A MAINLINE TO MY VEIN, LEADS TO A CENTER IN MY HEAD, AND THEN I'M BETTER OFF THAN DEAD.
THE VELVETS SUCCESSFULLY SCARE AWAY MUCH OF THE CROWD. A FEW STUDENTS ARE LEFT BEHIND, MESMERIZED.
MAN, THIS IS AWESOME.
EXIT
BACKSTAGE, THE MYDDLE CLASS LEAD IS NOT AMUSED.
WHAT THE FUCK, MAN? WE'RE GONNA BE PERFORMING TO AN EMPTY ROOM!!
I'M SO SORRY, DAVE, WE WERE JUST DOING OUR THING.
"DOING YOUR THING"? THAT WASN'T MUSIC! IT WAS **NAPALM!**

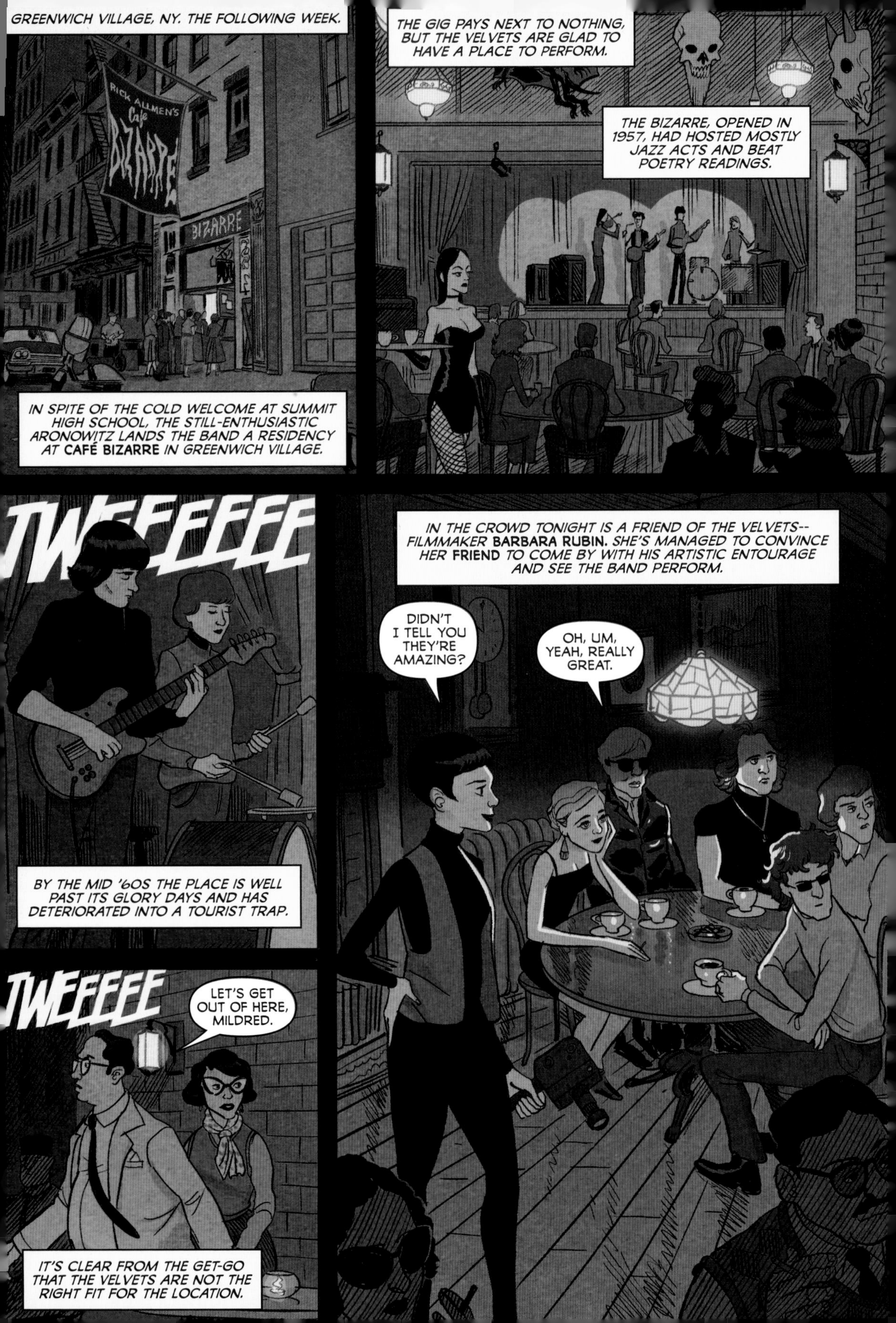
GREENWICH VILLAGE, NY. THE FOLLOWING WEEK.
RICK ALLMEN'S Café BIZARRE
BIZARRE
IN SPITE OF THE COLD WELCOME AT SUMMIT HIGH SCHOOL, THE STILL-ENTHUSIASTIC ARONOWITZ LANDS THE BAND A RESIDENCY AT **CAFÉ BIZARRE** IN GREENWICH VILLAGE.
THE GIG PAYS NEXT TO NOTHING, BUT THE VELVETS ARE GLAD TO HAVE A PLACE TO PERFORM.
THE BIZARRE, OPENED IN 1957, HAD HOSTED MOSTLY JAZZ ACTS AND BEAT POETRY READINGS.
TWEEEEEE
BY THE MID '60S THE PLACE IS WELL PAST ITS GLORY DAYS AND HAS DETERIORATED INTO A TOURIST TRAP.
TWEEEEE
LET'S GET OUT OF HERE, MILDRED.
IT'S CLEAR FROM THE GET-GO THAT THE VELVETS ARE NOT THE RIGHT FIT FOR THE LOCATION.
IN THE CROWD TONIGHT IS A FRIEND OF THE VELVETS-- FILMMAKER **BARBARA RUBIN.** SHE'S MANAGED TO CONVINCE HER **FRIEND** TO COME BY WITH HIS ARTISTIC ENTOURAGE AND SEE THE BAND PERFORM.
DIDN'T I TELL YOU THEY'RE AMAZING?
OH, UM, YEAH, REALLY GREAT.

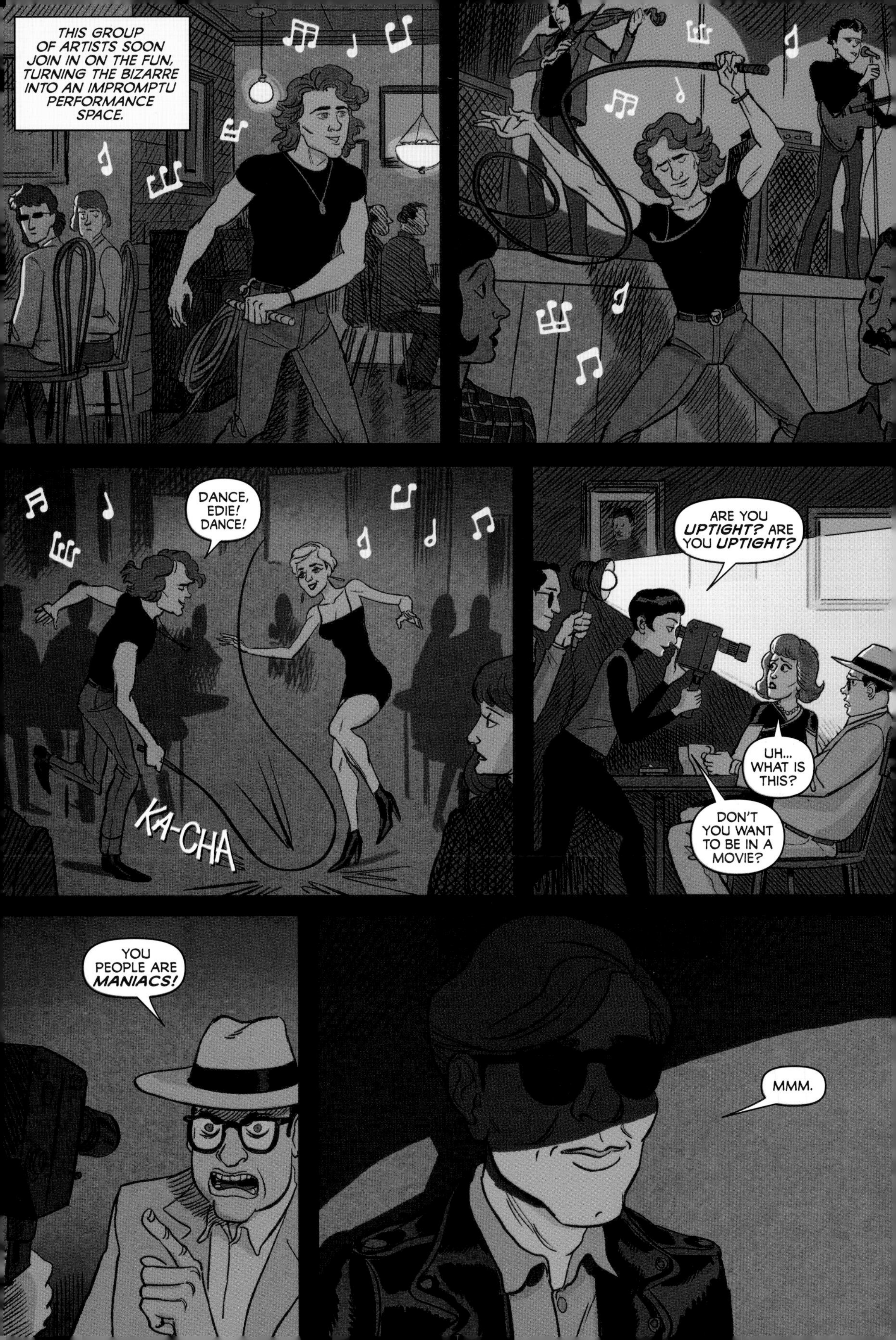
THIS GROUP OF ARTISTS SOON JOIN IN ON THE FUN, TURNING THE BIZARRE INTO AN IMPROMPTU PERFORMANCE SPACE.
DANCE, EDIE! DANCE!
KA-CHA
ARE YOU UPTIGHT? ARE YOU UPTIGHT?
UH... WHAT IS THIS?
DON'T YOU WANT TO BE IN A MOVIE?
YOU PEOPLE ARE MANIACS!
MMM.

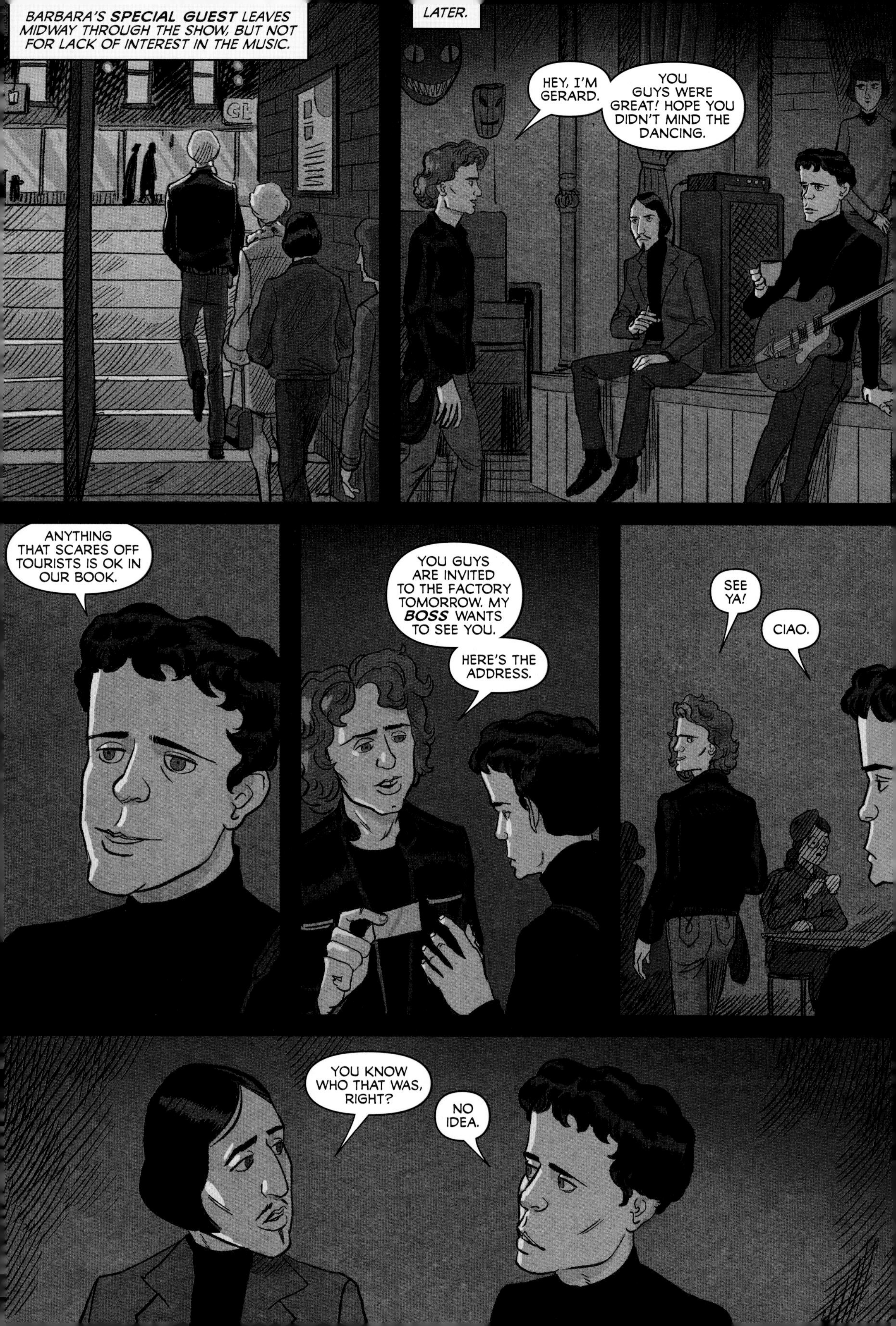
BARBARA'S **SPECIAL GUEST** LEAVES MIDWAY THROUGH THE SHOW, BUT NOT FOR LACK OF INTEREST IN THE MUSIC.
LATER.
HEY, I'M GERARD.
YOU GUYS WERE GREAT! HOPE YOU DIDN'T MIND THE DANCING.
ANYTHING THAT SCARES OFF TOURISTS IS OK IN OUR BOOK.
YOU GUYS ARE INVITED TO THE FACTORY TOMORROW. MY **BOSS** WANTS TO SEE YOU.
HERE'S THE ADDRESS.
SEE YA!
CIAO.
YOU KNOW WHO THAT WAS, RIGHT?
NO IDEA.

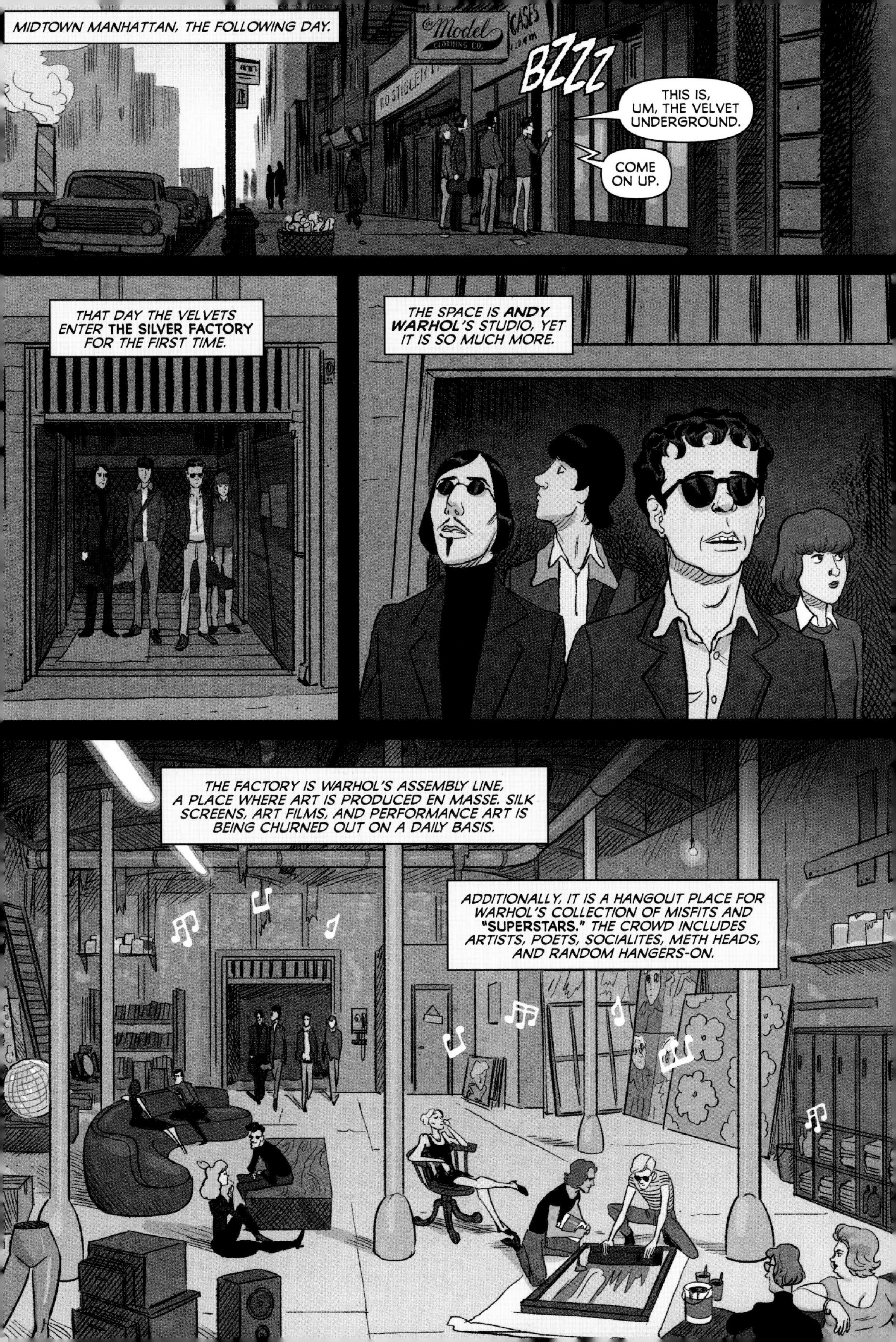
MIDTOWN MANHATTAN, THE FOLLOWING DAY.
The Model CLOTHING CO.
BZZZ
THIS IS, UM, THE VELVET UNDERGROUND.
COME ON UP.
THAT DAY THE VELVETS ENTER THE SILVER FACTORY FOR THE FIRST TIME.
THE SPACE IS ANDY WARHOL'S STUDIO, YET IT IS SO MUCH MORE.
THE FACTORY IS WARHOL'S ASSEMBLY LINE, A PLACE WHERE ART IS PRODUCED EN MASSE. SILK SCREENS, ART FILMS, AND PERFORMANCE ART IS BEING CHURNED OUT ON A DAILY BASIS.
ADDITIONALLY, IT IS A HANGOUT PLACE FOR WARHOL'S COLLECTION OF MISFITS AND "SUPERSTARS." THE CROWD INCLUDES ARTISTS, POETS, SOCIALITES, METH HEADS, AND RANDOM HANGERS-ON.

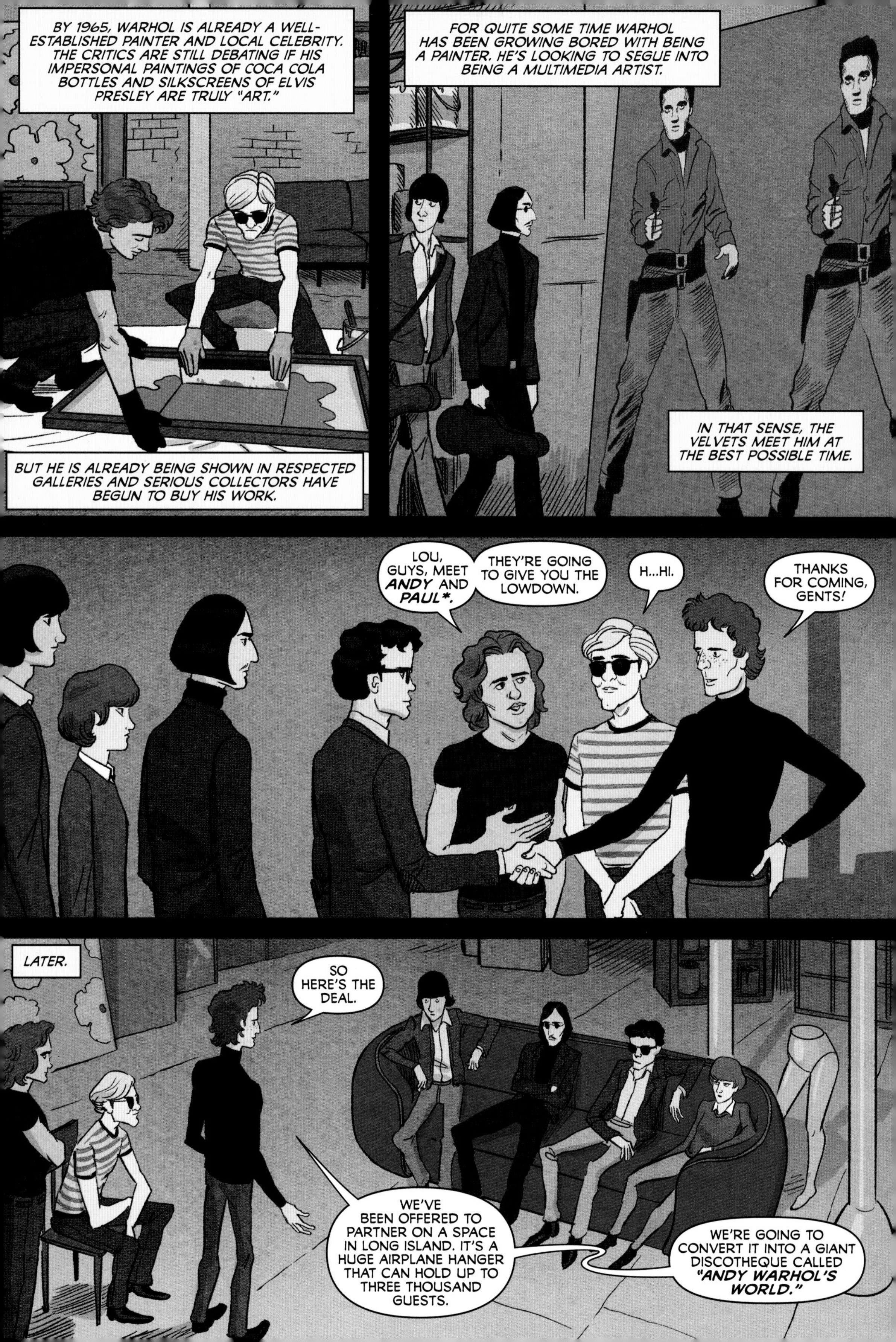

BY 1965, WARHOL IS ALREADY A WELL-ESTABLISHED PAINTER AND LOCAL CELEBRITY. THE CRITICS ARE STILL DEBATING IF HIS IMPERSONAL PAINTINGS OF COCA COLA BOTTLES AND SILKSCREENS OF ELVIS PRESLEY ARE TRULY "ART."
BUT HE IS ALREADY BEING SHOWN IN RESPECTED GALLERIES AND SERIOUS COLLECTORS HAVE BEGUN TO BUY HIS WORK.
FOR QUITE SOME TIME WARHOL HAS BEEN GROWING BORED WITH BEING A PAINTER. HE'S LOOKING TO SEGUE INTO BEING A MULTIMEDIA ARTIST.
IN THAT SENSE, THE VELVETS MEET HIM AT THE BEST POSSIBLE TIME.
LOU, GUYS, MEET ***ANDY*** AND ***PAUL****.
THEY'RE GOING TO GIVE YOU THE LOWDOWN.
H...HI.
THANKS FOR COMING, GENTS!
LATER.
SO HERE'S THE DEAL.
WE'VE BEEN OFFERED TO PARTNER ON A SPACE IN LONG ISLAND. IT'S A HUGE AIRPLANE HANGER THAT CAN HOLD UP TO THREE THOUSAND GUESTS.
WE'RE GOING TO CONVERT IT INTO A GIANT DISCOTHEQUE CALLED ***"ANDY WARHOL'S WORLD."***

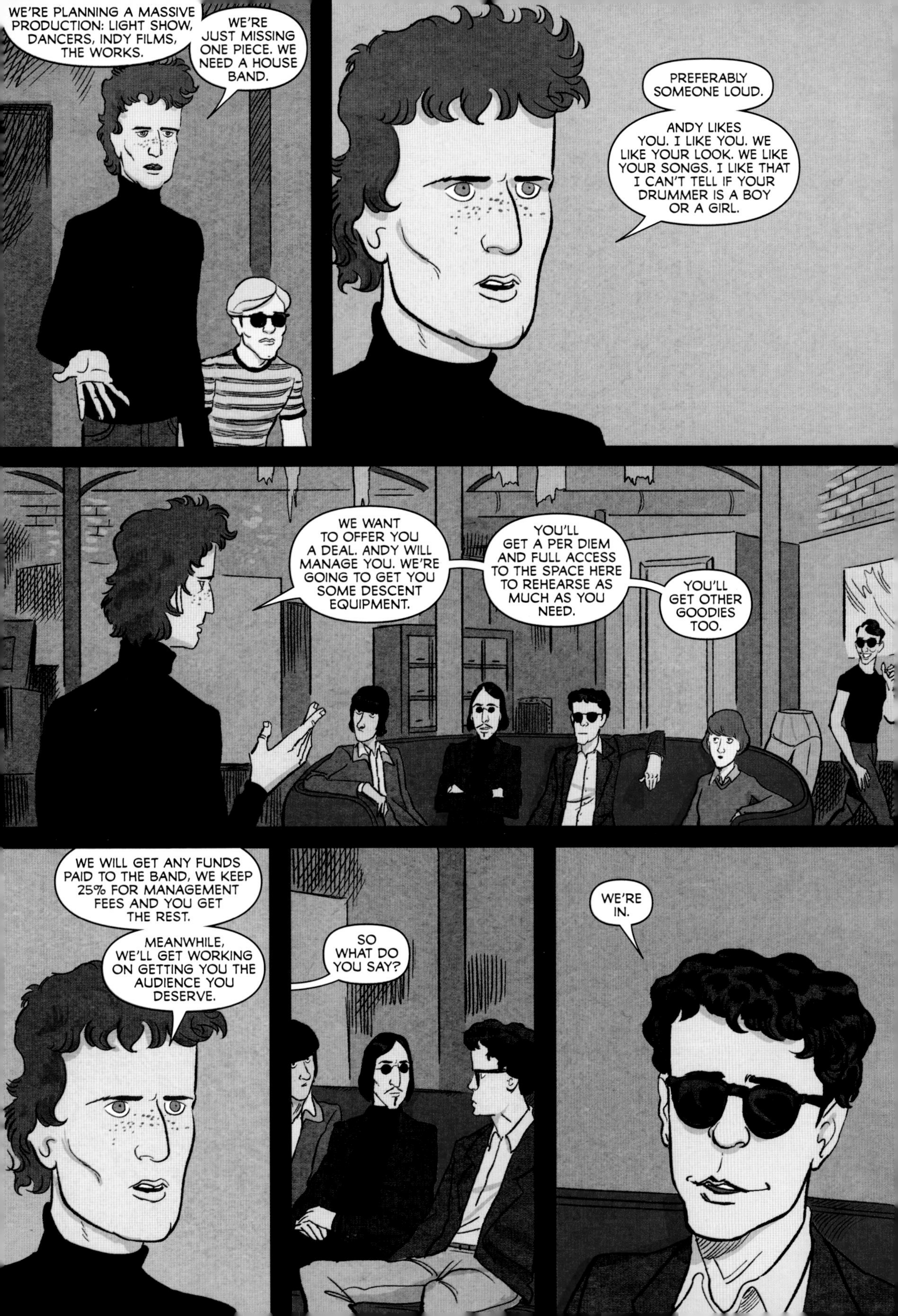
WE'RE PLANNING A MASSIVE PRODUCTION: LIGHT SHOW, DANCERS, INDY FILMS, THE WORKS.
WE'RE JUST MISSING ONE PIECE. WE NEED A HOUSE BAND.
PREFERABLY SOMEONE LOUD.
ANDY LIKES YOU. I LIKE YOU. WE LIKE YOUR LOOK. WE LIKE YOUR SONGS. I LIKE THAT I CAN'T TELL IF YOUR DRUMMER IS A BOY OR A GIRL.
WE WANT TO OFFER YOU A DEAL. ANDY WILL MANAGE YOU. WE'RE GOING TO GET YOU SOME DESCENT EQUIPMENT.
YOU'LL GET A PER DIEM AND FULL ACCESS TO THE SPACE HERE TO REHEARSE AS MUCH AS YOU NEED.
YOU'LL GET OTHER GOODIES TOO.
WE WILL GET ANY FUNDS PAID TO THE BAND, WE KEEP 25% FOR MANAGEMENT FEES AND YOU GET THE REST.
MEANWHILE, WE'LL GET WORKING ON GETTING YOU THE AUDIENCE YOU DESERVE.
SO WHAT DO YOU SAY?
WE'RE IN.

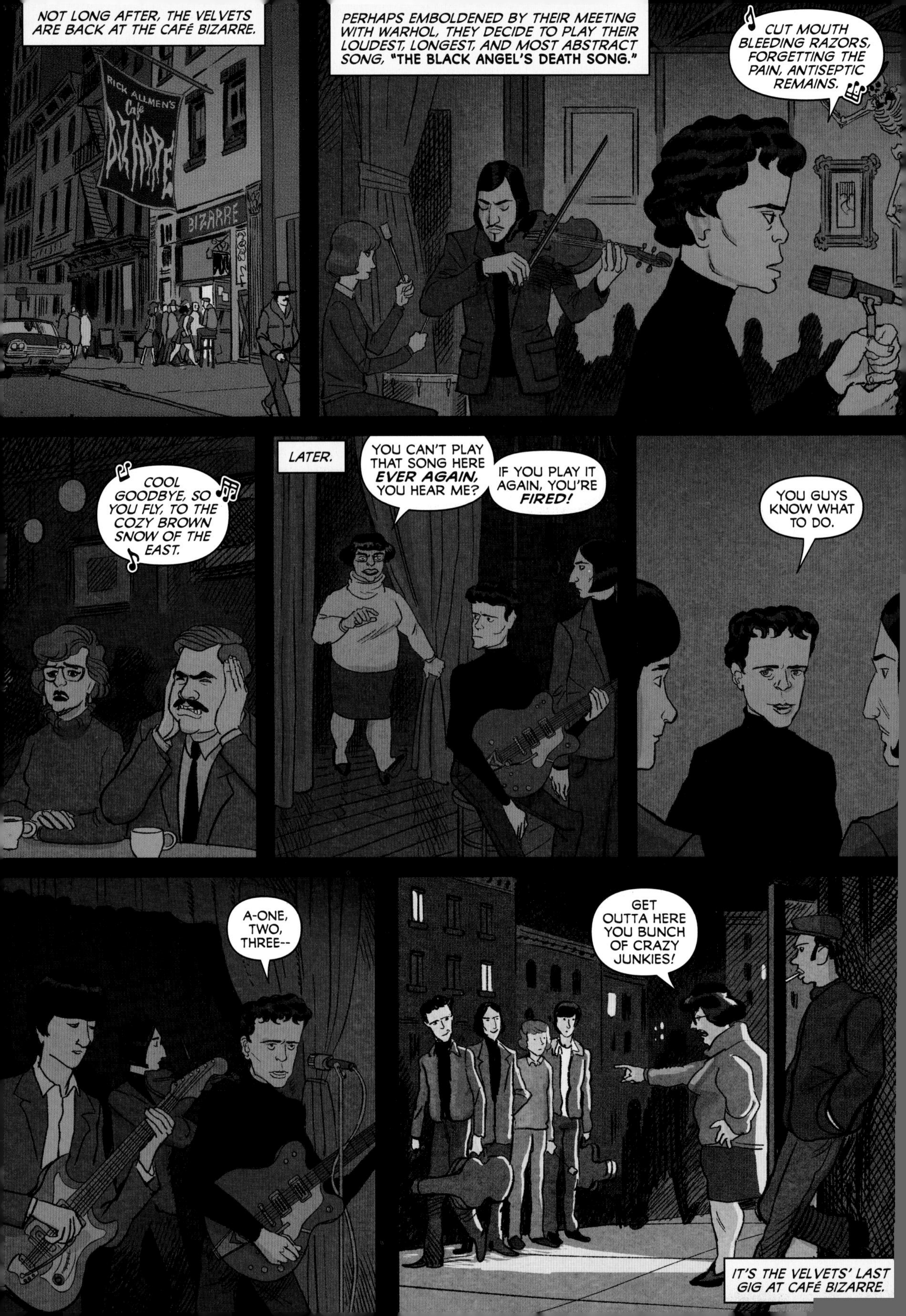
NOT LONG AFTER, THE VELVETS ARE BACK AT THE CAFÉ BIZARRE.
RICK ALLMEN'S Café BIZARRE
BIZARRE
PERHAPS EMBOLDENED BY THEIR MEETING WITH WARHOL, THEY DECIDE TO PLAY THEIR LOUDEST, LONGEST, AND MOST ABSTRACT SONG, "THE BLACK ANGEL'S DEATH SONG."
CUT MOUTH BLEEDING RAZORS, FORGETTING THE PAIN, ANTISEPTIC REMAINS.
COOL GOODBYE, SO YOU FLY, TO THE COZY BROWN SNOW OF THE EAST.
LATER.
YOU CAN'T PLAY THAT SONG HERE EVER AGAIN, YOU HEAR ME?
IF YOU PLAY IT AGAIN, YOU'RE FIRED!
YOU GUYS KNOW WHAT TO DO.
A-ONE, TWO, THREE--
GET OUTTA HERE YOU BUNCH OF CRAZY JUNKIES!
IT'S THE VELVETS' LAST GIG AT CAFÉ BIZARRE.

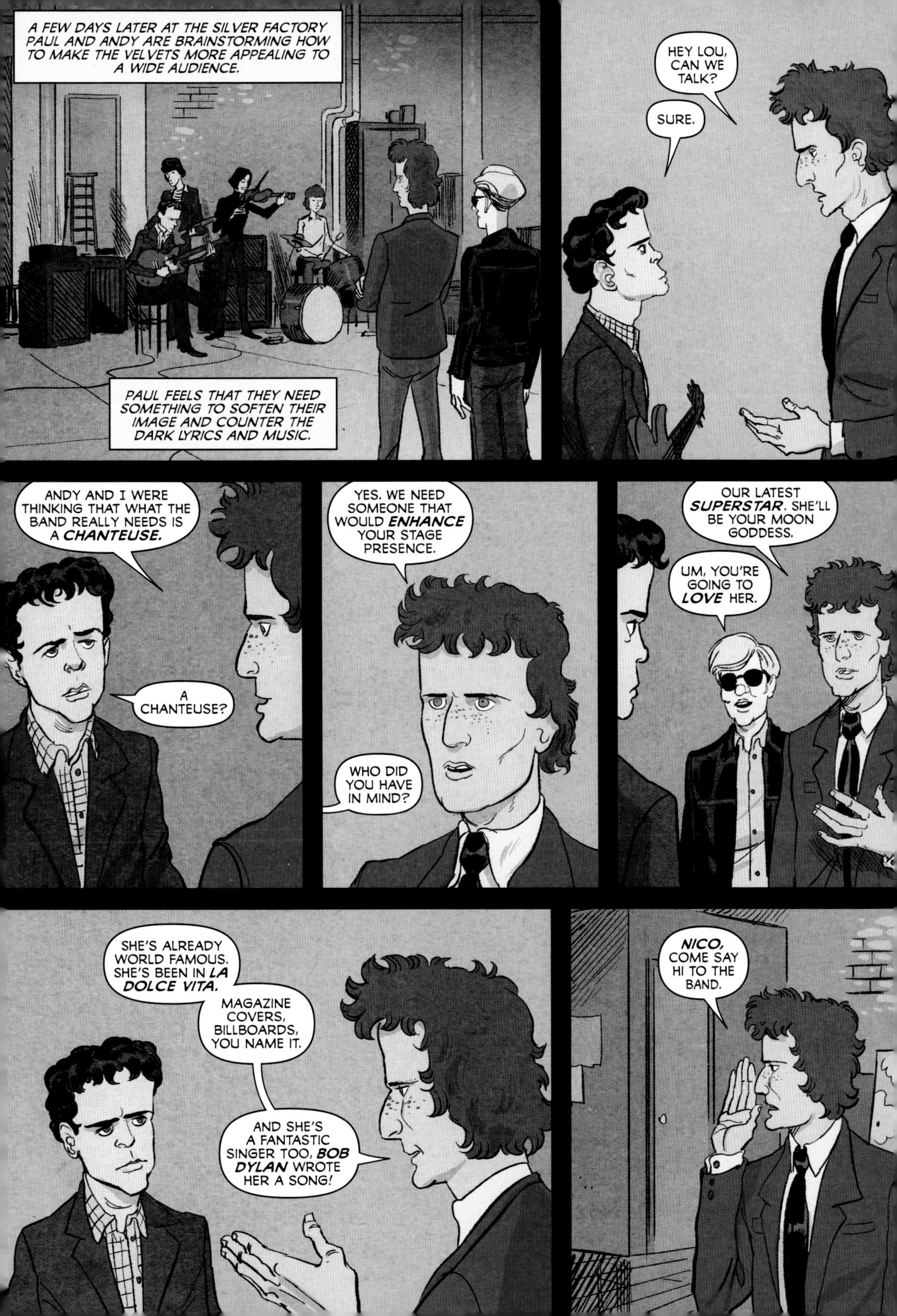
A FEW DAYS LATER AT THE SILVER FACTORY PAUL AND ANDY ARE BRAINSTORMING HOW TO MAKE THE VELVETS MORE APPEALING TO A WIDE AUDIENCE.
PAUL FEELS THAT THEY NEED SOMETHING TO SOFTEN THEIR IMAGE AND COUNTER THE DARK LYRICS AND MUSIC.
HEY LOU, CAN WE TALK?
SURE.
ANDY AND I WERE THINKING THAT WHAT THE BAND REALLY NEEDS IS A *CHANTEUSE.*
A CHANTEUSE?
YES. WE NEED SOMEONE THAT WOULD *ENHANCE* YOUR STAGE PRESENCE.
WHO DID YOU HAVE IN MIND?
OUR LATEST *SUPERSTAR*. SHE'LL BE YOUR MOON GODDESS.
UM, YOU'RE GOING TO *LOVE* HER.
SHE'S ALREADY WORLD FAMOUS. SHE'S BEEN IN *LA DOLCE VITA.*
MAGAZINE COVERS, BILLBOARDS, YOU NAME IT.
AND SHE'S A FANTASTIC SINGER TOO, *BOB DYLAN* WROTE HER A SONG!
NICO, COME SAY HI TO THE BAND.

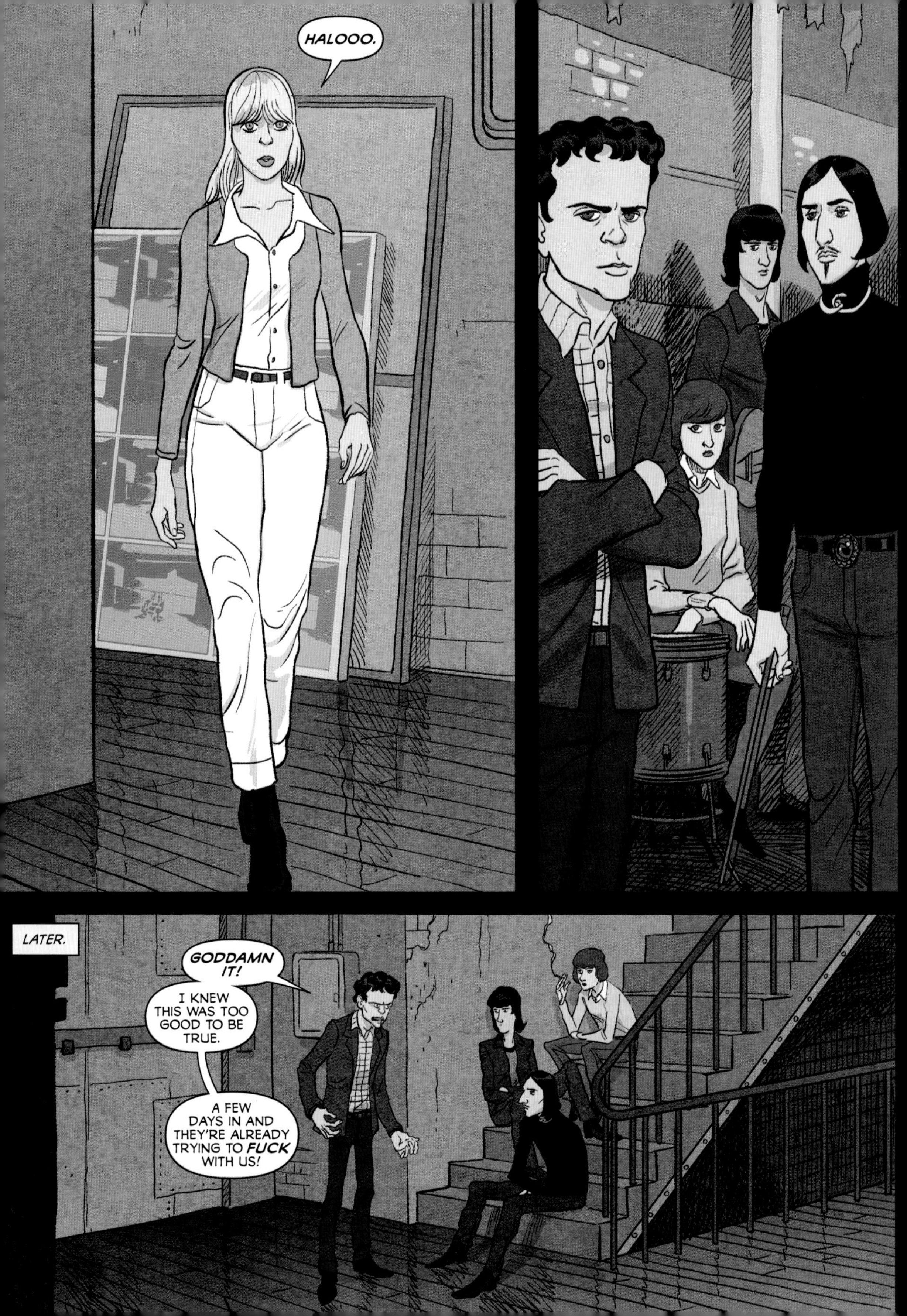
HALOOO.
LATER.
GODDAMN IT!
I KNEW THIS WAS TOO GOOD TO BE TRUE.
A FEW DAYS IN AND THEY'RE ALREADY TRYING TO FUCK WITH US!

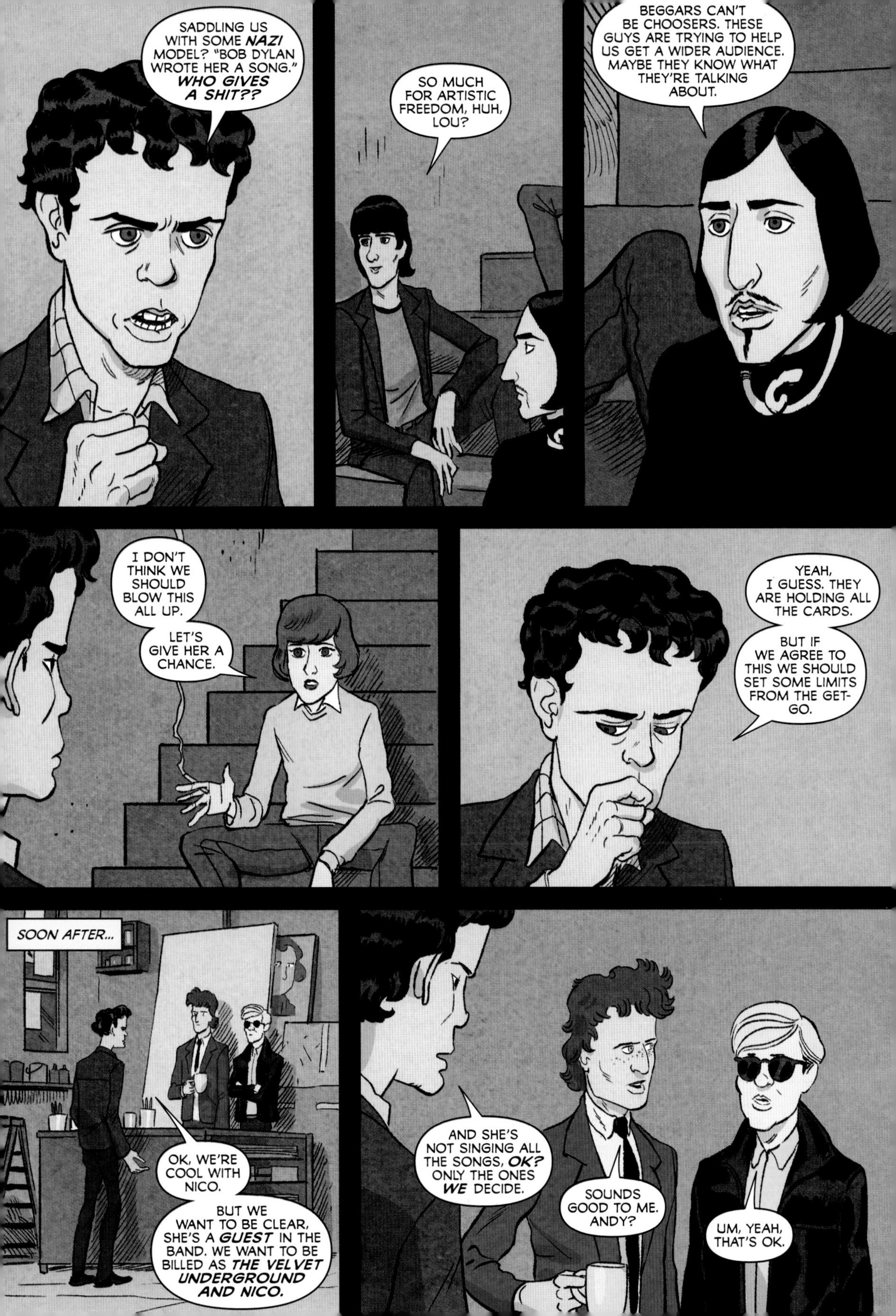
SADDLING US WITH SOME ***NAZI*** MODEL? "BOB DYLAN WROTE HER A SONG." ***WHO GIVES A SHIT??***
SO MUCH FOR ARTISTIC FREEDOM, HUH, LOU?
BEGGARS CAN'T BE CHOOSERS. THESE GUYS ARE TRYING TO HELP US GET A WIDER AUDIENCE. MAYBE THEY KNOW WHAT THEY'RE TALKING ABOUT.
I DON'T THINK WE SHOULD BLOW THIS ALL UP.
LET'S GIVE HER A CHANCE.
YEAH, I GUESS. THEY ARE HOLDING ALL THE CARDS.
BUT IF WE AGREE TO THIS WE SHOULD SET SOME LIMITS FROM THE GET-GO.
SOON AFTER...
OK, WE'RE COOL WITH NICO.
BUT WE WANT TO BE CLEAR, SHE'S A ***GUEST*** IN THE BAND. WE WANT TO BE BILLED AS ***THE VELVET UNDERGROUND AND NICO.***
AND SHE'S NOT SINGING ALL THE SONGS, ***OK?*** ONLY THE ONES ***WE*** DECIDE.
SOUNDS GOOD TO ME. ANDY?
UM, YEAH, THAT'S OK.

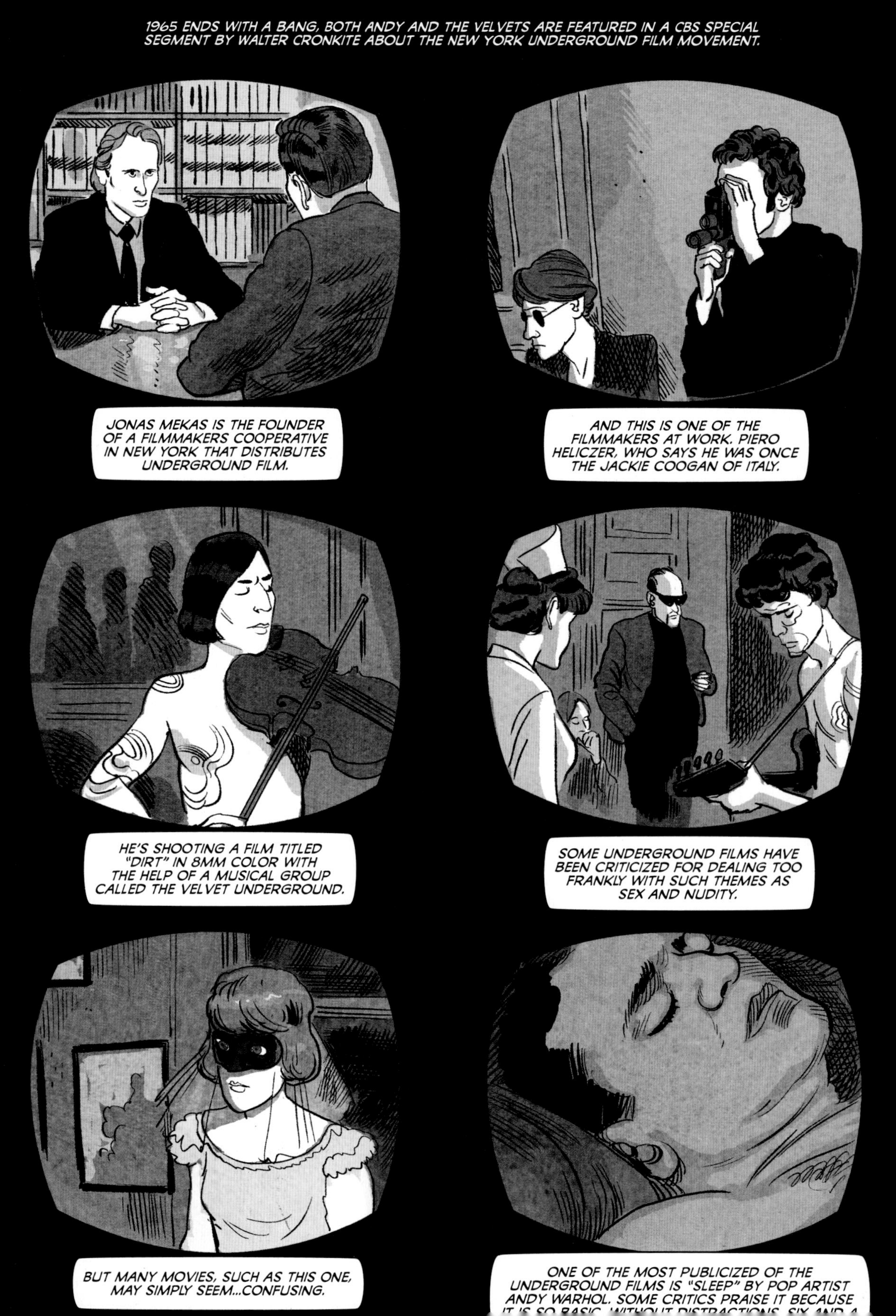
1965 ENDS WITH A BANG, BOTH ANDY AND THE VELVETS ARE FEATURED IN A CBS SPECIAL SEGMENT BY WALTER CRONKITE ABOUT THE NEW YORK UNDERGROUND FILM MOVEMENT.
JONAS MEKAS IS THE FOUNDER OF A FILMMAKERS COOPERATIVE IN NEW YORK THAT DISTRIBUTES UNDERGROUND FILM.
AND THIS IS ONE OF THE FILMMAKERS AT WORK. PIERO HELICZER, WHO SAYS HE WAS ONCE THE JACKIE COOGAN OF ITALY.
HE'S SHOOTING A FILM TITLED "DIRT" IN 8MM COLOR WITH THE HELP OF A MUSICAL GROUP CALLED THE VELVET UNDERGROUND.
SOME UNDERGROUND FILMS HAVE BEEN CRITICIZED FOR DEALING TOO FRANKLY WITH SUCH THEMES AS SEX AND NUDITY.
BUT MANY MOVIES, SUCH AS THIS ONE, MAY SIMPLY SEEM...CONFUSING.
ONE OF THE MOST PUBLICIZED OF THE UNDERGROUND FILMS IS "SLEEP" BY POP ARTIST ANDY WARHOL. SOME CRITICS PRAISE IT BECAUSE

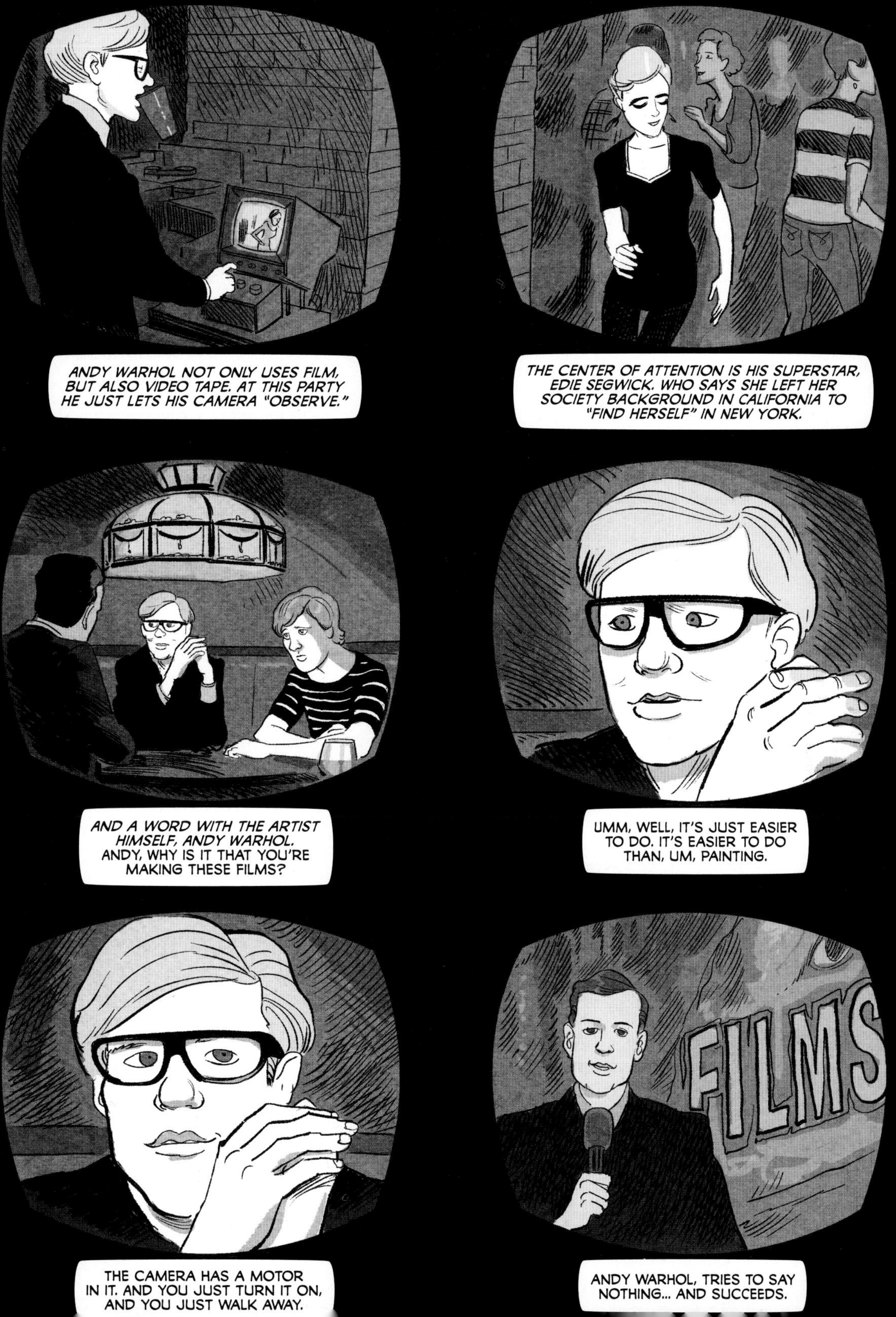
ANDY WARHOL NOT ONLY USES FILM, BUT ALSO VIDEO TAPE. AT THIS PARTY HE JUST LETS HIS CAMERA "OBSERVE."
THE CENTER OF ATTENTION IS HIS SUPERSTAR, EDIE SEGWICK. WHO SAYS SHE LEFT HER SOCIETY BACKGROUND IN CALIFORNIA TO "FIND HERSELF" IN NEW YORK.
AND A WORD WITH THE ARTIST HIMSELF, ANDY WARHOL. ANDY, WHY IS IT THAT YOU'RE MAKING THESE FILMS?
UMM, WELL, IT'S JUST EASIER TO DO. IT'S EASIER TO DO THAN, UM, PAINTING.
THE CAMERA HAS A MOTOR IN IT. AND YOU JUST TURN IT ON, AND YOU JUST WALK AWAY.
FILMS
ANDY WARHOL, TRIES TO SAY NOTHING... AND SUCCEEDS.

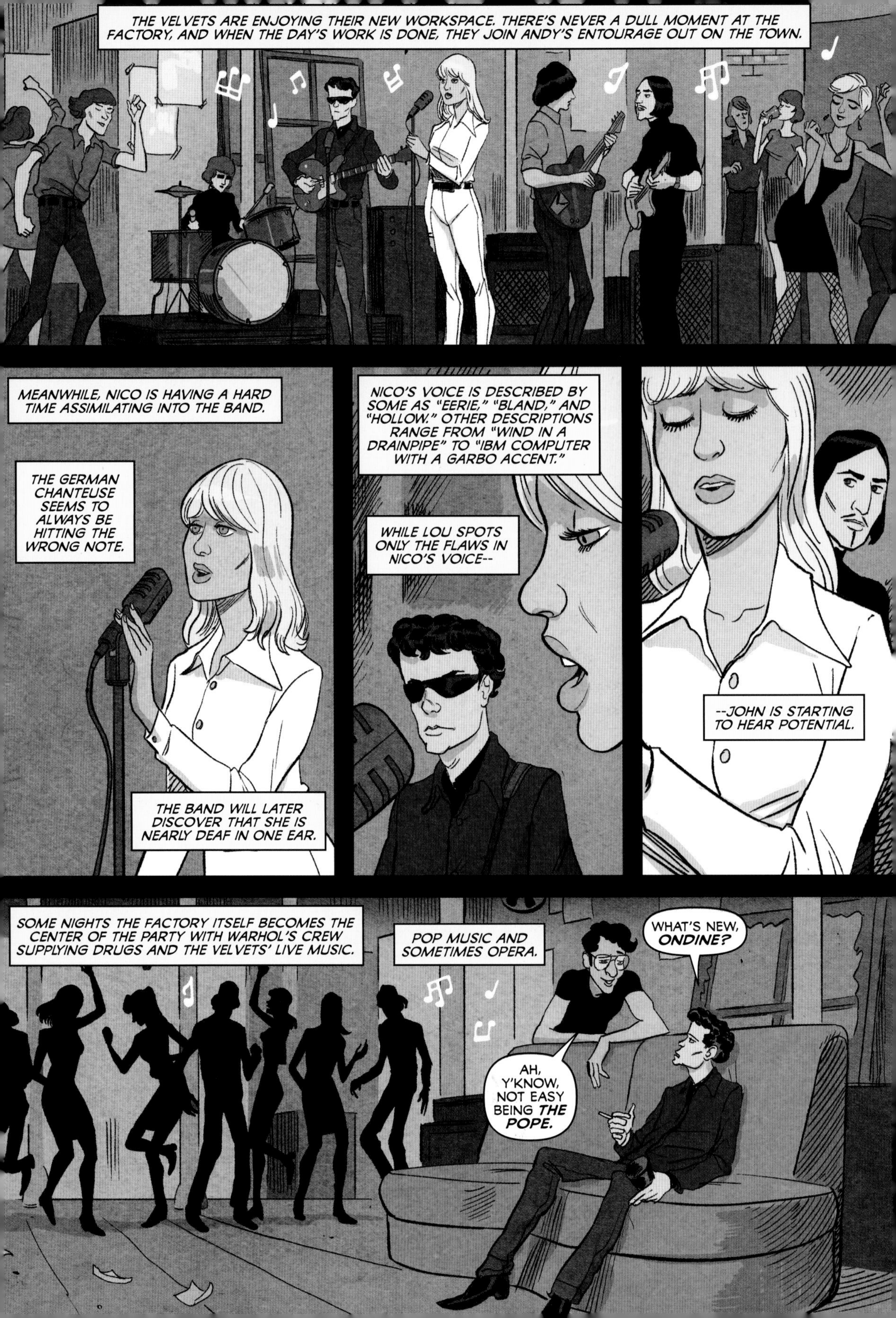

THE VELVETS ARE ENJOYING THEIR NEW WORKSPACE. THERE'S NEVER A DULL MOMENT AT THE FACTORY, AND WHEN THE DAY'S WORK IS DONE, THEY JOIN ANDY'S ENTOURAGE OUT ON THE TOWN.
MEANWHILE, NICO IS HAVING A HARD TIME ASSIMILATING INTO THE BAND.
THE GERMAN CHANTEUSE SEEMS TO ALWAYS BE HITTING THE WRONG NOTE.
THE BAND WILL LATER DISCOVER THAT SHE IS NEARLY DEAF IN ONE EAR.
NICO'S VOICE IS DESCRIBED BY SOME AS "EERIE," "BLAND," AND "HOLLOW." OTHER DESCRIPTIONS RANGE FROM "WIND IN A DRAINPIPE" TO "IBM COMPUTER WITH A GARBO ACCENT."
WHILE LOU SPOTS ONLY THE FLAWS IN NICO'S VOICE--
--JOHN IS STARTING TO HEAR POTENTIAL.
SOME NIGHTS THE FACTORY ITSELF BECOMES THE CENTER OF THE PARTY WITH WARHOL'S CREW SUPPLYING DRUGS AND THE VELVETS' LIVE MUSIC.
POP MUSIC AND SOMETIMES OPERA.
WHAT'S NEW, ONDINE?
AH, Y'KNOW, NOT EASY BEING THE POPE.

HEY, SOME GOOD STUFF CAME IN TODAY, YOU HAVE TO TRY IT.

HOW MUCH?

YOU'RE ANDY'S ROYAL GUESTS! FIRST TASTE'S ON THE HOUSE.

I USUALLY DO H.

OH, LOU, GET WITH THE PROGRAM! EVERYONE IN THE FACTORY IS AN A-HEAD*. YOU'RE GONNA LOVE IT. IT'LL MAKE YOU GO-GO-GO ALL NIGHT LONG!

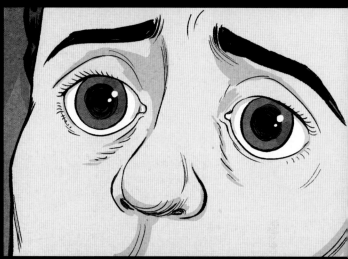

WHILE LOU IS GETTING AN INTRODUCTION TO THE FACTORY'S DRUG OF CHOICE, JOHN IS GETTING TO KNOW ONE OF ITS CENTRAL FIGURES, EDIE SEDGWICK.

I LOVE IT THAT WE HAVE A HOUSE BAND NOW!

GLAD TO BE OF SERVICE.

WHAT KIND OF ACCENT IS THAT?

WELSH.

I'VE NEVER MET A WELSHMAN! FAR OUT.

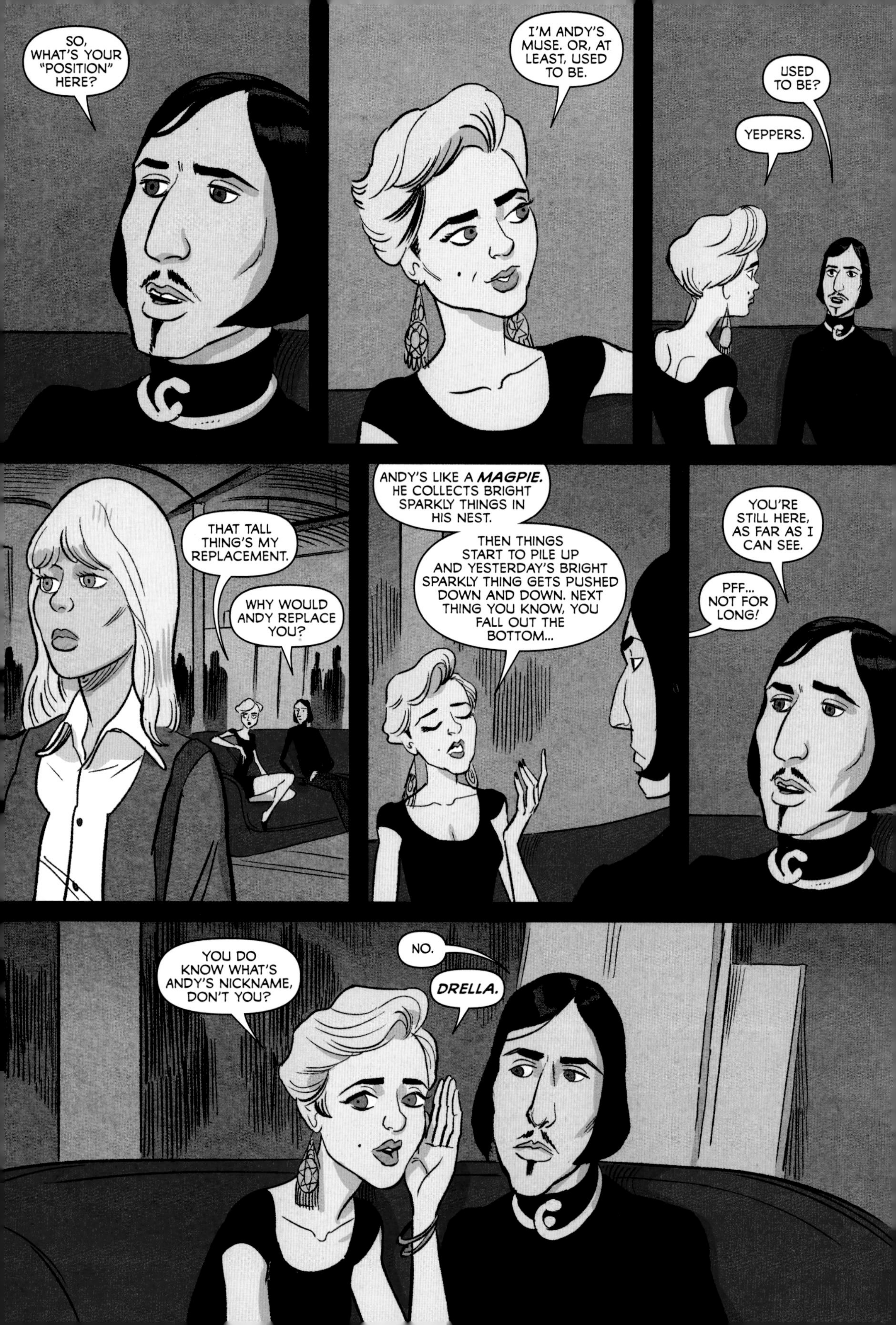
SO, WHAT'S YOUR "POSITION" HERE?
I'M ANDY'S MUSE. OR, AT LEAST, USED TO BE.
USED TO BE?
YEPPERS.
THAT TALL THING'S MY REPLACEMENT.
WHY WOULD ANDY REPLACE YOU?
ANDY'S LIKE A MAGPIE. HE COLLECTS BRIGHT SPARKLY THINGS IN HIS NEST.
THEN THINGS START TO PILE UP AND YESTERDAY'S BRIGHT SPARKLY THING GETS PUSHED DOWN AND DOWN. NEXT THING YOU KNOW, YOU FALL OUT THE BOTTOM...
YOU'RE STILL HERE, AS FAR AS I CAN SEE.
PFF... NOT FOR LONG!
YOU DO KNOW WHAT'S ANDY'S NICKNAME, DON'T YOU?
NO.
DRELLA.

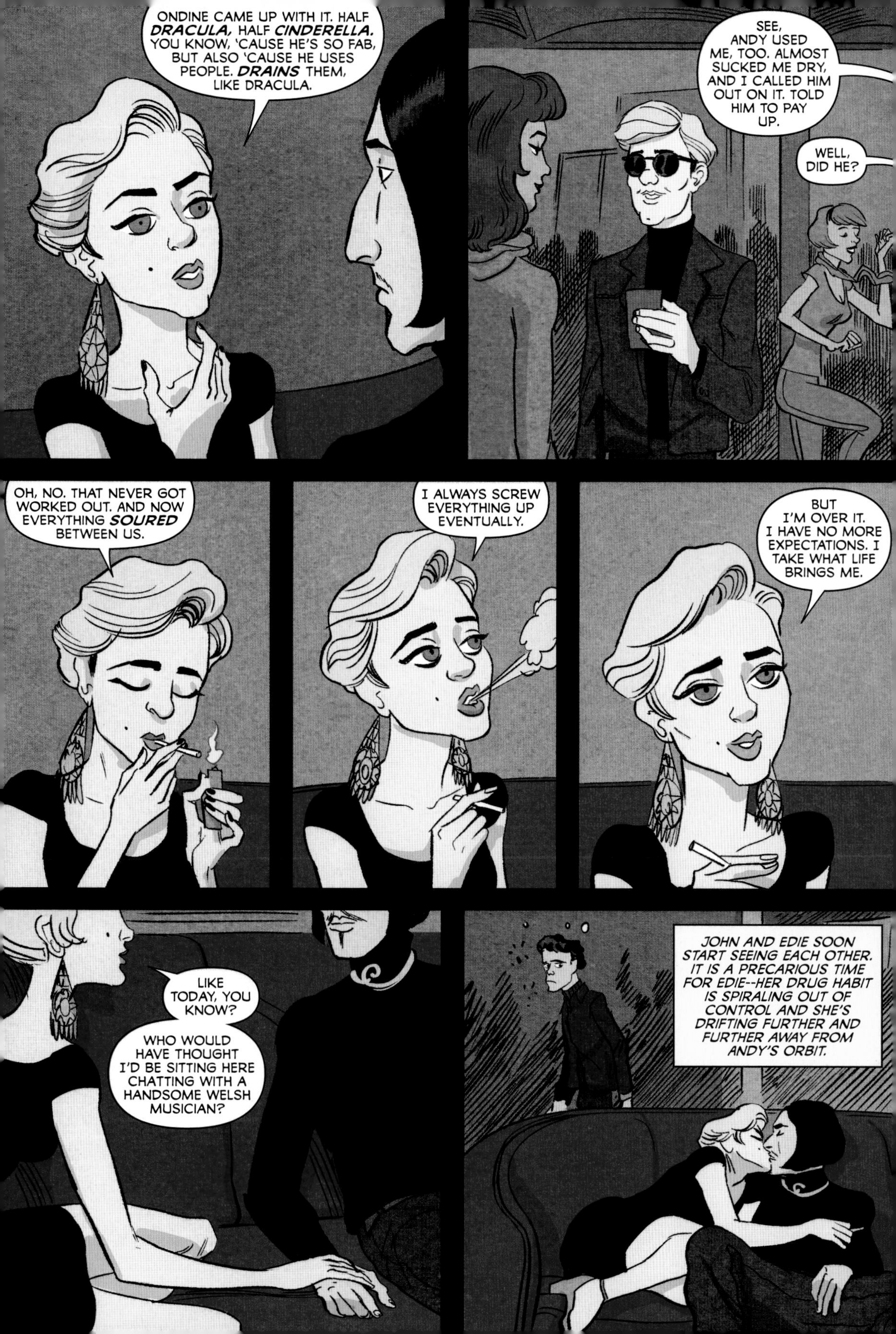
ONDINE CAME UP WITH IT. HALF DRACULA, HALF CINDERELLA. YOU KNOW, 'CAUSE HE'S SO FAB, BUT ALSO 'CAUSE HE USES PEOPLE. DRAINS THEM, LIKE DRACULA.
SEE, ANDY USED ME, TOO. ALMOST SUCKED ME DRY, AND I CALLED HIM OUT ON IT. TOLD HIM TO PAY UP.
WELL, DID HE?
OH, NO. THAT NEVER GOT WORKED OUT. AND NOW EVERYTHING SOURED BETWEEN US.
I ALWAYS SCREW EVERYTHING UP EVENTUALLY.
BUT I'M OVER IT. I HAVE NO MORE EXPECTATIONS. I TAKE WHAT LIFE BRINGS ME.
LIKE TODAY, YOU KNOW?
WHO WOULD HAVE THOUGHT I'D BE SITTING HERE CHATTING WITH A HANDSOME WELSH MUSICIAN?
JOHN AND EDIE SOON START SEEING EACH OTHER. IT IS A PRECARIOUS TIME FOR EDIE--HER DRUG HABIT IS SPIRALING OUT OF CONTROL AND SHE'S DRIFTING FURTHER AND FURTHER AWAY FROM ANDY'S ORBIT.

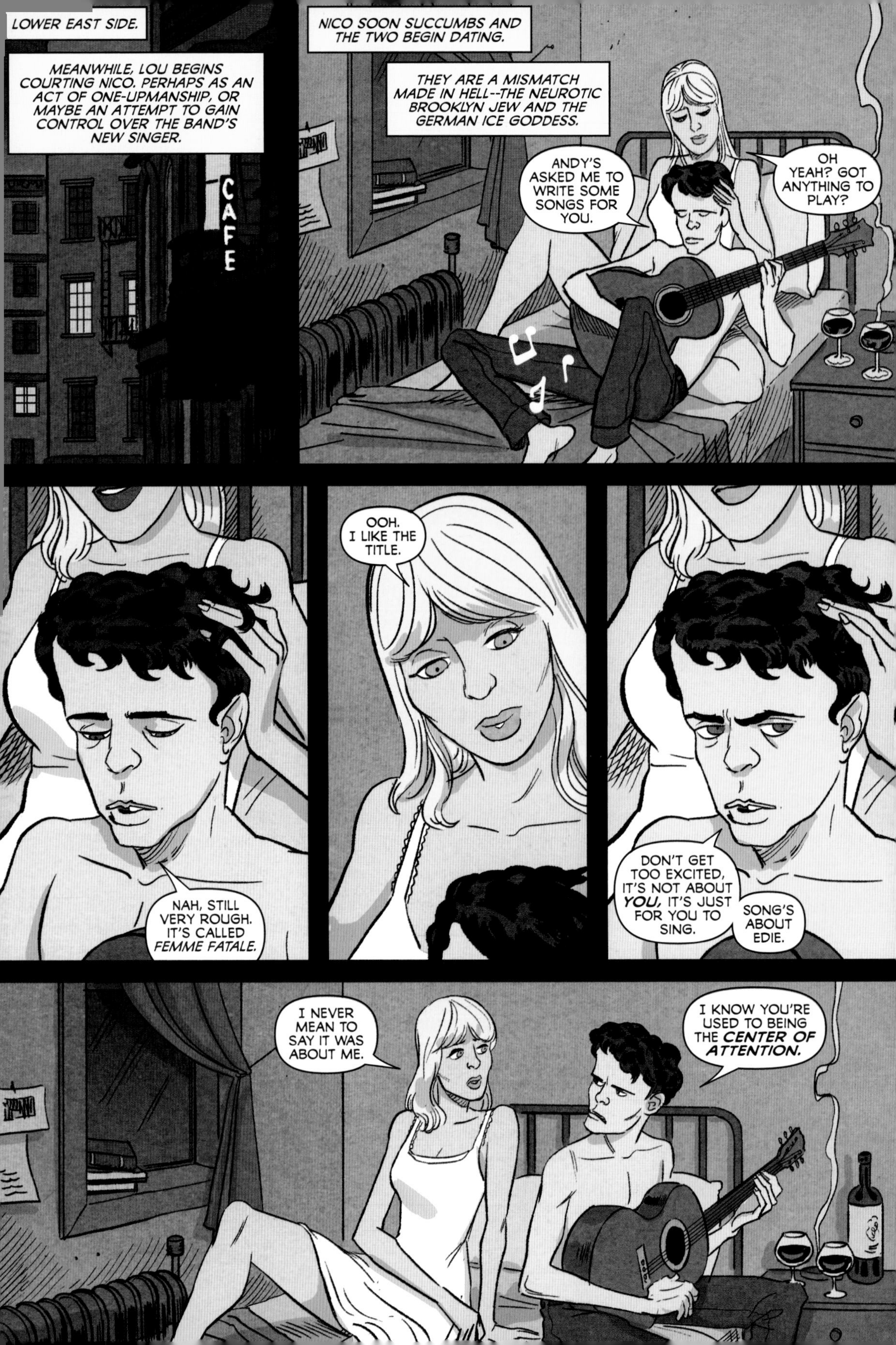
LOWER EAST SIDE.
MEANWHILE, LOU BEGINS COURTING NICO. PERHAPS AS AN ACT OF ONE-UPMANSHIP, OR MAYBE AN ATTEMPT TO GAIN CONTROL OVER THE BAND'S NEW SINGER.
CAFE
NICO SOON SUCCUMBS AND THE TWO BEGIN DATING.
THEY ARE A MISMATCH MADE IN HELL--THE NEUROTIC BROOKLYN JEW AND THE GERMAN ICE GODDESS.
ANDY'S ASKED ME TO WRITE SOME SONGS FOR YOU.
OH YEAH? GOT ANYTHING TO PLAY?
NAH, STILL VERY ROUGH. IT'S CALLED *FEMME FATALE.*
OOH. I LIKE THE TITLE.
DON'T GET TOO EXCITED, IT'S NOT ABOUT ***YOU,*** IT'S JUST FOR YOU TO SING.
SONG'S ABOUT EDIE.
I NEVER MEAN TO SAY IT WAS ABOUT ME.
I KNOW YOU'RE USED TO BEING THE ***CENTER OF ATTENTION.***

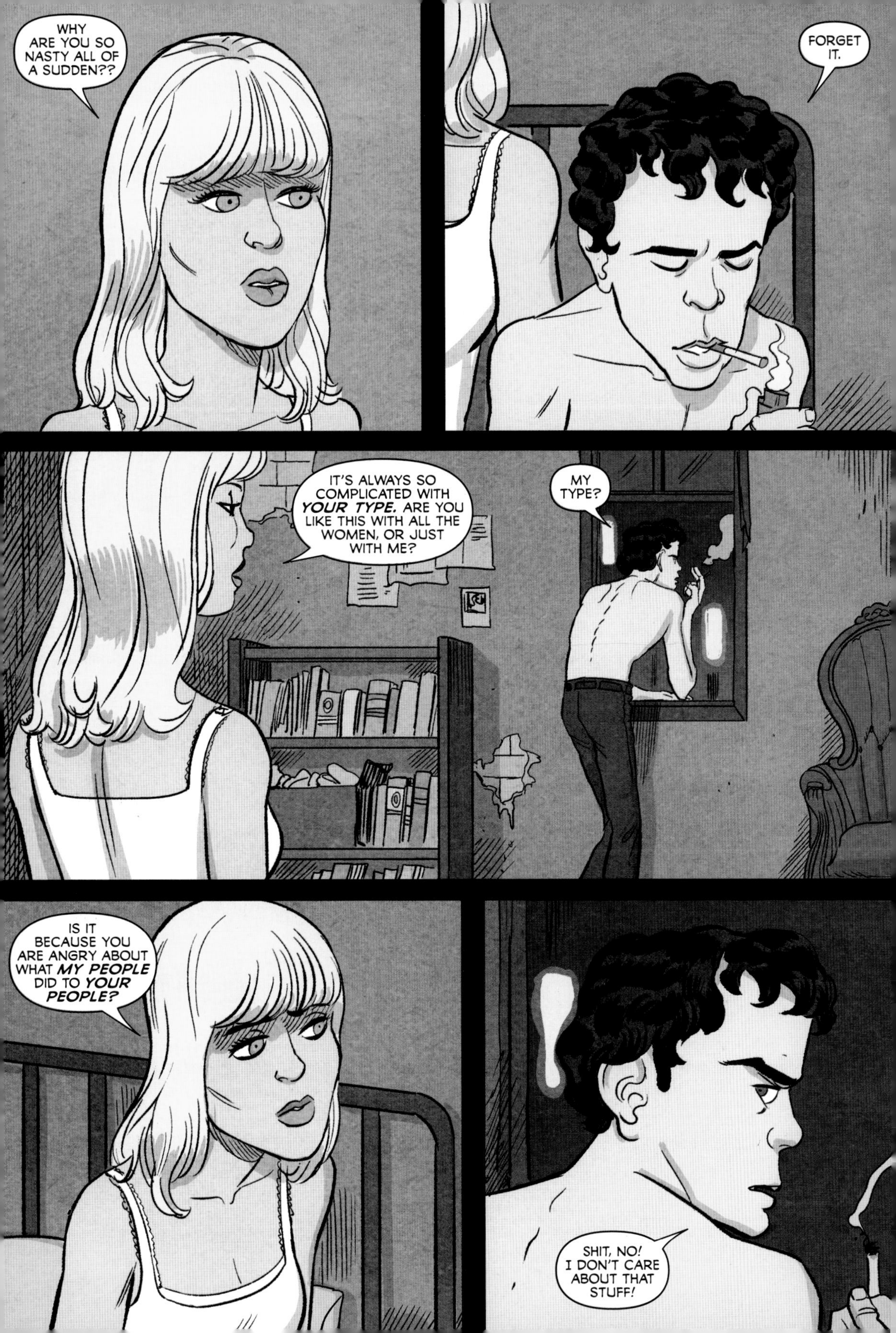
WHY ARE YOU SO NASTY ALL OF A SUDDEN??
FORGET IT.
IT'S ALWAYS SO COMPLICATED WITH *YOUR TYPE.* ARE YOU LIKE THIS WITH ALL THE WOMEN, OR JUST WITH ME?
MY TYPE?
IS IT BECAUSE YOU ARE ANGRY ABOUT WHAT *MY PEOPLE* DID TO *YOUR PEOPLE?*
SHIT, NO! I DON'T CARE ABOUT THAT STUFF!

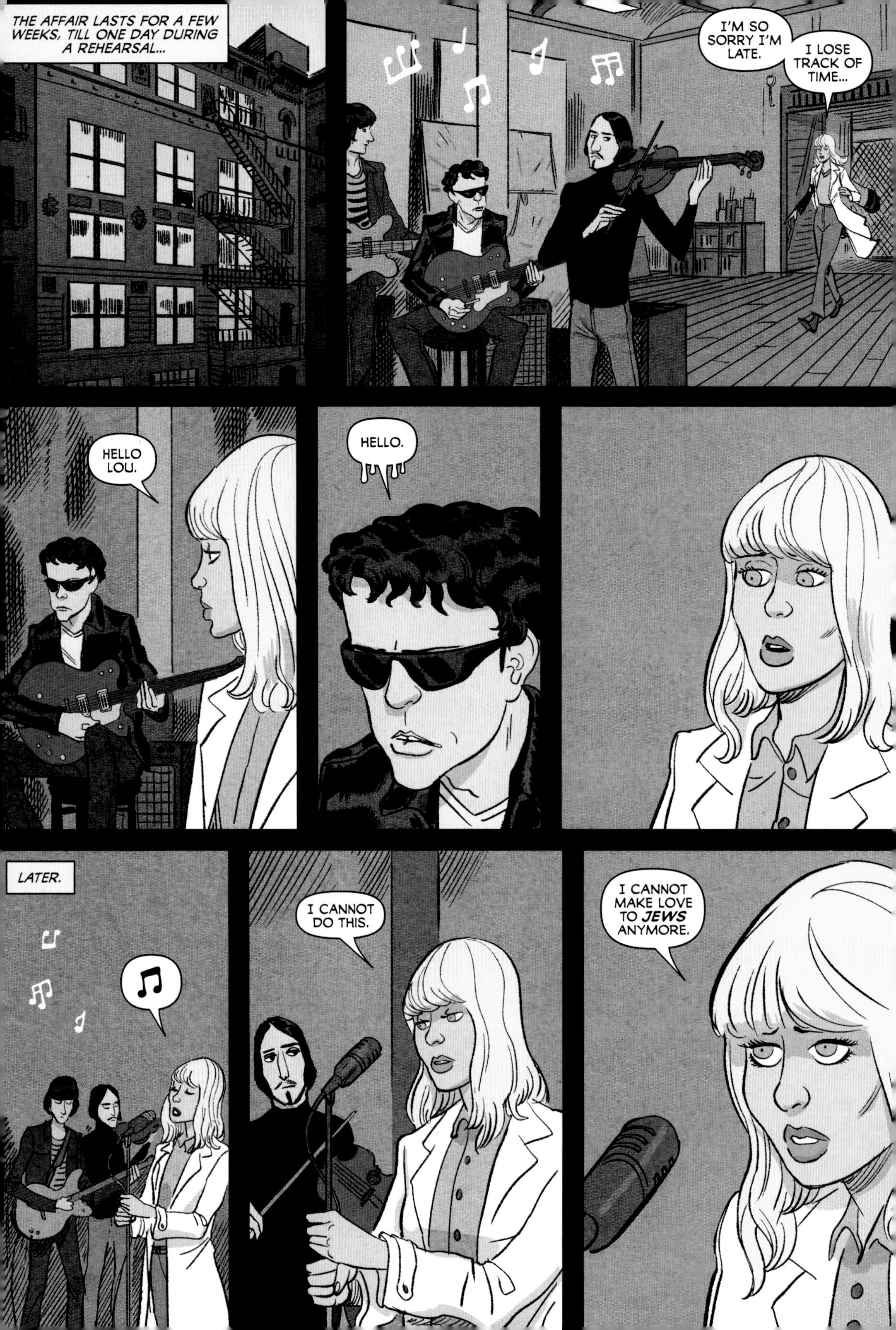
THE AFFAIR LASTS FOR A FEW WEEKS, TILL ONE DAY DURING A REHEARSAL...
I'M SO SORRY I'M LATE.
I LOSE TRACK OF TIME...
HELLO LOU.
HELLO.
LATER.
I CANNOT DO THIS.
I CANNOT MAKE LOVE TO JEWS ANYMORE.

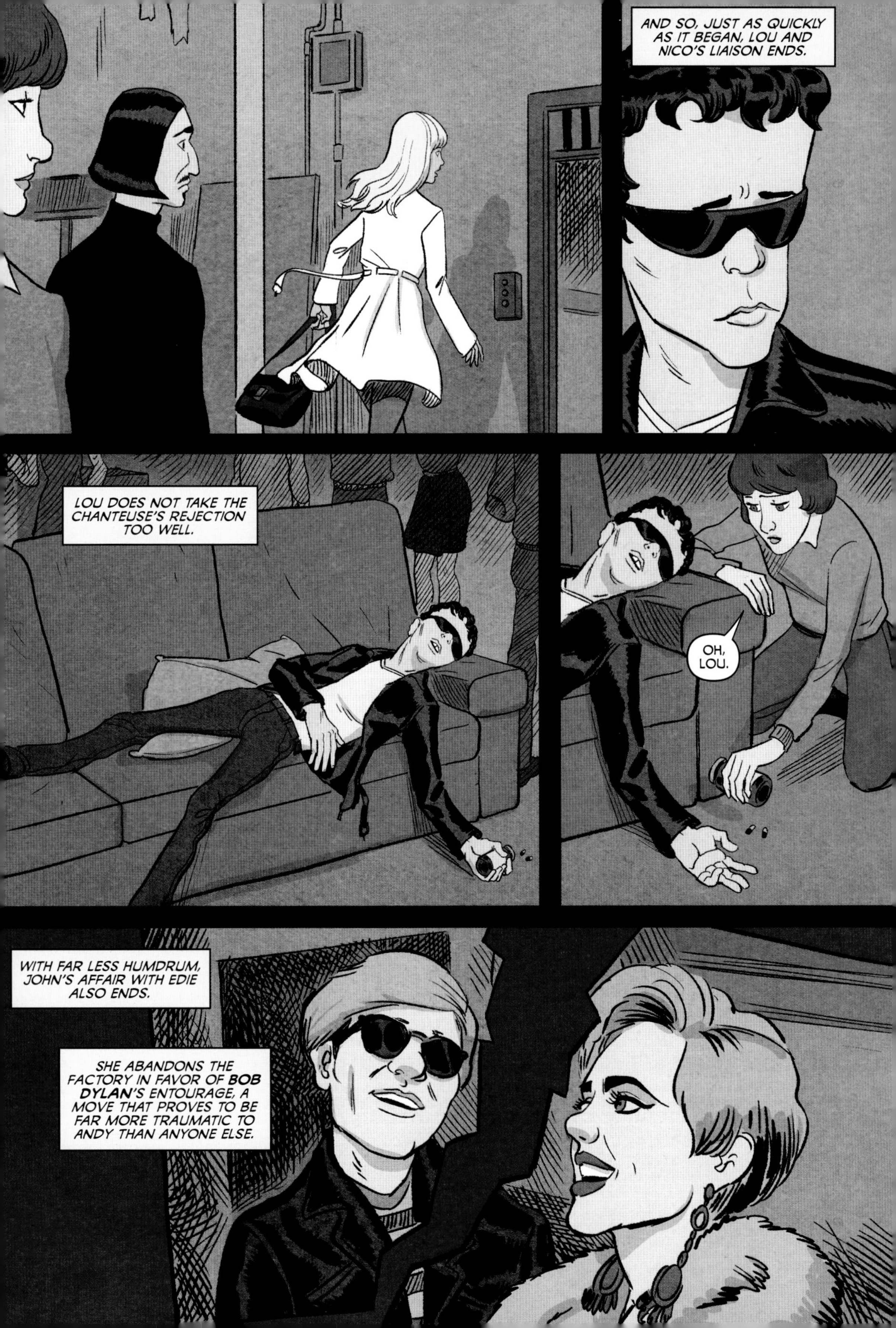
AND SO, JUST AS QUICKLY AS IT BEGAN, LOU AND NICO'S LIAISON ENDS.
LOU DOES NOT TAKE THE CHANTEUSE'S REJECTION TOO WELL.
OH, LOU.
WITH FAR LESS HUMDRUM, JOHN'S AFFAIR WITH EDIE ALSO ENDS.
SHE ABANDONS THE FACTORY IN FAVOR OF **BOB DYLAN**'S ENTOURAGE, A MOVE THAT PROVES TO BE FAR MORE TRAUMATIC TO ANDY THAN ANYONE ELSE.

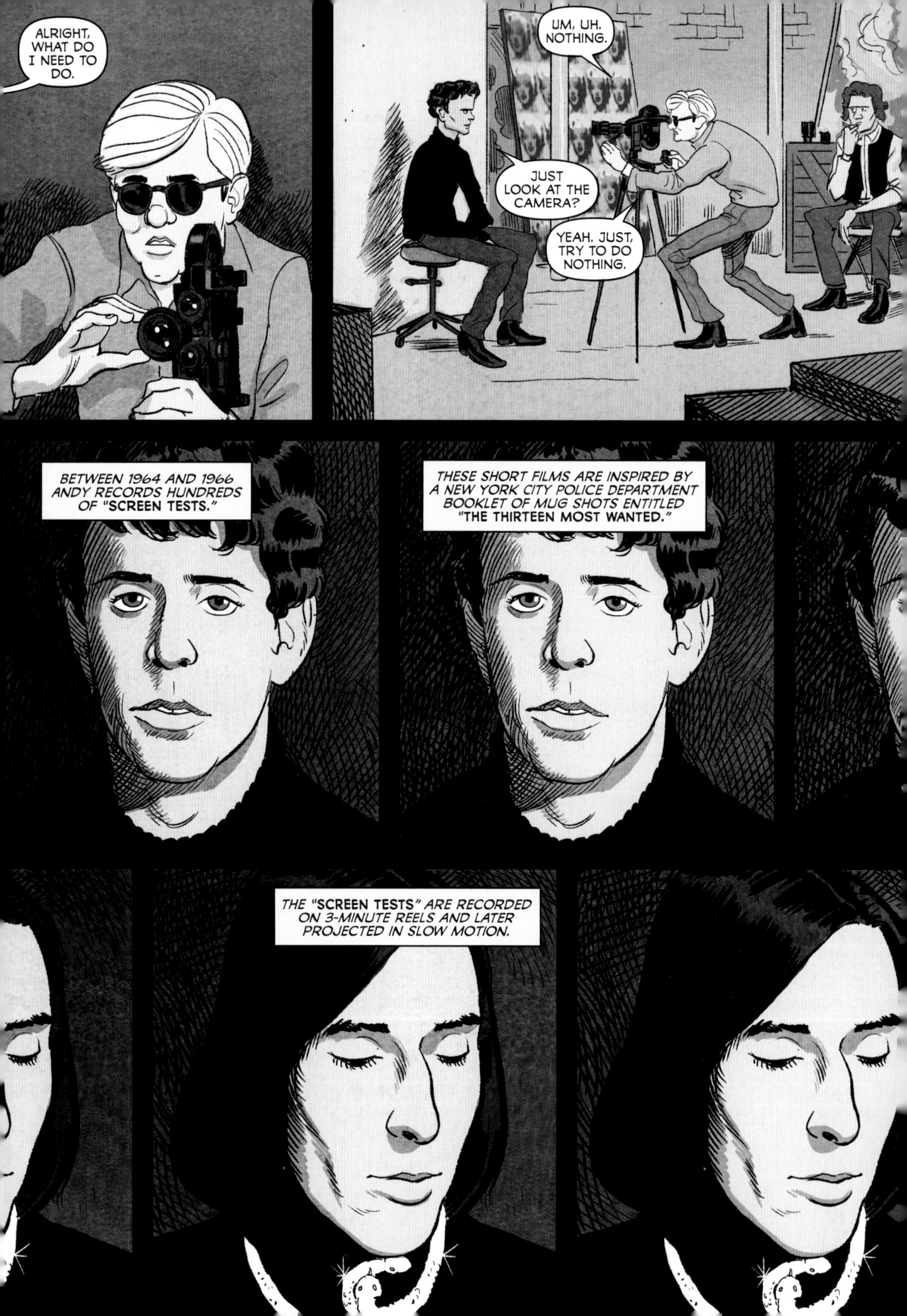
ALRIGHT, WHAT DO I NEED TO DO.
UM, UH. NOTHING.
JUST LOOK AT THE CAMERA?
YEAH. JUST, TRY TO DO NOTHING.
BETWEEN 1964 AND 1966 ANDY RECORDS HUNDREDS OF "SCREEN TESTS."
THESE SHORT FILMS ARE INSPIRED BY A NEW YORK CITY POLICE DEPARTMENT BOOKLET OF MUG SHOTS ENTITLED "THE THIRTEEN MOST WANTED."
THE "SCREEN TESTS" ARE RECORDED ON 3-MINUTE REELS AND LATER PROJECTED IN SLOW MOTION.

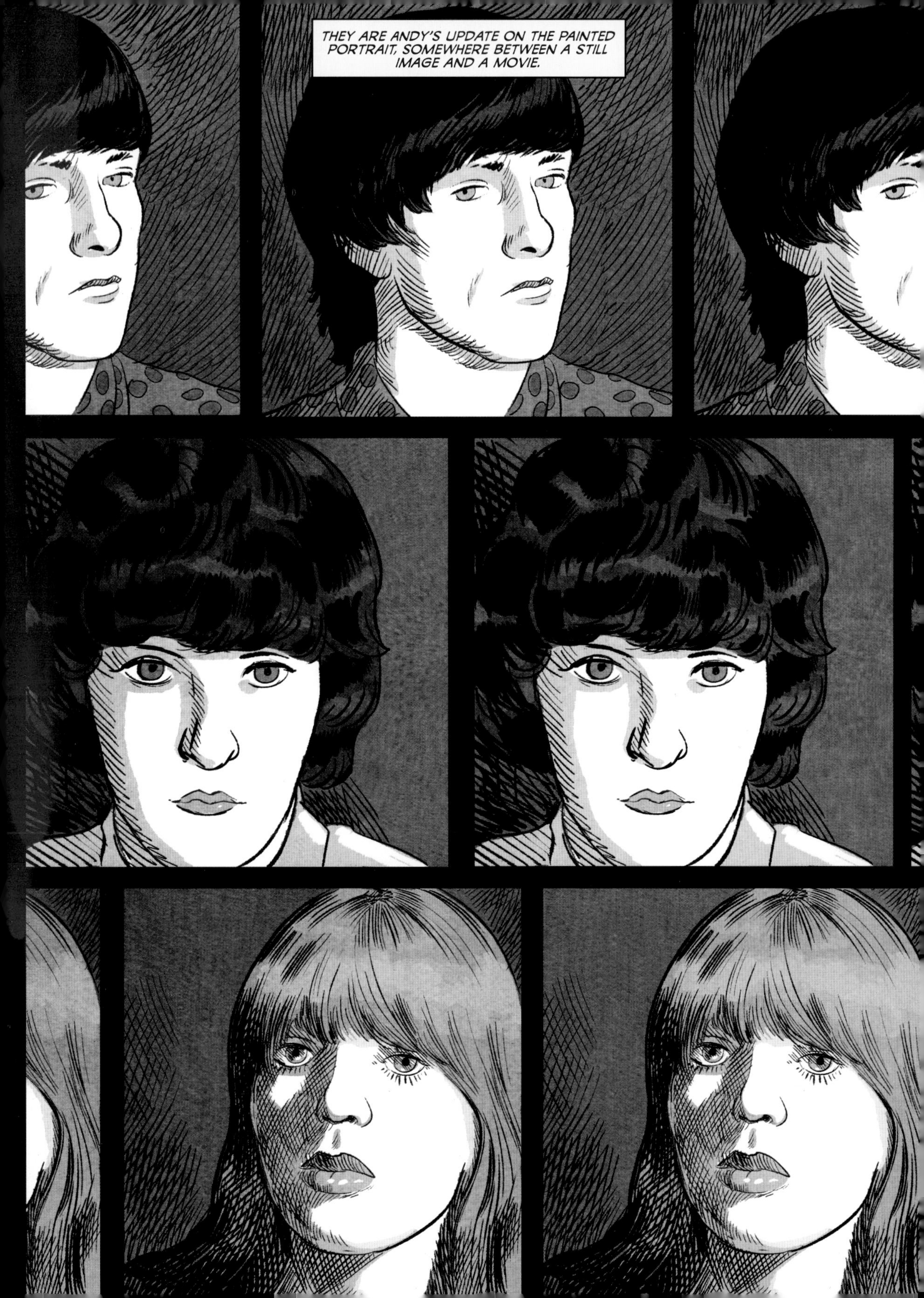
THEY ARE ANDY'S UPDATE ON THE PAINTED PORTRAIT, SOMEWHERE BETWEEN A STILL IMAGE AND A MOVIE.

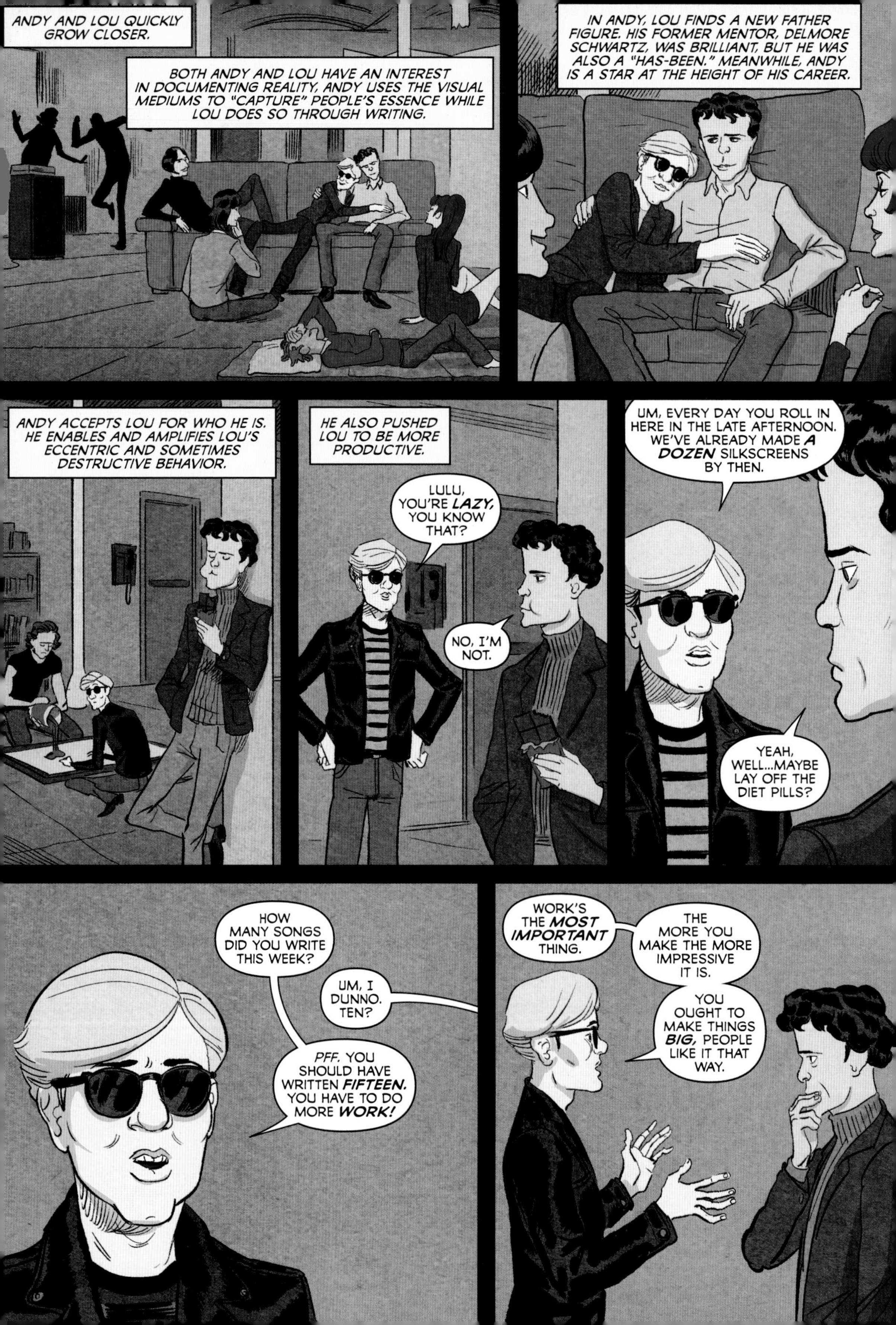

ANDY AND LOU QUICKLY GROW CLOSER.
BOTH ANDY AND LOU HAVE AN INTEREST IN DOCUMENTING REALITY, ANDY USES THE VISUAL MEDIUMS TO "CAPTURE" PEOPLE'S ESSENCE WHILE LOU DOES SO THROUGH WRITING.
IN ANDY, LOU FINDS A NEW FATHER FIGURE. HIS FORMER MENTOR, DELMORE SCHWARTZ, WAS BRILLIANT, BUT HE WAS ALSO A "HAS-BEEN." MEANWHILE, ANDY IS A STAR AT THE HEIGHT OF HIS CAREER.
ANDY ACCEPTS LOU FOR WHO HE IS. HE ENABLES AND AMPLIFIES LOU'S ECCENTRIC AND SOMETIMES DESTRUCTIVE BEHAVIOR.
HE ALSO PUSHED LOU TO BE MORE PRODUCTIVE.
LULU, YOU'RE *LAZY,* YOU KNOW THAT?
NO, I'M NOT.
UM, EVERY DAY YOU ROLL IN HERE IN THE LATE AFTERNOON. WE'VE ALREADY MADE ***A DOZEN*** SILKSCREENS BY THEN.
YEAH, WELL...MAYBE LAY OFF THE DIET PILLS?
HOW MANY SONGS DID YOU WRITE THIS WEEK?
UM, I DUNNO. TEN?
PFF. YOU SHOULD HAVE WRITTEN ***FIFTEEN.*** YOU HAVE TO DO MORE ***WORK!***
WORK'S THE ***MOST IMPORTANT*** THING.
THE MORE YOU MAKE THE MORE IMPRESSIVE IT IS.
YOU OUGHT TO MAKE THINGS ***BIG,*** PEOPLE LIKE IT THAT WAY.

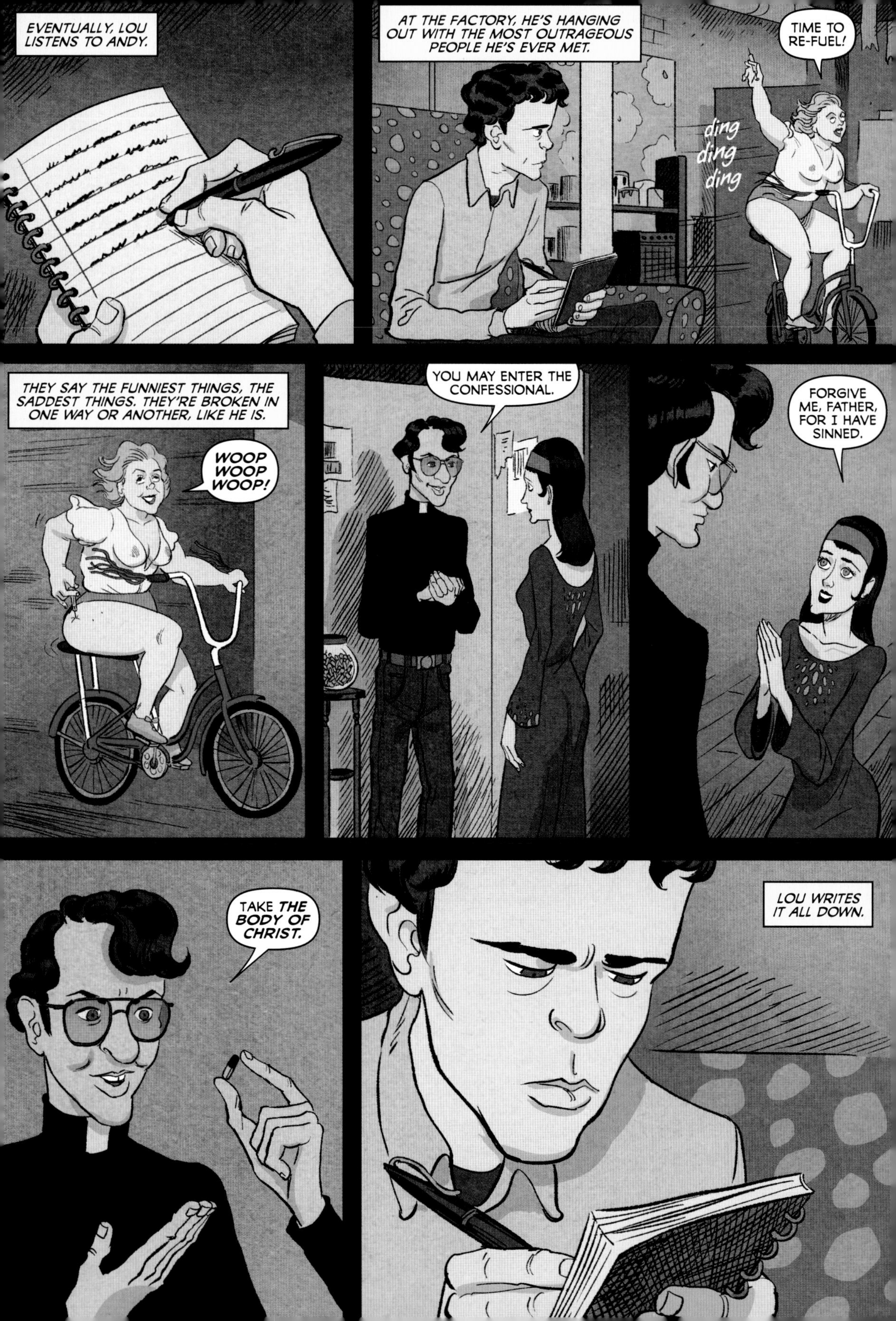
EVENTUALLY, LOU LISTENS TO ANDY.
AT THE FACTORY, HE'S HANGING OUT WITH THE MOST OUTRAGEOUS PEOPLE HE'S EVER MET.
TIME TO RE-FUEL!
ding ding ding
THEY SAY THE FUNNIEST THINGS, THE SADDEST THINGS. THEY'RE BROKEN IN ONE WAY OR ANOTHER, LIKE HE IS.
WOOP WOOP WOOP!
YOU MAY ENTER THE CONFESSIONAL.
FORGIVE ME, FATHER, FOR I HAVE SINNED.
TAKE THE BODY OF CHRIST.
LOU WRITES IT ALL DOWN.

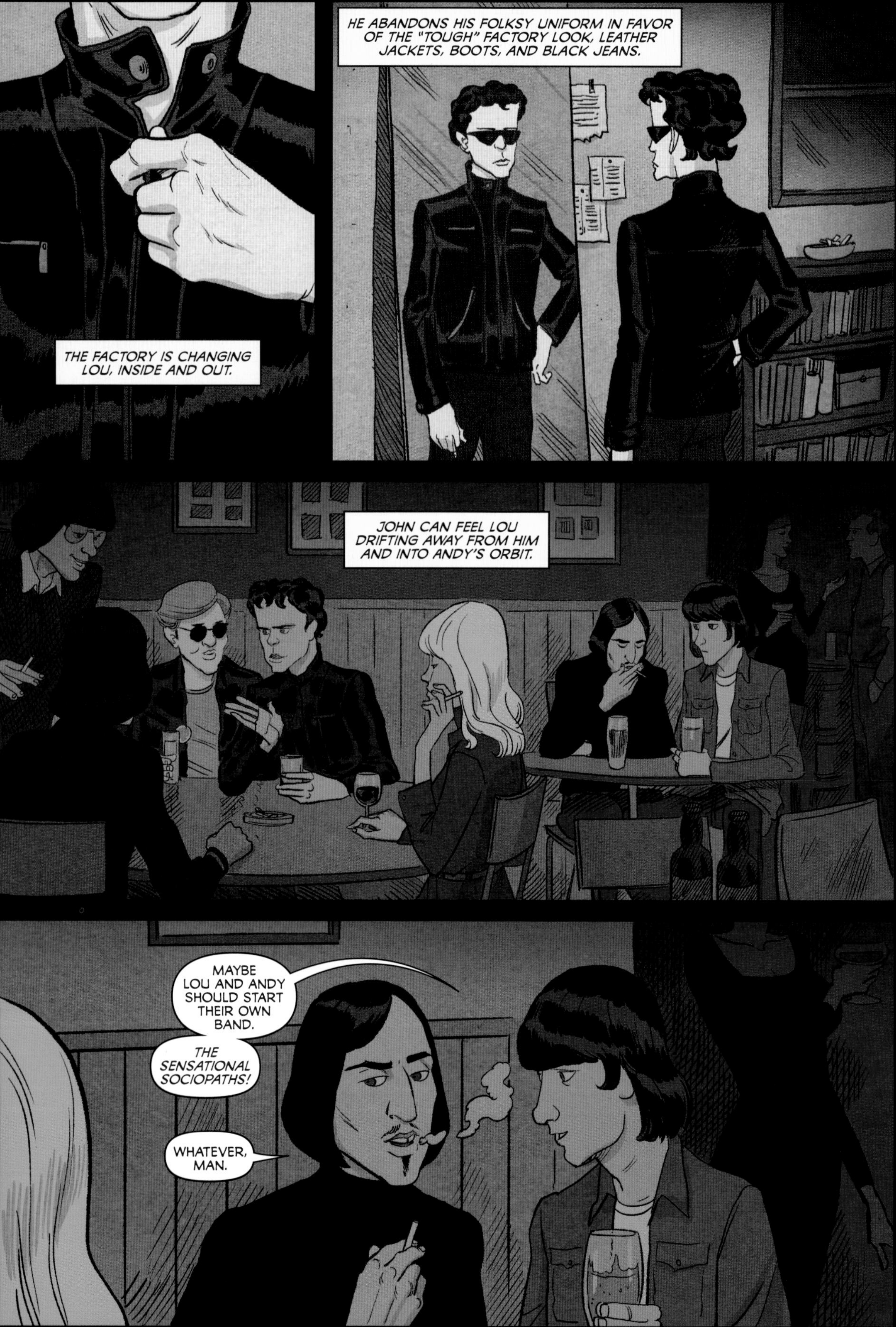
THE FACTORY IS CHANGING LOU, INSIDE AND OUT.
HE ABANDONS HIS FOLKSY UNIFORM IN FAVOR OF THE "TOUGH" FACTORY LOOK, LEATHER JACKETS, BOOTS, AND BLACK JEANS.
JOHN CAN FEEL LOU DRIFTING AWAY FROM HIM AND INTO ANDY'S ORBIT.
MAYBE LOU AND ANDY SHOULD START THEIR OWN BAND.
THE SENSATIONAL SOCIOPATHS!
WHATEVER, MAN.

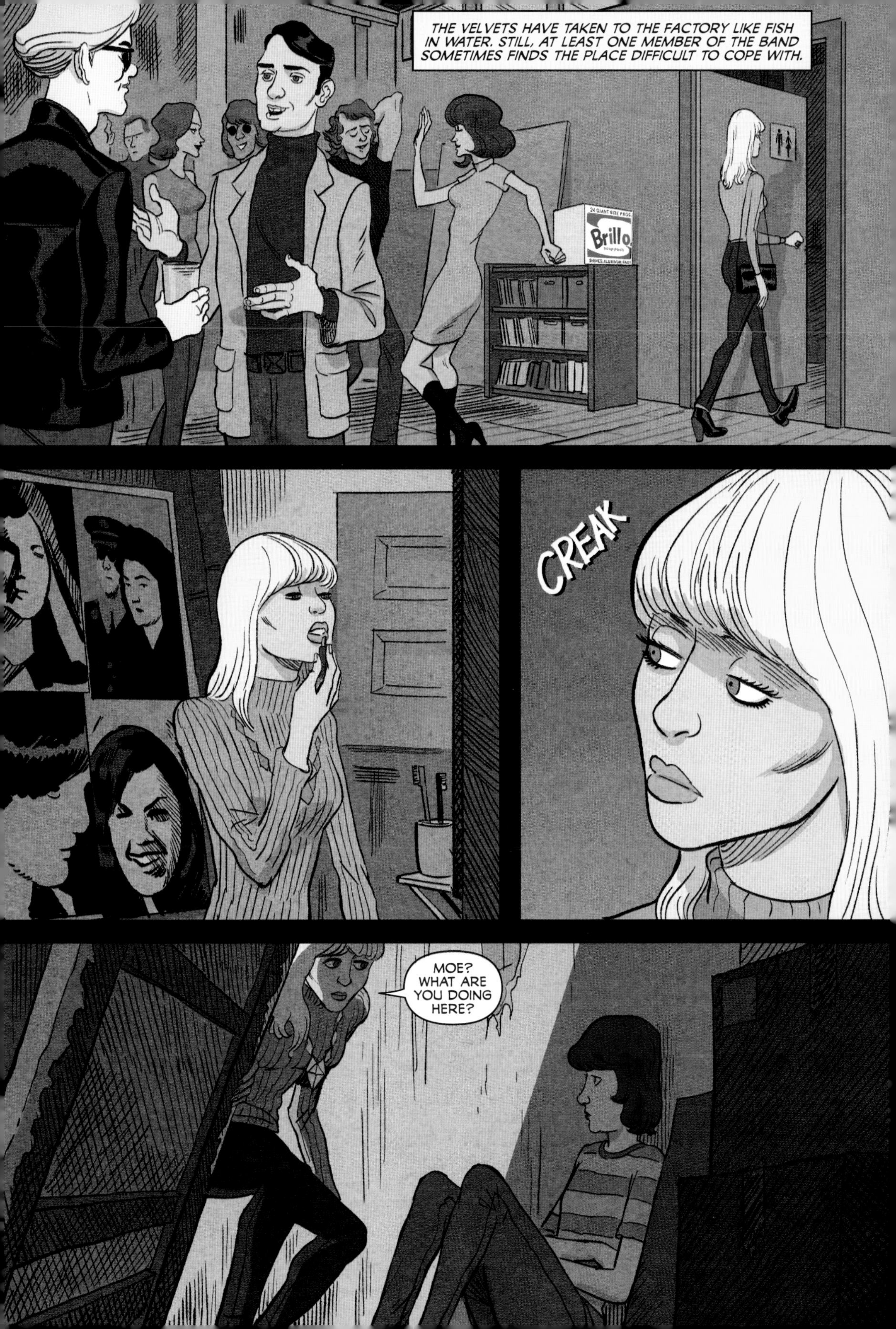

THE VELVETS HAVE TAKEN TO THE FACTORY LIKE FISH IN WATER. STILL, AT LEAST ONE MEMBER OF THE BAND SOMETIMES FINDS THE PLACE DIFFICULT TO COPE WITH.
24 GIANT SIZE PKGS.
Brillo
SHINES ALUMINUM FAST
CREAK
MOE? WHAT ARE YOU DOING HERE?

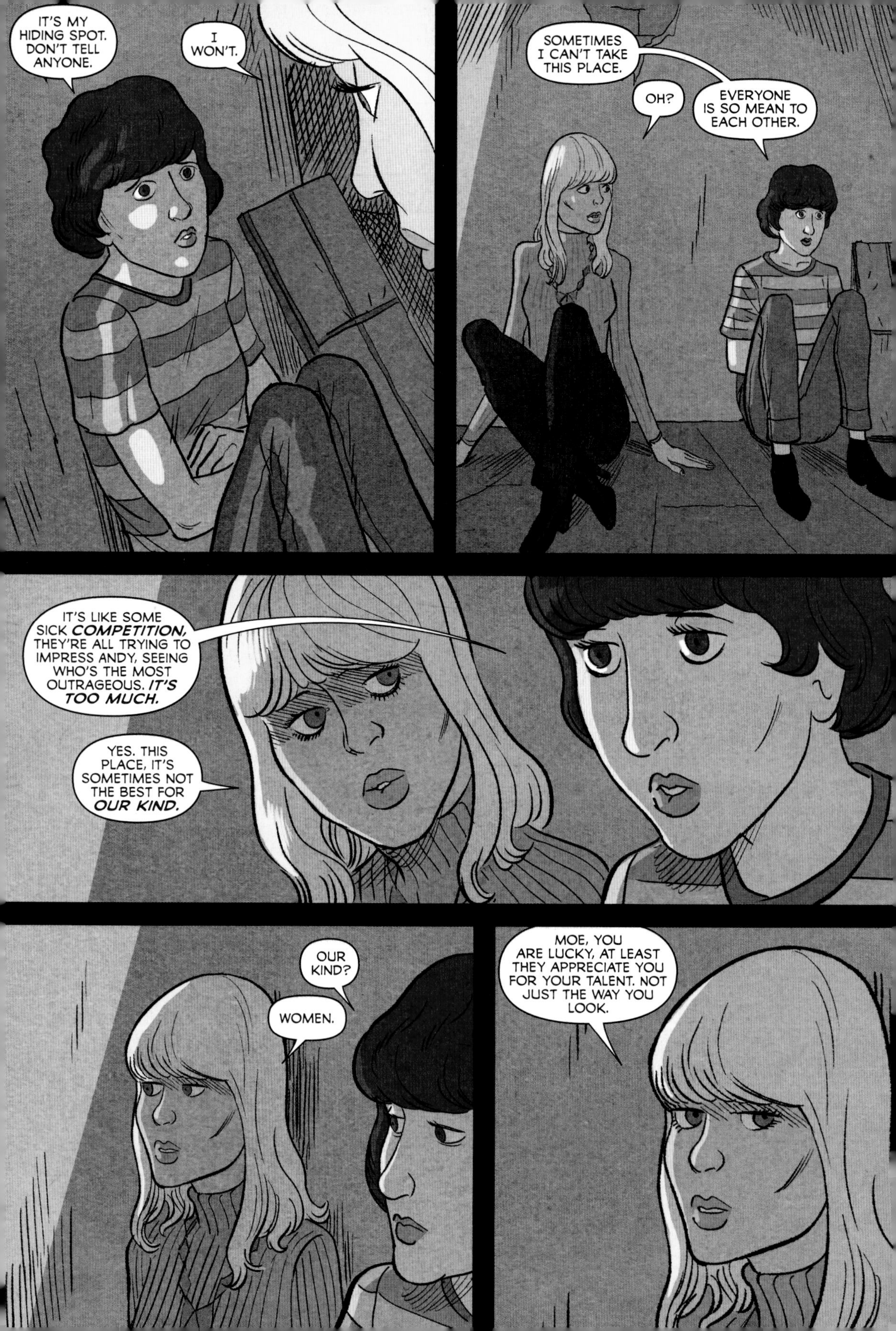

IT'S MY HIDING SPOT. DON'T TELL ANYONE.
I WON'T.
SOMETIMES I CAN'T TAKE THIS PLACE.
OH?
EVERYONE IS SO MEAN TO EACH OTHER.
IT'S LIKE SOME SICK *COMPETITION,* THEY'RE ALL TRYING TO IMPRESS ANDY, SEEING WHO'S THE MOST OUTRAGEOUS. *IT'S TOO MUCH.*
YES. THIS PLACE, IT'S SOMETIMES NOT THE BEST FOR *OUR KIND.*
OUR KIND?
WOMEN.
MOE, YOU ARE LUCKY, AT LEAST THEY APPRECIATE YOU FOR YOUR TALENT. NOT JUST THE WAY YOU LOOK.

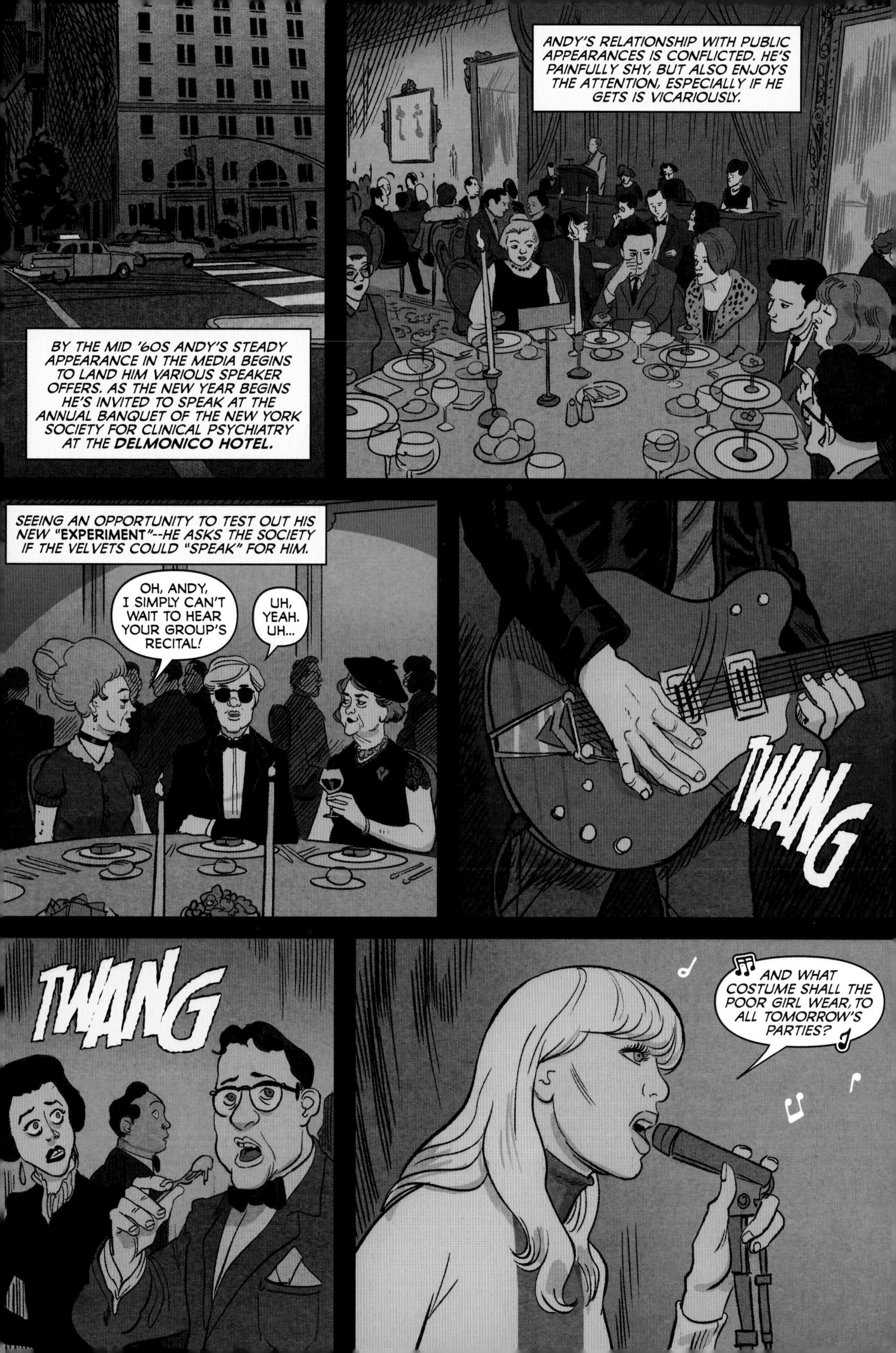
BY THE MID '60S ANDY'S STEADY APPEARANCE IN THE MEDIA BEGINS TO LAND HIM VARIOUS SPEAKER OFFERS. AS THE NEW YEAR BEGINS HE'S INVITED TO SPEAK AT THE ANNUAL BANQUET OF THE NEW YORK SOCIETY FOR CLINICAL PSYCHIATRY AT THE DELMONICO HOTEL.
ANDY'S RELATIONSHIP WITH PUBLIC APPEARANCES IS CONFLICTED. HE'S PAINFULLY SHY, BUT ALSO ENJOYS THE ATTENTION, ESPECIALLY IF HE GETS IS VICARIOUSLY.
SEEING AN OPPORTUNITY TO TEST OUT HIS NEW "EXPERIMENT"--HE ASKS THE SOCIETY IF THE VELVETS COULD "SPEAK" FOR HIM.
OH, ANDY, I SIMPLY CAN'T WAIT TO HEAR YOUR GROUP'S RECITAL!
UH, YEAH. UH...
TWANG
TWANG
AND WHAT COSTUME SHALL THE POOR GIRL WEAR, TO ALL TOMORROW'S PARTIES?

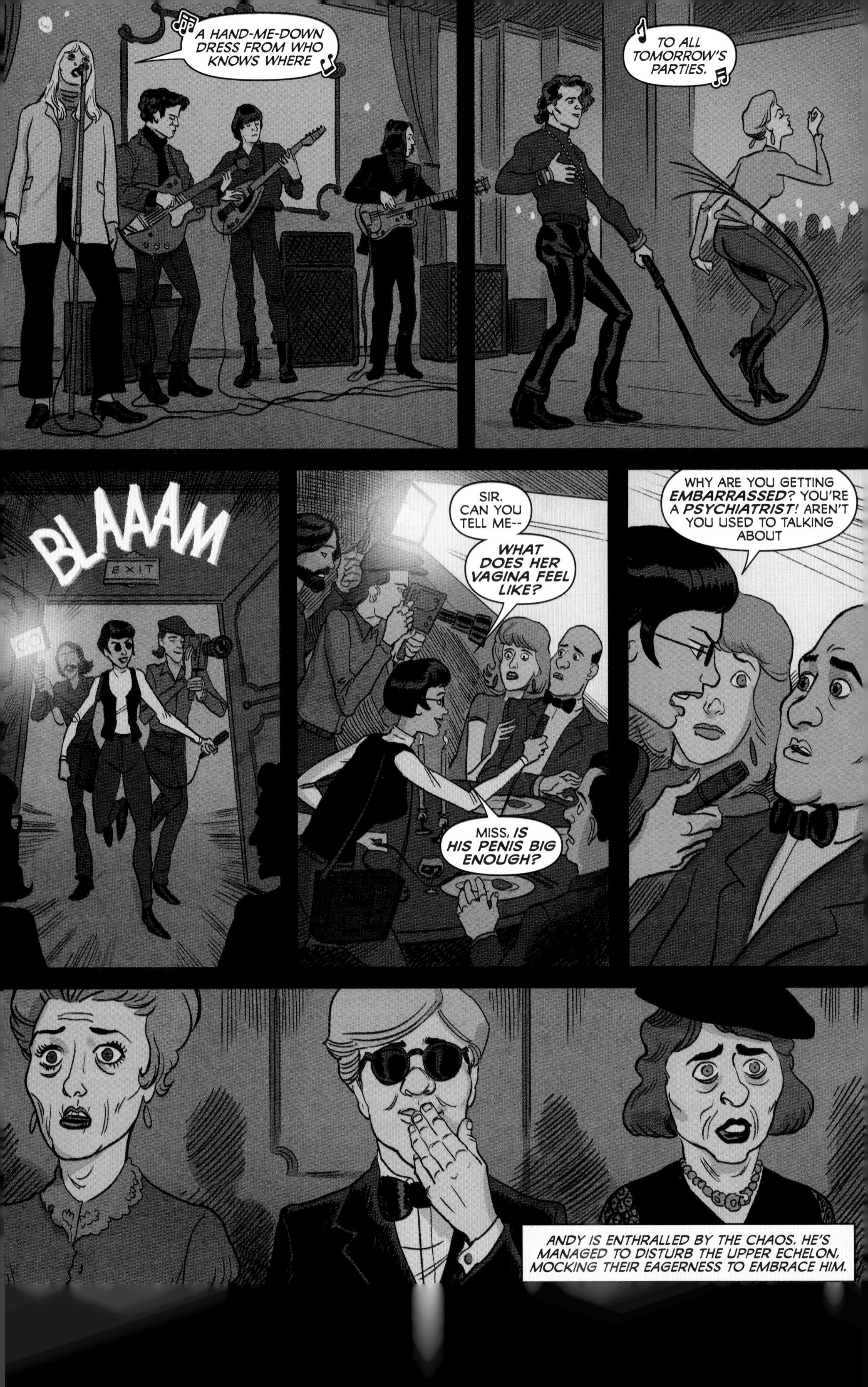
A HAND-ME-DOWN DRESS FROM WHO KNOWS WHERE
TO ALL TOMORROW'S PARTIES.
BLAAAM
EXIT
SIR. CAN YOU TELL ME--
WHAT DOES HER VAGINA FEEL LIKE?
MISS, IS HIS PENIS BIG ENOUGH?
WHY ARE YOU GETTING EMBARRASSED? YOU'RE A PSYCHIATRIST! AREN'T YOU USED TO TALKING ABOUT
ANDY IS ENTHRALLED BY THE CHAOS. HE'S MANAGED TO DISTURB THE UPPER ECHELON, MOCKING THEIR EAGERNESS TO EMBRACE HIM.

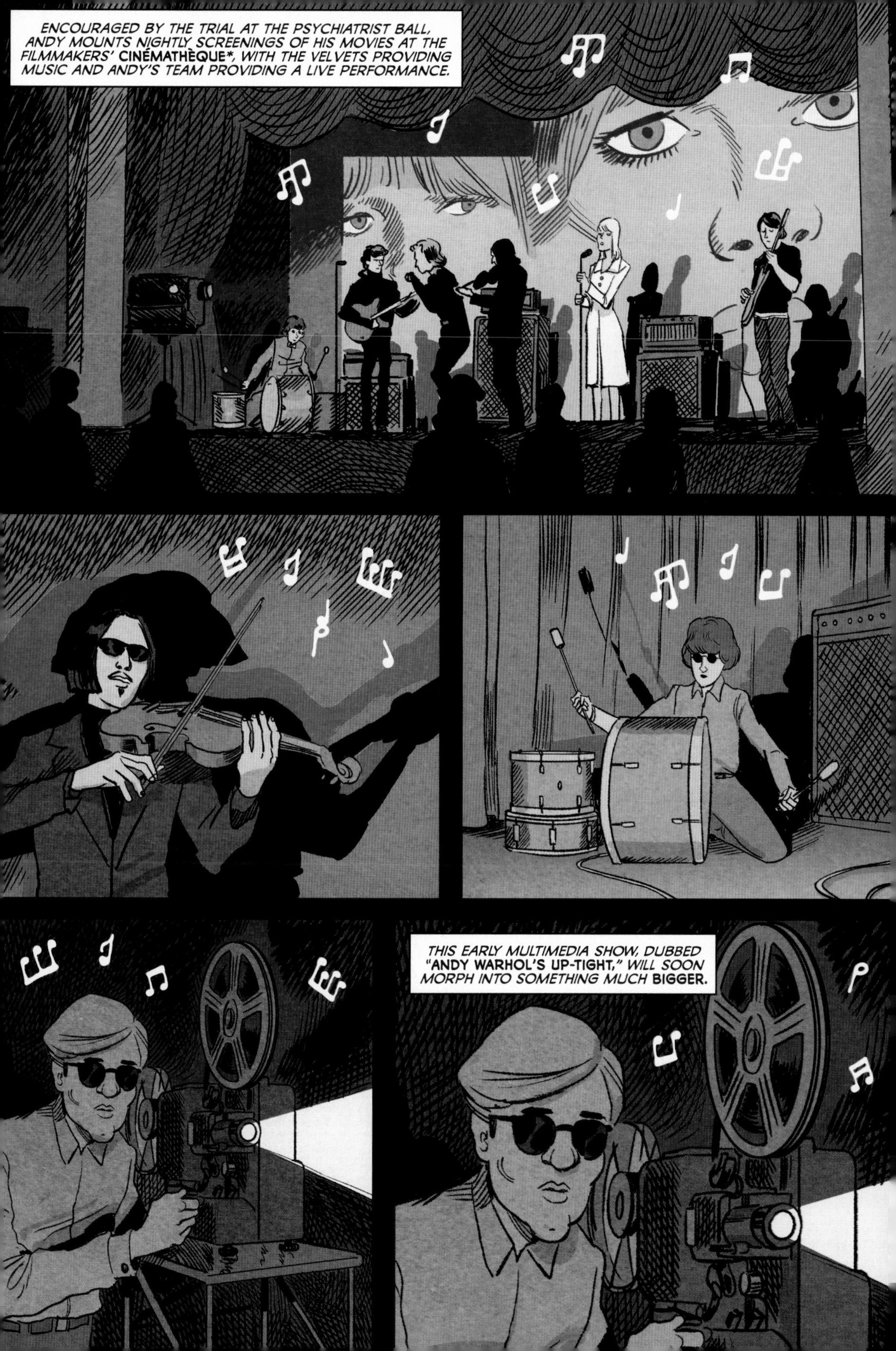
ENCOURAGED BY THE TRIAL AT THE PSYCHIATRIST BALL, ANDY MOUNTS NIGHTLY SCREENINGS OF HIS MOVIES AT THE FILMMAKERS' CINÉMATHÈQUE*, WITH THE VELVETS PROVIDING MUSIC AND ANDY'S TEAM PROVIDING A LIVE PERFORMANCE.
THIS EARLY MULTIMEDIA SHOW, DUBBED "ANDY WARHOL'S UP-TIGHT," WILL SOON MORPH INTO SOMETHING MUCH BIGGER.

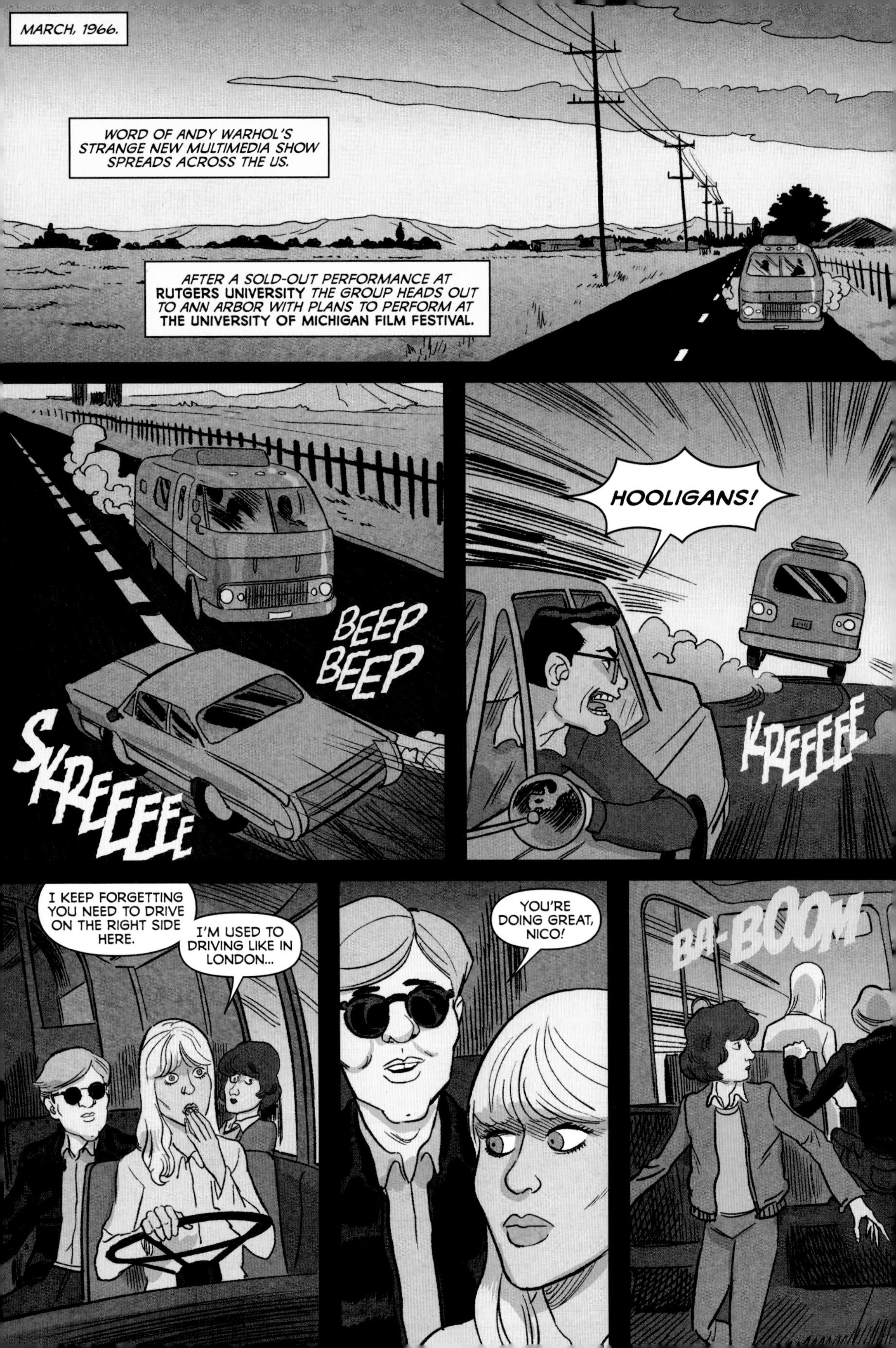
MARCH, 1966.
WORD OF ANDY WARHOL'S STRANGE NEW MULTIMEDIA SHOW SPREADS ACROSS THE US.
AFTER A SOLD-OUT PERFORMANCE AT RUTGERS UNIVERSITY THE GROUP HEADS OUT TO ANN ARBOR WITH PLANS TO PERFORM AT THE UNIVERSITY OF MICHIGAN FILM FESTIVAL.
BEEP BEEP
SKREEEEEE
HOOLIGANS!
KREEEEE
I KEEP FORGETTING YOU NEED TO DRIVE ON THE RIGHT SIDE HERE.
I'M USED TO DRIVING LIKE IN LONDON...
YOU'RE DOING GREAT, NICO!
BA-BOOM

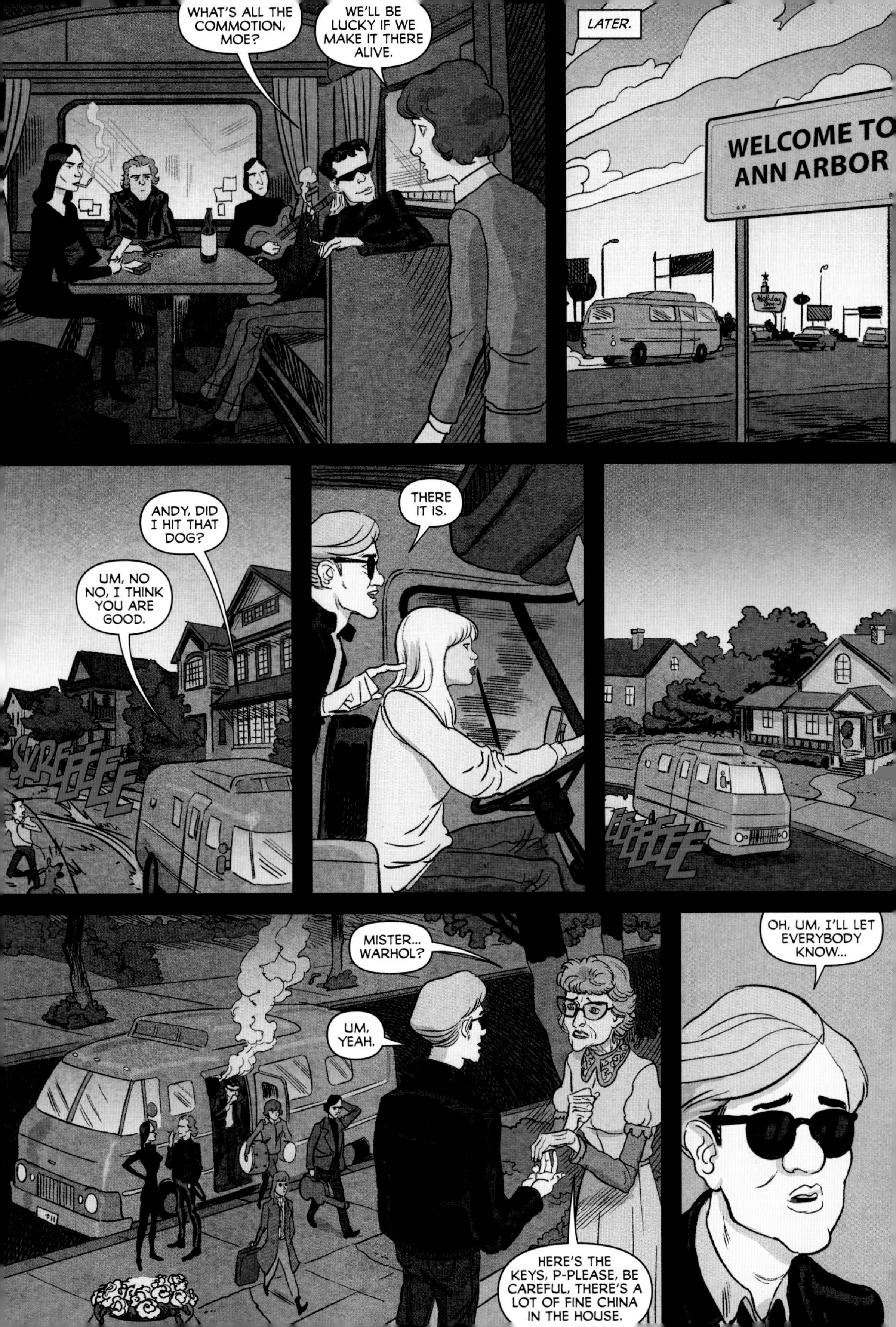
WHAT'S ALL THE COMMOTION, MOE?
WE'LL BE LUCKY IF WE MAKE IT THERE ALIVE.
LATER.
WELCOME TO ANN ARBOR
ANDY, DID I HIT THAT DOG?
UM, NO NO, I THINK YOU ARE GOOD.
THERE IT IS.
MISTER... WARHOL?
UM, YEAH.
HERE'S THE KEYS, P-PLEASE, BE CAREFUL, THERE'S A LOT OF FINE CHINA IN THE HOUSE.
OH, UM, I'LL LET EVERYBODY KNOW...

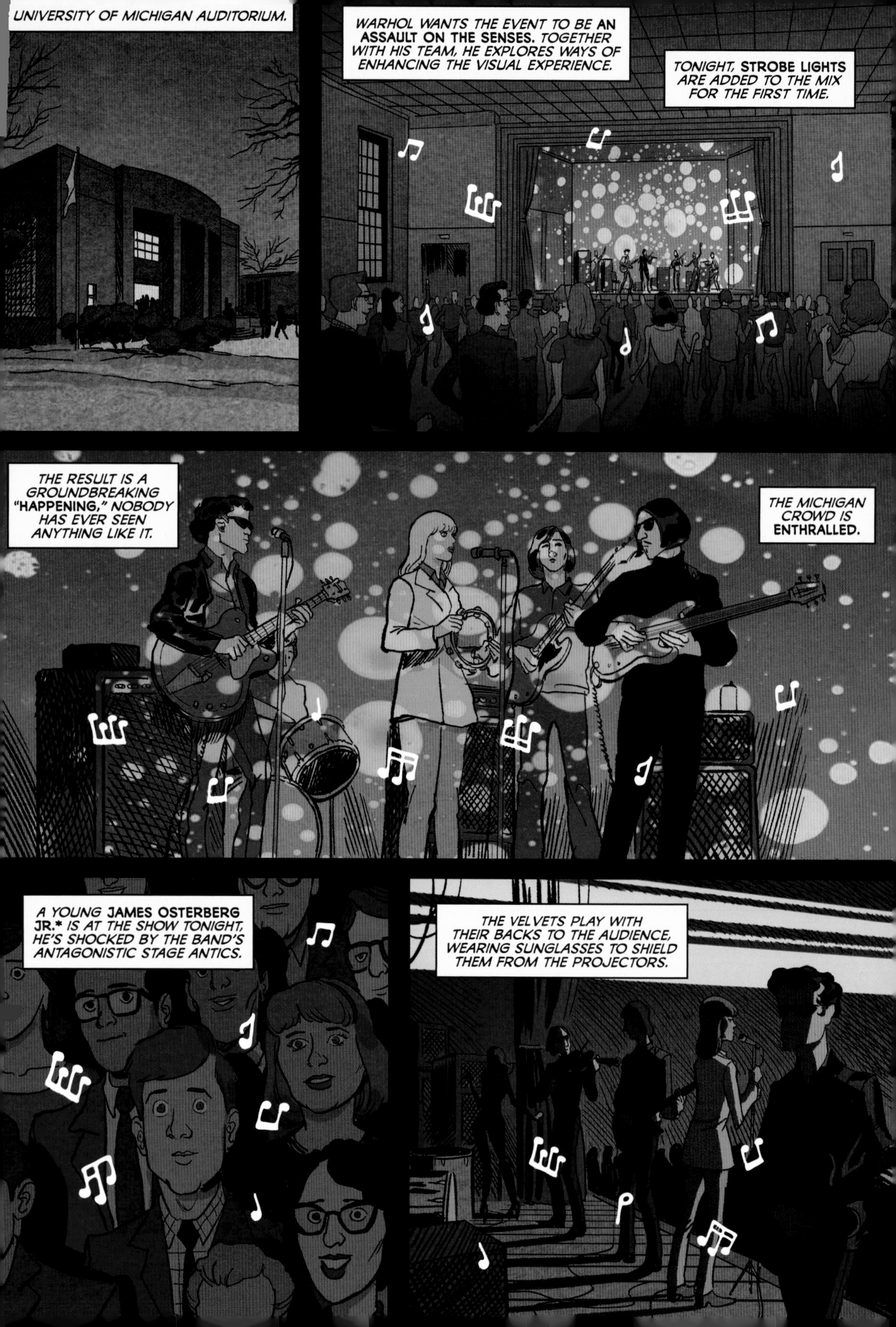
UNIVERSITY OF MICHIGAN AUDITORIUM.
WARHOL WANTS THE EVENT TO BE AN ASSAULT ON THE SENSES. TOGETHER WITH HIS TEAM, HE EXPLORES WAYS OF ENHANCING THE VISUAL EXPERIENCE.
TONIGHT, STROBE LIGHTS ARE ADDED TO THE MIX FOR THE FIRST TIME.
THE RESULT IS A GROUNDBREAKING "HAPPENING," NOBODY HAS EVER SEEN ANYTHING LIKE IT.
THE MICHIGAN CROWD IS ENTHRALLED.
A YOUNG JAMES OSTERBERG JR.* IS AT THE SHOW TONIGHT, HE'S SHOCKED BY THE BAND'S ANTAGONISTIC STAGE ANTICS.
THE VELVETS PLAY WITH THEIR BACKS TO THE AUDIENCE, WEARING SUNGLASSES TO SHIELD THEM FROM THE PROJECTORS.

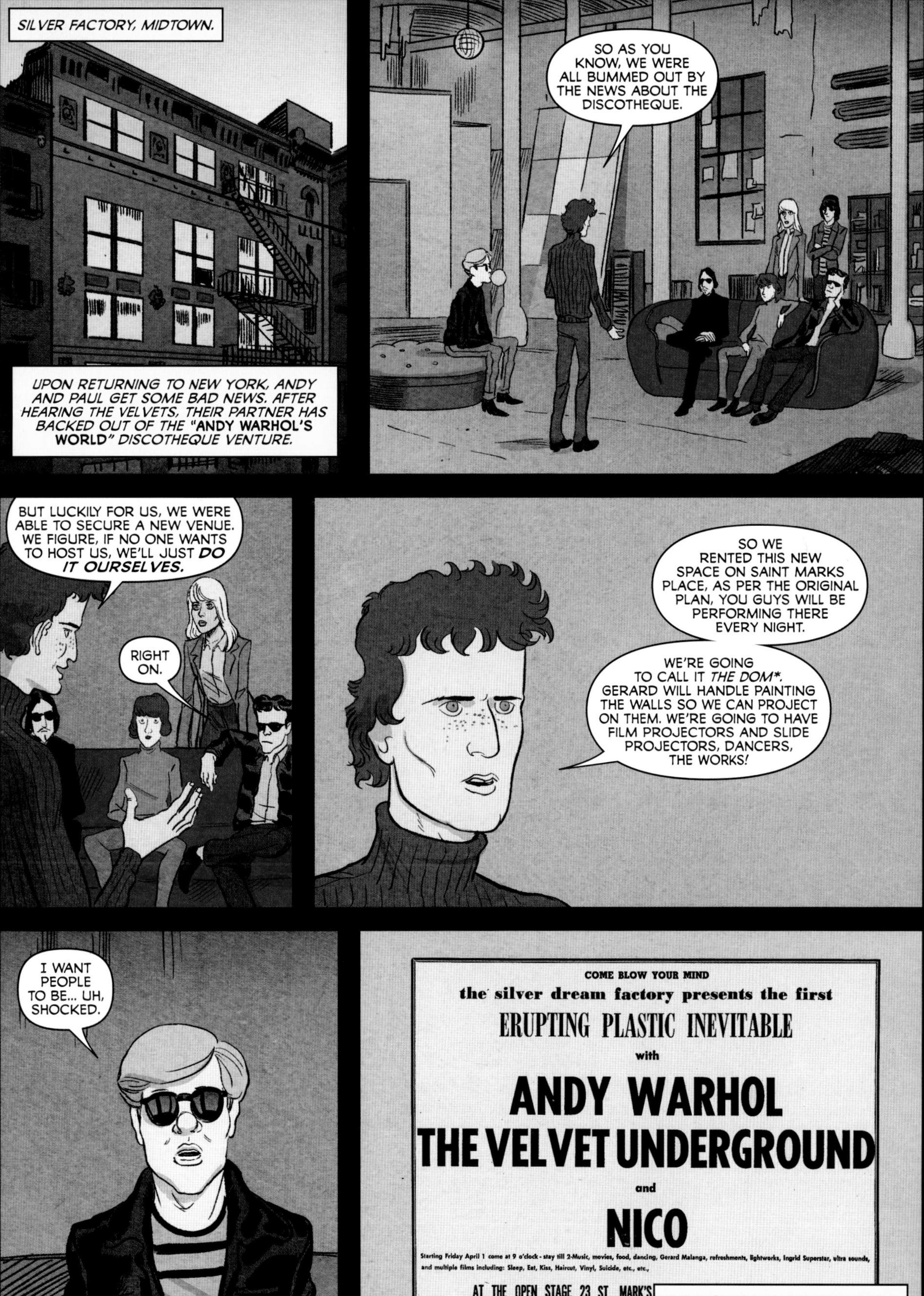

SILVER FACTORY, MIDTOWN.
UPON RETURNING TO NEW YORK, ANDY AND PAUL GET SOME BAD NEWS. AFTER HEARING THE VELVETS, THEIR PARTNER HAS BACKED OUT OF THE "ANDY WARHOL'S WORLD" DISCOTHEQUE VENTURE.
SO AS YOU KNOW, WE WERE ALL BUMMED OUT BY THE NEWS ABOUT THE DISCOTHEQUE.
BUT LUCKILY FOR US, WE WERE ABLE TO SECURE A NEW VENUE. WE FIGURE, IF NO ONE WANTS TO HOST US, WE'LL JUST DO IT OURSELVES.
RIGHT ON.
SO WE RENTED THIS NEW SPACE ON SAINT MARKS PLACE, AS PER THE ORIGINAL PLAN, YOU GUYS WILL BE PERFORMING THERE EVERY NIGHT.
WE'RE GOING TO CALL IT THE DOM*. GERARD WILL HANDLE PAINTING THE WALLS SO WE CAN PROJECT ON THEM. WE'RE GOING TO HAVE FILM PROJECTORS AND SLIDE PROJECTORS, DANCERS, THE WORKS!
I WANT PEOPLE TO BE... UH, SHOCKED.
COME BLOW YOUR MIND
the silver dream factory presents the first
ERUPTING PLASTIC INEVITABLE
with
ANDY WARHOL
THE VELVET UNDERGROUND
and
NICO
Starting Friday April 1 come at 9 o'clock - stay till 2-Music, movies, food, dancing, Gerard Malanga, refreshments, lightworks, Ingrid Superstar, ultra sounds, and multiple films including: Sleep, Eat, Kiss, Haircut, Vinyl, Suicide, etc., etc.,
AT THE OPEN STAGE 23 ST. MARK'S
NO PERFORMANCE SATURDAY APRIL 2ND,
THE SHOW'S NAME IS CHANGED A WEEK LATER TO "THE EXPLODING PLASTIC INEVITABLE."

*THE SPACE WAS ORIGINALLY CALLED POLSKY DOM NARODWY--OR "POLISH NATIONAL HOME." WARHOL OFTEN LIKED TO LEAVE THINGS AS THEY WERE.

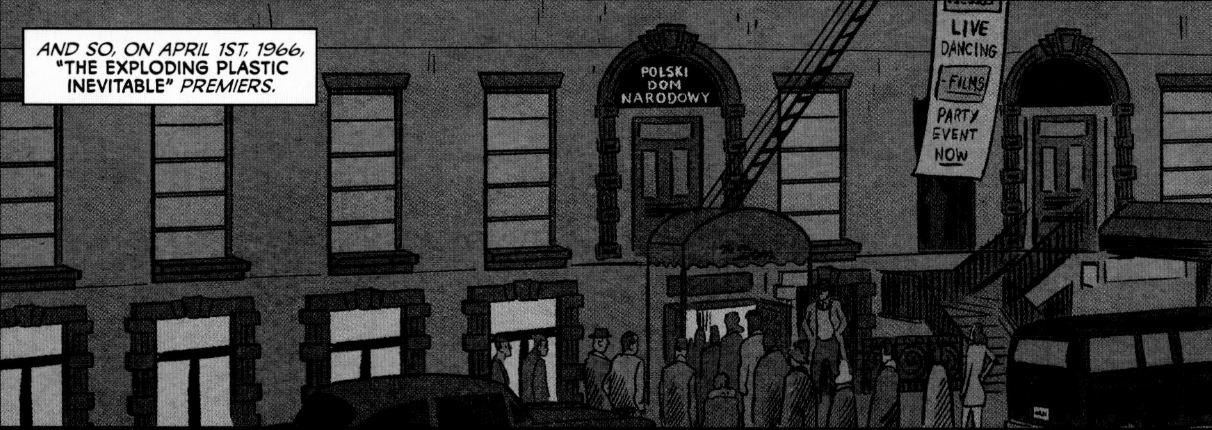
AND SO, ON APRIL 1ST, 1966, "THE EXPLODING PLASTIC INEVITABLE" PREMIERS.
POLSKI DOM NARODOWY
LIVE DANCING FILMS PARTY EVENT NOW

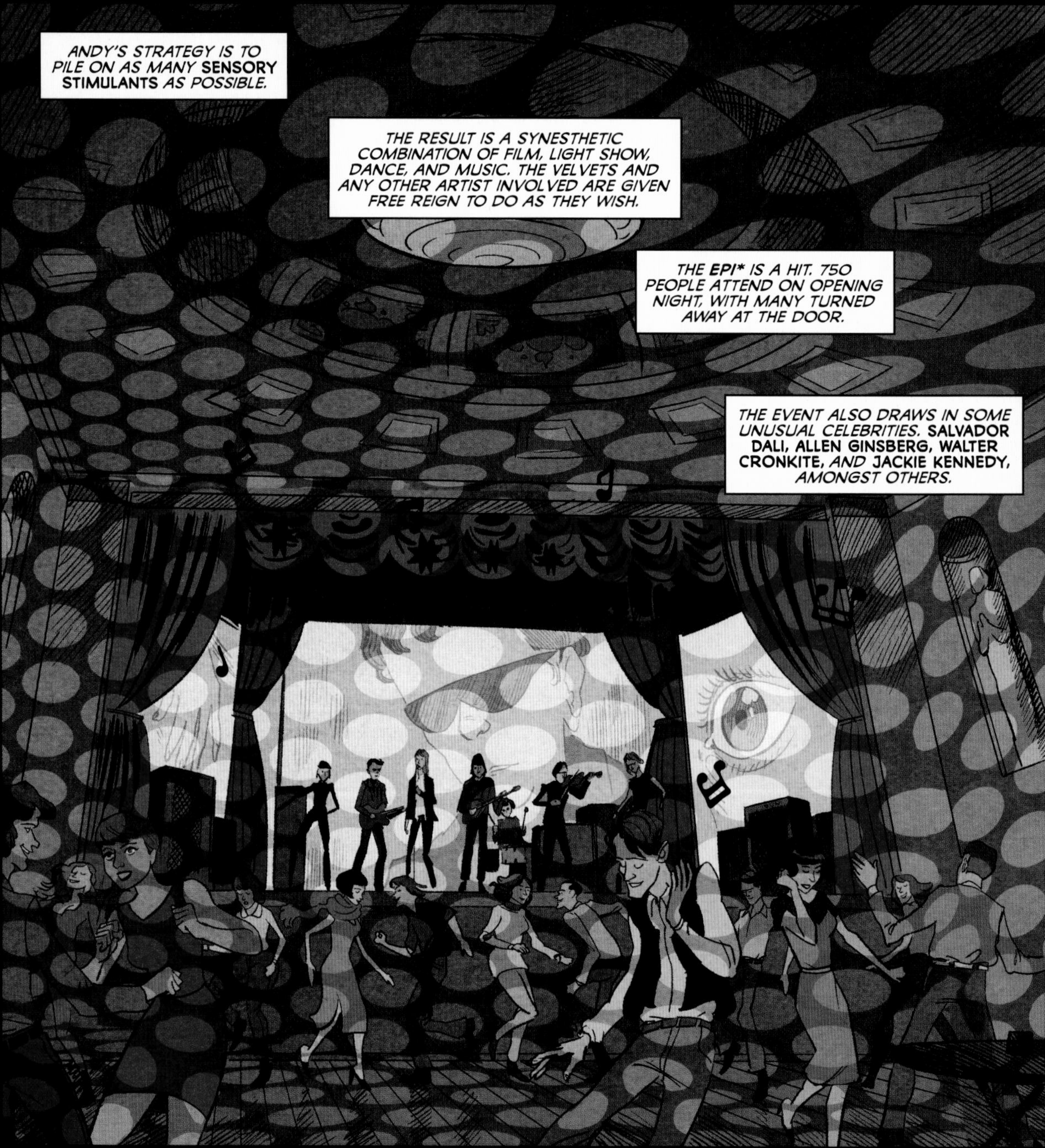
ANDY'S STRATEGY IS TO PILE ON AS MANY SENSORY STIMULANTS AS POSSIBLE.
THE RESULT IS A SYNESTHETIC COMBINATION OF FILM, LIGHT SHOW, DANCE, AND MUSIC. THE VELVETS AND ANY OTHER ARTIST INVOLVED ARE GIVEN FREE REIGN TO DO AS THEY WISH.
THE EPI* IS A HIT. 750 PEOPLE ATTEND ON OPENING NIGHT, WITH MANY TURNED AWAY AT THE DOOR.
THE EVENT ALSO DRAWS IN SOME UNUSUAL CELEBRITIES. SALVADOR DALI, ALLEN GINSBERG, WALTER CRONKITE, AND JACKIE KENNEDY, AMONGST OTHERS.

*EXPLODING PLASTIC INEVITABLE.

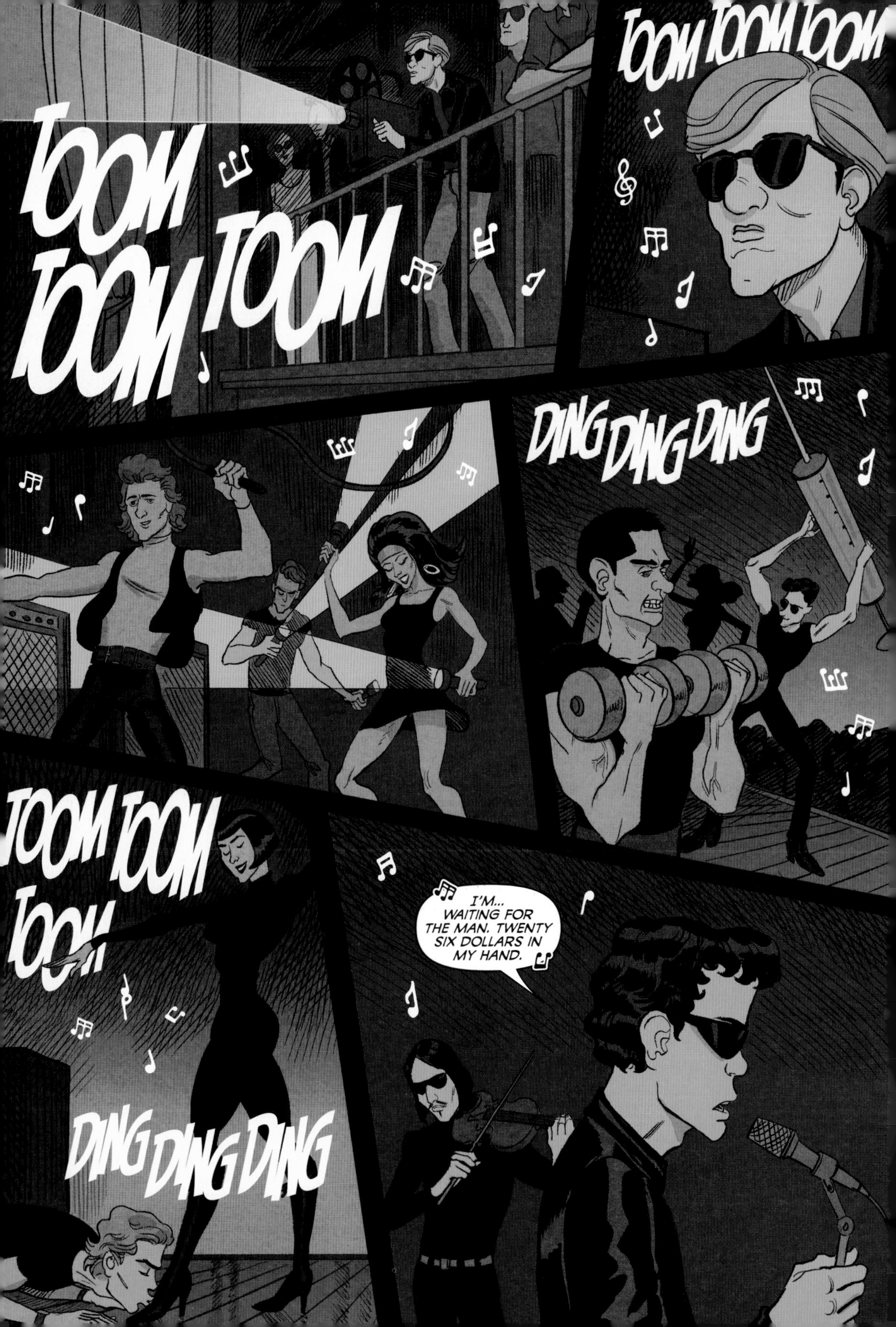
TOOM TOOM TOOM TOOM
TOOM TOOM TOOM
DING DING DING
TOOM TOOM TOOM
DING DING DING
I'M... WAITING FOR THE MAN. TWENTY SIX DOLLARS IN MY HAND.

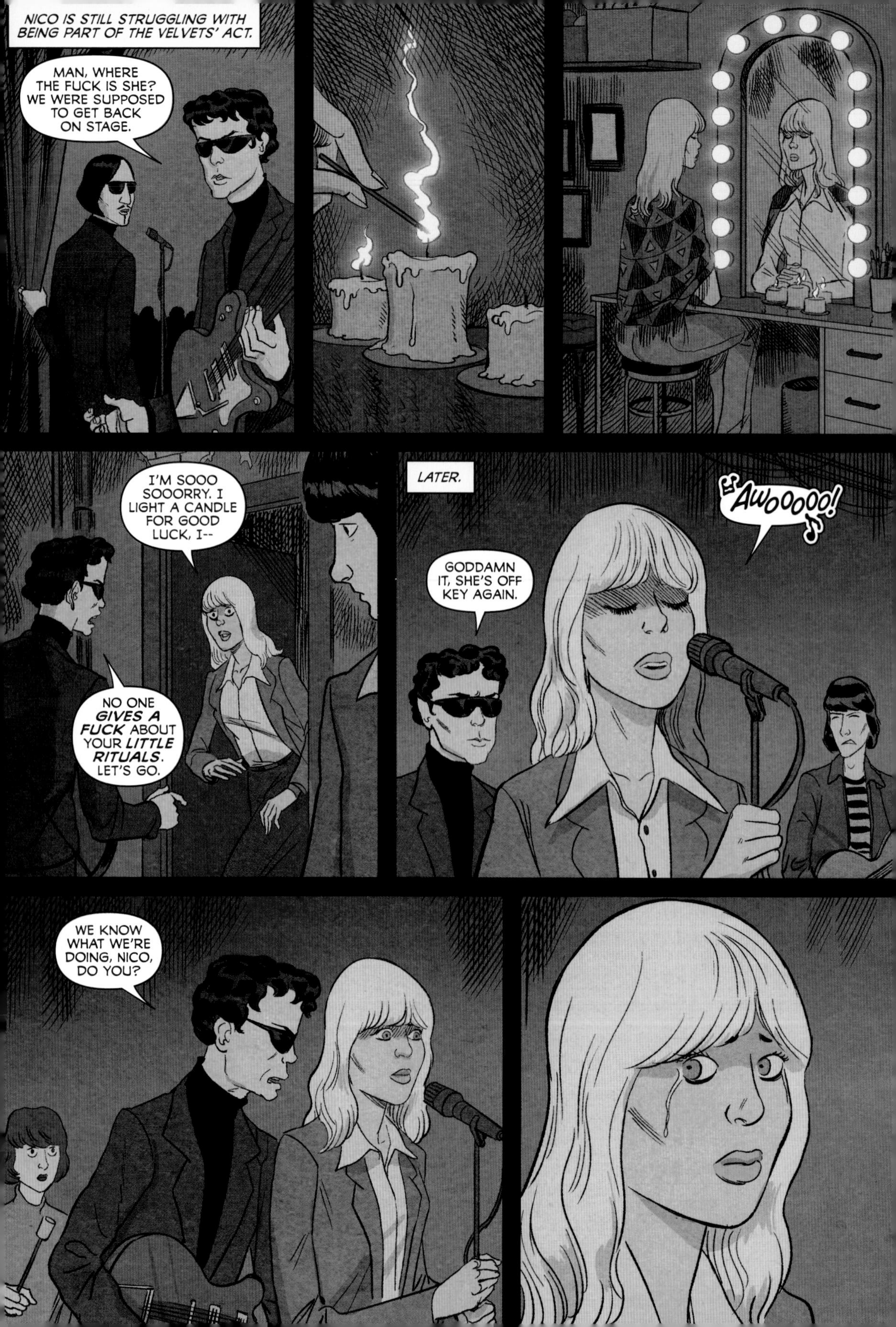
NICO IS STILL STRUGGLING WITH BEING PART OF THE VELVETS' ACT.
MAN, WHERE THE FUCK IS SHE? WE WERE SUPPOSED TO GET BACK ON STAGE.
I'M SOOO SOOORRY. I LIGHT A CANDLE FOR GOOD LUCK, I--
NO ONE *GIVES A FUCK* ABOUT YOUR *LITTLE RITUALS*. LET'S GO.
LATER.
AWOOOOO!
GODDAMN IT, SHE'S OFF KEY AGAIN.
WE KNOW WHAT WE'RE DOING, NICO, DO YOU?

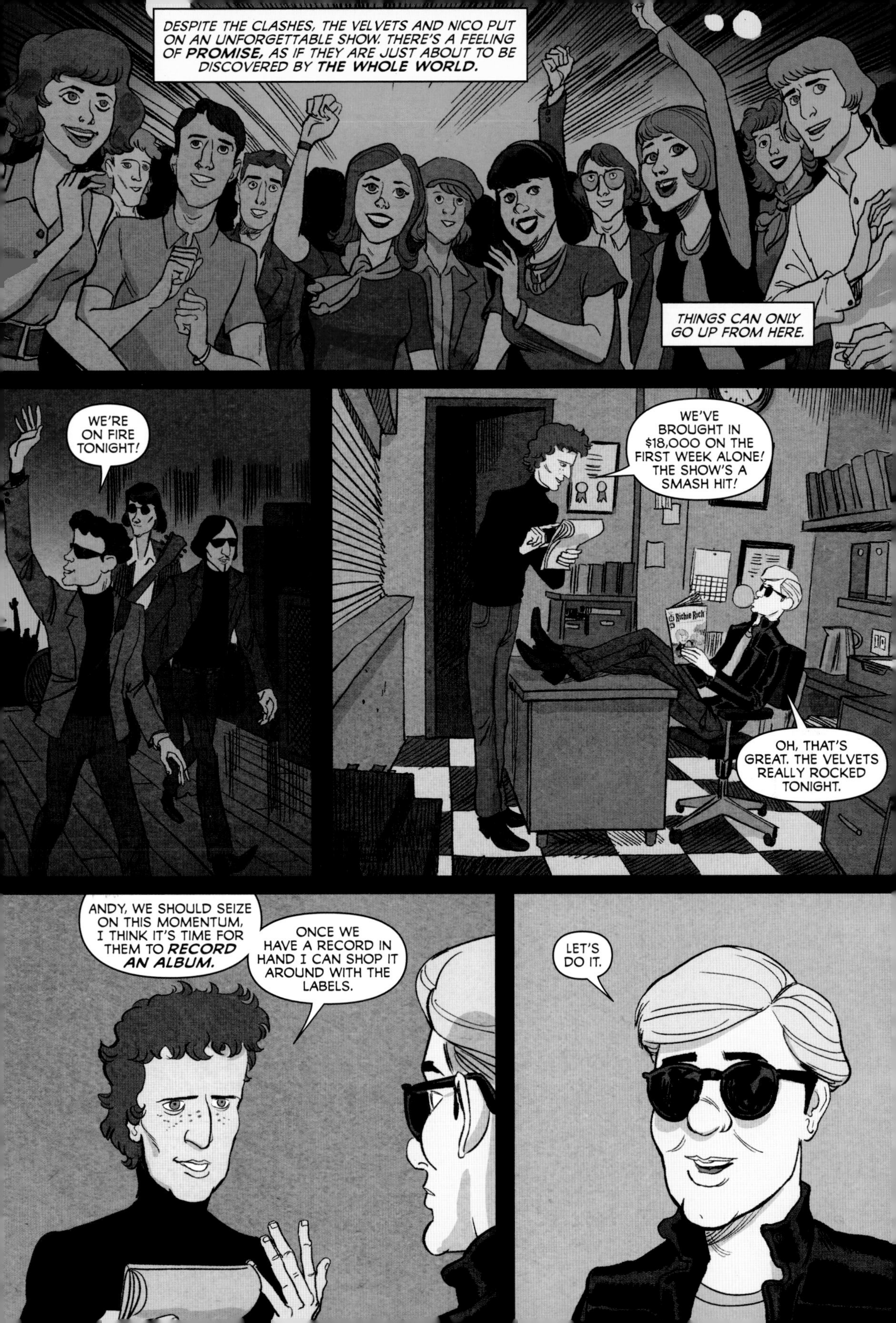
DESPITE THE CLASHES, THE VELVETS AND NICO PUT ON AN UNFORGETTABLE SHOW. THERE'S A FEELING OF PROMISE, AS IF THEY ARE JUST ABOUT TO BE DISCOVERED BY THE WHOLE WORLD.
THINGS CAN ONLY GO UP FROM HERE.
WE'RE ON FIRE TONIGHT!
WE'VE BROUGHT IN $18,000 ON THE FIRST WEEK ALONE! THE SHOW'S A SMASH HIT!
Richie Rich
OH, THAT'S GREAT. THE VELVETS REALLY ROCKED TONIGHT.
ANDY, WE SHOULD SEIZE ON THIS MOMENTUM, I THINK IT'S TIME FOR THEM TO RECORD AN ALBUM.
ONCE WE HAVE A RECORD IN HAND I CAN SHOP IT AROUND WITH THE LABELS.
LET'S DO IT.

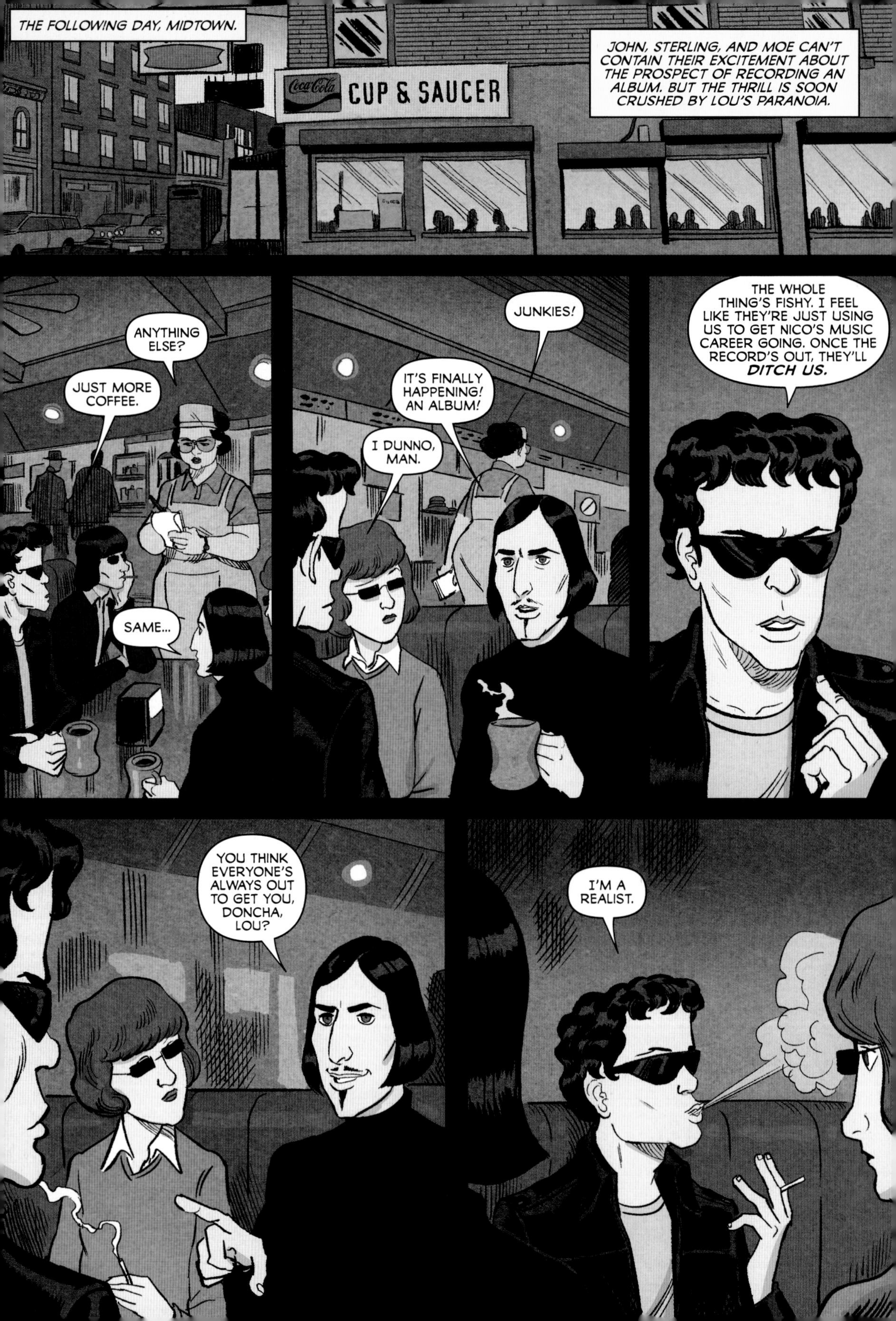
THE FOLLOWING DAY, MIDTOWN.
Coca-Cola CUP & SAUCER
JOHN, STERLING, AND MOE CAN'T CONTAIN THEIR EXCITEMENT ABOUT THE PROSPECT OF RECORDING AN ALBUM. BUT THE THRILL IS SOON CRUSHED BY LOU'S PARANOIA.
ANYTHING ELSE?
JUST MORE COFFEE.
SAME...
JUNKIES!
IT'S FINALLY HAPPENING! AN ALBUM!
I DUNNO, MAN.
THE WHOLE THING'S FISHY. I FEEL LIKE THEY'RE JUST USING US TO GET NICO'S MUSIC CAREER GOING. ONCE THE RECORD'S OUT, THEY'LL DITCH US.
YOU THINK EVERYONE'S ALWAYS OUT TO GET YOU, DONCHA, LOU?
I'M A REALIST.

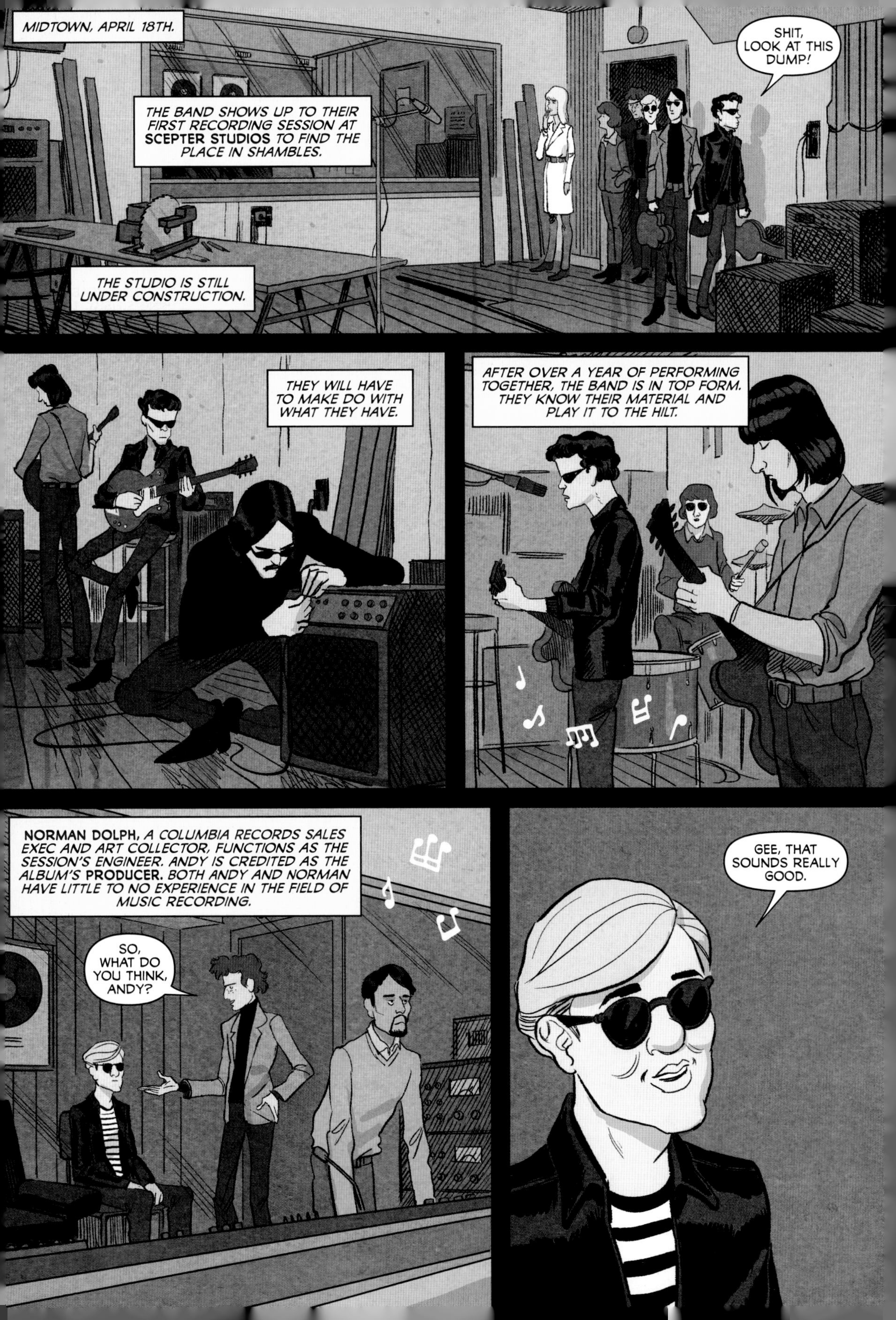
MIDTOWN, APRIL 18TH.
THE BAND SHOWS UP TO THEIR FIRST RECORDING SESSION AT SCEPTER STUDIOS TO FIND THE PLACE IN SHAMBLES.
SHIT, LOOK AT THIS DUMP!
THE STUDIO IS STILL UNDER CONSTRUCTION.
THEY WILL HAVE TO MAKE DO WITH WHAT THEY HAVE.
AFTER OVER A YEAR OF PERFORMING TOGETHER, THE BAND IS IN TOP FORM. THEY KNOW THEIR MATERIAL AND PLAY IT TO THE HILT.
NORMAN DOLPH, A COLUMBIA RECORDS SALES EXEC AND ART COLLECTOR, FUNCTIONS AS THE SESSION'S ENGINEER. ANDY IS CREDITED AS THE ALBUM'S PRODUCER. BOTH ANDY AND NORMAN HAVE LITTLE TO NO EXPERIENCE IN THE FIELD OF MUSIC RECORDING.
SO, WHAT DO YOU THINK, ANDY?
GEE, THAT SOUNDS REALLY GOOD.

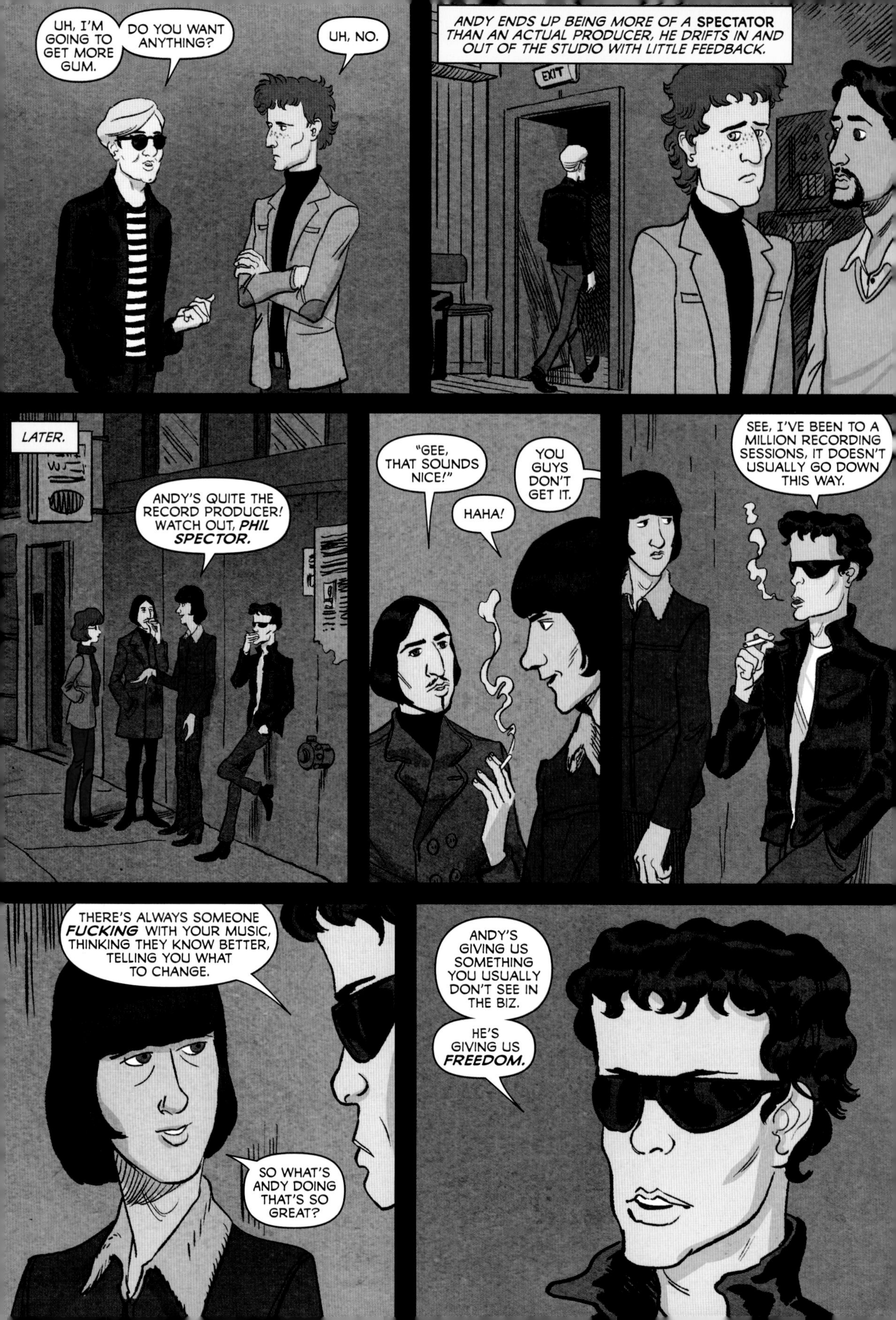
UH, I'M GOING TO GET MORE GUM.
DO YOU WANT ANYTHING?
UH, NO.
ANDY ENDS UP BEING MORE OF A SPECTATOR THAN AN ACTUAL PRODUCER, HE DRIFTS IN AND OUT OF THE STUDIO WITH LITTLE FEEDBACK.
EXIT
LATER.
ANDY'S QUITE THE RECORD PRODUCER! WATCH OUT, PHIL SPECTOR.
"GEE, THAT SOUNDS NICE!"
HAHA!
YOU GUYS DON'T GET IT.
SEE, I'VE BEEN TO A MILLION RECORDING SESSIONS, IT DOESN'T USUALLY GO DOWN THIS WAY.
THERE'S ALWAYS SOMEONE FUCKING WITH YOUR MUSIC, THINKING THEY KNOW BETTER, TELLING YOU WHAT TO CHANGE.
SO WHAT'S ANDY DOING THAT'S SO GREAT?
ANDY'S GIVING US SOMETHING YOU USUALLY DON'T SEE IN THE BIZ.
HE'S GIVING US FREEDOM.

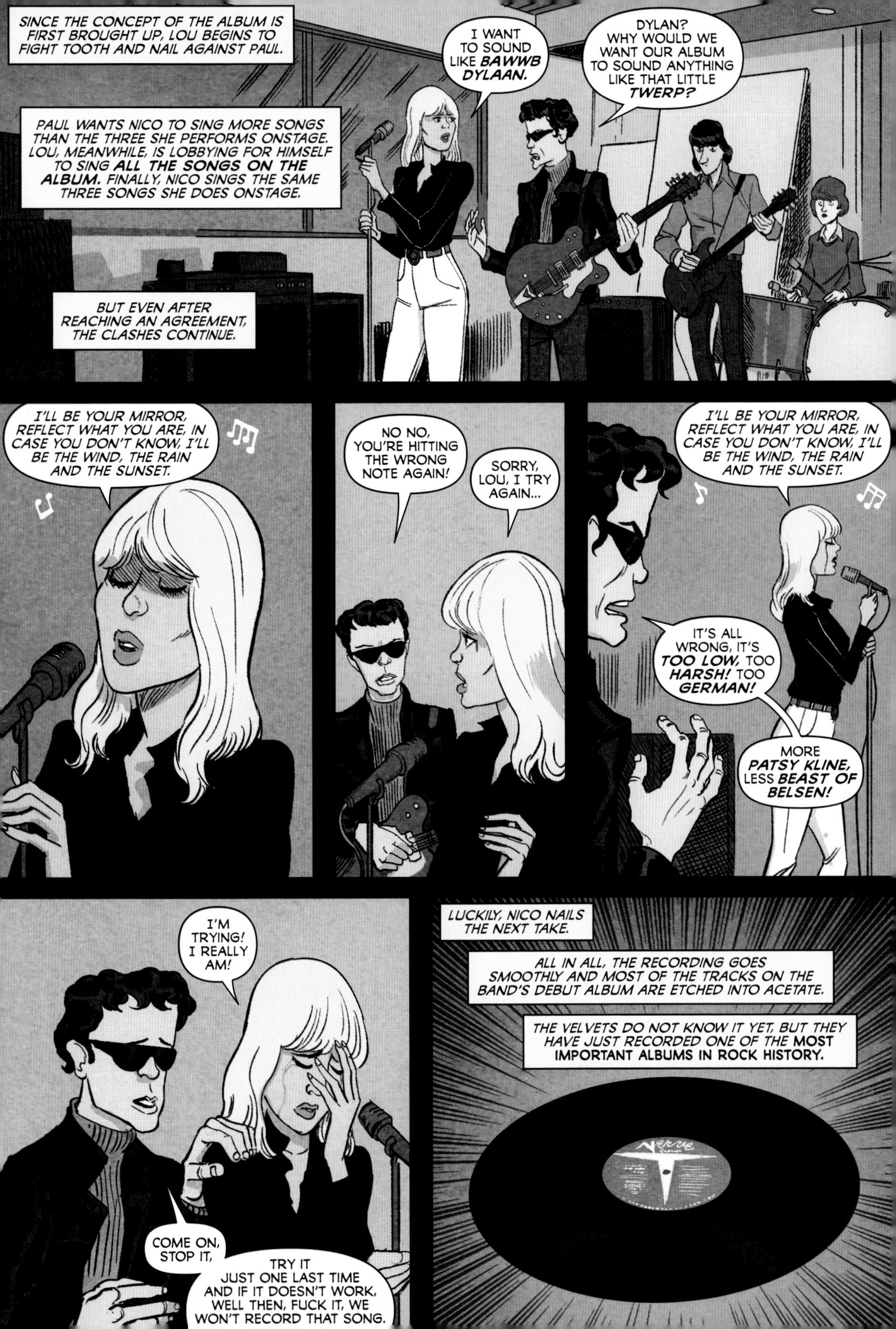

SINCE THE CONCEPT OF THE ALBUM IS FIRST BROUGHT UP, LOU BEGINS TO FIGHT TOOTH AND NAIL AGAINST PAUL.
I WANT TO SOUND LIKE BAWWB DYLAAN.
DYLAN? WHY WOULD WE WANT OUR ALBUM TO SOUND ANYTHING LIKE THAT LITTLE TWERP?
PAUL WANTS NICO TO SING MORE SONGS THAN THE THREE SHE PERFORMS ONSTAGE. LOU, MEANWHILE, IS LOBBYING FOR HIMSELF TO SING ALL THE SONGS ON THE ALBUM. FINALLY, NICO SINGS THE SAME THREE SONGS SHE DOES ONSTAGE.
BUT EVEN AFTER REACHING AN AGREEMENT, THE CLASHES CONTINUE.
I'LL BE YOUR MIRROR, REFLECT WHAT YOU ARE, IN CASE YOU DON'T KNOW, I'LL BE THE WIND, THE RAIN AND THE SUNSET.
NO NO, YOU'RE HITTING THE WRONG NOTE AGAIN!
SORRY, LOU, I TRY AGAIN...
I'LL BE YOUR MIRROR, REFLECT WHAT YOU ARE, IN CASE YOU DON'T KNOW, I'LL BE THE WIND, THE RAIN AND THE SUNSET.
IT'S ALL WRONG, IT'S TOO LOW, TOO HARSH! TOO GERMAN!
MORE PATSY KLINE, LESS BEAST OF BELSEN!
I'M TRYING! I REALLY AM!
COME ON, STOP IT,
TRY IT JUST ONE LAST TIME AND IF IT DOESN'T WORK, WELL THEN, FUCK IT, WE WON'T RECORD THAT SONG.
LUCKILY, NICO NAILS THE NEXT TAKE.
ALL IN ALL, THE RECORDING GOES SMOOTHLY AND MOST OF THE TRACKS ON THE BAND'S DEBUT ALBUM ARE ETCHED INTO ACETATE.
THE VELVETS DO NOT KNOW IT YET, BUT THEY HAVE JUST RECORDED ONE OF THE MOST IMPORTANT ALBUMS IN ROCK HISTORY.

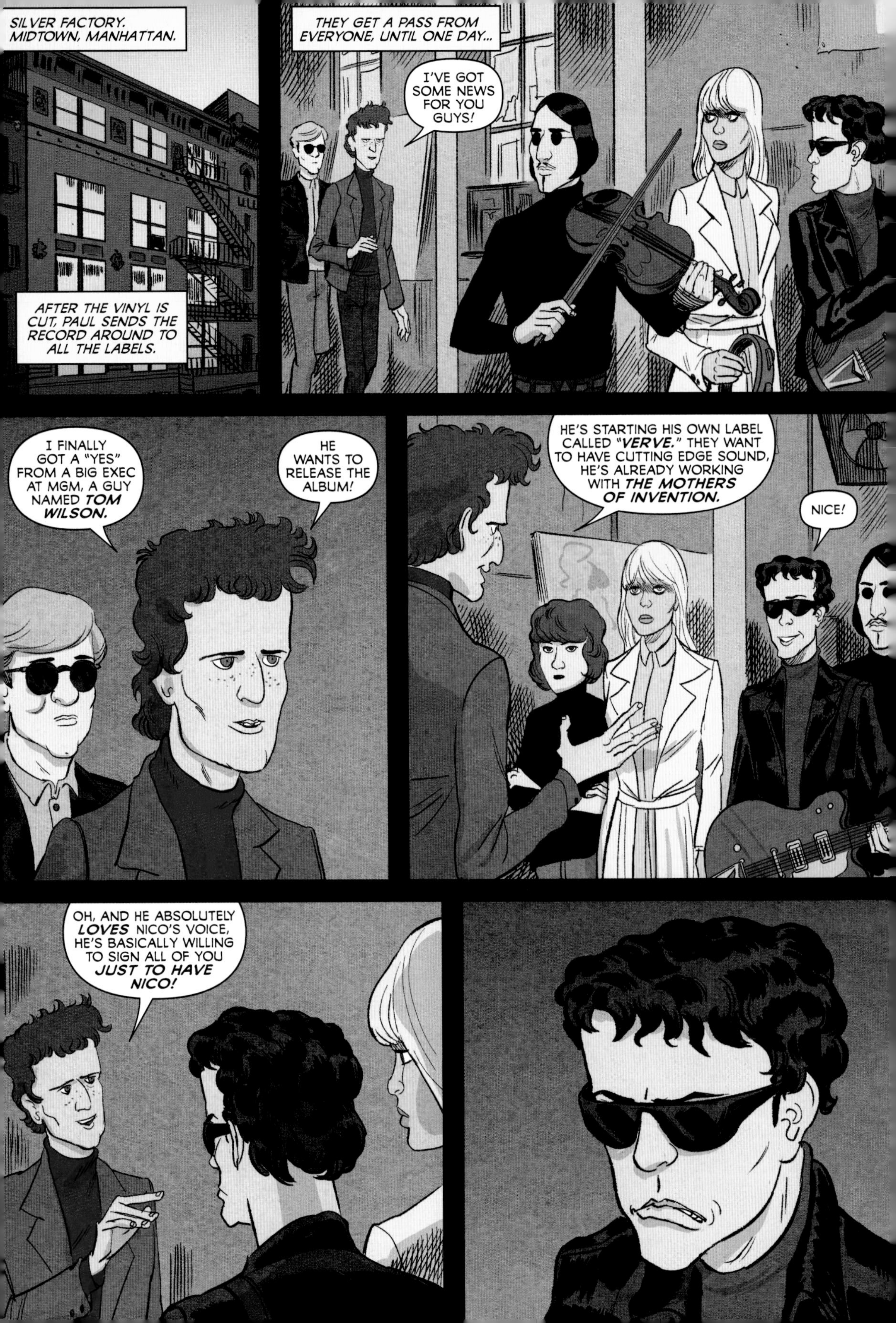
SILVER FACTORY. MIDTOWN, MANHATTAN.
AFTER THE VINYL IS CUT, PAUL SENDS THE RECORD AROUND TO ALL THE LABELS.
THEY GET A PASS FROM EVERYONE, UNTIL ONE DAY...
I'VE GOT SOME NEWS FOR YOU GUYS!
I FINALLY GOT A "YES" FROM A BIG EXEC AT MGM, A GUY NAMED TOM WILSON.
HE WANTS TO RELEASE THE ALBUM!
HE'S STARTING HIS OWN LABEL CALLED "VERVE." THEY WANT TO HAVE CUTTING EDGE SOUND, HE'S ALREADY WORKING WITH THE MOTHERS OF INVENTION.
NICE!
OH, AND HE ABSOLUTELY LOVES NICO'S VOICE, HE'S BASICALLY WILLING TO SIGN ALL OF YOU JUST TO HAVE NICO!

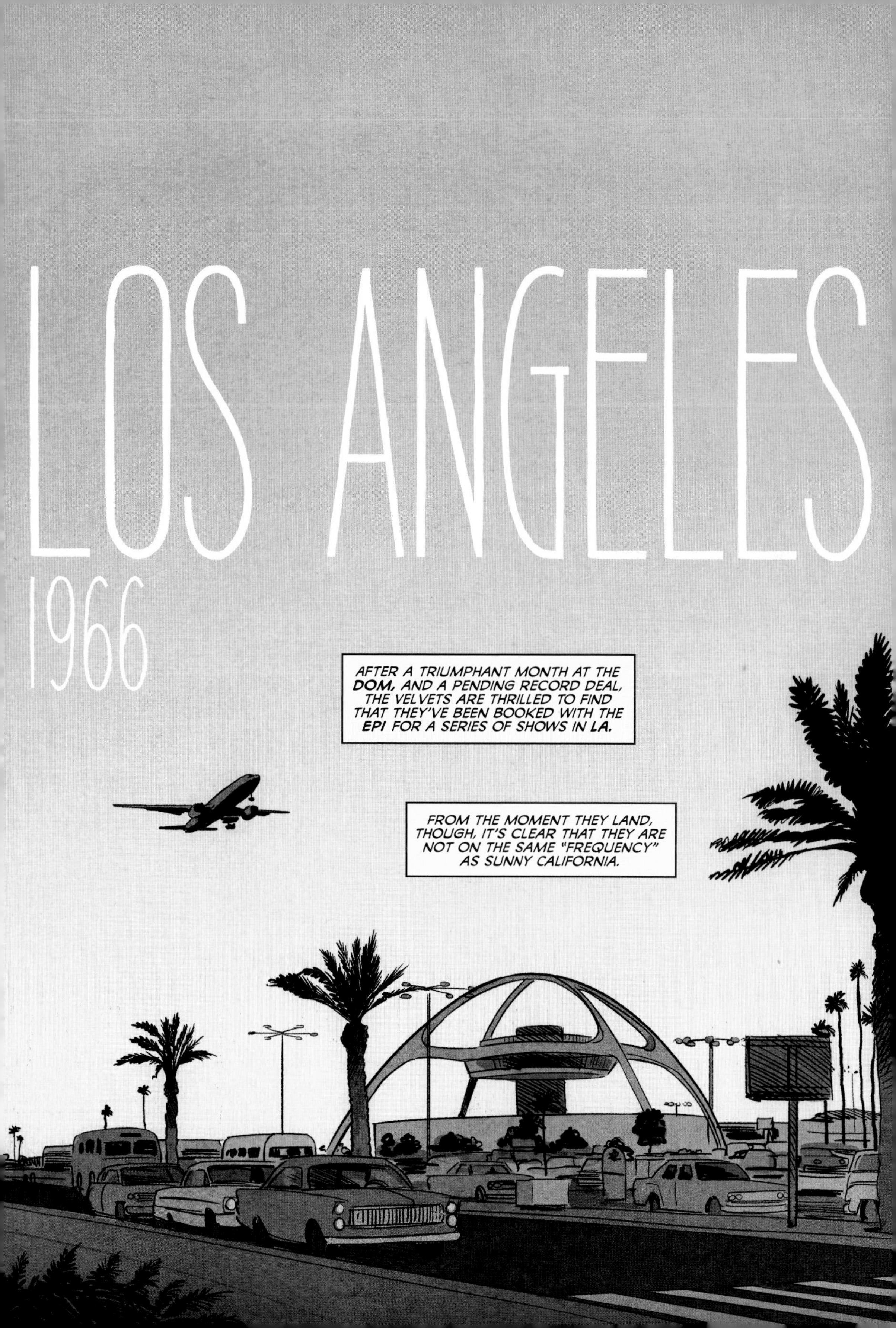
LOS ANGELES
1966
AFTER A TRIUMPHANT MONTH AT THE DOM, AND A PENDING RECORD DEAL, THE VELVETS ARE THRILLED TO FIND THAT THEY'VE BEEN BOOKED WITH THE EPI FOR A SERIES OF SHOWS IN LA.
FROM THE MOMENT THEY LAND, THOUGH, IT'S CLEAR THAT THEY ARE NOT ON THE SAME "FREQUENCY" AS SUNNY CALIFORNIA.

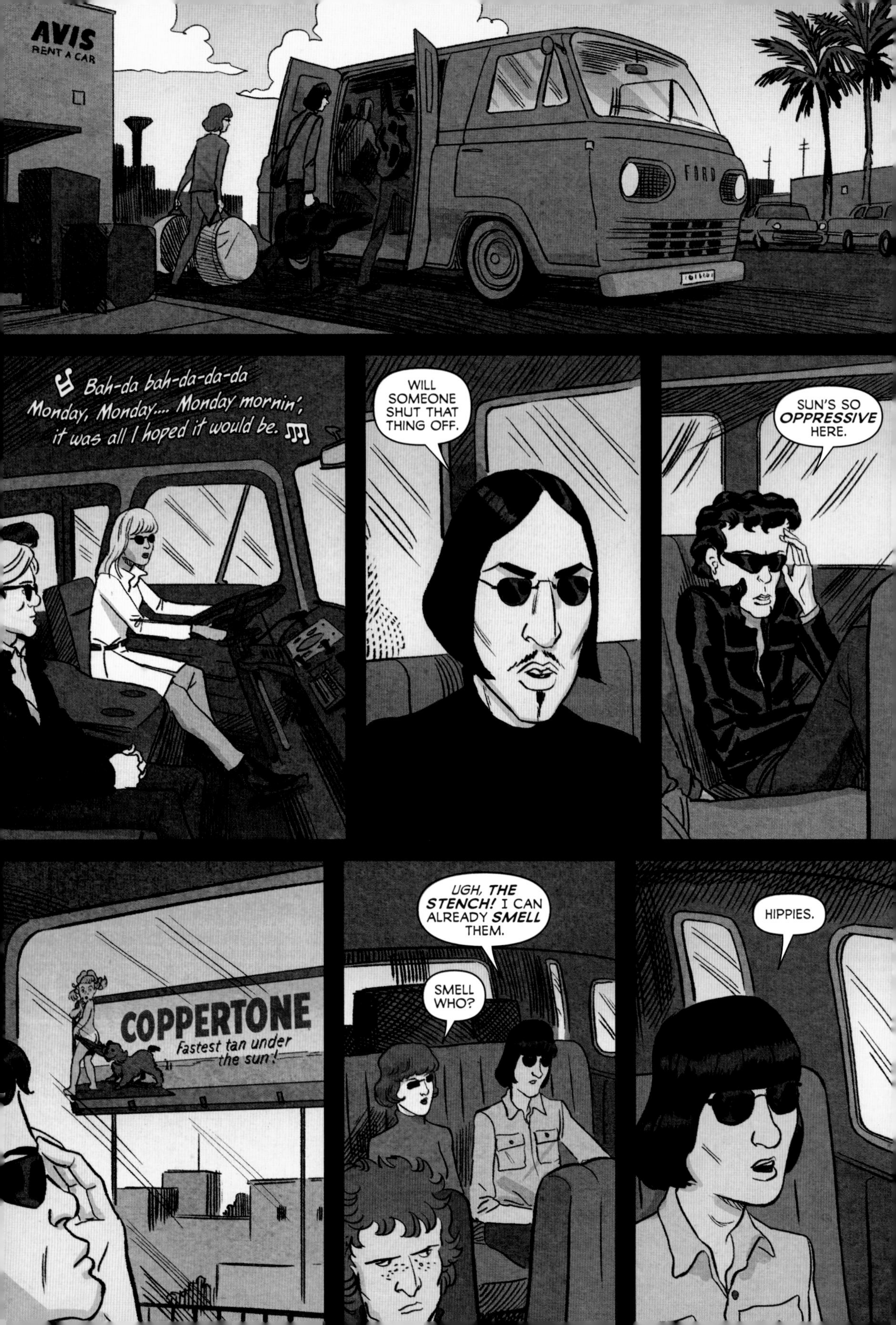
AVIS
RENT A CAR
FORD
Bah-da bah-da-da-da Monday, Monday.... Monday mornin', it was all I hoped it would be.
WILL SOMEONE SHUT THAT THING OFF.
SUN'S SO *OPPRESSIVE* HERE.
COPPERTONE
Fastest tan under the sun!
UGH, ***THE STENCH!*** I CAN ALREADY ***SMELL*** THEM.
SMELL WHO?
HIPPIES.

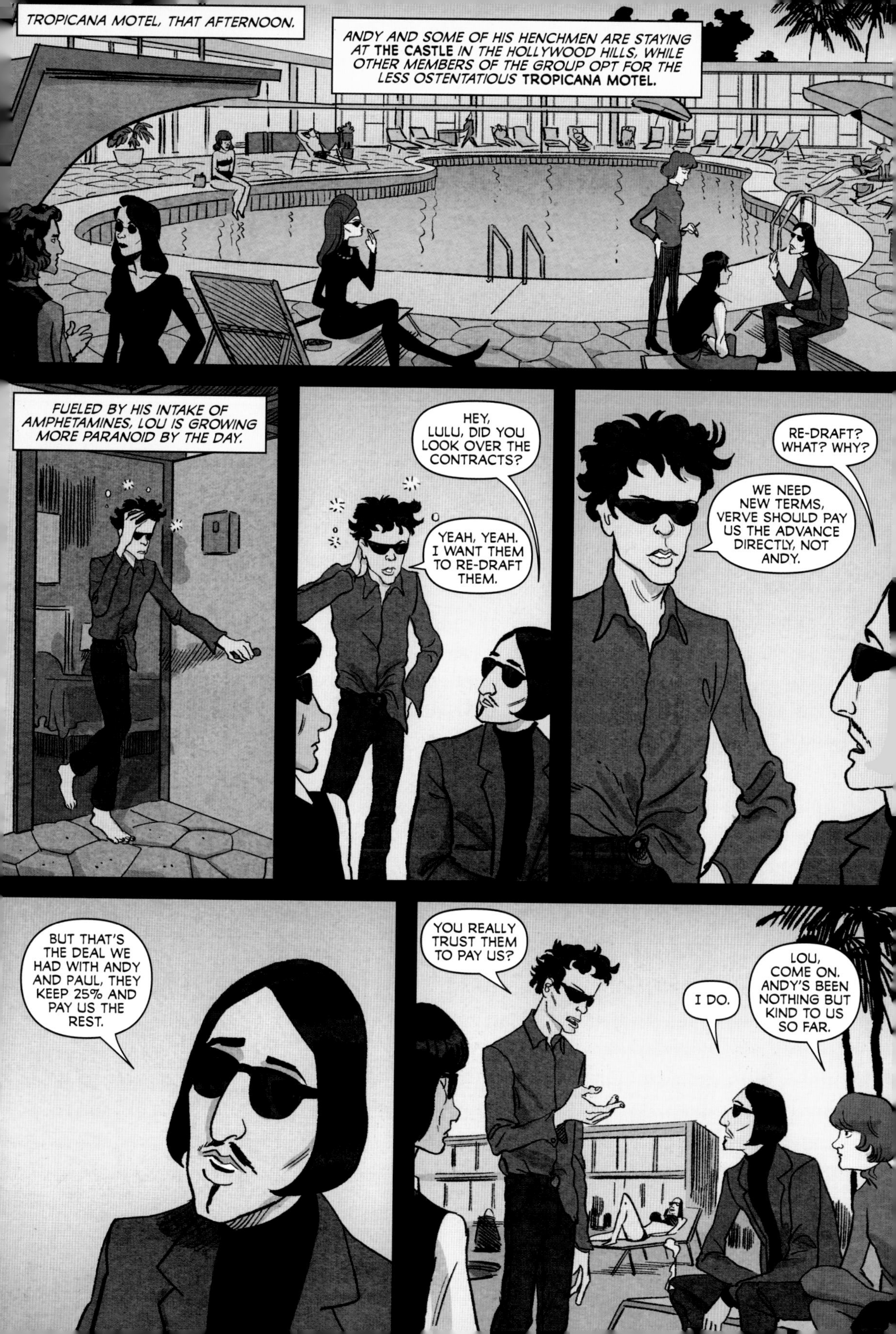
TROPICANA MOTEL, THAT AFTERNOON.
ANDY AND SOME OF HIS HENCHMEN ARE STAYING AT THE CASTLE IN THE HOLLYWOOD HILLS, WHILE OTHER MEMBERS OF THE GROUP OPT FOR THE LESS OSTENTATIOUS TROPICANA MOTEL.
FUELED BY HIS INTAKE OF AMPHETAMINES, LOU IS GROWING MORE PARANOID BY THE DAY.
HEY, LULU, DID YOU LOOK OVER THE CONTRACTS?
YEAH, YEAH. I WANT THEM TO RE-DRAFT THEM.
RE-DRAFT? WHAT? WHY?
WE NEED NEW TERMS, VERVE SHOULD PAY US THE ADVANCE DIRECTLY, NOT ANDY.
BUT THAT'S THE DEAL WE HAD WITH ANDY AND PAUL, THEY KEEP 25% AND PAY US THE REST.
YOU REALLY TRUST THEM TO PAY US?
I DO.
LOU, COME ON. ANDY'S BEEN NOTHING BUT KIND TO US SO FAR.

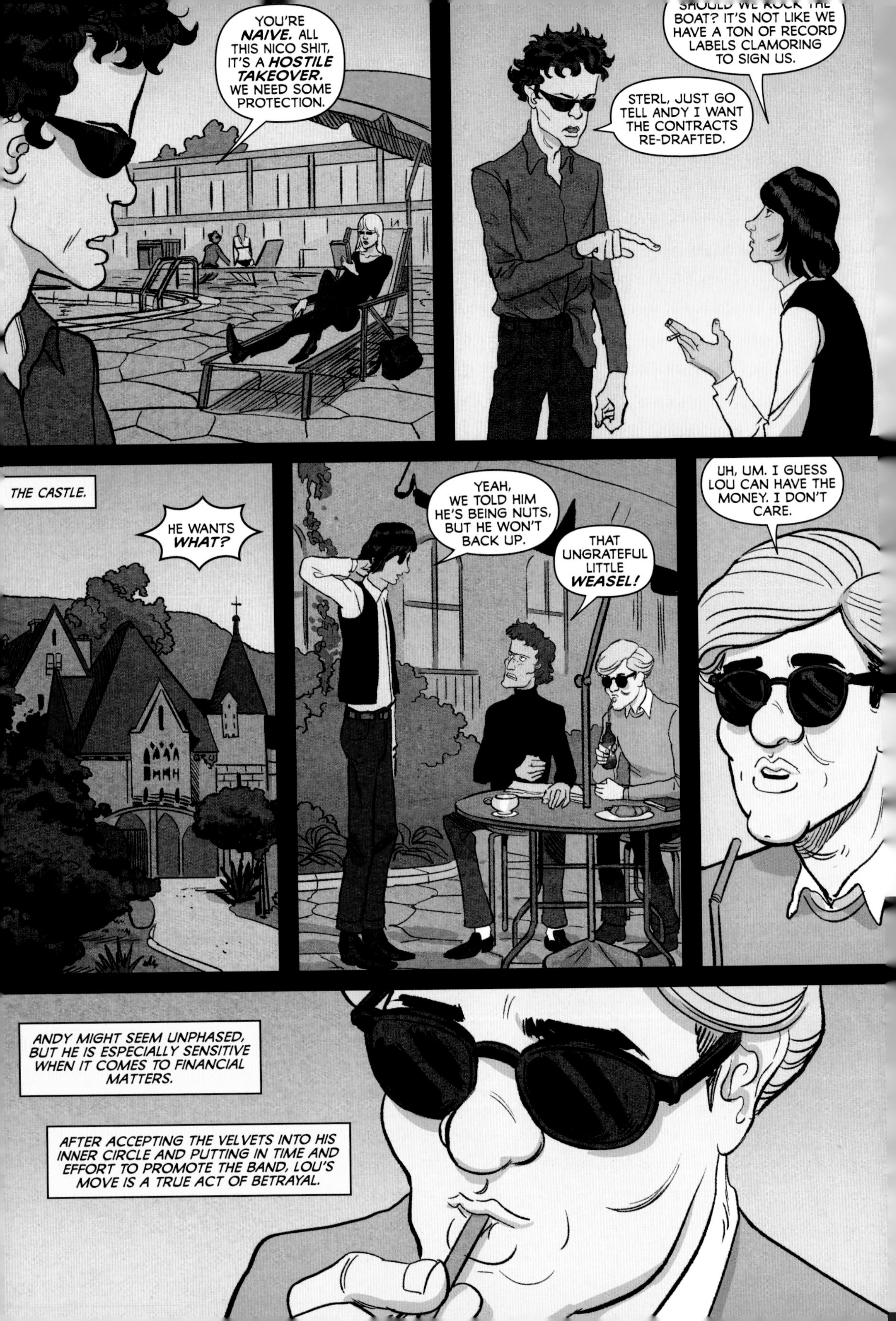
YOU'RE NAIVE. ALL THIS NICO SHIT, IT'S A HOSTILE TAKEOVER. WE NEED SOME PROTECTION.
BOAT? IT'S NOT LIKE WE HAVE A TON OF RECORD LABELS CLAMORING TO SIGN US.
STERL, JUST GO TELL ANDY I WANT THE CONTRACTS RE-DRAFTED.
THE CASTLE.
HE WANTS WHAT?
YEAH, WE TOLD HIM HE'S BEING NUTS, BUT HE WON'T BACK UP.
THAT UNGRATEFUL LITTLE WEASEL!
UH, UM. I GUESS LOU CAN HAVE THE MONEY. I DON'T CARE.
ANDY MIGHT SEEM UNPHASED, BUT HE IS ESPECIALLY SENSITIVE WHEN IT COMES TO FINANCIAL MATTERS.
AFTER ACCEPTING THE VELVETS INTO HIS INNER CIRCLE AND PUTTING IN TIME AND EFFORT TO PROMOTE THE BAND, LOU'S MOVE IS A TRUE ACT OF BETRAYAL.

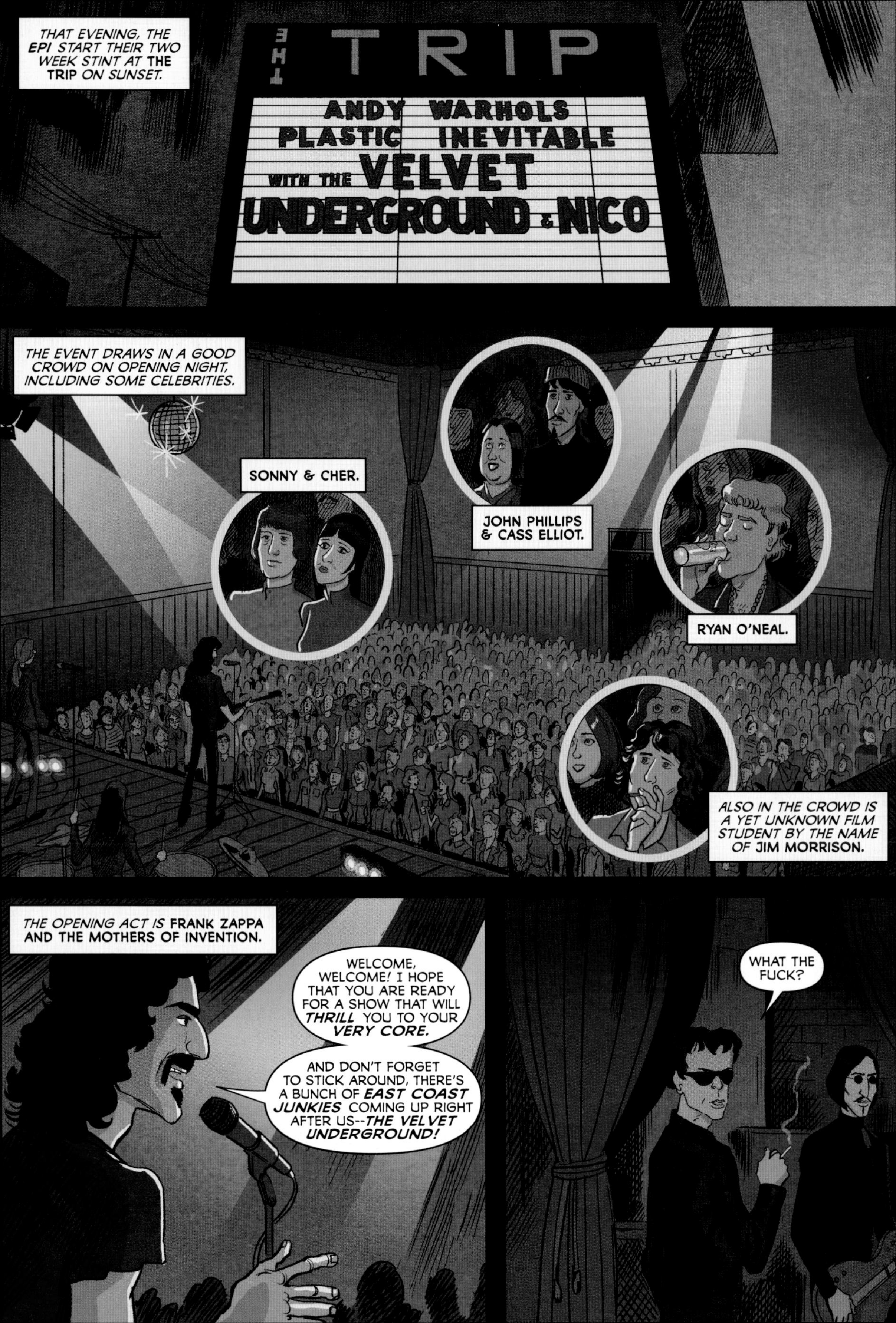

THAT EVENING, THE EPI START THEIR TWO WEEK STINT AT THE TRIP ON SUNSET.
THE TRIP
ANDY WARHOLS PLASTIC INEVITABLE WITH THE VELVET UNDERGROUND & NICO
THE EVENT DRAWS IN A GOOD CROWD ON OPENING NIGHT, INCLUDING SOME CELEBRITIES.
SONNY & CHER.
JOHN PHILLIPS & CASS ELLIOT.
RYAN O'NEAL.
ALSO IN THE CROWD IS A YET UNKNOWN FILM STUDENT BY THE NAME OF JIM MORRISON.
THE OPENING ACT IS FRANK ZAPPA AND THE MOTHERS OF INVENTION.
WELCOME, WELCOME! I HOPE THAT YOU ARE READY FOR A SHOW THAT WILL THRILL YOU TO YOUR VERY CORE.
AND DON'T FORGET TO STICK AROUND, THERE'S A BUNCH OF EAST COAST JUNKIES COMING UP RIGHT AFTER US--THE VELVET UNDERGROUND!
WHAT THE FUCK?

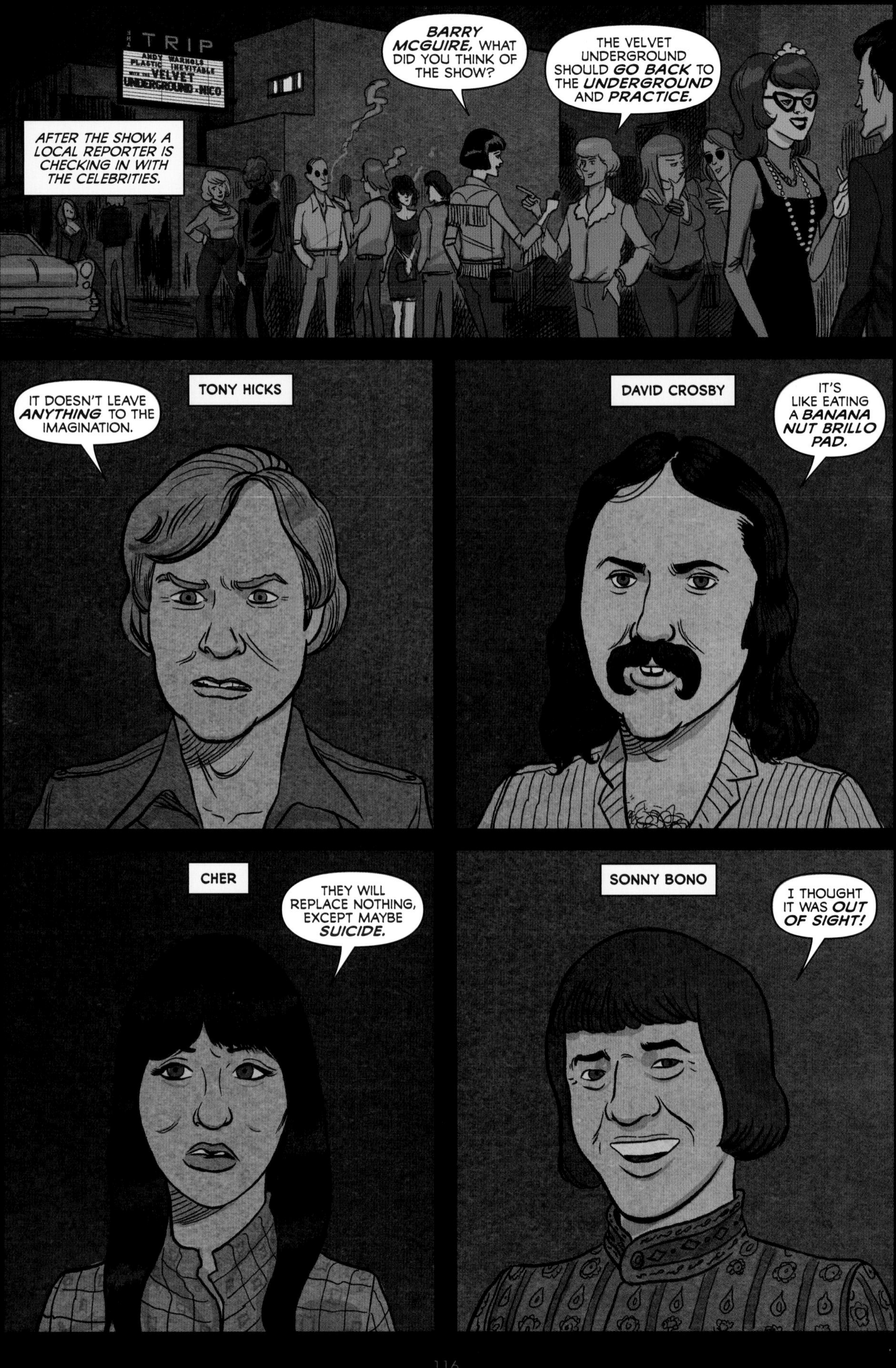
TRIP
ANDY WARHOLS
PLASTIC INEVITABLE
VELVET
UNDERGROUND - NICO
AFTER THE SHOW, A LOCAL REPORTER IS CHECKING IN WITH THE CELEBRITIES.
BARRY MCGUIRE, WHAT DID YOU THINK OF THE SHOW?
THE VELVET UNDERGROUND SHOULD GO BACK TO THE UNDERGROUND AND PRACTICE.
TONY HICKS
IT DOESN'T LEAVE ANYTHING TO THE IMAGINATION.
DAVID CROSBY
IT'S LIKE EATING A BANANA NUT BRILLO PAD.
CHER
THEY WILL REPLACE NOTHING, EXCEPT MAYBE SUICIDE.
SONNY BONO
I THOUGHT IT WAS OUT OF SIGHT!

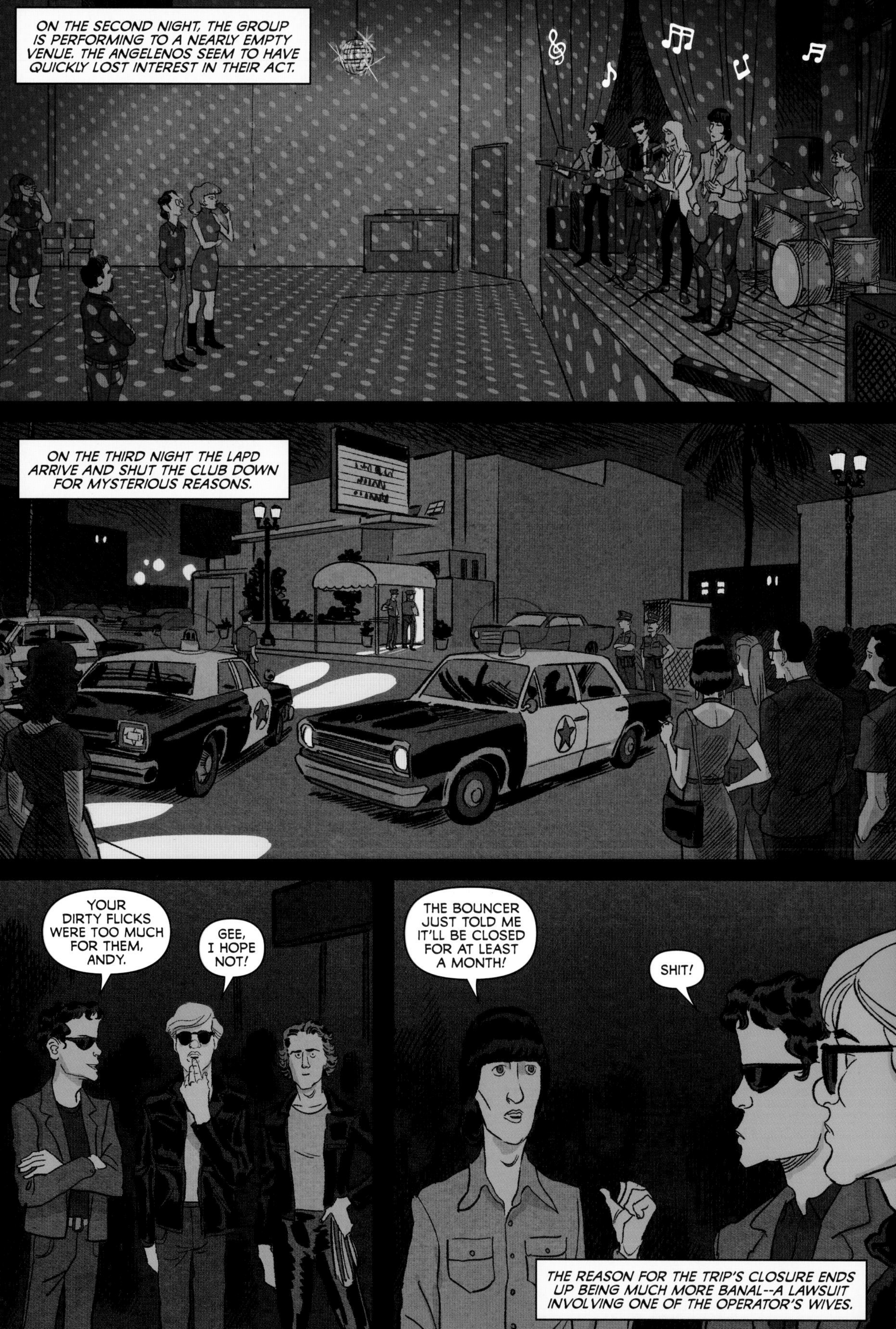
ON THE SECOND NIGHT, THE GROUP IS PERFORMING TO A NEARLY EMPTY VENUE. THE ANGELENOS SEEM TO HAVE QUICKLY LOST INTEREST IN THEIR ACT.
ON THE THIRD NIGHT THE LAPD ARRIVE AND SHUT THE CLUB DOWN FOR MYSTERIOUS REASONS.
YOUR DIRTY FLICKS WERE TOO MUCH FOR THEM, ANDY.
GEE, I HOPE NOT!
THE BOUNCER JUST TOLD ME IT'LL BE CLOSED FOR AT LEAST A MONTH!
SHIT!
THE REASON FOR THE TRIP'S CLOSURE ENDS UP BEING MUCH MORE BANAL--A LAWSUIT INVOLVING ONE OF THE OPERATOR'S WIVES.

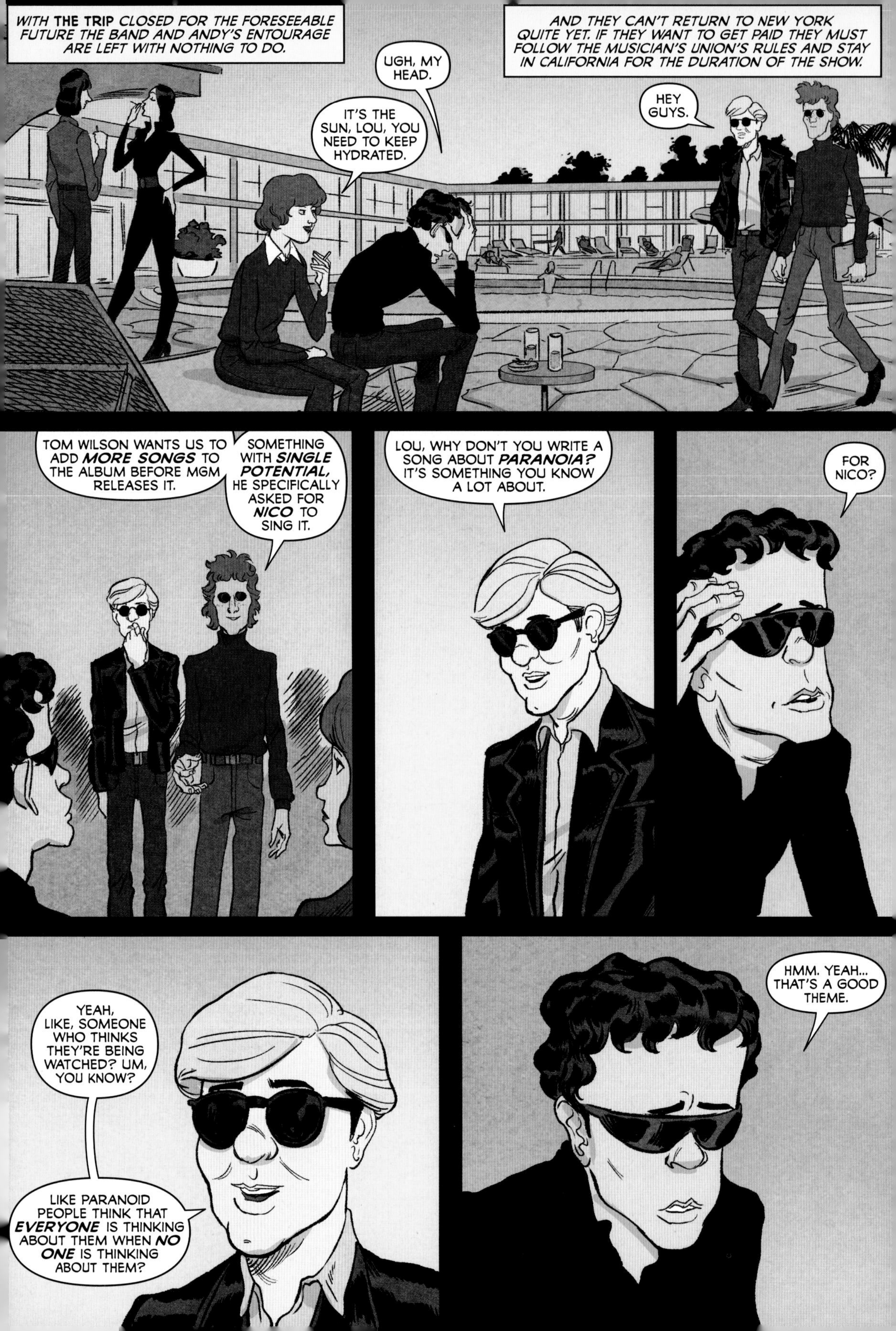
WITH THE TRIP CLOSED FOR THE FORESEEABLE FUTURE THE BAND AND ANDY'S ENTOURAGE ARE LEFT WITH NOTHING TO DO.
UGH, MY HEAD.
IT'S THE SUN, LOU, YOU NEED TO KEEP HYDRATED.
AND THEY CAN'T RETURN TO NEW YORK QUITE YET. IF THEY WANT TO GET PAID THEY MUST FOLLOW THE MUSICIAN'S UNION'S RULES AND STAY IN CALIFORNIA FOR THE DURATION OF THE SHOW.
HEY GUYS.
TOM WILSON WANTS US TO ADD MORE SONGS TO THE ALBUM BEFORE MGM RELEASES IT.
SOMETHING WITH SINGLE POTENTIAL, HE SPECIFICALLY ASKED FOR NICO TO SING IT.
LOU, WHY DON'T YOU WRITE A SONG ABOUT PARANOIA? IT'S SOMETHING YOU KNOW A LOT ABOUT.
FOR NICO?
YEAH, LIKE, SOMEONE WHO THINKS THEY'RE BEING WATCHED? UM, YOU KNOW?
LIKE PARANOID PEOPLE THINK THAT EVERYONE IS THINKING ABOUT THEM WHEN NO ONE IS THINKING ABOUT THEM?
HMM. YEAH... THAT'S A GOOD THEME.

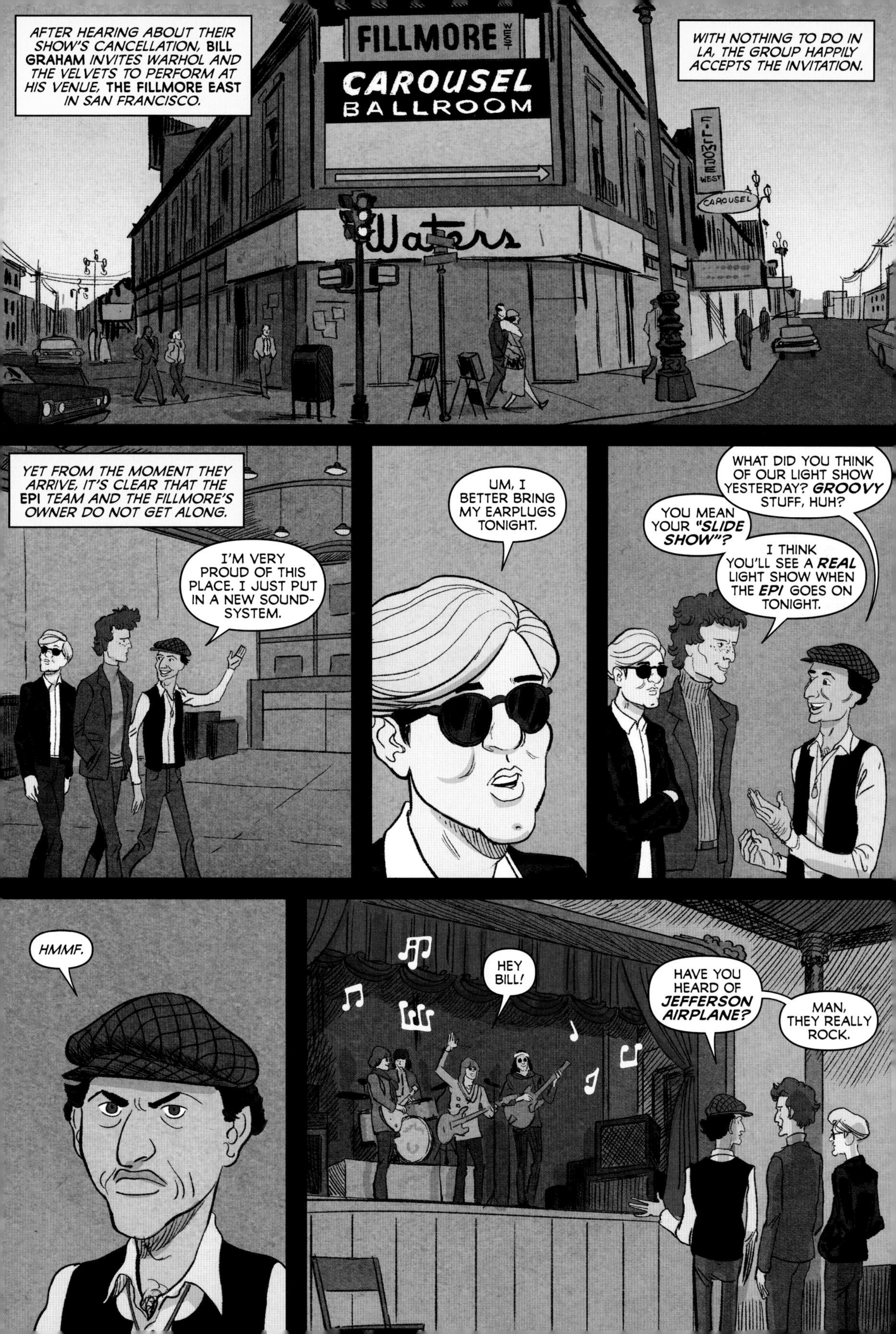

AFTER HEARING ABOUT THEIR SHOW'S CANCELLATION, BILL GRAHAM INVITES WARHOL AND THE VELVETS TO PERFORM AT HIS VENUE, THE FILLMORE EAST IN SAN FRANCISCO.
FILLMORE WEST
CAROUSEL BALLROOM
FILLMORE WEST
CAROUSEL
Waters
WITH NOTHING TO DO IN LA, THE GROUP HAPPILY ACCEPTS THE INVITATION.
YET FROM THE MOMENT THEY ARRIVE, IT'S CLEAR THAT THE EPI TEAM AND THE FILLMORE'S OWNER DO NOT GET ALONG.
I'M VERY PROUD OF THIS PLACE. I JUST PUT IN A NEW SOUND-SYSTEM.
UM, I BETTER BRING MY EARPLUGS TONIGHT.
WHAT DID YOU THINK OF OUR LIGHT SHOW YESTERDAY? GROOVY STUFF, HUH?
YOU MEAN YOUR "SLIDE SHOW"?
I THINK YOU'LL SEE A REAL LIGHT SHOW WHEN THE EPI GOES ON TONIGHT.
HMMF.
HEY BILL!
HAVE YOU HEARD OF JEFFERSON AIRPLANE?
MAN, THEY REALLY ROCK.

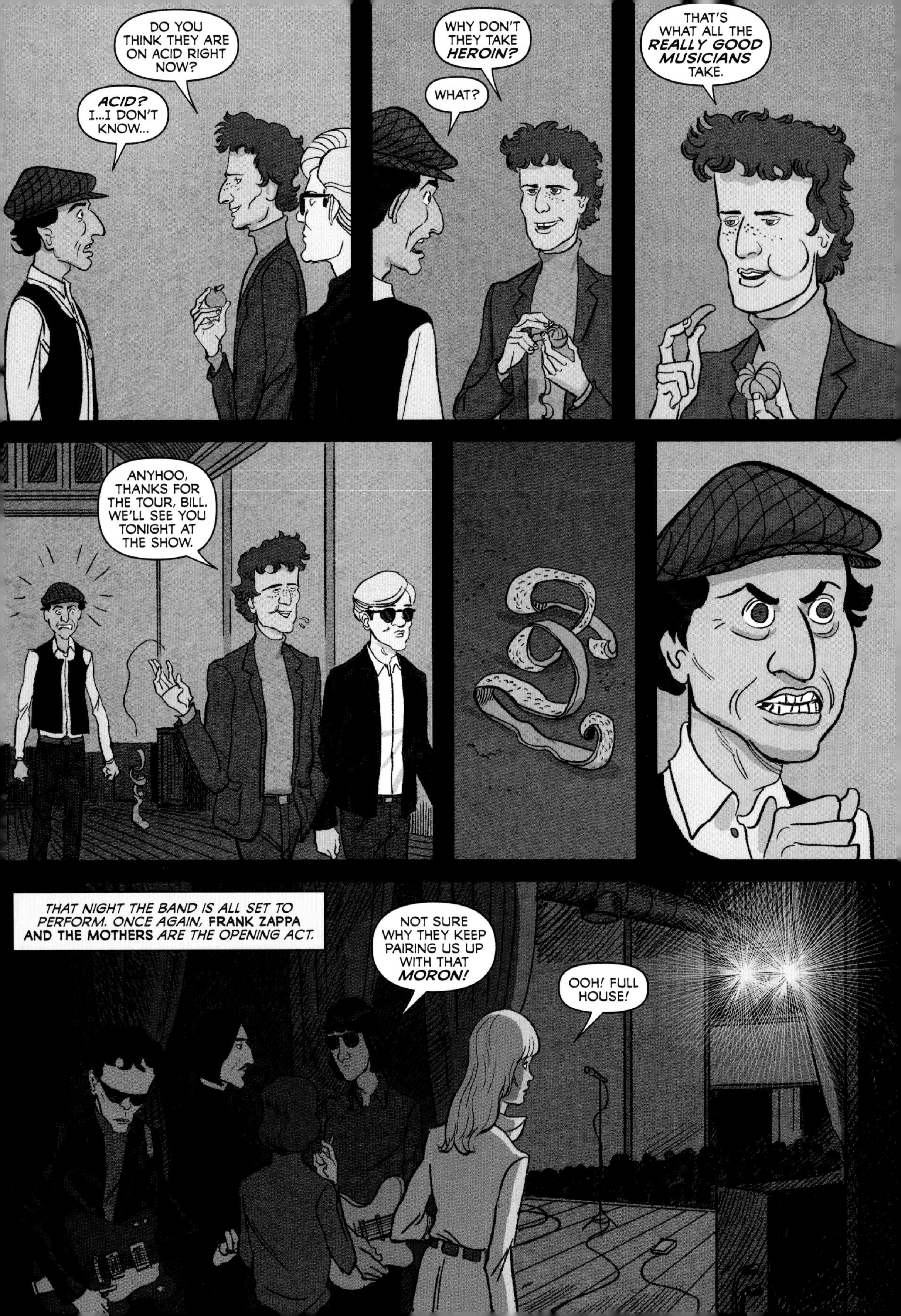
ACID? I...I DON'T KNOW...
DO YOU THINK THEY ARE ON ACID RIGHT NOW?
WHAT?
WHY DON'T THEY TAKE HEROIN?
THAT'S WHAT ALL THE REALLY GOOD MUSICIANS TAKE.
ANYHOO, THANKS FOR THE TOUR, BILL. WE'LL SEE YOU TONIGHT AT THE SHOW.
THAT NIGHT THE BAND IS ALL SET TO PERFORM. ONCE AGAIN, FRANK ZAPPA AND THE MOTHERS ARE THE OPENING ACT.
NOT SURE WHY THEY KEEP PAIRING US UP WITH THAT MORON!
OOH! FULL HOUSE!

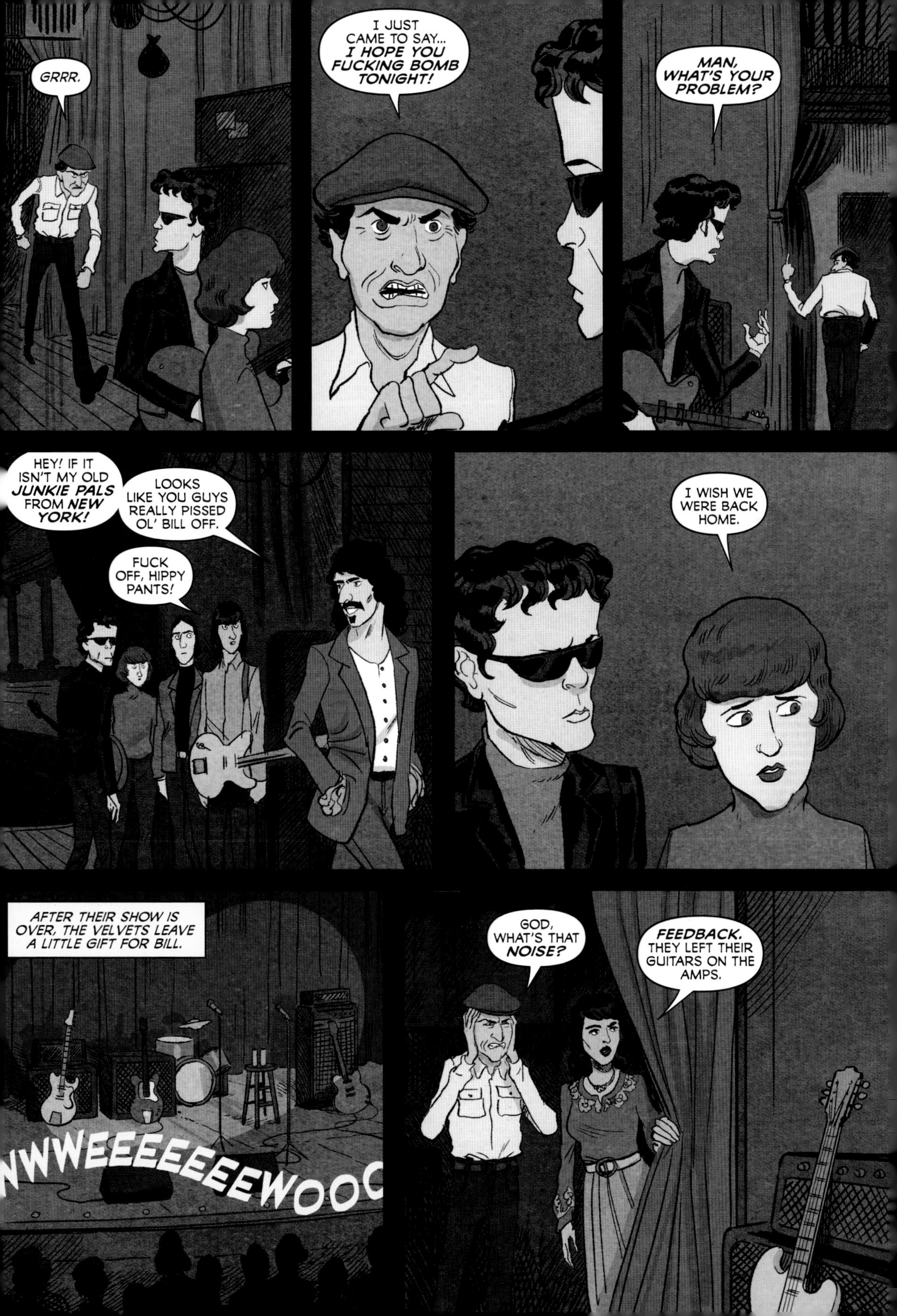
GRRR.
I JUST CAME TO SAY... I HOPE YOU FUCKING BOMB TONIGHT!
MAN, WHAT'S YOUR PROBLEM?
HEY! IF IT ISN'T MY OLD JUNKIE PALS FROM NEW YORK!
LOOKS LIKE YOU GUYS REALLY PISSED OL' BILL OFF.
FUCK OFF, HIPPY PANTS!
I WISH WE WERE BACK HOME.
AFTER THEIR SHOW IS OVER, THE VELVETS LEAVE A LITTLE GIFT FOR BILL.
NWWEEEEEEEEEWOOO
GOD, WHAT'S THAT NOISE?
FEEDBACK. THEY LEFT THEIR GUITARS ON THE AMPS.

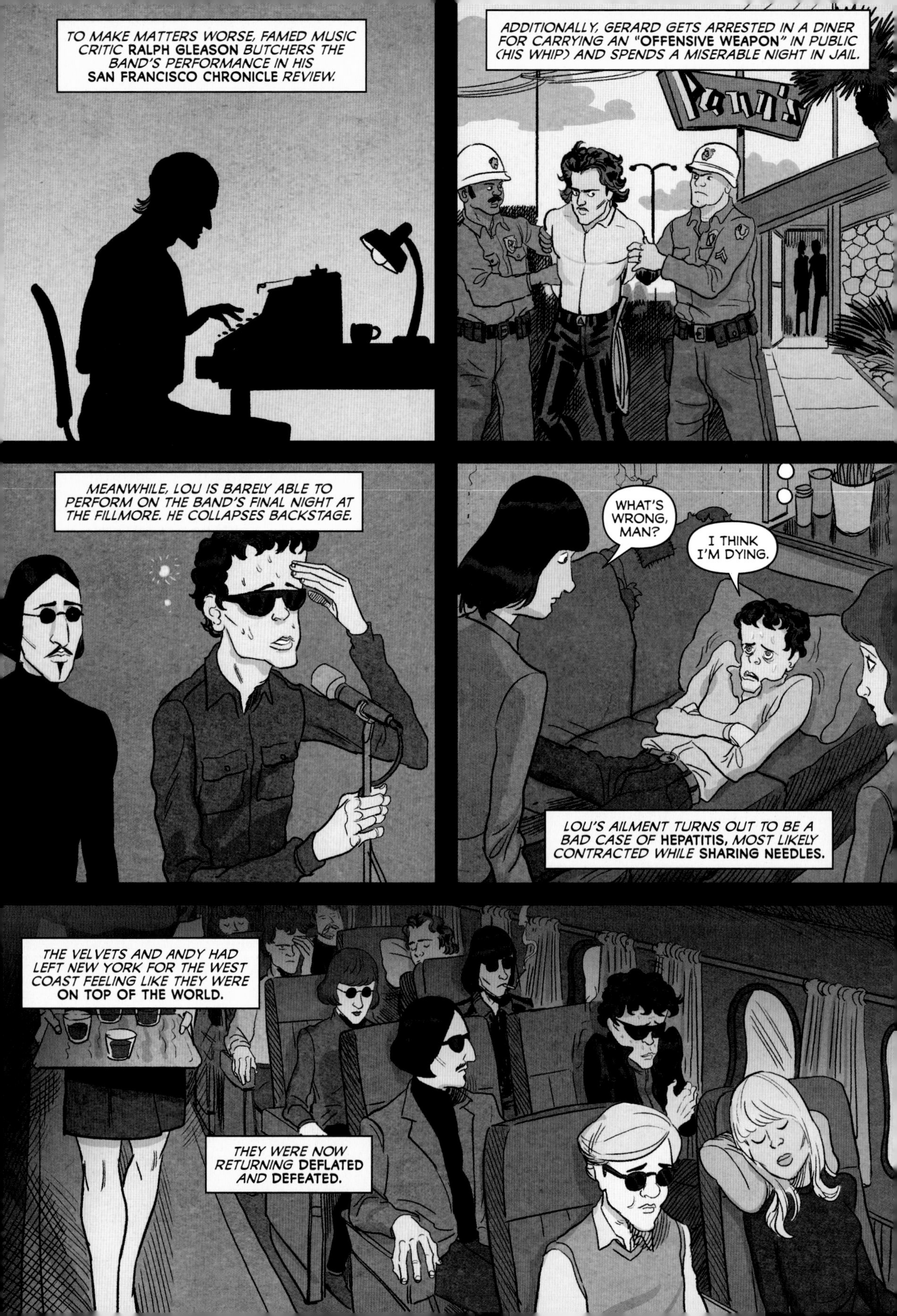
TO MAKE MATTERS WORSE, FAMED MUSIC CRITIC RALPH GLEASON BUTCHERS THE BAND'S PERFORMANCE IN HIS SAN FRANCISCO CHRONICLE REVIEW.
ADDITIONALLY, GERARD GETS ARRESTED IN A DINER FOR CARRYING AN "OFFENSIVE WEAPON" IN PUBLIC (HIS WHIP) AND SPENDS A MISERABLE NIGHT IN JAIL.
MEANWHILE, LOU IS BARELY ABLE TO PERFORM ON THE BAND'S FINAL NIGHT AT THE FILLMORE. HE COLLAPSES BACKSTAGE.
WHAT'S WRONG, MAN?
I THINK I'M DYING.
LOU'S AILMENT TURNS OUT TO BE A BAD CASE OF HEPATITIS, MOST LIKELY CONTRACTED WHILE SHARING NEEDLES.
THE VELVETS AND ANDY HAD LEFT NEW YORK FOR THE WEST COAST FEELING LIKE THEY WERE ON TOP OF THE WORLD.
THEY WERE NOW RETURNING DEFLATED AND DEFEATED.

ADDING INSULT TO INJURY, THE GROUP FINDS OUT THAT WHILE THEY WERE GONE THE DOM WAS RENTED OUT TO BOB DYLAN'S MANAGER, WHO HAD EFFECTIVELY STOLEN THEIR IDEA, RENAMING THE VENUE THE BALLOON FARM.

LOU CHECKS HIMSELF INTO BETH ISRAEL HOSPITAL.

NICO GOES ON A SOJOURN TO IBIZA, SPENDING TIME WITH HER MOTHER AND SON, ARI.

ANDY, DISAPPOINTED WITH THE LACK OF INCOME FROM THE EPI, THROWS HIMSELF BACK INTO FILMMAKING.

THE LEFTOVER VELVETS ACCEPT A WEEK-LONG STINT AT POOR RICHARD'S IN CHICAGO.

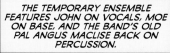

THE TEMPORARY ENSEMBLE FEATURES JOHN ON VOCALS, MOE ON BASE, AND THE BAND'S OLD PAL ANGUS MACLISE BACK ON PERCUSSION.

THE BAND'S SHOWS IN CHICAGO ARE A HIT, AND THEY ARE EXTENDED FOR ANOTHER WEEK.

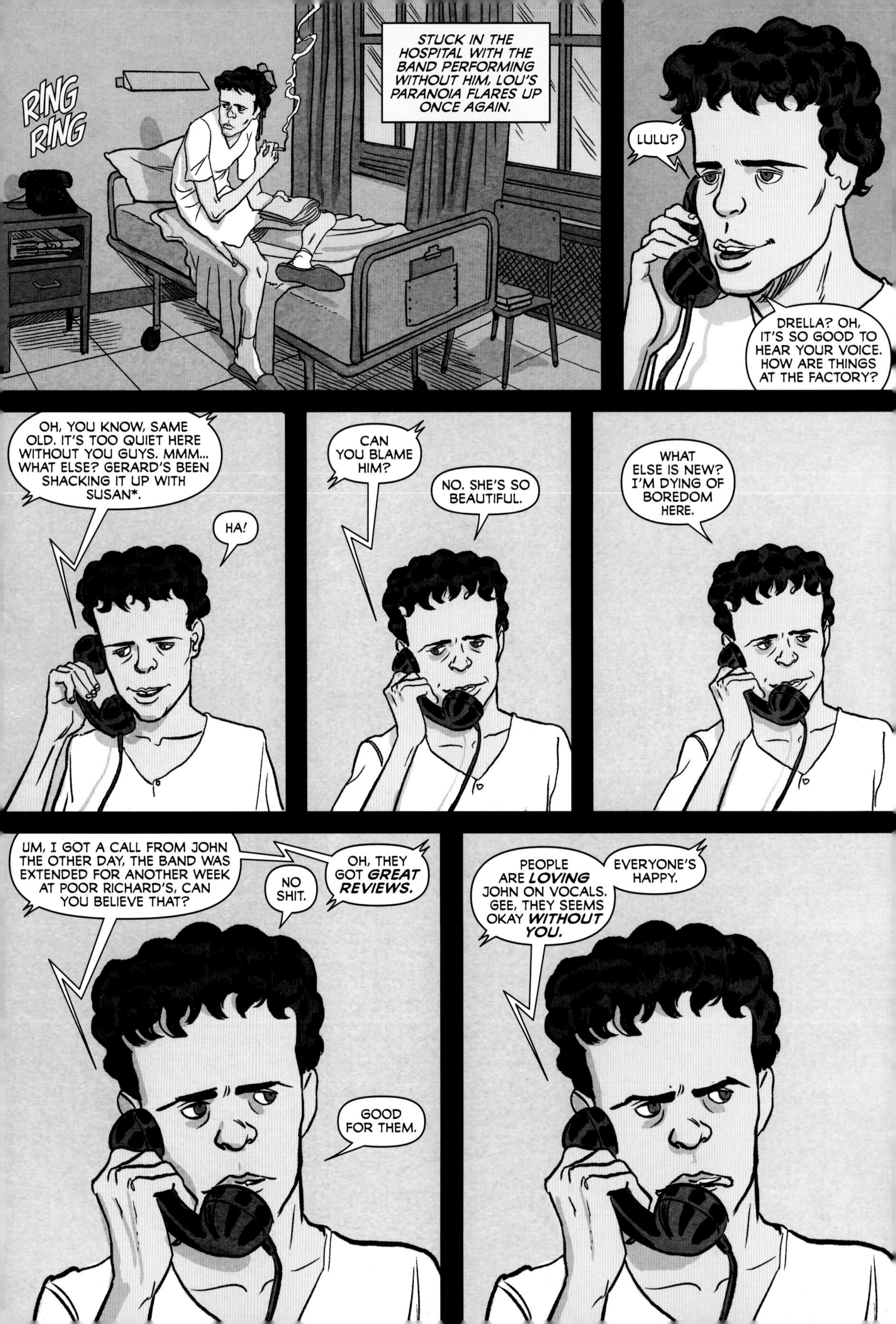
STUCK IN THE HOSPITAL WITH THE BAND PERFORMING WITHOUT HIM, LOU'S PARANOIA FLARES UP ONCE AGAIN.
RING RING
LULU?
DRELLA? OH, IT'S SO GOOD TO HEAR YOUR VOICE. HOW ARE THINGS AT THE FACTORY?
OH, YOU KNOW, SAME OLD. IT'S TOO QUIET HERE WITHOUT YOU GUYS. MMM... WHAT ELSE? GERARD'S BEEN SHACKING IT UP WITH SUSAN*.
HA!
CAN YOU BLAME HIM?
NO. SHE'S SO BEAUTIFUL.
WHAT ELSE IS NEW? I'M DYING OF BOREDOM HERE.
UM, I GOT A CALL FROM JOHN THE OTHER DAY, THE BAND WAS EXTENDED FOR ANOTHER WEEK AT POOR RICHARD'S, CAN YOU BELIEVE THAT?
NO SHIT.
OH, THEY GOT GREAT REVIEWS.
GOOD FOR THEM.
EVERYONE'S HAPPY.
PEOPLE ARE LOVING JOHN ON VOCALS. GEE, THEY SEEMS OKAY WITHOUT YOU.

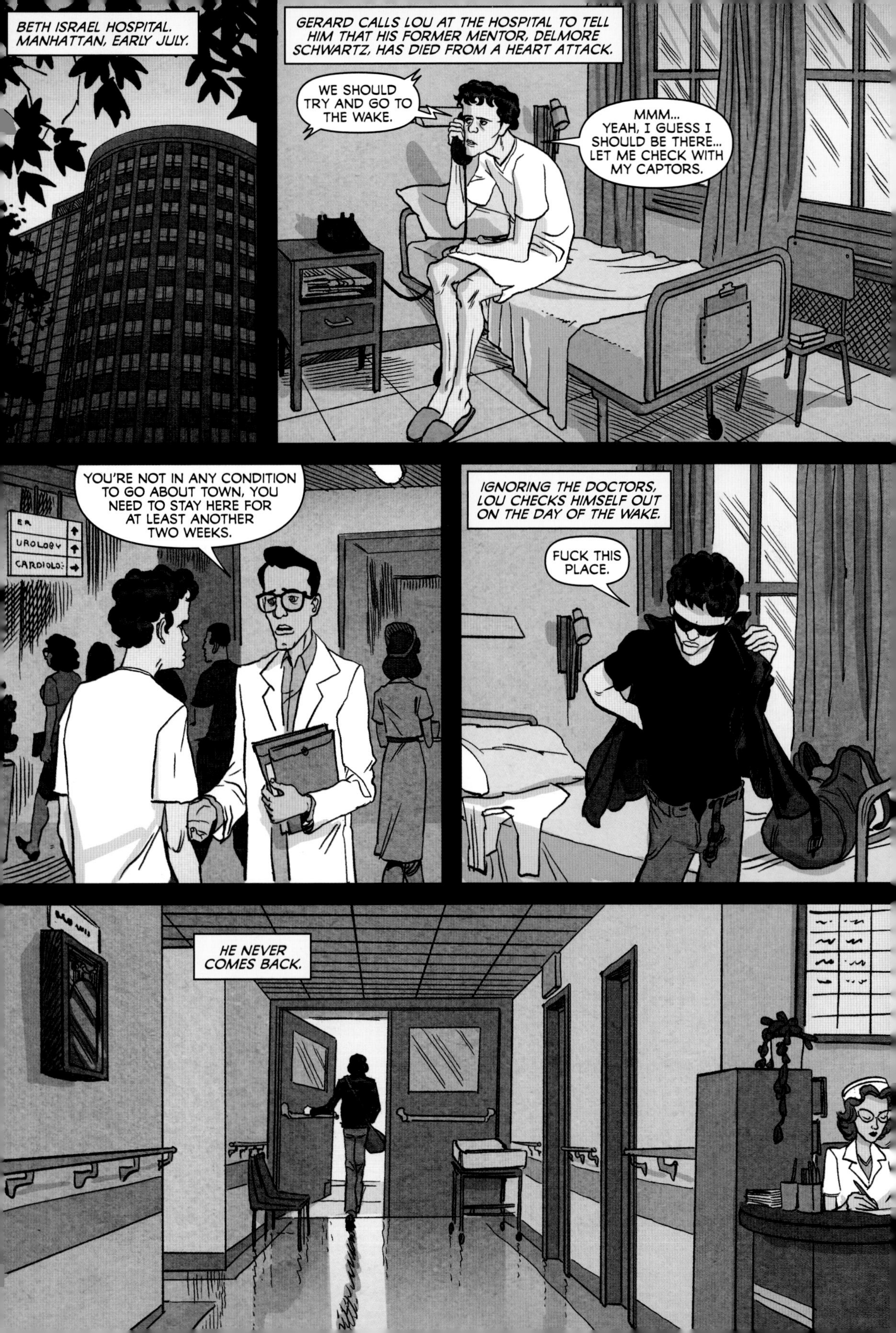
BETH ISRAEL HOSPITAL. MANHATTAN, EARLY JULY.
GERARD CALLS LOU AT THE HOSPITAL TO TELL HIM THAT HIS FORMER MENTOR, DELMORE SCHWARTZ, HAS DIED FROM A HEART ATTACK.
WE SHOULD TRY AND GO TO THE WAKE.
MMM... YEAH, I GUESS I SHOULD BE THERE... LET ME CHECK WITH MY CAPTORS.
ER
UROLOGY
CARDIOLO:
YOU'RE NOT IN ANY CONDITION TO GO ABOUT TOWN, YOU NEED TO STAY HERE FOR AT LEAST ANOTHER TWO WEEKS.
IGNORING THE DOCTORS, LOU CHECKS HIMSELF OUT ON THE DAY OF THE WAKE.
FUCK THIS PLACE.
HE NEVER COMES BACK.

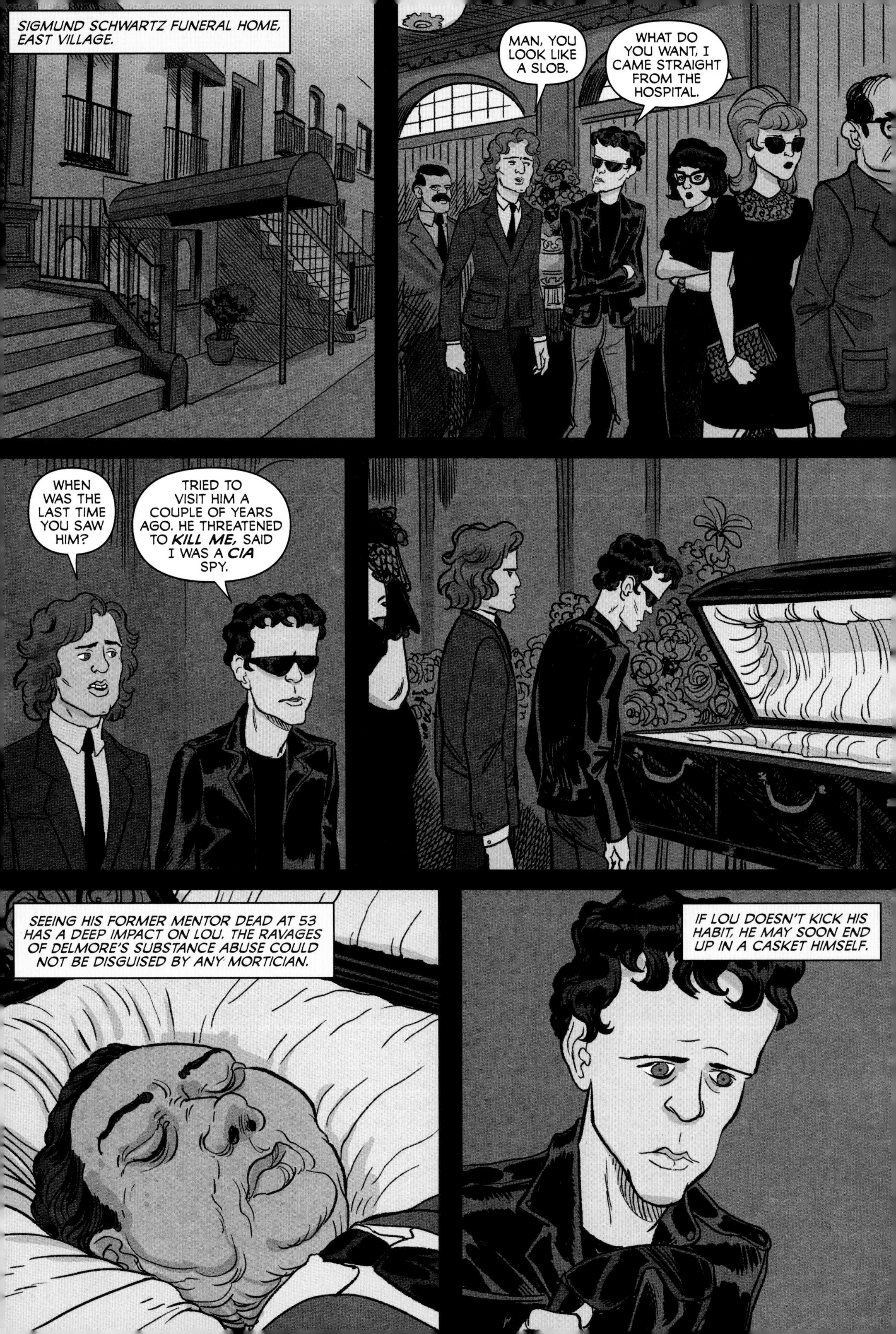
SIGMUND SCHWARTZ FUNERAL HOME, EAST VILLAGE.
MAN, YOU LOOK LIKE A SLOB.
WHAT DO YOU WANT, I CAME STRAIGHT FROM THE HOSPITAL.
WHEN WAS THE LAST TIME YOU SAW HIM?
TRIED TO VISIT HIM A COUPLE OF YEARS AGO. HE THREATENED TO KILL ME, SAID I WAS A CIA SPY.
SEEING HIS FORMER MENTOR DEAD AT 53 HAS A DEEP IMPACT ON LOU. THE RAVAGES OF DELMORE'S SUBSTANCE ABUSE COULD NOT BE DISGUISED BY ANY MORTICIAN.
IF LOU DOESN'T KICK HIS HABIT, HE MAY SOON END UP IN A CASKET HIMSELF.

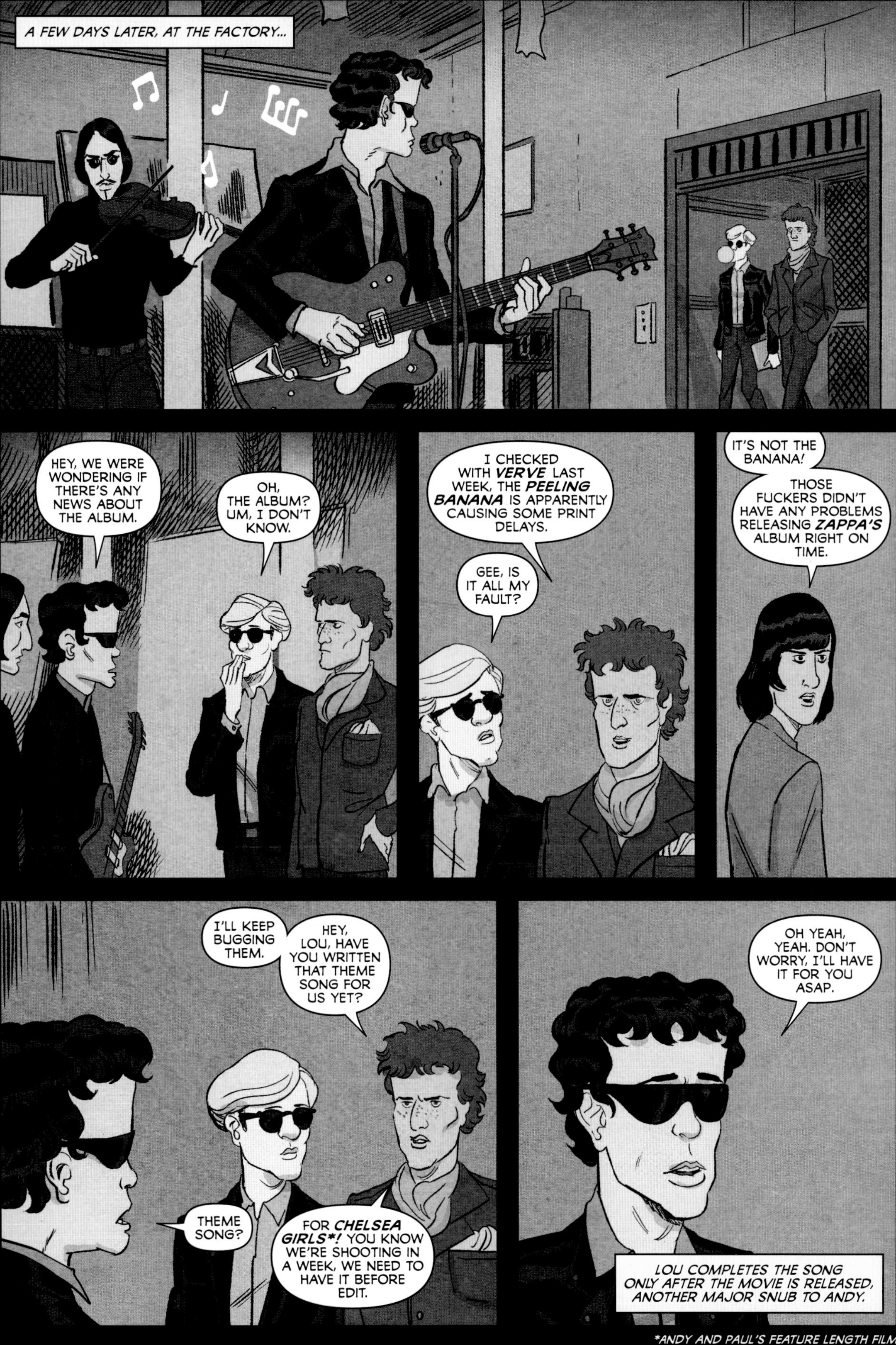
A FEW DAYS LATER, AT THE FACTORY...
HEY, WE WERE WONDERING IF THERE'S ANY NEWS ABOUT THE ALBUM.
OH, THE ALBUM? UM, I DON'T KNOW.
I CHECKED WITH VERVE LAST WEEK, THE PEELING BANANA IS APPARENTLY CAUSING SOME PRINT DELAYS.
GEE, IS IT ALL MY FAULT?
IT'S NOT THE BANANA!
THOSE FUCKERS DIDN'T HAVE ANY PROBLEMS RELEASING ZAPPA'S ALBUM RIGHT ON TIME.
I'LL KEEP BUGGING THEM.
HEY, LOU, HAVE YOU WRITTEN THAT THEME SONG FOR US YET?
THEME SONG?
FOR CHELSEA GIRLS*! YOU KNOW WE'RE SHOOTING IN A WEEK, WE NEED TO HAVE IT BEFORE EDIT.
OH YEAH, YEAH. DON'T WORRY, I'LL HAVE IT FOR YOU ASAP.
LOU COMPLETES THE SONG ONLY AFTER THE MOVIE IS RELEASED, ANOTHER MAJOR SNUB TO ANDY.
*ANDY AND PAUL'S FEATURE LENGTH FILM

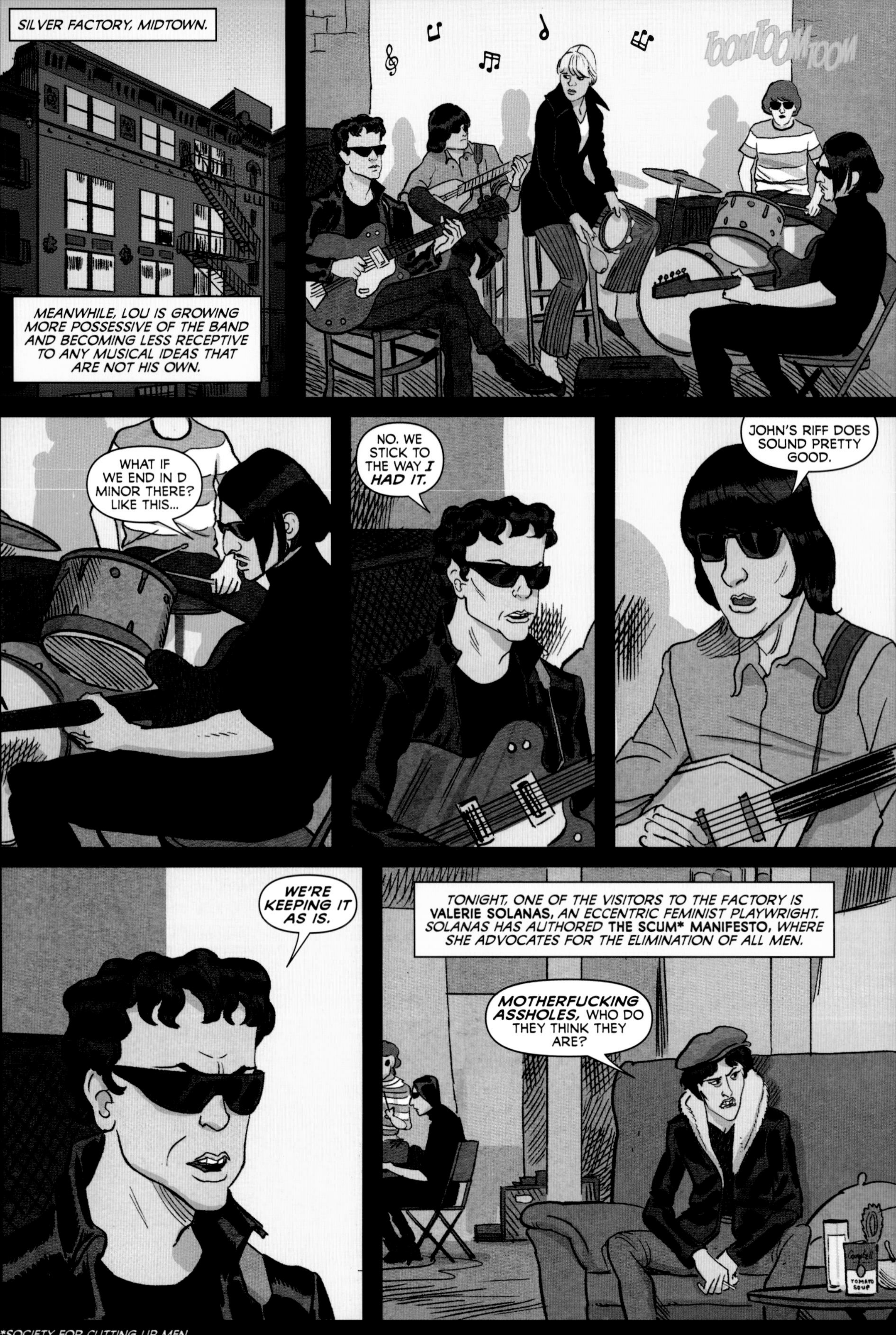
SILVER FACTORY, MIDTOWN.
MEANWHILE, LOU IS GROWING MORE POSSESSIVE OF THE BAND AND BECOMING LESS RECEPTIVE TO ANY MUSICAL IDEAS THAT ARE NOT HIS OWN.
TOOM TOOM TOOM
WHAT IF WE END IN D MINOR THERE? LIKE THIS...
NO. WE STICK TO THE WAY *I HAD IT.*
JOHN'S RIFF DOES SOUND PRETTY GOOD.
WE'RE KEEPING IT AS IS.
TONIGHT, ONE OF THE VISITORS TO THE FACTORY IS **VALERIE SOLANAS**, AN ECCENTRIC FEMINIST PLAYWRIGHT. SOLANAS HAS AUTHORED **THE SCUM* MANIFESTO**, WHERE SHE ADVOCATES FOR THE ELIMINATION OF ALL MEN.
MOTHERFUCKING ASSHOLES, WHO DO THEY THINK THEY ARE?

*SOCIETY FOR CUTTING UP MEN.

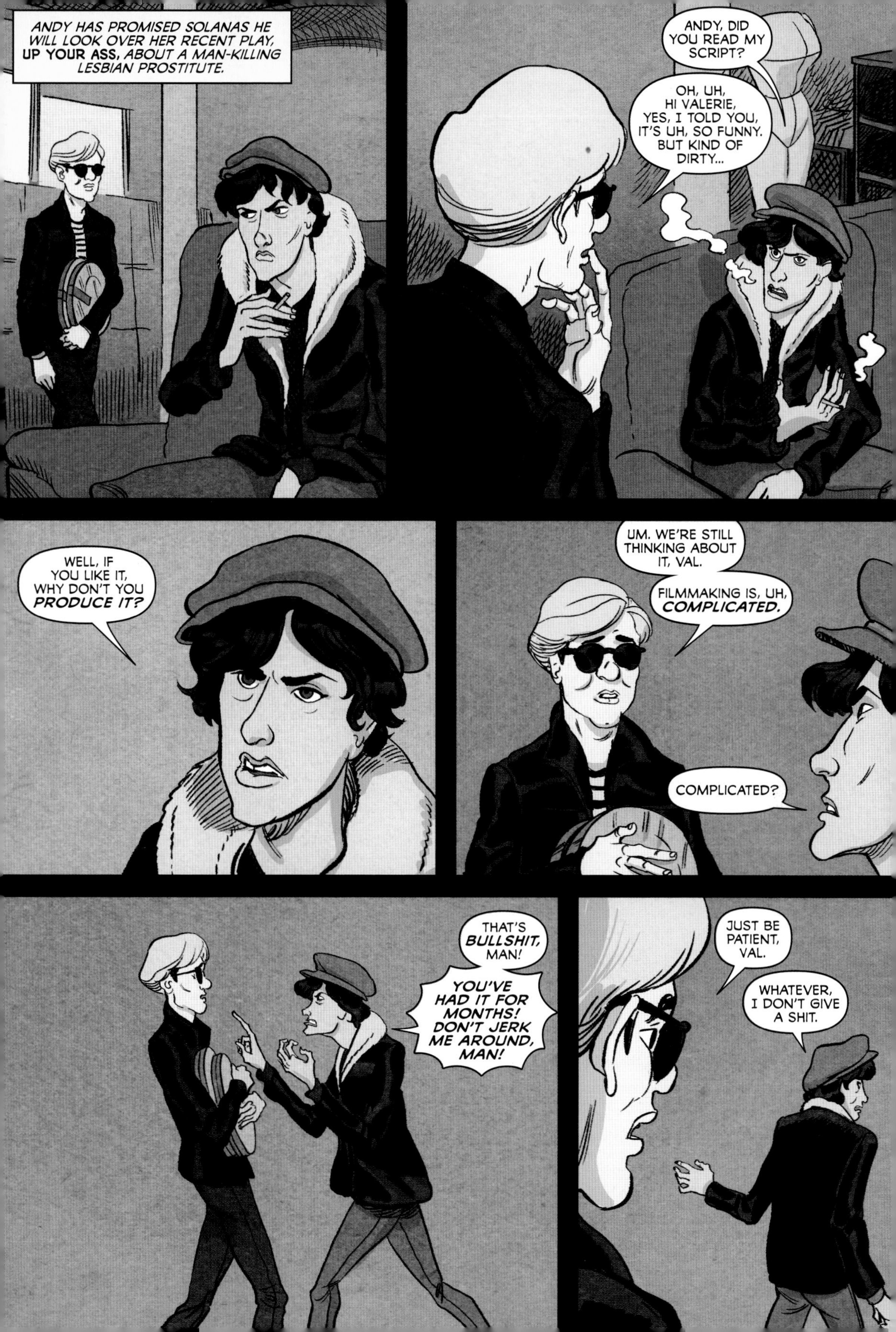
ANDY HAS PROMISED SOLANAS HE WILL LOOK OVER HER RECENT PLAY, UP YOUR ASS, ABOUT A MAN-KILLING LESBIAN PROSTITUTE.
ANDY, DID YOU READ MY SCRIPT?
OH, UH, HI VALERIE, YES, I TOLD YOU, IT'S UH, SO FUNNY. BUT KIND OF DIRTY...
WELL, IF YOU LIKE IT, WHY DON'T YOU PRODUCE IT?
UM. WE'RE STILL THINKING ABOUT IT, VAL.
FILMMAKING IS, UH, COMPLICATED.
COMPLICATED?
THAT'S BULLSHIT, MAN!
YOU'VE HAD IT FOR MONTHS! DON'T JERK ME AROUND, MAN!
JUST BE PATIENT, VAL.
WHATEVER, I DON'T GIVE A SHIT.

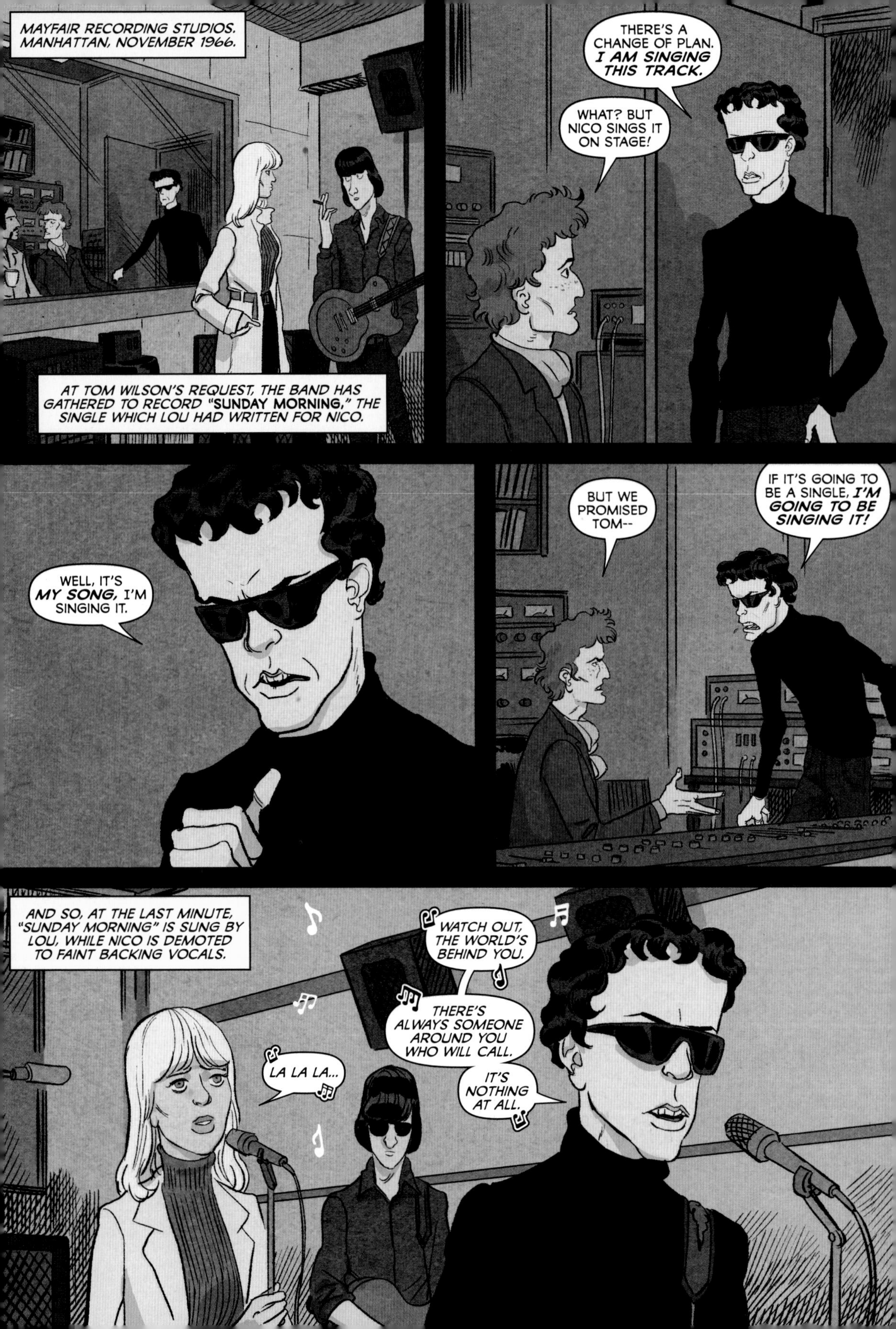
MAYFAIR RECORDING STUDIOS. MANHATTAN, NOVEMBER 1966.
AT TOM WILSON'S REQUEST, THE BAND HAS GATHERED TO RECORD "SUNDAY MORNING," THE SINGLE WHICH LOU HAD WRITTEN FOR NICO.
THERE'S A CHANGE OF PLAN. I AM SINGING THIS TRACK.
WHAT? BUT NICO SINGS IT ON STAGE!
WELL, IT'S MY SONG, I'M SINGING IT.
BUT WE PROMISED TOM--
IF IT'S GOING TO BE A SINGLE, I'M GOING TO BE SINGING IT!
AND SO, AT THE LAST MINUTE, "SUNDAY MORNING" IS SUNG BY LOU, WHILE NICO IS DEMOTED TO FAINT BACKING VOCALS.
WATCH OUT, THE WORLD'S BEHIND YOU.
THERE'S ALWAYS SOMEONE AROUND YOU WHO WILL CALL.
IT'S NOTHING AT ALL.
LA LA LA...

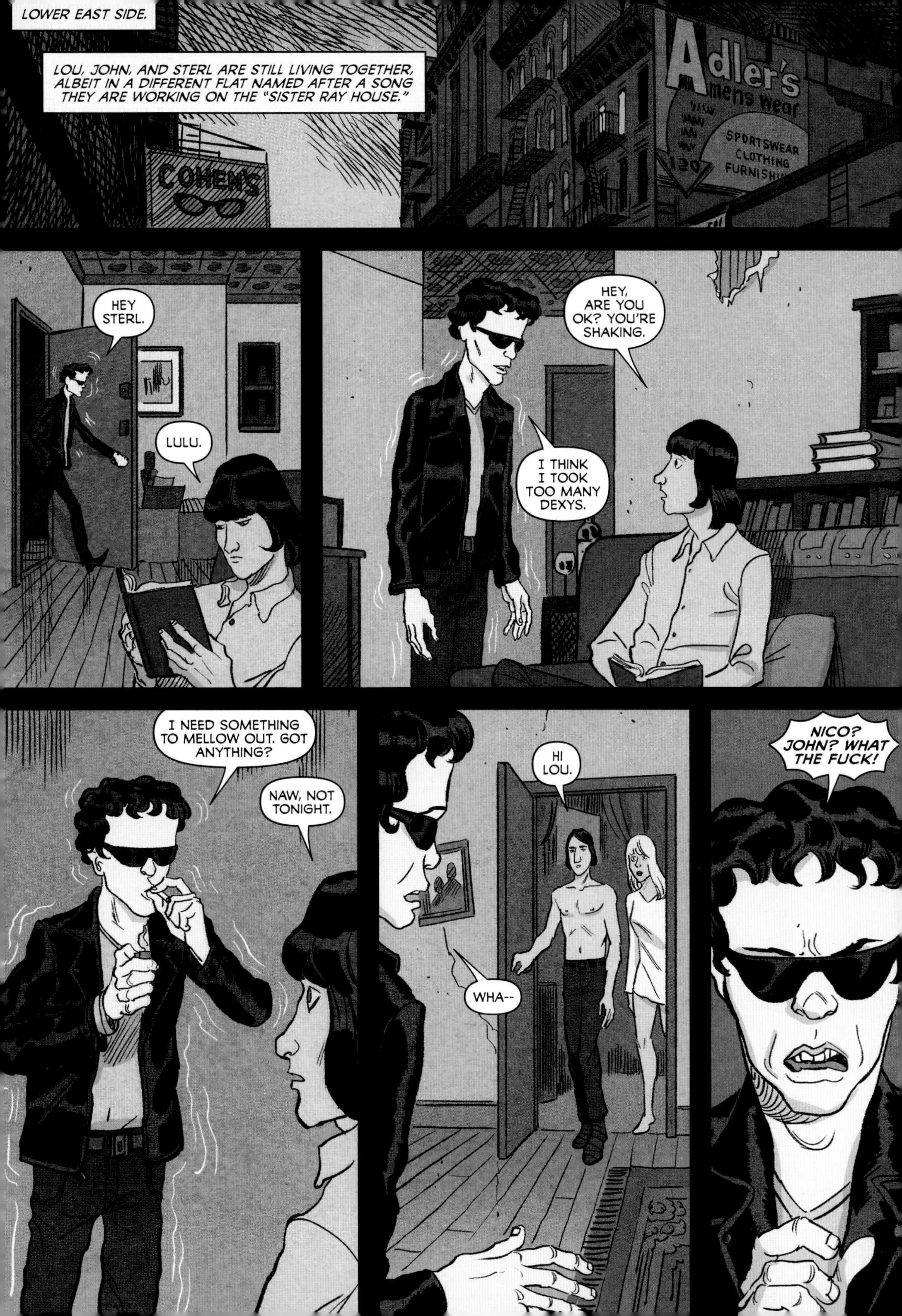
LOWER EAST SIDE.
LOU, JOHN, AND STERL ARE STILL LIVING TOGETHER, ALBEIT IN A DIFFERENT FLAT NAMED AFTER A SONG THEY ARE WORKING ON THE "SISTER RAY HOUSE."
COHEN'S
Adler's mens wear
SPORTSWEAR
CLOTHING
120
HEY STERL.
LULU.
HEY, ARE YOU OK? YOU'RE SHAKING.
I THINK I TOOK TOO MANY DEXYS.
I NEED SOMETHING TO MELLOW OUT. GOT ANYTHING?
NAW, NOT TONIGHT.
HI LOU.
WHA--
NICO? JOHN? WHAT THE FUCK!

COME ON, LOU, LET'S ALL STAY CALM.

CALM? YOU GOTTA FUCK ALL THE WOMEN I'VE BEEN WITH?

IS THAT YOUR THING?

YOU GUYS BARELY DATED. ANYWAY, WHAT IS SHE, YOUR PROPERTY?

WHATEVER, MAN.

AFTER YOU'RE DONE WITH NICO YOU SHOULD FLY BACK TO SCOTLAND AND GO *FUCK* SOME *SHEEP*.

LOU, PLEASE, WHY DON'T WE ALL JUST GET ALONG?

WE CAN GET ALONG WHEN YOU FINALLY *LEARN TO SING*.

I DON'T NEED THIS BULLSHIT.

KA·KLUNK

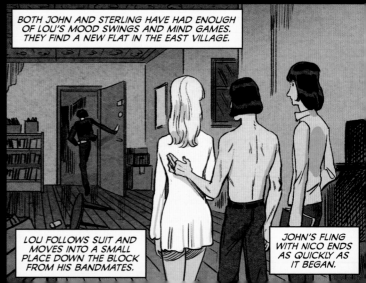

BOTH JOHN AND STERLING HAVE HAD ENOUGH OF LOU'S MOOD SWINGS AND MIND GAMES. THEY FIND A NEW FLAT IN THE EAST VILLAGE.

LOU FOLLOWS SUIT AND MOVES INTO A SMALL PLACE DOWN THE BLOCK FROM HIS BANDMATES.

JOHN'S FLING WITH NICO ENDS AS QUICKLY AS IT BEGAN.

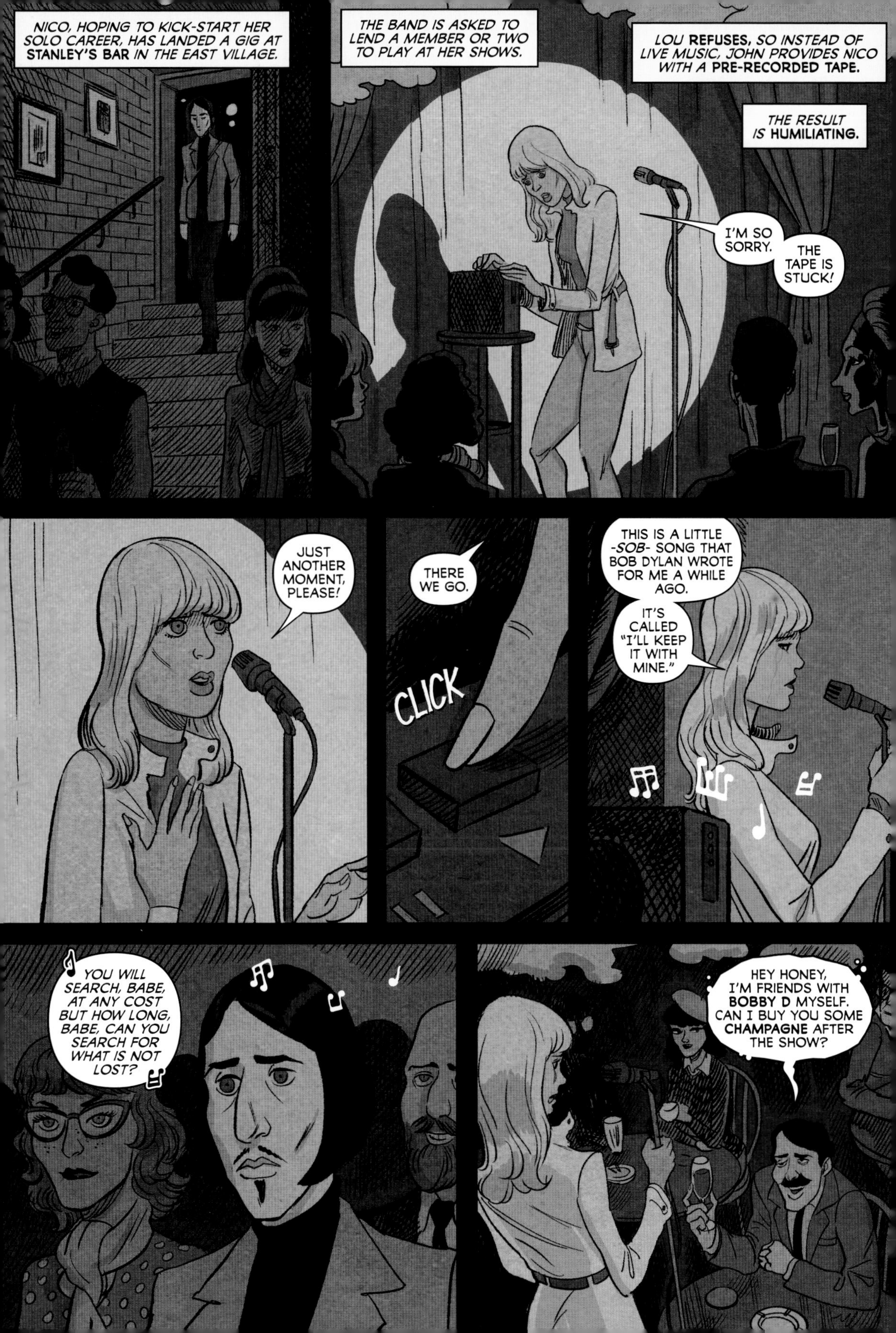

NICO, HOPING TO KICK-START HER SOLO CAREER, HAS LANDED A GIG AT STANLEY'S BAR IN THE EAST VILLAGE.
THE BAND IS ASKED TO LEND A MEMBER OR TWO TO PLAY AT HER SHOWS.
LOU REFUSES, SO INSTEAD OF LIVE MUSIC, JOHN PROVIDES NICO WITH A PRE-RECORDED TAPE.
THE RESULT IS HUMILIATING.
I'M SO SORRY.
THE TAPE IS STUCK!
JUST ANOTHER MOMENT, PLEASE!
THERE WE GO.
CLICK
THIS IS A LITTLE -SOB- SONG THAT BOB DYLAN WROTE FOR ME A WHILE AGO.
IT'S CALLED "I'LL KEEP IT WITH MINE."
YOU WILL SEARCH, BABE, AT ANY COST BUT HOW LONG, BABE, CAN YOU SEARCH FOR WHAT IS NOT LOST?
HEY HONEY, I'M FRIENDS WITH BOBBY D MYSELF. CAN I BUY YOU SOME CHAMPAGNE AFTER THE SHOW?

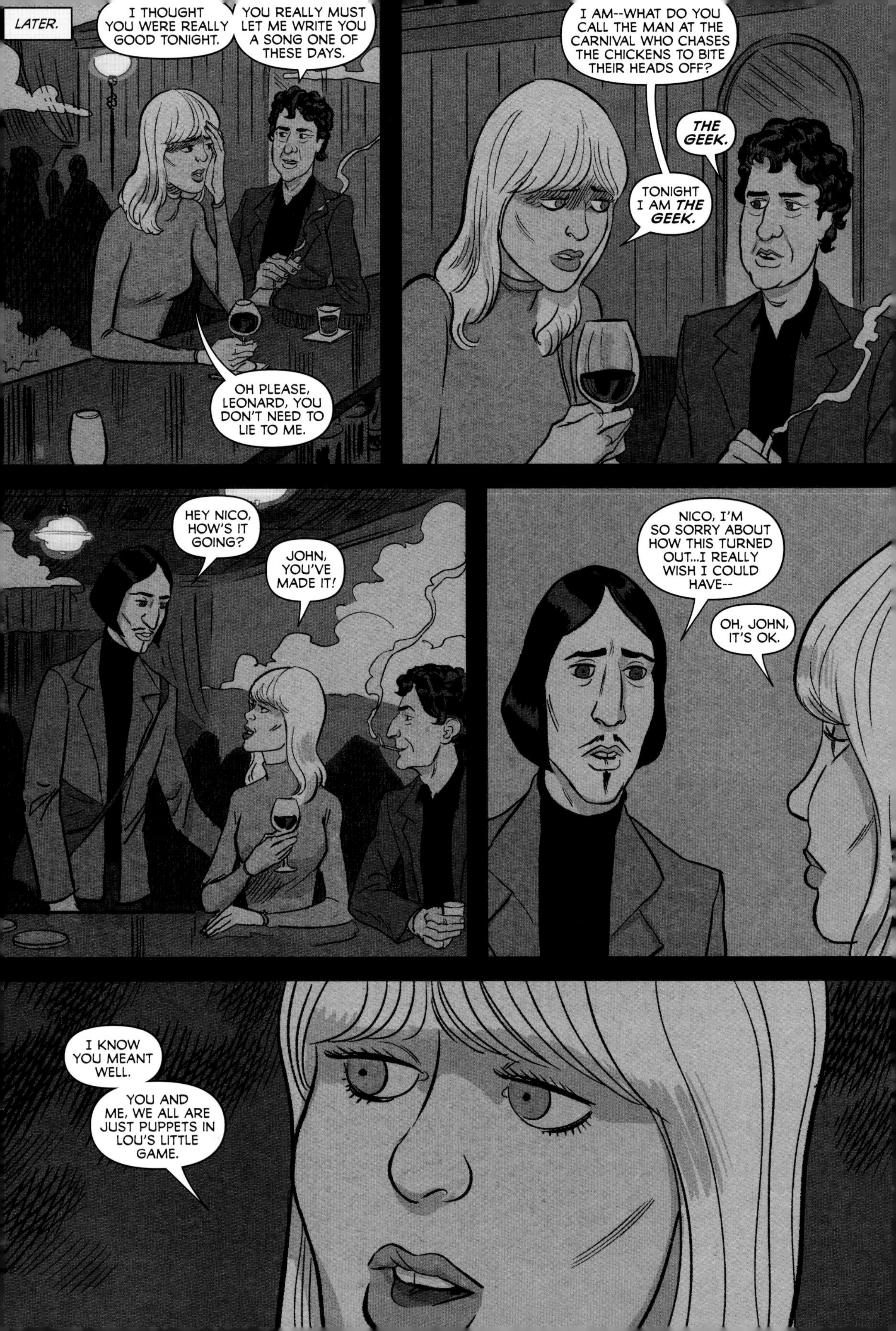
LATER.
I THOUGHT YOU WERE REALLY GOOD TONIGHT.
YOU REALLY MUST LET ME WRITE YOU A SONG ONE OF THESE DAYS.
OH PLEASE, LEONARD, YOU DON'T NEED TO LIE TO ME.
I AM--WHAT DO YOU CALL THE MAN AT THE CARNIVAL WHO CHASES THE CHICKENS TO BITE THEIR HEADS OFF?
THE GEEK.
TONIGHT I AM *THE GEEK.*
HEY NICO, HOW'S IT GOING?
JOHN, YOU'VE MADE IT!
NICO, I'M SO SORRY ABOUT HOW THIS TURNED OUT...I REALLY WISH I COULD HAVE--
OH, JOHN, IT'S OK.
I KNOW YOU MEANT WELL.
YOU AND ME, WE ALL ARE JUST PUPPETS IN LOU'S LITTLE GAME.

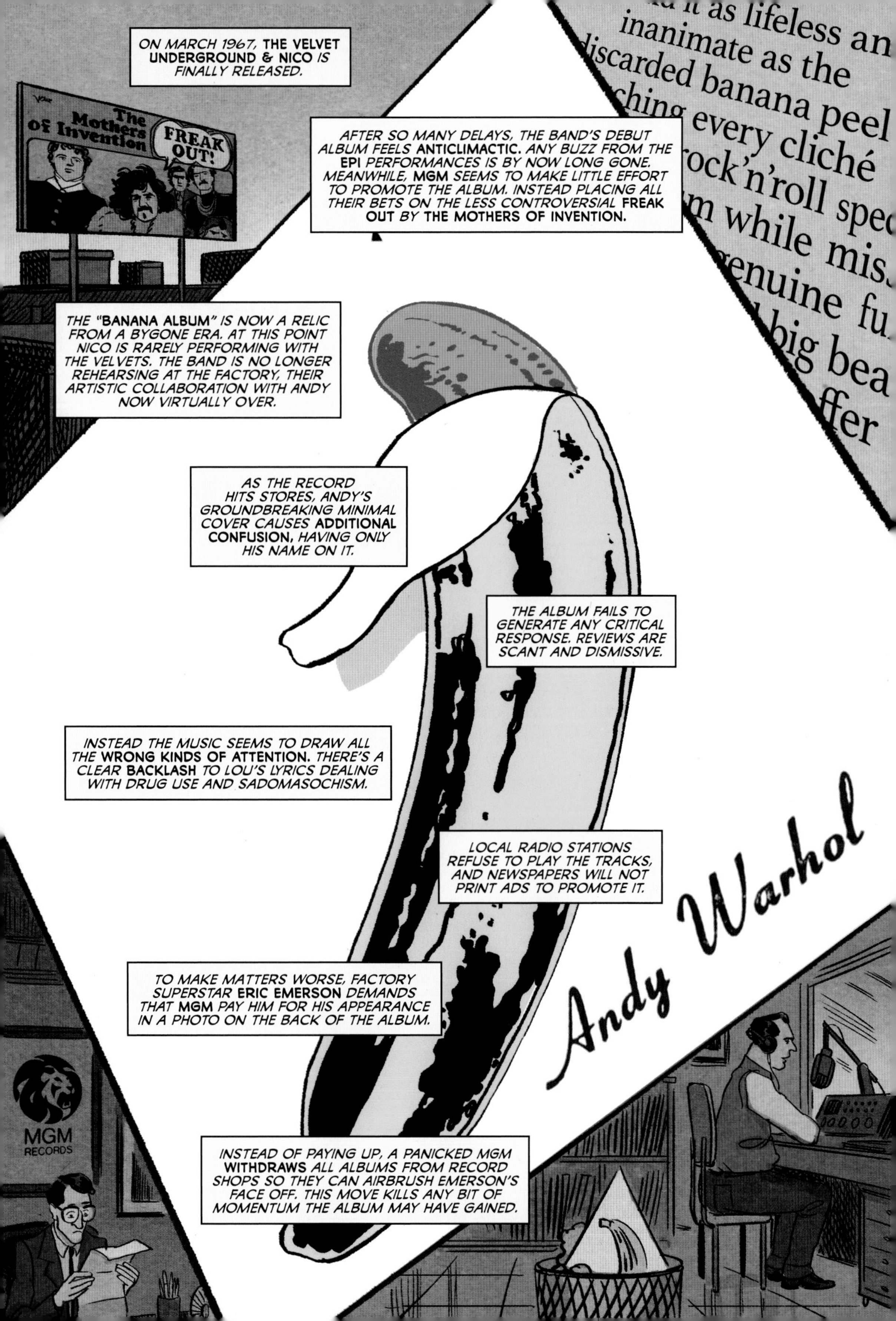

ON MARCH 1967, THE VELVET UNDERGROUND & NICO IS FINALLY RELEASED.
The Mothers of Invention
FREAK OUT!
AFTER SO MANY DELAYS, THE BAND'S DEBUT ALBUM FEELS ANTICLIMACTIC. ANY BUZZ FROM THE EPI PERFORMANCES IS BY NOW LONG GONE. MEANWHILE, MGM SEEMS TO MAKE LITTLE EFFORT TO PROMOTE THE ALBUM. INSTEAD PLACING ALL THEIR BETS ON THE LESS CONTROVERSIAL FREAK OUT BY THE MOTHERS OF INVENTION.
it as lifeless an
inanimate as the
discarded banana peel
every cliché
rock'n'roll spe
while mis
genuine fu
big bea
THE "BANANA ALBUM" IS NOW A RELIC FROM A BYGONE ERA. AT THIS POINT NICO IS RARELY PERFORMING WITH THE VELVETS. THE BAND IS NO LONGER REHEARSING AT THE FACTORY, THEIR ARTISTIC COLLABORATION WITH ANDY NOW VIRTUALLY OVER.
AS THE RECORD HITS STORES, ANDY'S GROUNDBREAKING MINIMAL COVER CAUSES ADDITIONAL CONFUSION, HAVING ONLY HIS NAME ON IT.
THE ALBUM FAILS TO GENERATE ANY CRITICAL RESPONSE. REVIEWS ARE SCANT AND DISMISSIVE.
INSTEAD THE MUSIC SEEMS TO DRAW ALL THE WRONG KINDS OF ATTENTION. THERE'S A CLEAR BACKLASH TO LOU'S LYRICS DEALING WITH DRUG USE AND SADOMASOCHISM.
LOCAL RADIO STATIONS REFUSE TO PLAY THE TRACKS, AND NEWSPAPERS WILL NOT PRINT ADS TO PROMOTE IT.
Andy Warhol
TO MAKE MATTERS WORSE, FACTORY SUPERSTAR ERIC EMERSON DEMANDS THAT MGM PAY HIM FOR HIS APPEARANCE IN A PHOTO ON THE BACK OF THE ALBUM.
MGM
RECORDS
INSTEAD OF PAYING UP, A PANICKED MGM WITHDRAWS ALL ALBUMS FROM RECORD SHOPS SO THEY CAN AIRBRUSH EMERSON'S FACE OFF. THIS MOVE KILLS ANY BIT OF MOMENTUM THE ALBUM MAY HAVE GAINED.

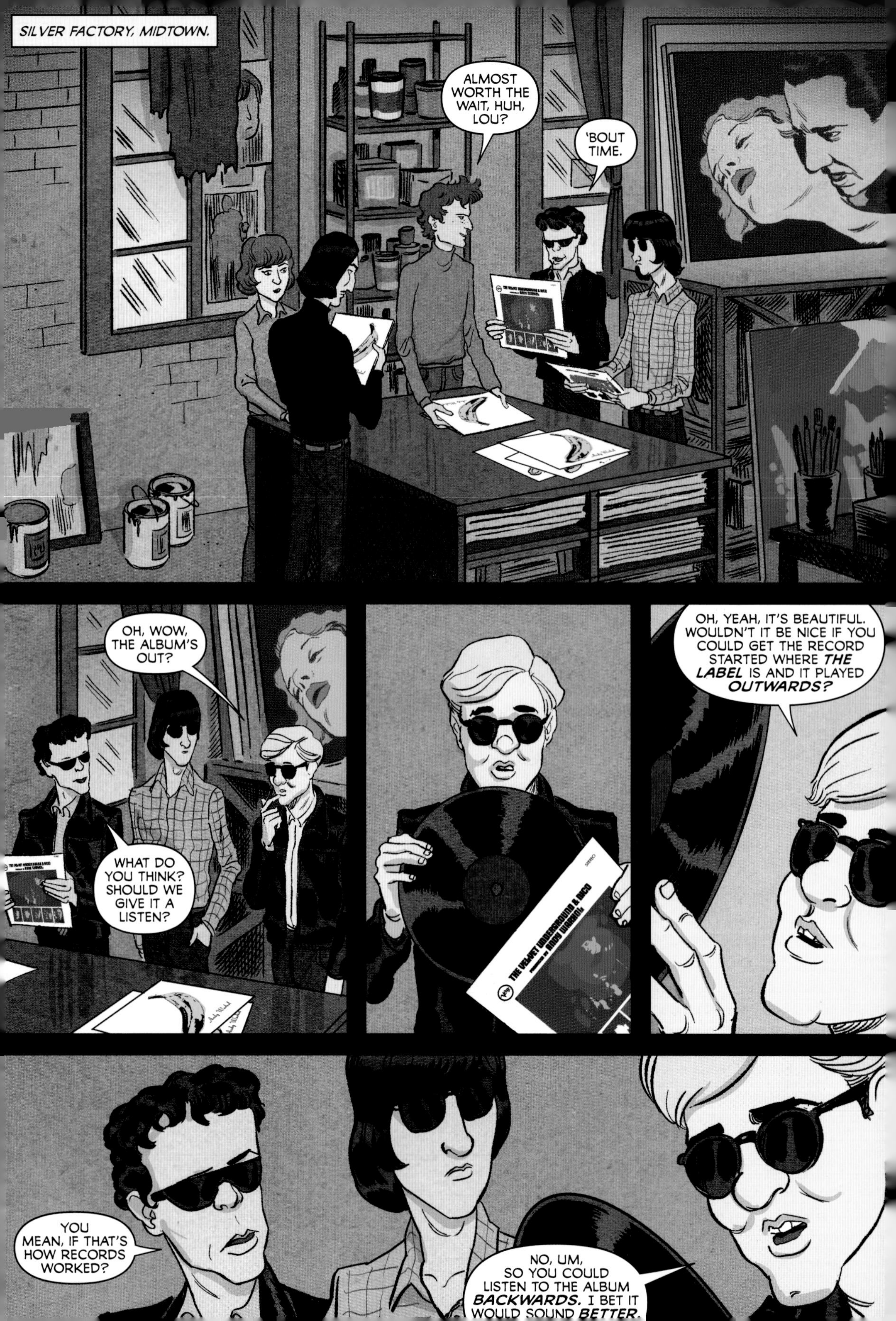
SILVER FACTORY, MIDTOWN.
ALMOST WORTH THE WAIT, HUH, LOU?
'BOUT TIME.
OH, WOW, THE ALBUM'S OUT?
WHAT DO YOU THINK? SHOULD WE GIVE IT A LISTEN?
OH, YEAH, IT'S BEAUTIFUL. WOULDN'T IT BE NICE IF YOU COULD GET THE RECORD STARTED WHERE *THE LABEL* IS AND IT PLAYED *OUTWARDS?*
YOU MEAN, IF THAT'S HOW RECORDS WORKED?
NO, UM, SO YOU COULD LISTEN TO THE ALBUM *BACKWARDS.* I BET IT WOULD SOUND *BETTER.*

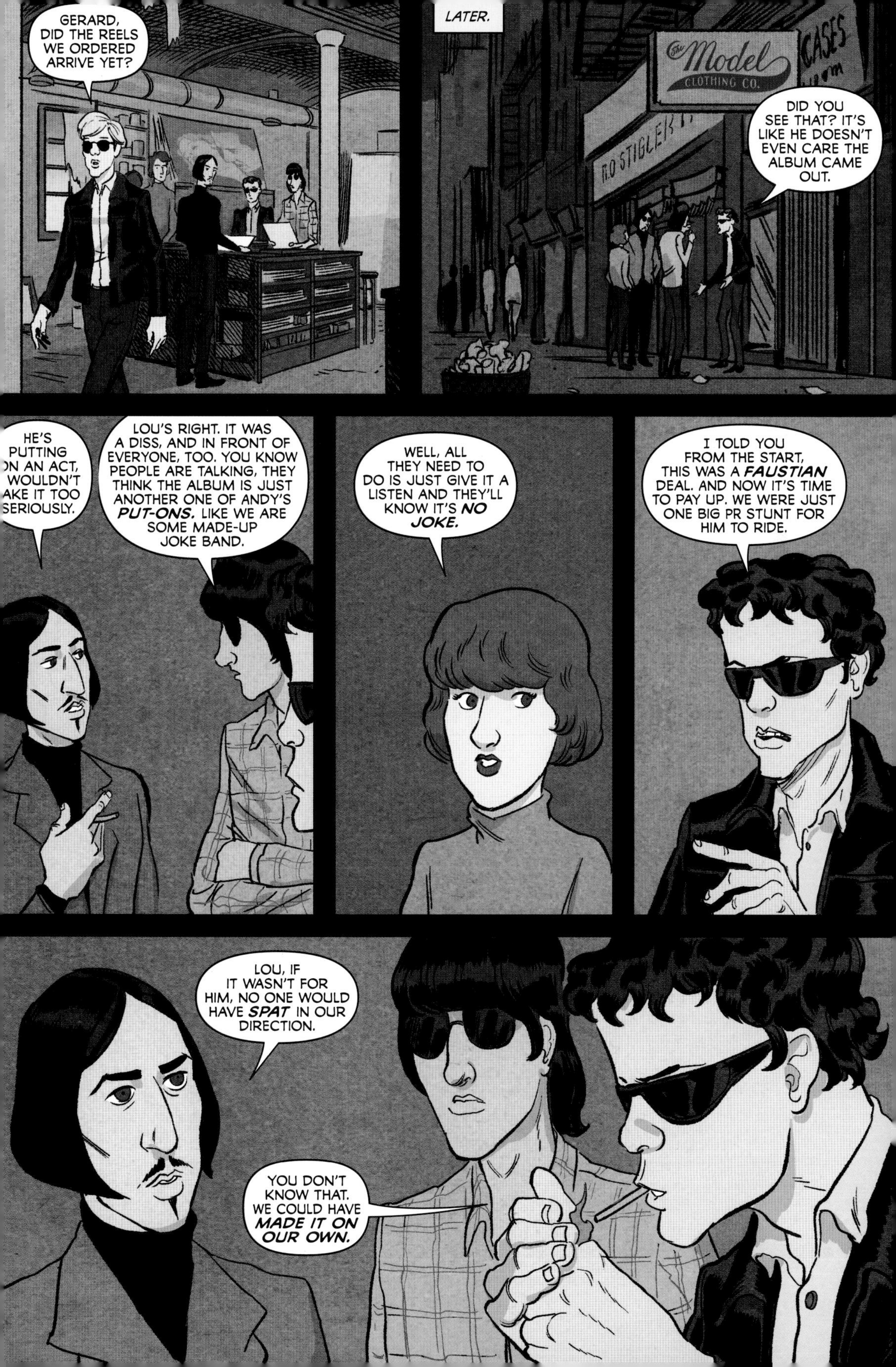
GERARD, DID THE REELS WE ORDERED ARRIVE YET?
LATER.
The Model CLOTHING CO.
DID YOU SEE THAT? IT'S LIKE HE DOESN'T EVEN CARE THE ALBUM CAME OUT.
HE'S PUTTING ON AN ACT, WOULDN'T AKE IT TOO SERIOUSLY.
LOU'S RIGHT. IT WAS A DISS, AND IN FRONT OF EVERYONE, TOO. YOU KNOW PEOPLE ARE TALKING, THEY THINK THE ALBUM IS JUST ANOTHER ONE OF ANDY'S PUT-ONS. LIKE WE ARE SOME MADE-UP JOKE BAND.
WELL, ALL THEY NEED TO DO IS JUST GIVE IT A LISTEN AND THEY'LL KNOW IT'S NO JOKE.
I TOLD YOU FROM THE START, THIS WAS A FAUSTIAN DEAL. AND NOW IT'S TIME TO PAY UP. WE WERE JUST ONE BIG PR STUNT FOR HIM TO RIDE.
LOU, IF IT WASN'T FOR HIM, NO ONE WOULD HAVE SPAT IN OUR DIRECTION.
YOU DON'T KNOW THAT. WE COULD HAVE MADE IT ON OUR OWN.

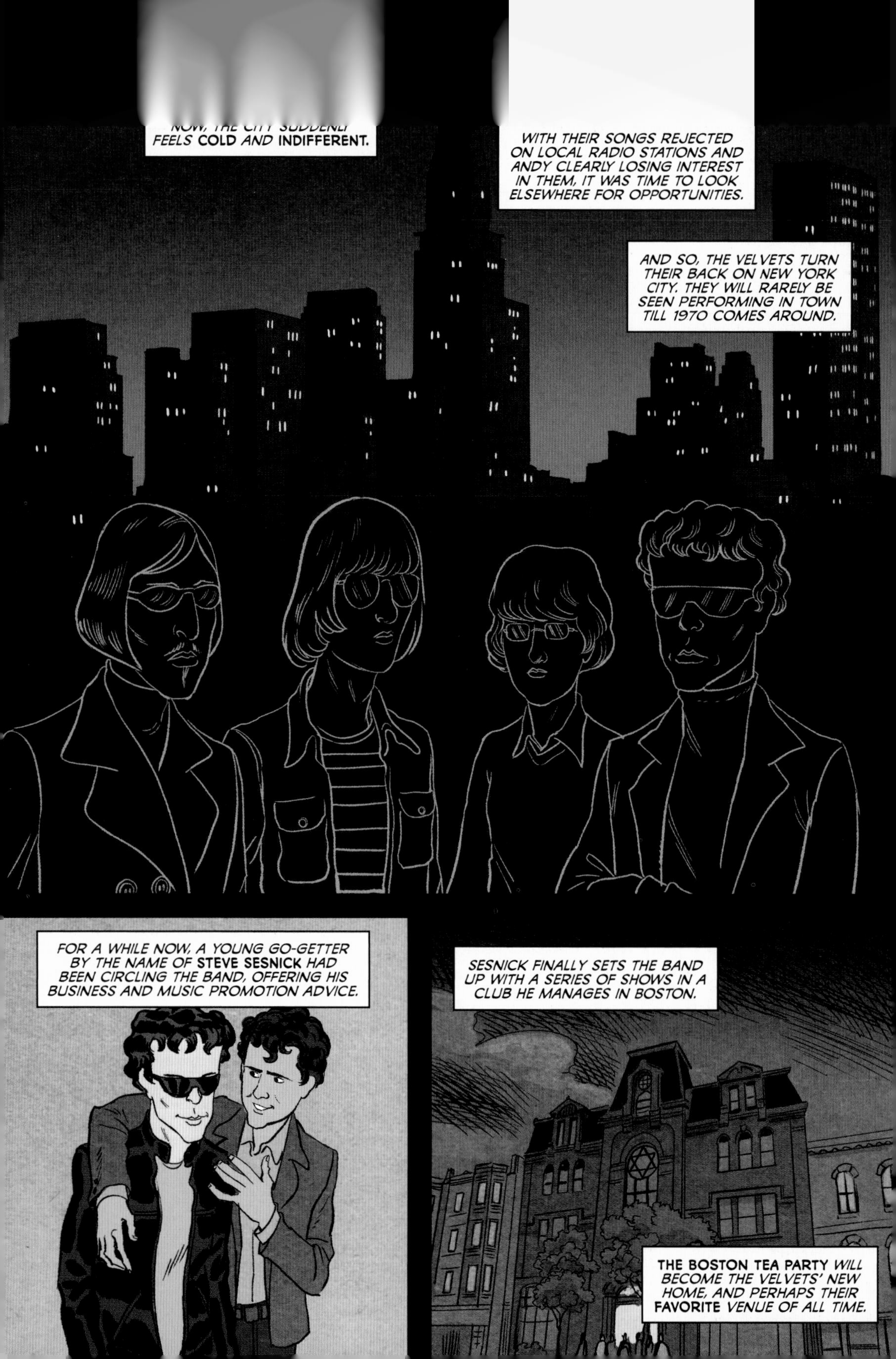
FEELS COLD AND INDIFFERENT.
WITH THEIR SONGS REJECTED ON LOCAL RADIO STATIONS AND ANDY CLEARLY LOSING INTEREST IN THEM, IT WAS TIME TO LOOK ELSEWHERE FOR OPPORTUNITIES.
AND SO, THE VELVETS TURN THEIR BACK ON NEW YORK CITY. THEY WILL RARELY BE SEEN PERFORMING IN TOWN TILL 1970 COMES AROUND.
FOR A WHILE NOW, A YOUNG GO-GETTER BY THE NAME OF STEVE SESNICK HAD BEEN CIRCLING THE BAND, OFFERING HIS BUSINESS AND MUSIC PROMOTION ADVICE.
SESNICK FINALLY SETS THE BAND UP WITH A SERIES OF SHOWS IN A CLUB HE MANAGES IN BOSTON.
THE BOSTON TEA PARTY WILL BECOME THE VELVETS' NEW HOME, AND PERHAPS THEIR FAVORITE VENUE OF ALL TIME.

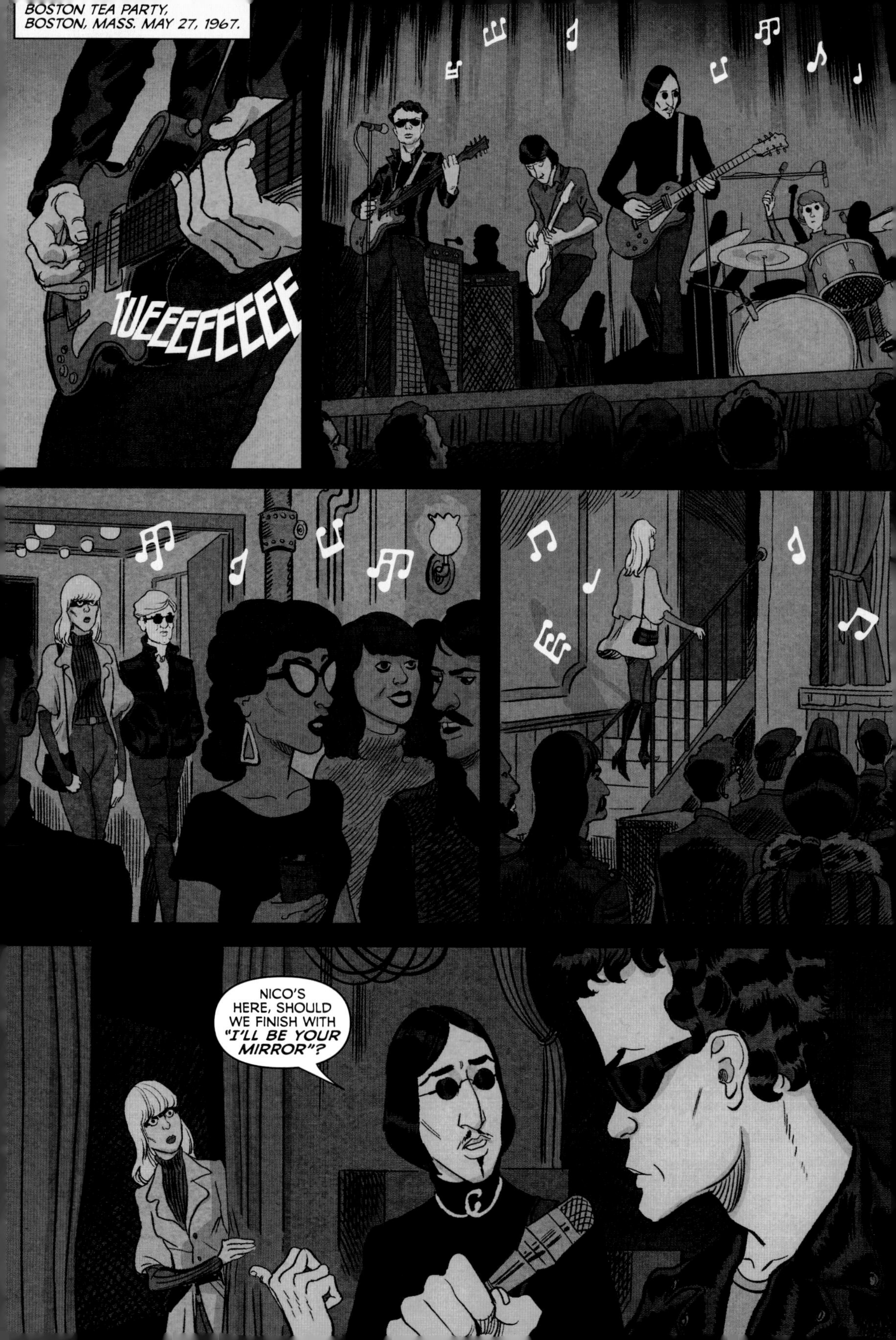
BOSTON TEA PARTY, BOSTON, MASS. MAY 27, 1967.
TUEEEEEEEEF
NICO'S HERE, SHOULD WE FINISH WITH "I'LL BE YOUR MIRROR"?

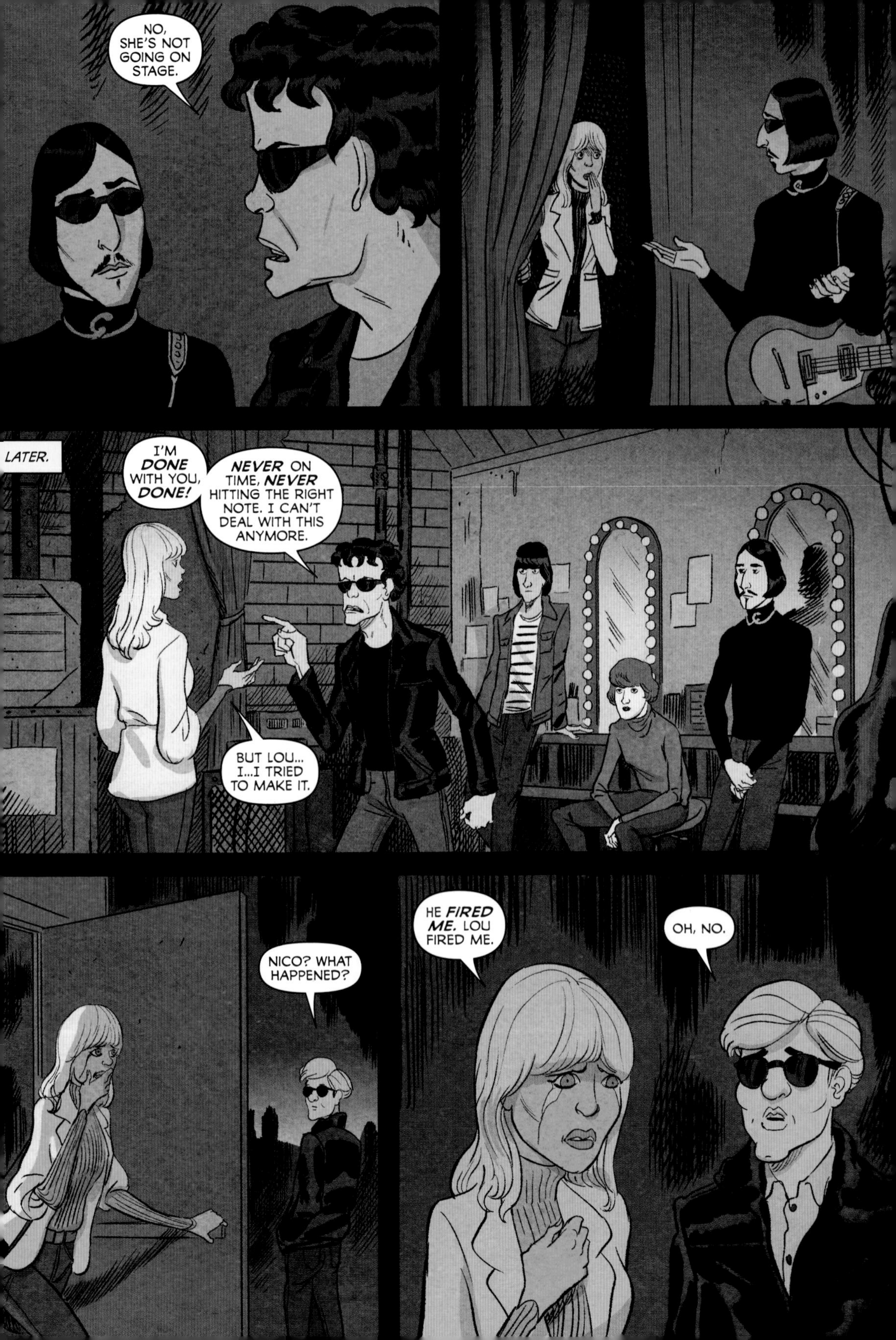
NO, SHE'S NOT GOING ON STAGE.
LATER.
I'M **DONE** WITH YOU, **DONE!**
NEVER ON TIME, **NEVER** HITTING THE RIGHT NOTE. I CAN'T DEAL WITH THIS ANYMORE.
BUT LOU... I...I TRIED TO MAKE IT.
NICO? WHAT HAPPENED?
HE **FIRED ME.** LOU FIRED ME.
OH, NO.

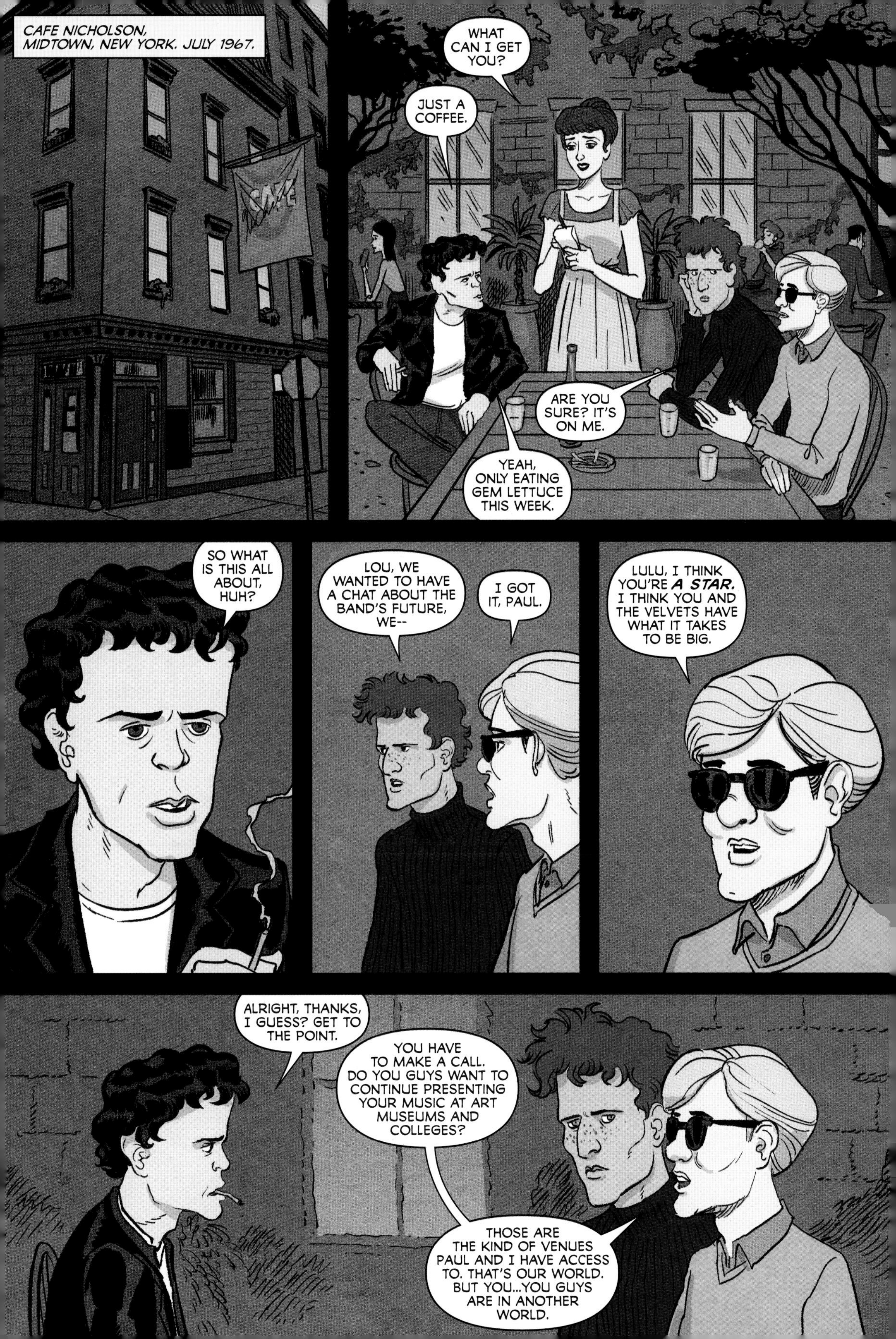
CAFE NICHOLSON, MIDTOWN, NEW YORK. JULY 1967.
WHAT CAN I GET YOU?
JUST A COFFEE.
ARE YOU SURE? IT'S ON ME.
YEAH, ONLY EATING GEM LETTUCE THIS WEEK.
SO WHAT IS THIS ALL ABOUT, HUH?
LOU, WE WANTED TO HAVE A CHAT ABOUT THE BAND'S FUTURE, WE--
I GOT IT, PAUL.
LULU, I THINK YOU'RE A STAR. I THINK YOU AND THE VELVETS HAVE WHAT IT TAKES TO BE BIG.
ALRIGHT, THANKS, I GUESS? GET TO THE POINT.
YOU HAVE TO MAKE A CALL. DO YOU GUYS WANT TO CONTINUE PRESENTING YOUR MUSIC AT ART MUSEUMS AND COLLEGES?
THOSE ARE THE KIND OF VENUES PAUL AND I HAVE ACCESS TO. THAT'S OUR WORLD. BUT YOU...YOU GUYS ARE IN ANOTHER WORLD.

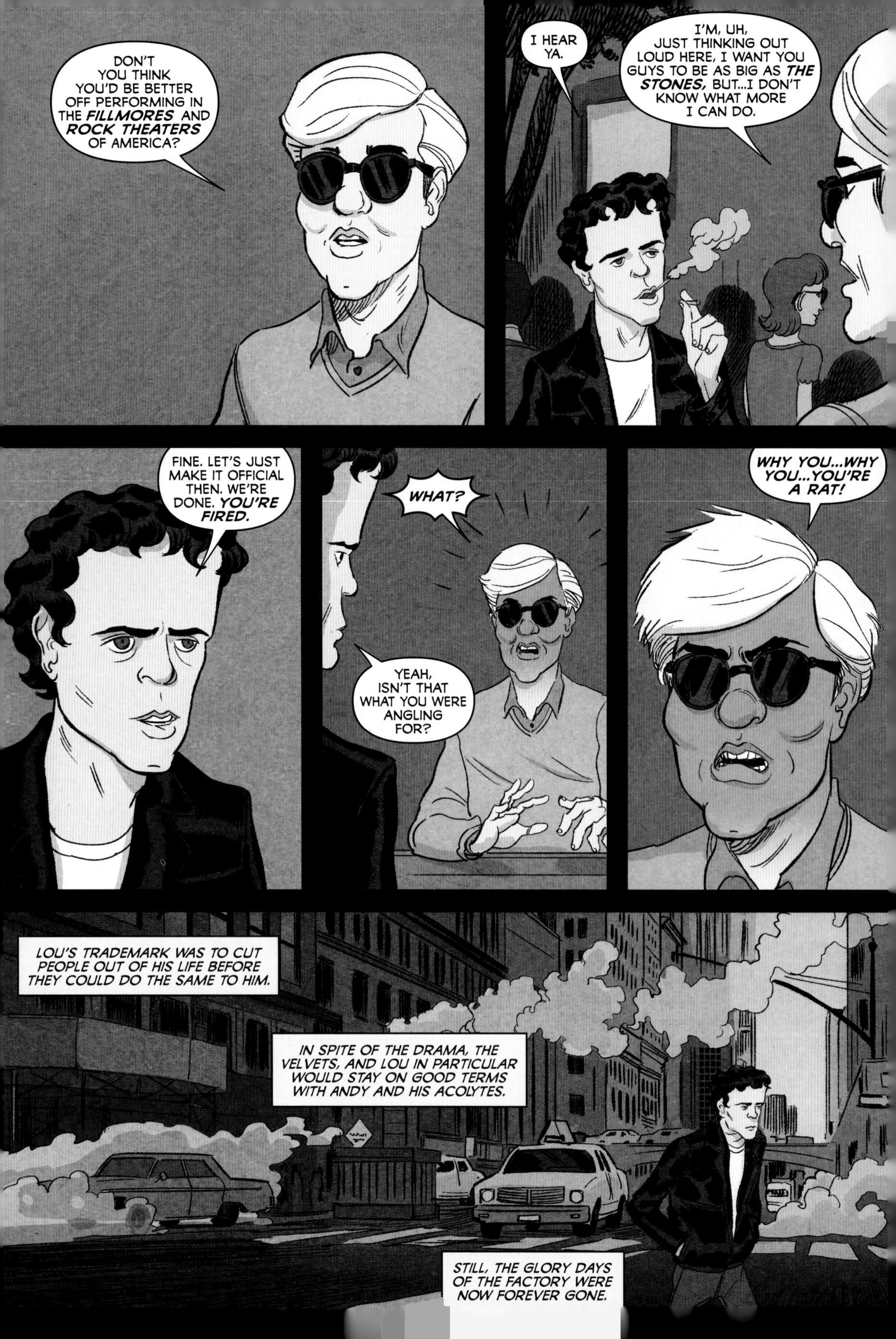
DON'T YOU THINK YOU'D BE BETTER OFF PERFORMING IN THE FILLMORES AND ROCK THEATERS OF AMERICA?
I HEAR YA.
I'M, UH, JUST THINKING OUT LOUD HERE, I WANT YOU GUYS TO BE AS BIG AS THE STONES, BUT...I DON'T KNOW WHAT MORE I CAN DO.
FINE. LET'S JUST MAKE IT OFFICIAL THEN. WE'RE DONE. YOU'RE FIRED.
WHAT?
YEAH, ISN'T THAT WHAT YOU WERE ANGLING FOR?
WHY YOU...WHY YOU...YOU'RE A RAT!
LOU'S TRADEMARK WAS TO CUT PEOPLE OUT OF HIS LIFE BEFORE THEY COULD DO THE SAME TO HIM.
IN SPITE OF THE DRAMA, THE VELVETS, AND LOU IN PARTICULAR WOULD STAY ON GOOD TERMS WITH ANDY AND HIS ACOLYTES.
STILL, THE GLORY DAYS OF THE FACTORY WERE NOW FOREVER GONE.

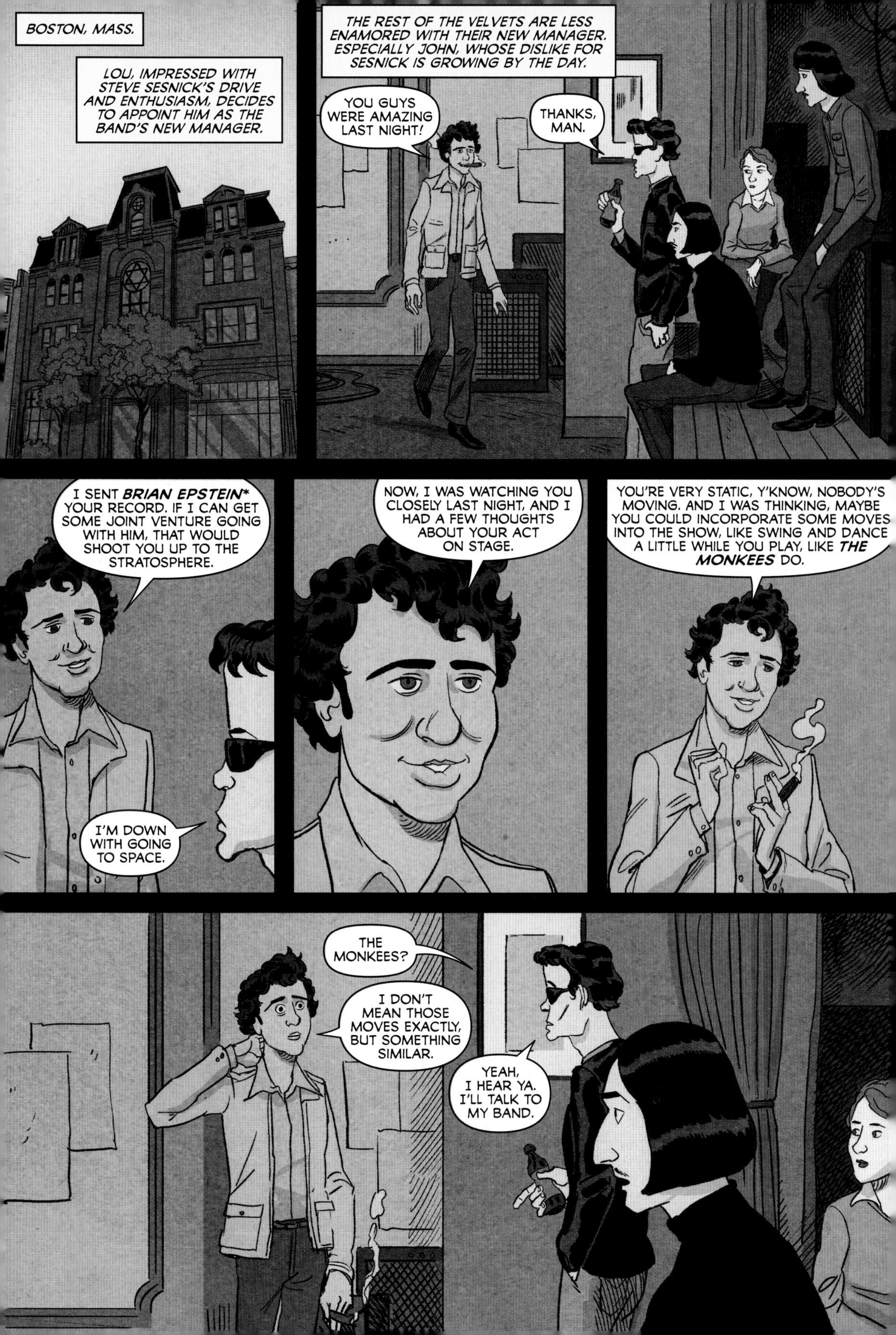
BOSTON, MASS.
LOU, IMPRESSED WITH STEVE SESNICK'S DRIVE AND ENTHUSIASM, DECIDES TO APPOINT HIM AS THE BAND'S NEW MANAGER.
THE REST OF THE VELVETS ARE LESS ENAMORED WITH THEIR NEW MANAGER. ESPECIALLY JOHN, WHOSE DISLIKE FOR SESNICK IS GROWING BY THE DAY.
YOU GUYS WERE AMAZING LAST NIGHT!
THANKS, MAN.
I SENT BRIAN EPSTEIN* YOUR RECORD. IF I CAN GET SOME JOINT VENTURE GOING WITH HIM, THAT WOULD SHOOT YOU UP TO THE STRATOSPHERE.
I'M DOWN WITH GOING TO SPACE.
NOW, I WAS WATCHING YOU CLOSELY LAST NIGHT, AND I HAD A FEW THOUGHTS ABOUT YOUR ACT ON STAGE.
YOU'RE VERY STATIC, Y'KNOW, NOBODY'S MOVING. AND I WAS THINKING, MAYBE YOU COULD INCORPORATE SOME MOVES INTO THE SHOW, LIKE SWING AND DANCE A LITTLE WHILE YOU PLAY, LIKE THE MONKEES DO.
THE MONKEES?
I DON'T MEAN THOSE MOVES EXACTLY, BUT SOMETHING SIMILAR.
YEAH, I HEAR YA. I'LL TALK TO MY BAND.

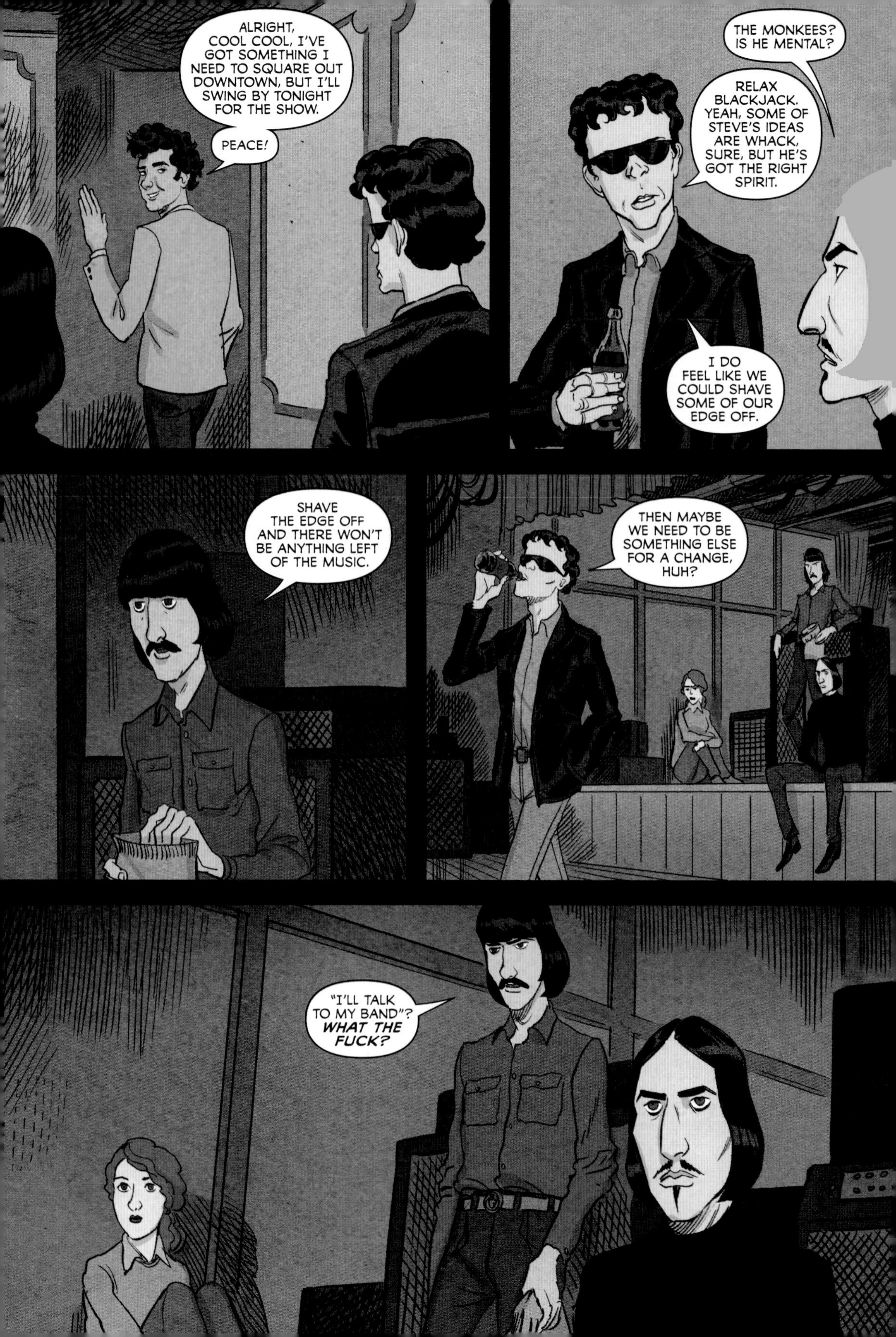
ALRIGHT, COOL COOL, I'VE GOT SOMETHING I NEED TO SQUARE OUT DOWNTOWN, BUT I'LL SWING BY TONIGHT FOR THE SHOW.
PEACE!
THE MONKEES? IS HE MENTAL?
RELAX BLACKJACK. YEAH, SOME OF STEVE'S IDEAS ARE WHACK, SURE, BUT HE'S GOT THE RIGHT SPIRIT.
I DO FEEL LIKE WE COULD SHAVE SOME OF OUR EDGE OFF.
SHAVE THE EDGE OFF AND THERE WON'T BE ANYTHING LEFT OF THE MUSIC.
THEN MAYBE WE NEED TO BE SOMETHING ELSE FOR A CHANGE, HUH?
"I'LL TALK TO MY BAND"? *WHAT THE FUCK?*

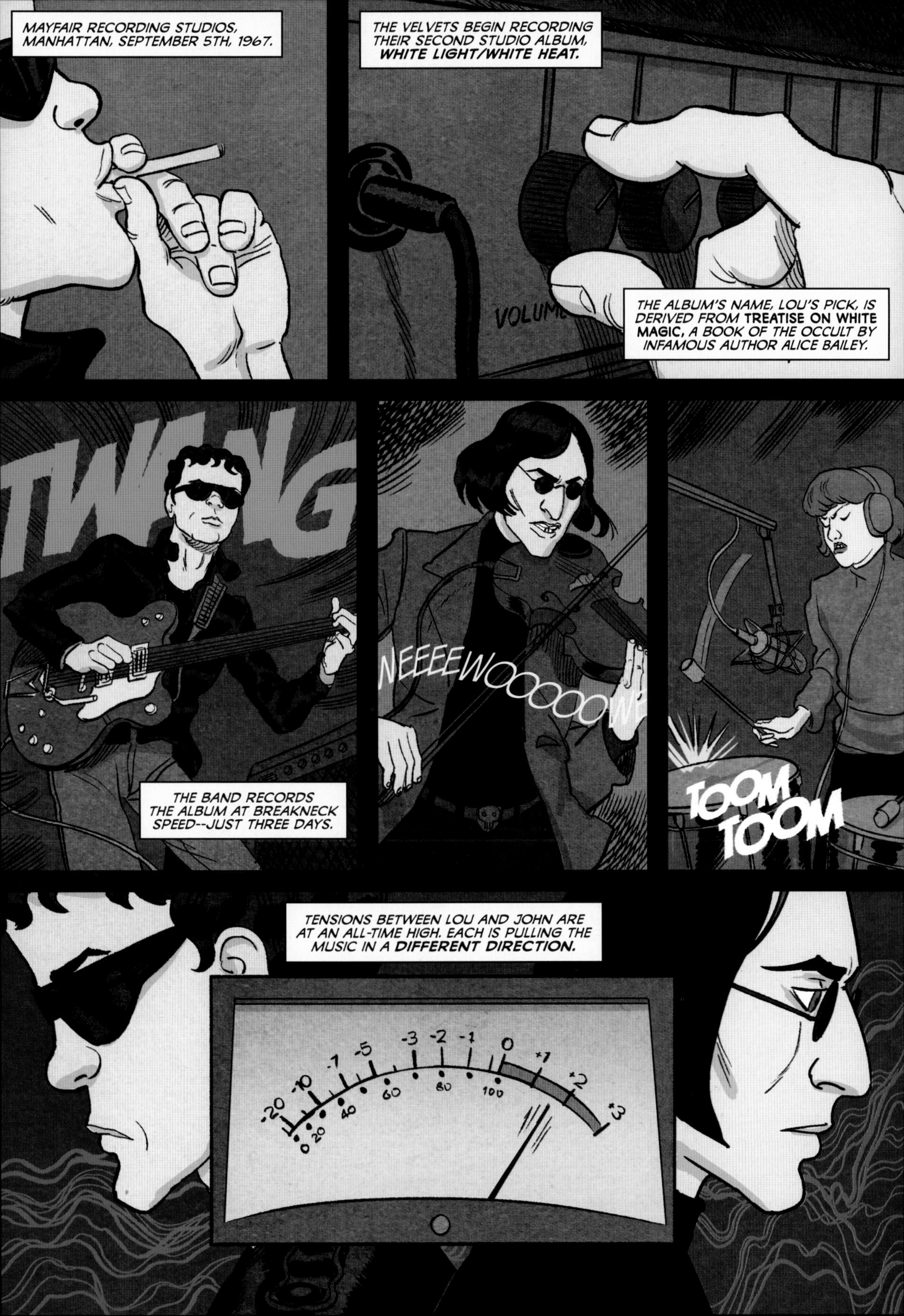
MAYFAIR RECORDING STUDIOS, MANHATTAN, SEPTEMBER 5TH, 1967.
THE VELVETS BEGIN RECORDING THEIR SECOND STUDIO ALBUM, **WHITE LIGHT/WHITE HEAT.**
VOLUME
THE ALBUM'S NAME, LOU'S PICK, IS DERIVED FROM **TREATISE ON WHITE MAGIC**, A BOOK OF THE OCCULT BY INFAMOUS AUTHOR ALICE BAILEY.
TWANG
THE BAND RECORDS THE ALBUM AT BREAKNECK SPEED--JUST THREE DAYS.
NEEEEWOOOOOOW
TOOM TOOM
TENSIONS BETWEEN LOU AND JOHN ARE AT AN ALL-TIME HIGH. EACH IS PULLING THE MUSIC IN A **DIFFERENT DIRECTION.**
-20 -10 -7 -5 -3 -2 -1 0 +1 +2 +3
0 20 40 60 80 100

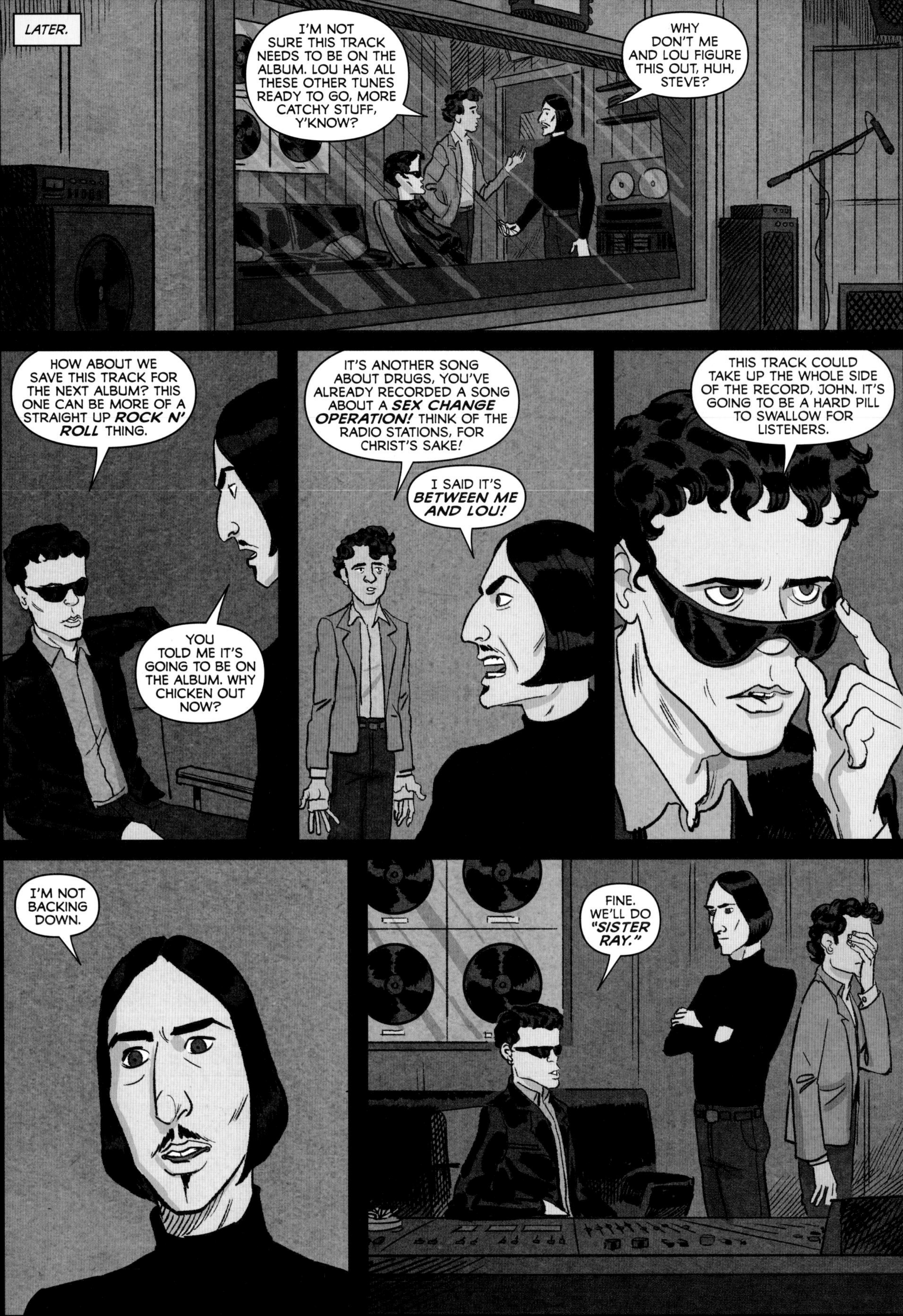

LATER.
I'M NOT SURE THIS TRACK NEEDS TO BE ON THE ALBUM. LOU HAS ALL THESE OTHER TUNES READY TO GO, MORE CATCHY STUFF, Y'KNOW?
WHY DON'T ME AND LOU FIGURE THIS OUT, HUH, STEVE?
HOW ABOUT WE SAVE THIS TRACK FOR THE NEXT ALBUM? THIS ONE CAN BE MORE OF A STRAIGHT UP ROCK N' ROLL THING.
YOU TOLD ME IT'S GOING TO BE ON THE ALBUM. WHY CHICKEN OUT NOW?
IT'S ANOTHER SONG ABOUT DRUGS, YOU'VE ALREADY RECORDED A SONG ABOUT A SEX CHANGE OPERATION! THINK OF THE RADIO STATIONS, FOR CHRIST'S SAKE!
I SAID IT'S BETWEEN ME AND LOU!
THIS TRACK COULD TAKE UP THE WHOLE SIDE OF THE RECORD, JOHN. IT'S GOING TO BE A HARD PILL TO SWALLOW FOR LISTENERS.
I'M NOT BACKING DOWN.
FINE. WE'LL DO "SISTER RAY."

BLANG ♪ BLANG BLING ♫

TOOM TOOM TOOM

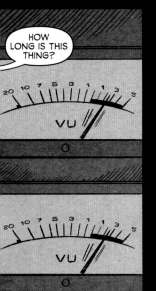

VU
20 10 7 5 3 1 1 3 5
0

VU
20 10 7 5 3 1 1 3 5
0

HOW LONG IS THIS THING?

YOU GUYS ARE *IN THE RED* AGAIN, *WAYYY IN THE RED.* THERE'S MAJOR *LEAKAGE.* I CAN'T MAKE HEADS OR TAILS OUT OF THIS.

I DON'T HAVE TO LISTEN TO THIS. I'M HITTING THE RECORD BUTTON. WHEN YOU'RE DONE, *YOU* TURN IT OFF.

THE RESULTING RECORD IS A FRENETIC, SPEED-INDUCED FEVER DREAM.

AFTER THE RECORDING SESSIONS ARE COMPLETED, LOU SNEAKS INTO THE STUDIO AND REMIXES THE SONG "I HEARD HER CALL MY NAME."

HE MAKES HIS VOCALS MORE PROMINENT, DOWNPLAYING *THE REST* OF THE BAND'S WORK.

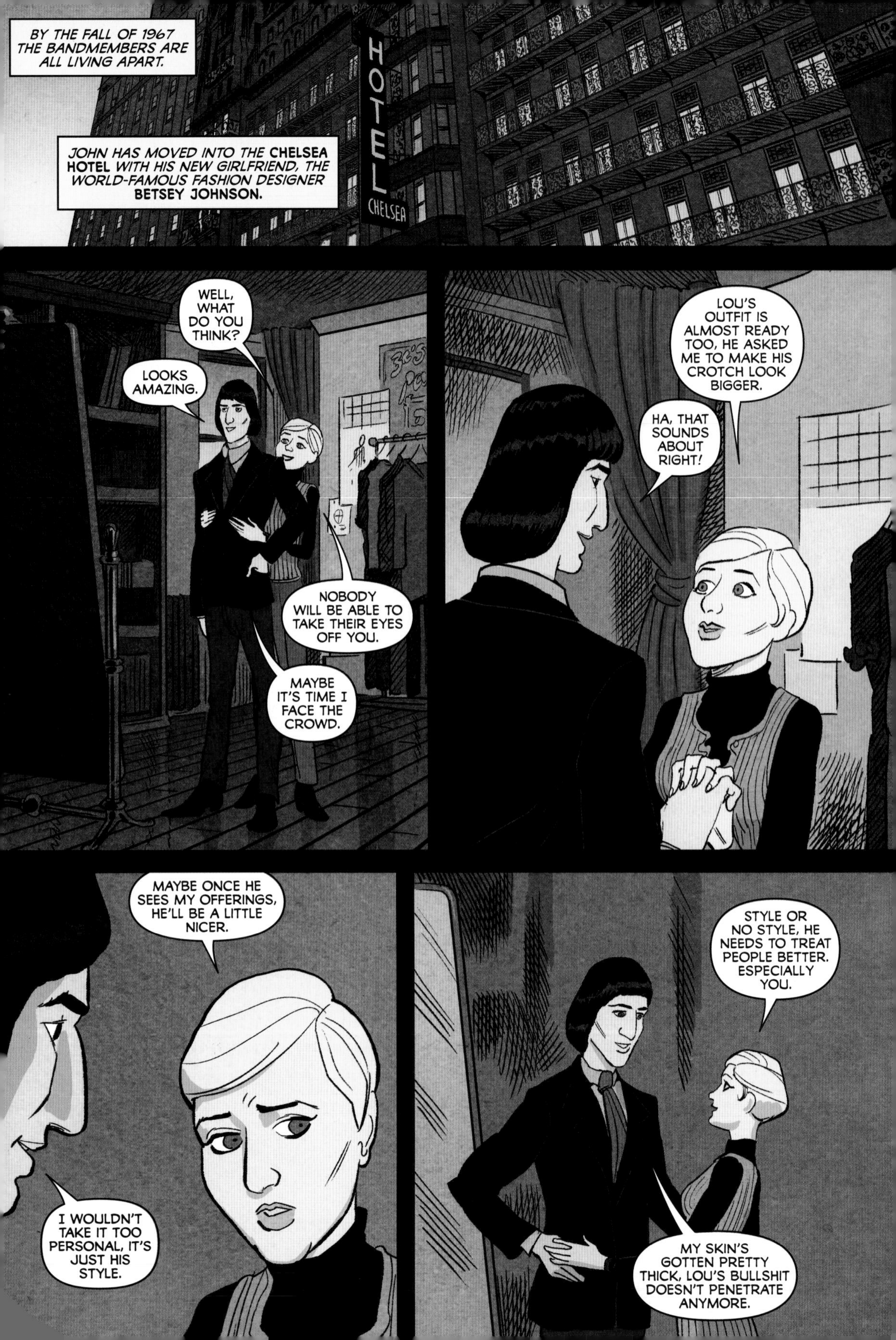
BY THE FALL OF 1967 THE BANDMEMBERS ARE ALL LIVING APART.
JOHN HAS MOVED INTO THE CHELSEA HOTEL WITH HIS NEW GIRLFRIEND, THE WORLD-FAMOUS FASHION DESIGNER BETSEY JOHNSON.
HOTEL
CHELSEA
WELL, WHAT DO YOU THINK?
LOOKS AMAZING.
NOBODY WILL BE ABLE TO TAKE THEIR EYES OFF YOU.
MAYBE IT'S TIME I FACE THE CROWD.
LOU'S OUTFIT IS ALMOST READY TOO, HE ASKED ME TO MAKE HIS CROTCH LOOK BIGGER.
HA, THAT SOUNDS ABOUT RIGHT!
MAYBE ONCE HE SEES MY OFFERINGS, HE'LL BE A LITTLE NICER.
I WOULDN'T TAKE IT TOO PERSONAL, IT'S JUST HIS STYLE.
STYLE OR NO STYLE, HE NEEDS TO TREAT PEOPLE BETTER. ESPECIALLY YOU.
MY SKIN'S GOTTEN PRETTY THICK, LOU'S BULLSHIT DOESN'T PENETRATE ANYMORE.

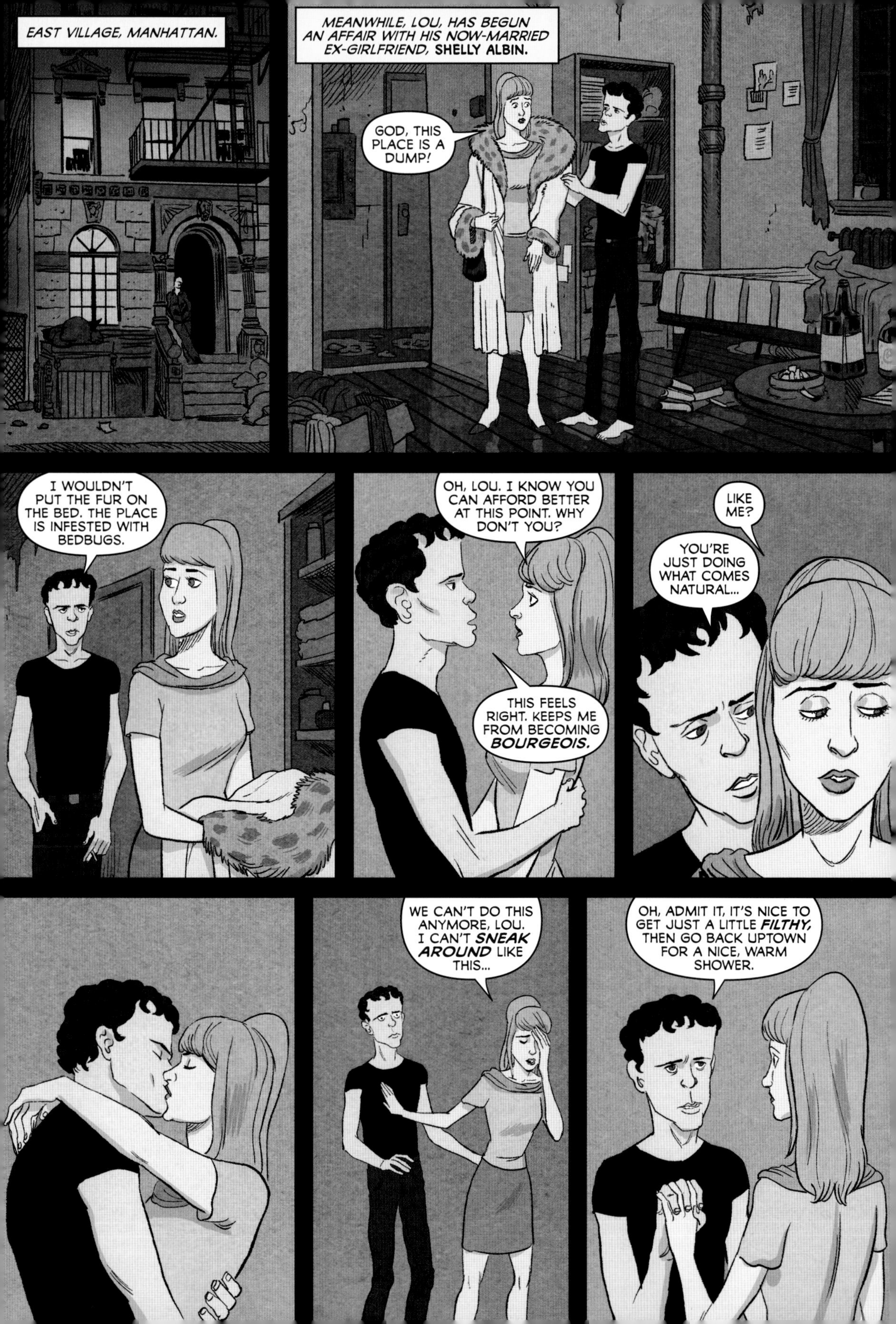

EAST VILLAGE, MANHATTAN.
MEANWHILE, LOU, HAS BEGUN AN AFFAIR WITH HIS NOW-MARRIED EX-GIRLFRIEND, SHELLY ALBIN.
GOD, THIS PLACE IS A DUMP!
I WOULDN'T PUT THE FUR ON THE BED. THE PLACE IS INFESTED WITH BEDBUGS.
OH, LOU. I KNOW YOU CAN AFFORD BETTER AT THIS POINT. WHY DON'T YOU?
THIS FEELS RIGHT. KEEPS ME FROM BECOMING *BOURGEOIS.*
LIKE ME?
YOU'RE JUST DOING WHAT COMES NATURAL...
WE CAN'T DO THIS ANYMORE, LOU. I CAN'T *SNEAK AROUND* LIKE THIS...
OH, ADMIT IT, IT'S NICE TO GET JUST A LITTLE *FILTHY,* THEN GO BACK UPTOWN FOR A NICE, WARM SHOWER.

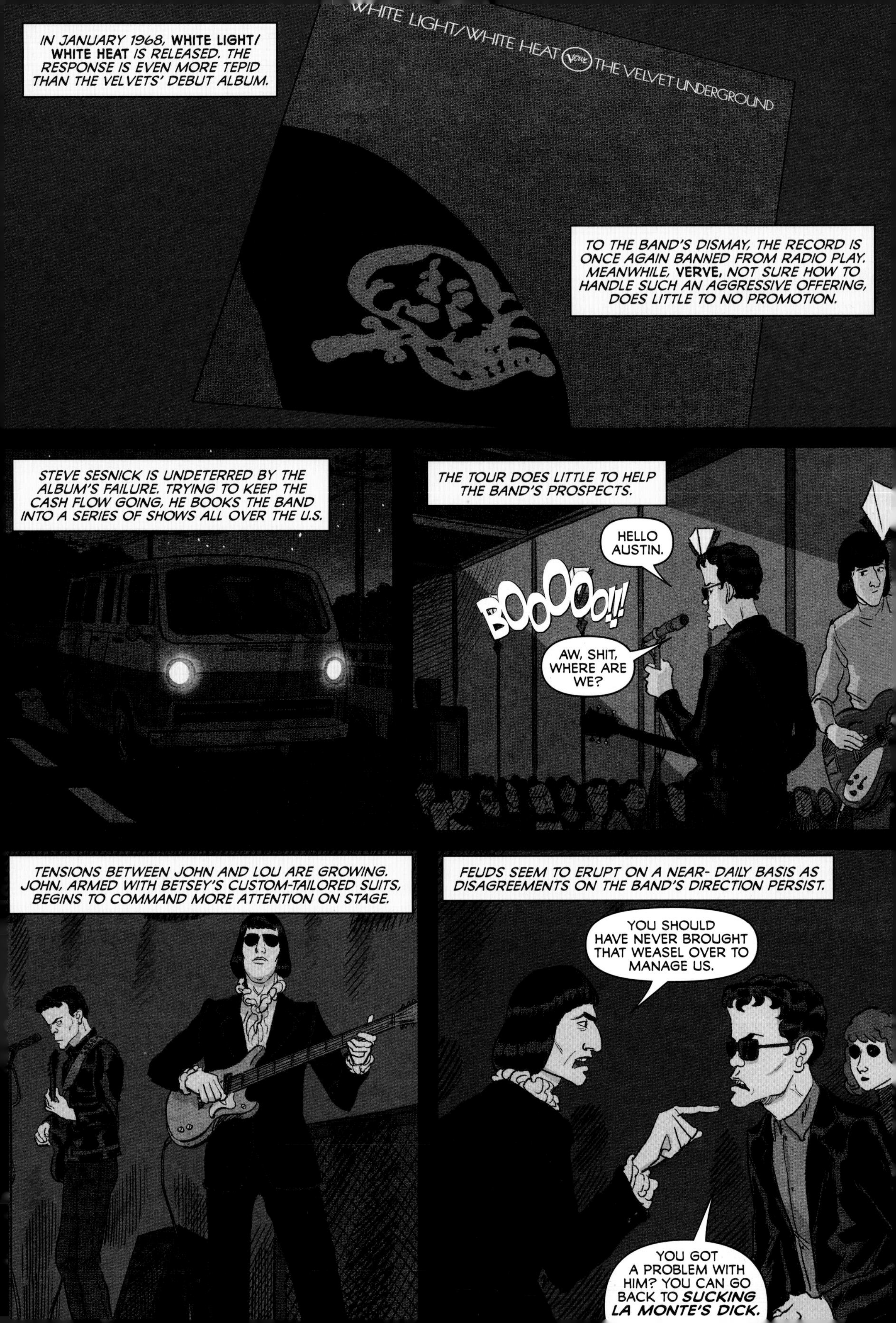
IN JANUARY 1968, WHITE LIGHT/ WHITE HEAT IS RELEASED. THE RESPONSE IS EVEN MORE TEPID THAN THE VELVETS' DEBUT ALBUM.
WHITE LIGHT/WHITE HEAT Verve THE VELVET UNDERGROUND
TO THE BAND'S DISMAY, THE RECORD IS ONCE AGAIN BANNED FROM RADIO PLAY. MEANWHILE, VERVE, NOT SURE HOW TO HANDLE SUCH AN AGGRESSIVE OFFERING, DOES LITTLE TO NO PROMOTION.
STEVE SESNICK IS UNDETERRED BY THE ALBUM'S FAILURE. TRYING TO KEEP THE CASH FLOW GOING, HE BOOKS THE BAND INTO A SERIES OF SHOWS ALL OVER THE U.S.
THE TOUR DOES LITTLE TO HELP THE BAND'S PROSPECTS.
HELLO AUSTIN.
BOOOOO!!!
AW, SHIT, WHERE ARE WE?
TENSIONS BETWEEN JOHN AND LOU ARE GROWING. JOHN, ARMED WITH BETSEY'S CUSTOM-TAILORED SUITS, BEGINS TO COMMAND MORE ATTENTION ON STAGE.
FEUDS SEEM TO ERUPT ON A NEAR- DAILY BASIS AS DISAGREEMENTS ON THE BAND'S DIRECTION PERSIST.
YOU SHOULD HAVE NEVER BROUGHT THAT WEASEL OVER TO MANAGE US.
YOU GOT A PROBLEM WITH HIM? YOU CAN GO BACK TO SUCKING LA MONTE'S DICK.

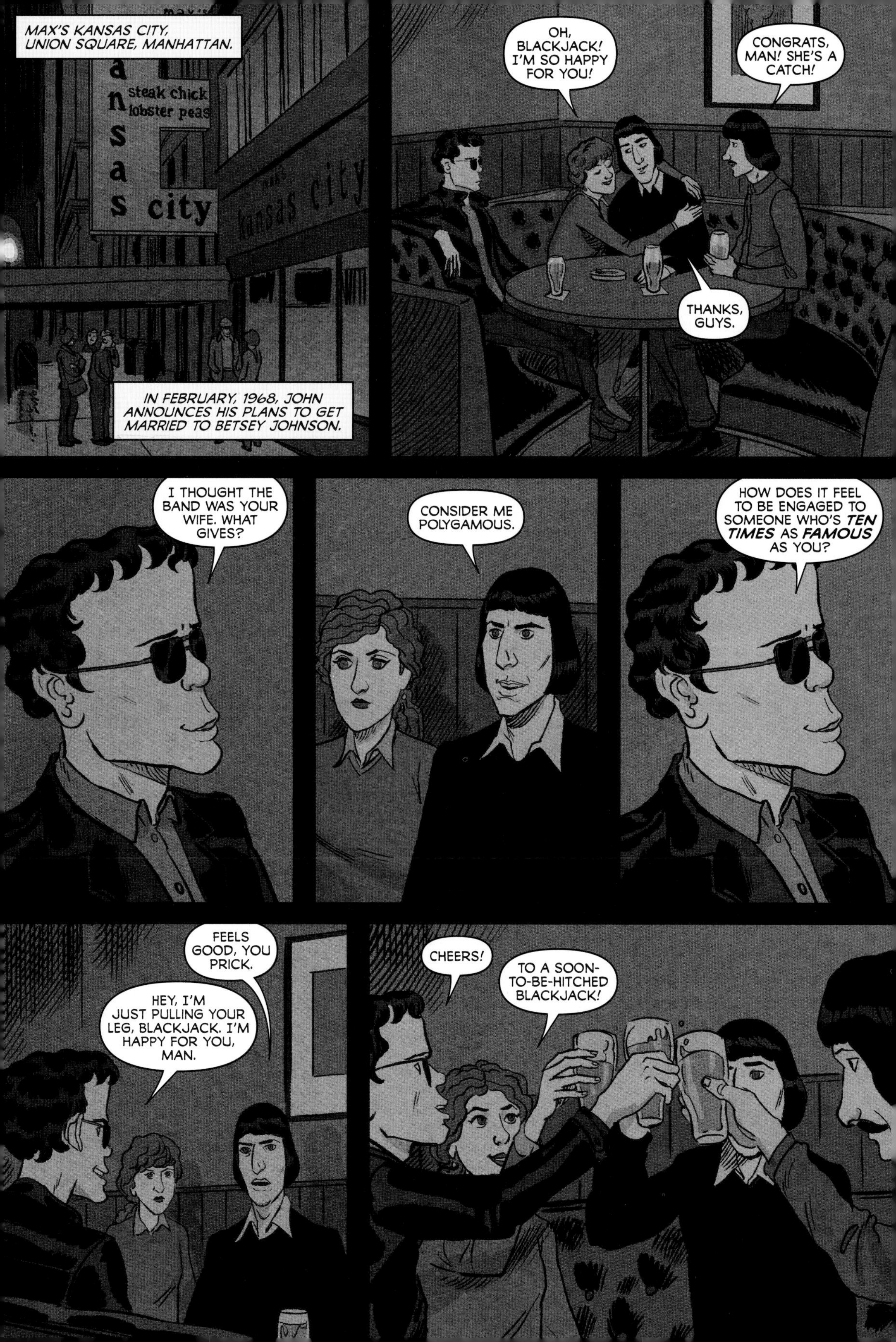
MAX'S KANSAS CITY, UNION SQUARE, MANHATTAN.
steak chick lobster peas
kansas city
IN FEBRUARY, 1968, JOHN ANNOUNCES HIS PLANS TO GET MARRIED TO BETSEY JOHNSON.
OH, BLACKJACK! I'M SO HAPPY FOR YOU!
CONGRATS, MAN! SHE'S A CATCH!
THANKS, GUYS.
I THOUGHT THE BAND WAS YOUR WIFE. WHAT GIVES?
CONSIDER ME POLYGAMOUS.
HOW DOES IT FEEL TO BE ENGAGED TO SOMEONE WHO'S *TEN TIMES* AS *FAMOUS* AS YOU?
FEELS GOOD, YOU PRICK.
HEY, I'M JUST PULLING YOUR LEG, BLACKJACK. I'M HAPPY FOR YOU, MAN.
CHEERS!
TO A SOON-TO-BE-HITCHED BLACKJACK!

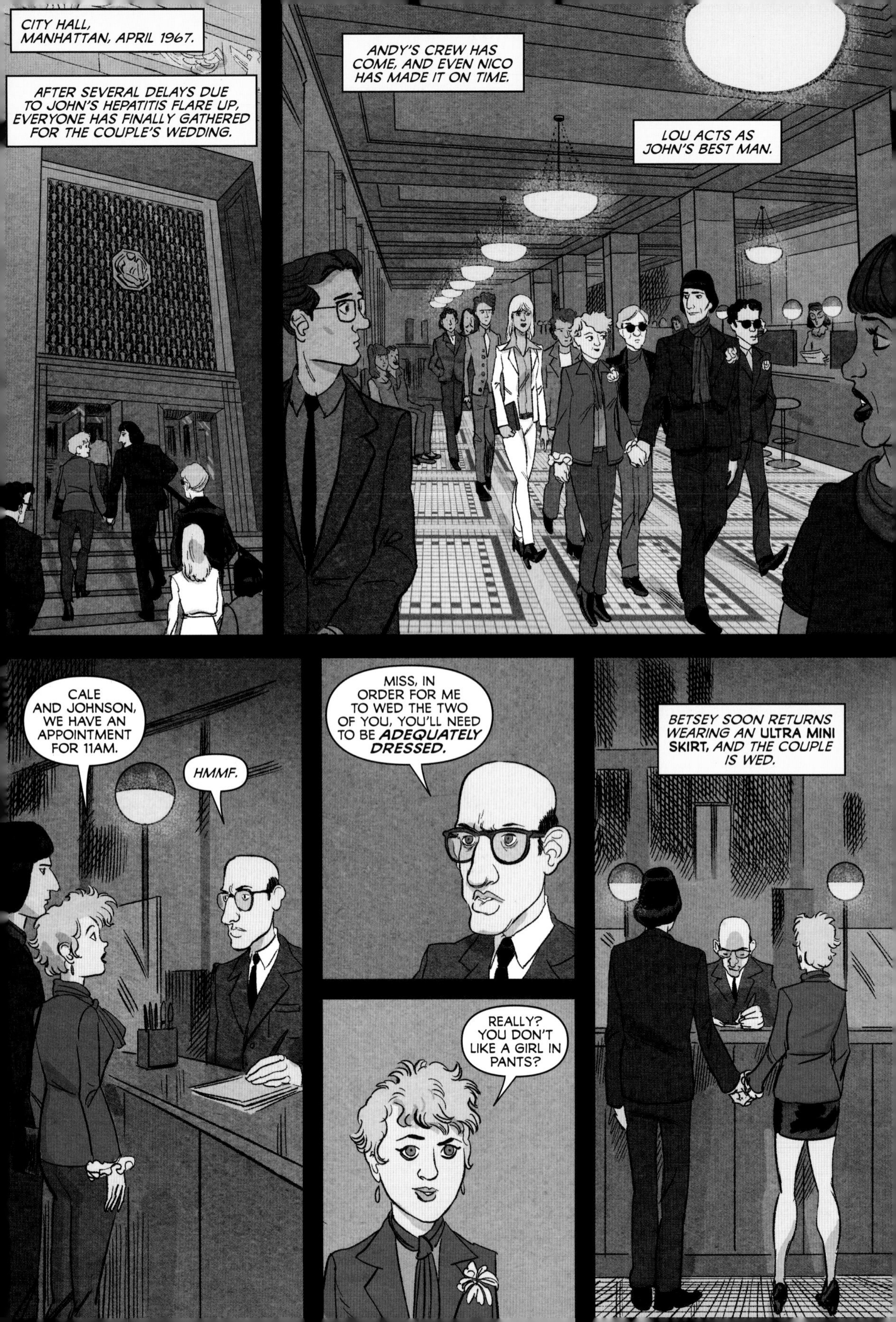
CITY HALL, MANHATTAN, APRIL 1967.
AFTER SEVERAL DELAYS DUE TO JOHN'S HEPATITIS FLARE UP, EVERYONE HAS FINALLY GATHERED FOR THE COUPLE'S WEDDING.
ANDY'S CREW HAS COME, AND EVEN NICO HAS MADE IT ON TIME.
LOU ACTS AS JOHN'S BEST MAN.
CALE AND JOHNSON, WE HAVE AN APPOINTMENT FOR 11AM.
HMMF.
MISS, IN ORDER FOR ME TO WED THE TWO OF YOU, YOU'LL NEED TO BE ADEQUATELY DRESSED.
REALLY? YOU DON'T LIKE A GIRL IN PANTS?
BETSEY SOON RETURNS WEARING AN ULTRA MINI SKIRT, AND THE COUPLE IS WED.

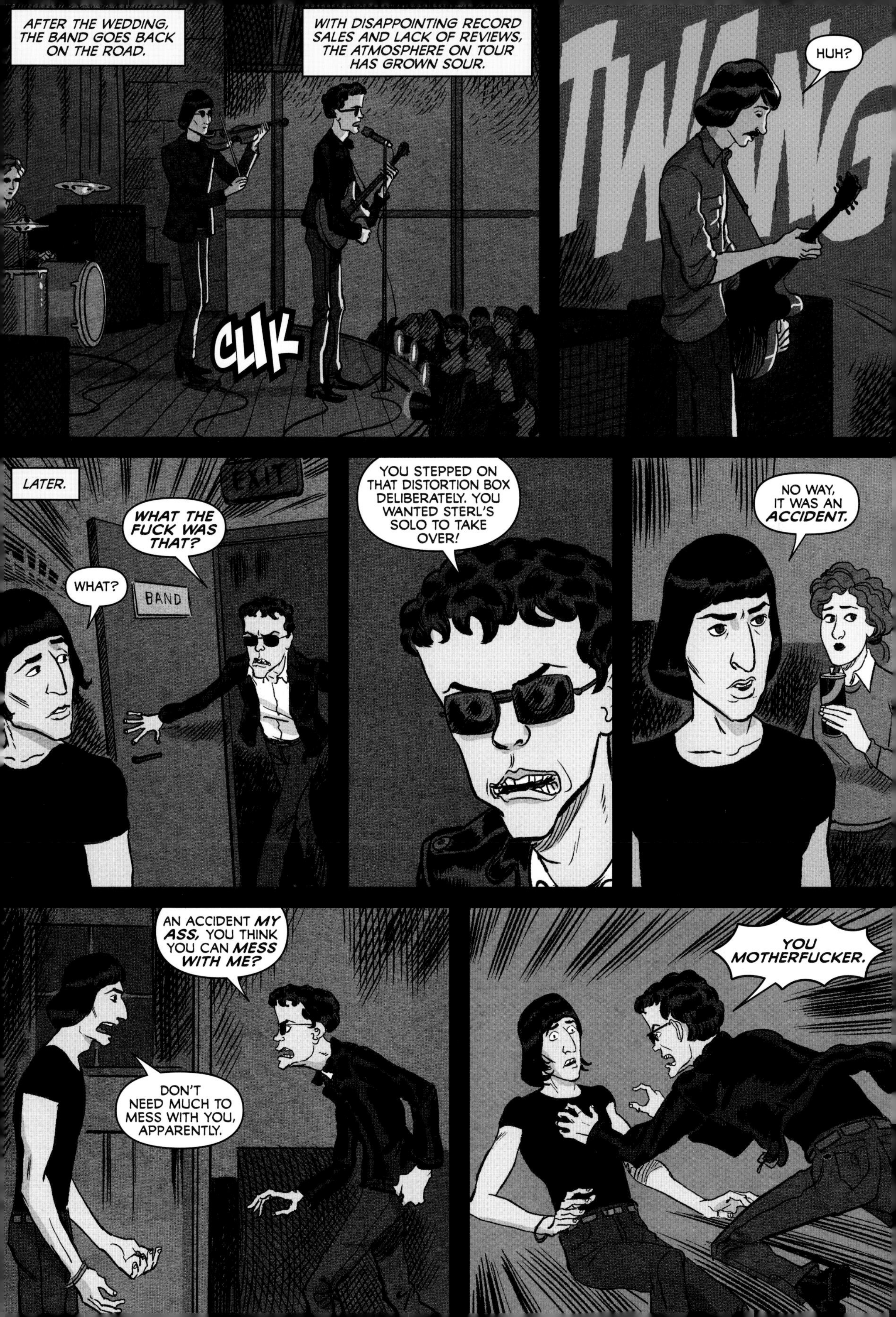
AFTER THE WEDDING, THE BAND GOES BACK ON THE ROAD.
WITH DISAPPOINTING RECORD SALES AND LACK OF REVIEWS, THE ATMOSPHERE ON TOUR HAS GROWN SOUR.
CLIK
TWANG
HUH?
LATER.
EXIT
WHAT THE FUCK WAS THAT?
WHAT?
BAND
YOU STEPPED ON THAT DISTORTION BOX DELIBERATELY. YOU WANTED STERL'S SOLO TO TAKE OVER!
NO WAY, IT WAS AN ACCIDENT.
AN ACCIDENT MY ASS, YOU THINK YOU CAN MESS WITH ME?
DON'T NEED MUCH TO MESS WITH YOU, APPARENTLY.
YOU MOTHERFUCKER.

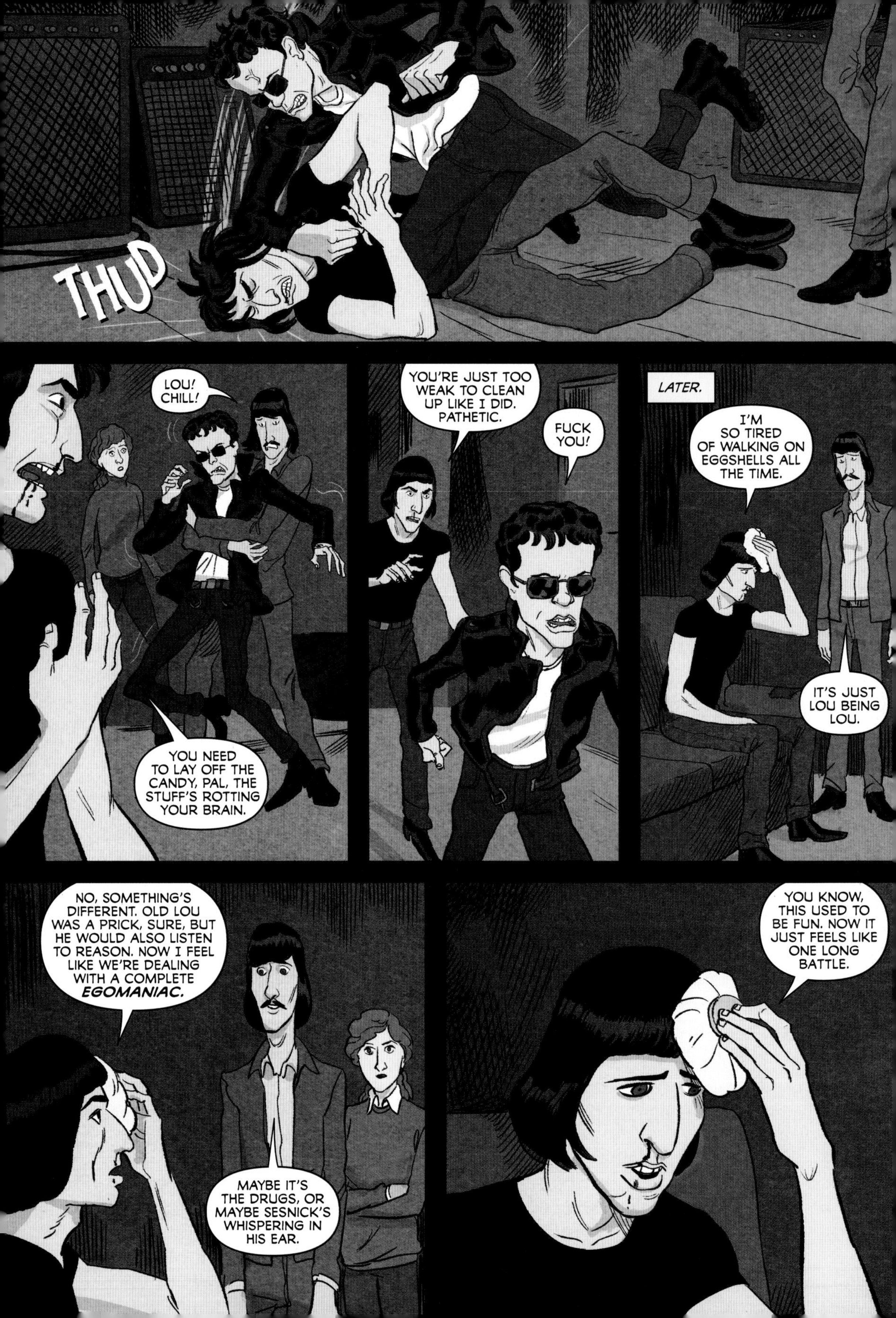
THUD
LOU! CHILL!
YOU NEED TO LAY OFF THE CANDY, PAL, THE STUFF'S ROTTING YOUR BRAIN.
YOU'RE JUST TOO WEAK TO CLEAN UP LIKE I DID. PATHETIC.
FUCK YOU!
LATER.
I'M SO TIRED OF WALKING ON EGGSHELLS ALL THE TIME.
IT'S JUST LOU BEING LOU.
NO, SOMETHING'S DIFFERENT. OLD LOU WAS A PRICK, SURE, BUT HE WOULD ALSO LISTEN TO REASON. NOW I FEEL LIKE WE'RE DEALING WITH A COMPLETE *EGOMANIAC.*
MAYBE IT'S THE DRUGS, OR MAYBE SESNICK'S WHISPERING IN HIS EAR.
YOU KNOW, THIS USED TO BE FUN. NOW IT JUST FEELS LIKE ONE LONG BATTLE.

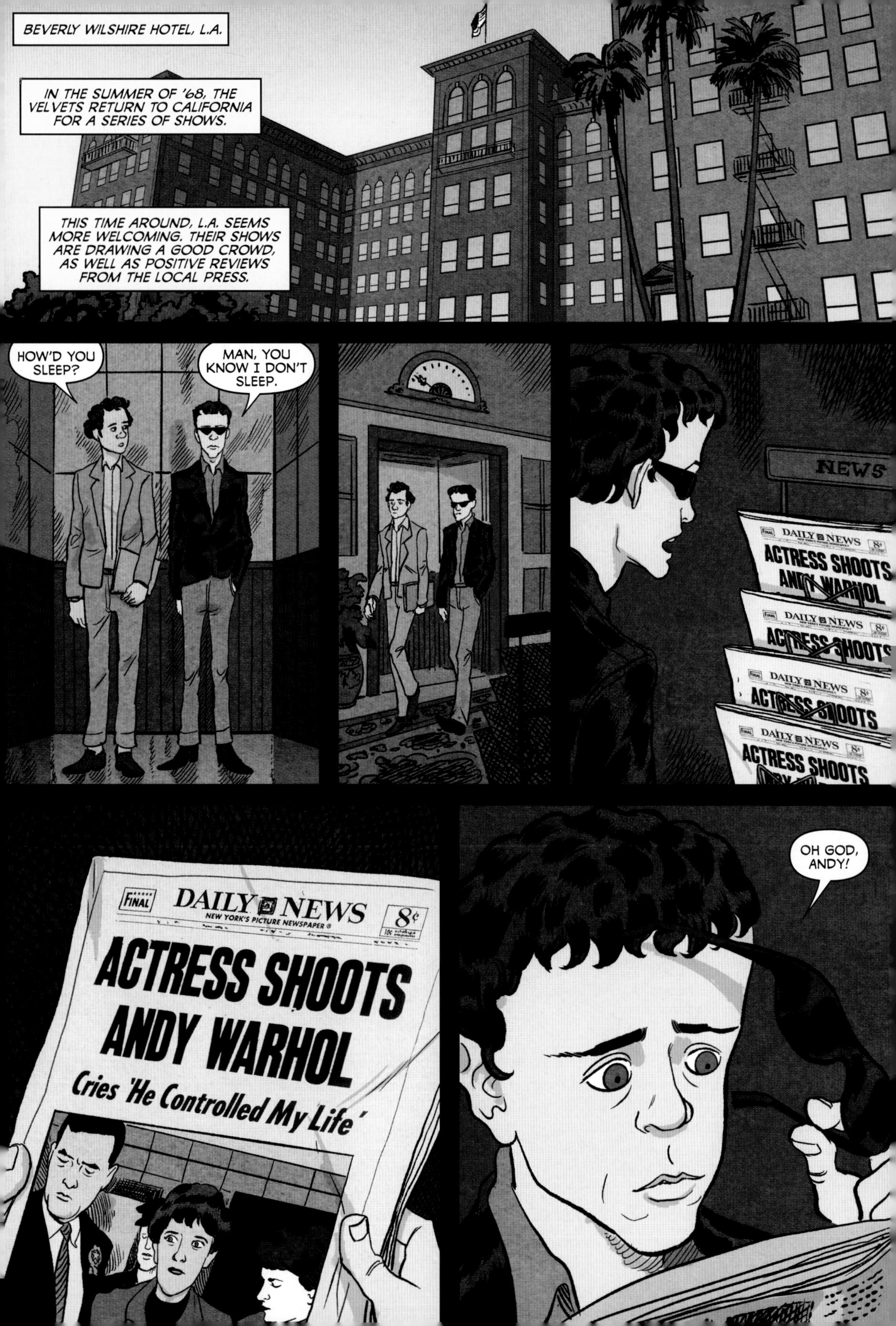
BEVERLY WILSHIRE HOTEL, L.A.
IN THE SUMMER OF '68, THE VELVETS RETURN TO CALIFORNIA FOR A SERIES OF SHOWS.
THIS TIME AROUND, L.A. SEEMS MORE WELCOMING. THEIR SHOWS ARE DRAWING A GOOD CROWD, AS WELL AS POSITIVE REVIEWS FROM THE LOCAL PRESS.
HOW'D YOU SLEEP?
MAN, YOU KNOW I DON'T SLEEP.
NEWS
DAILY NEWS
ACTRESS SHOOTS ANDY WARHOL
FINAL
DAILY NEWS
NEW YORK'S PICTURE NEWSPAPER
8¢
ACTRESS SHOOTS ANDY WARHOL
Cries 'He Controlled My Life'
OH GOD, ANDY!

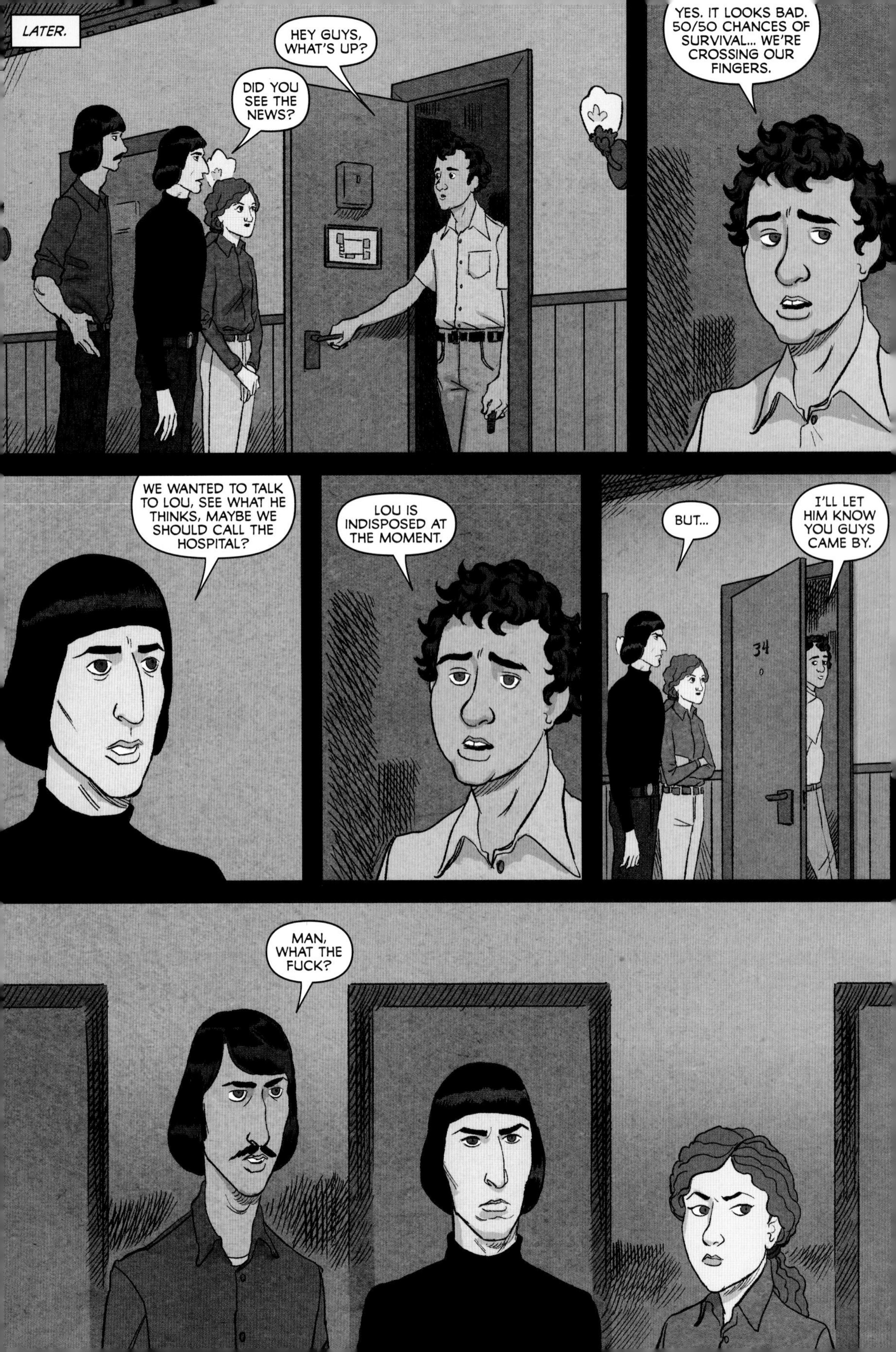
LATER.
HEY GUYS, WHAT'S UP?
DID YOU SEE THE NEWS?
YES. IT LOOKS BAD. 50/50 CHANCES OF SURVIVAL... WE'RE CROSSING OUR FINGERS.
WE WANTED TO TALK TO LOU, SEE WHAT HE THINKS, MAYBE WE SHOULD CALL THE HOSPITAL?
LOU IS INDISPOSED AT THE MOMENT.
BUT...
I'LL LET HIM KNOW YOU GUYS CAME BY.
34
MAN, WHAT THE FUCK?

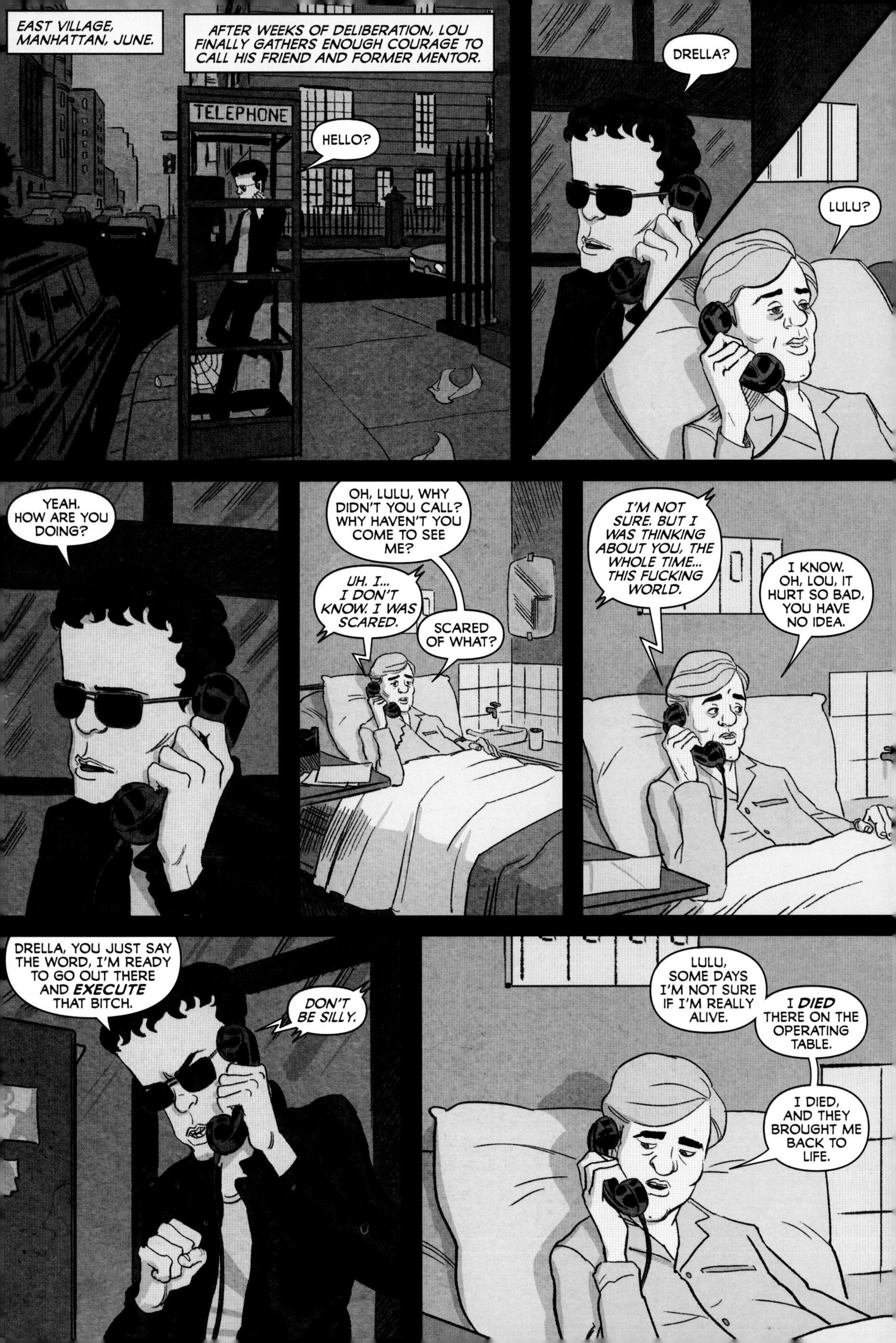
EAST VILLAGE, MANHATTAN, JUNE.
AFTER WEEKS OF DELIBERATION, LOU FINALLY GATHERS ENOUGH COURAGE TO CALL HIS FRIEND AND FORMER MENTOR.
TELEPHONE
HELLO?
DRELLA?
LULU?
YEAH. HOW ARE YOU DOING?
OH, LULU, WHY DIDN'T YOU CALL? WHY HAVEN'T YOU COME TO SEE ME?
UH. I... I DON'T KNOW. I WAS SCARED.
SCARED OF WHAT?
I'M NOT SURE. BUT I WAS THINKING ABOUT YOU, THE WHOLE TIME... THIS FUCKING WORLD.
I KNOW. OH, LOU, IT HURT SO BAD, YOU HAVE NO IDEA.
DRELLA, YOU JUST SAY THE WORD, I'M READY TO GO OUT THERE AND EXECUTE THAT BITCH.
DON'T BE SILLY.
LULU, SOME DAYS I'M NOT SURE IF I'M REALLY ALIVE.
I DIED THERE ON THE OPERATING TABLE.
I DIED, AND THEY BROUGHT ME BACK TO LIFE.

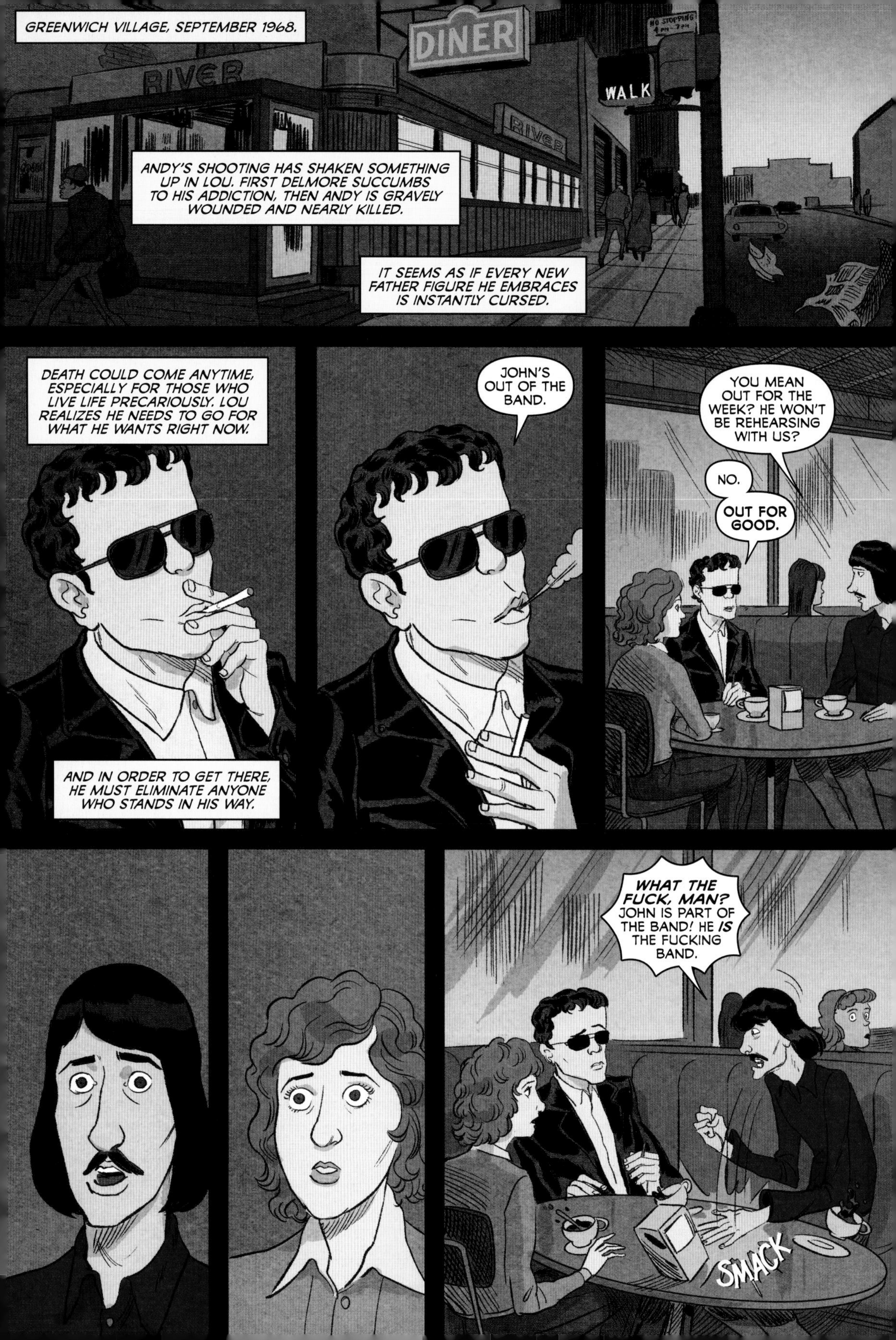
GREENWICH VILLAGE, SEPTEMBER 1968.
DINER
RIVER
NO STOPPING 4 PM–7 PM
WALK
ANDY'S SHOOTING HAS SHAKEN SOMETHING UP IN LOU. FIRST DELMORE SUCCUMBS TO HIS ADDICTION, THEN ANDY IS GRAVELY WOUNDED AND NEARLY KILLED.
IT SEEMS AS IF EVERY NEW FATHER FIGURE HE EMBRACES IS INSTANTLY CURSED.
DEATH COULD COME ANYTIME, ESPECIALLY FOR THOSE WHO LIVE LIFE PRECARIOUSLY. LOU REALIZES HE NEEDS TO GO FOR WHAT HE WANTS RIGHT NOW.
AND IN ORDER TO GET THERE, HE MUST ELIMINATE ANYONE WHO STANDS IN HIS WAY.
JOHN'S OUT OF THE BAND.
YOU MEAN OUT FOR THE WEEK? HE WON'T BE REHEARSING WITH US?
NO.
OUT FOR GOOD.
WHAT THE FUCK, MAN? JOHN IS PART OF THE BAND! HE IS THE FUCKING BAND.
SMACK

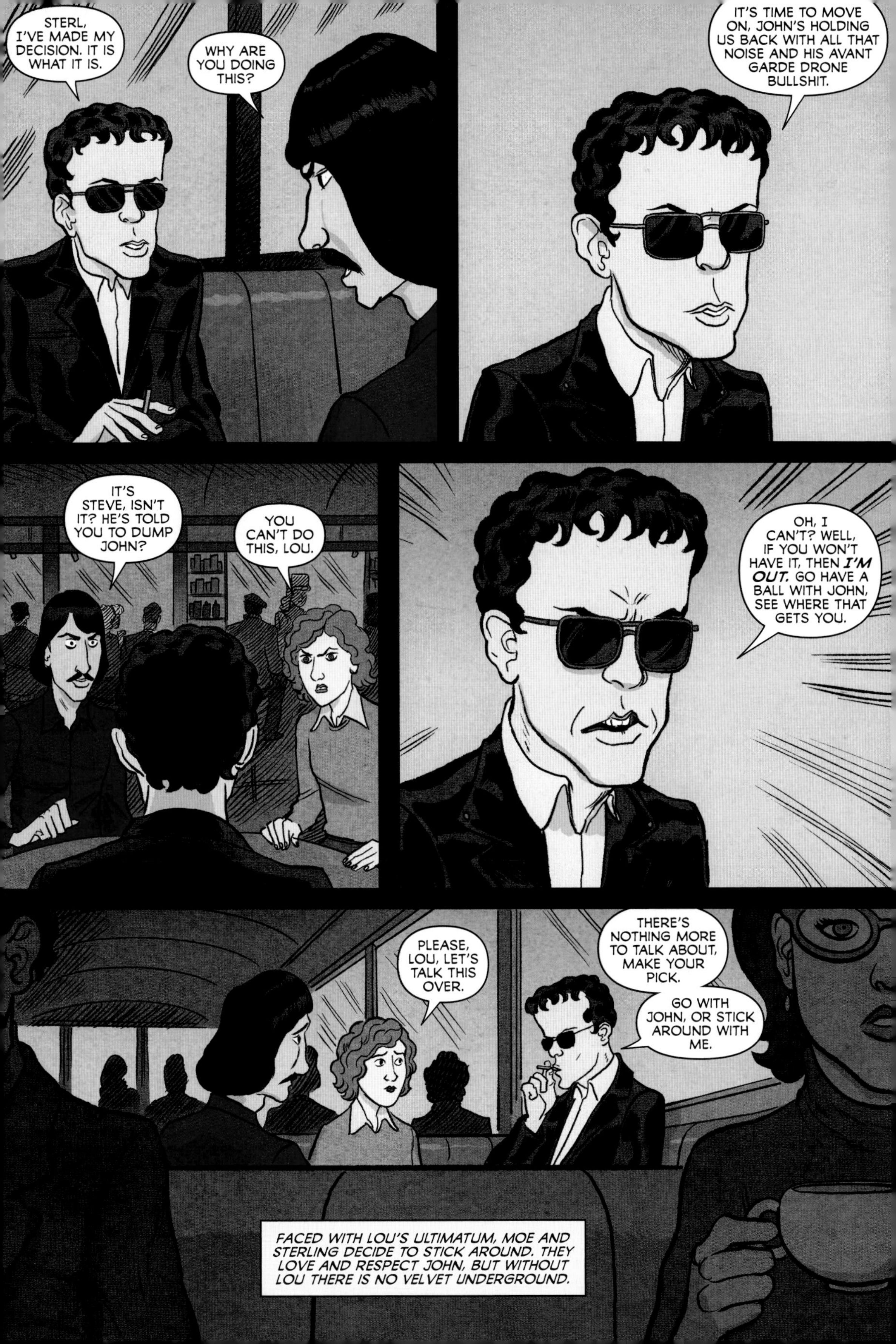
STERL, I'VE MADE MY DECISION. IT IS WHAT IT IS.
WHY ARE YOU DOING THIS?
IT'S TIME TO MOVE ON, JOHN'S HOLDING US BACK WITH ALL THAT NOISE AND HIS AVANT GARDE DRONE BULLSHIT.
IT'S STEVE, ISN'T IT? HE'S TOLD YOU TO DUMP JOHN?
YOU CAN'T DO THIS, LOU.
OH, I CAN'T? WELL, IF YOU WON'T HAVE IT, THEN ***I'M OUT.*** GO HAVE A BALL WITH JOHN, SEE WHERE THAT GETS YOU.
PLEASE, LOU, LET'S TALK THIS OVER.
THERE'S NOTHING MORE TO TALK ABOUT, MAKE YOUR PICK.
GO WITH JOHN, OR STICK AROUND WITH ME.
FACED WITH LOU'S ULTIMATUM, MOE AND STERLING DECIDE TO STICK AROUND. THEY LOVE AND RESPECT JOHN, BUT WITHOUT LOU THERE IS NO VELVET UNDERGROUND.

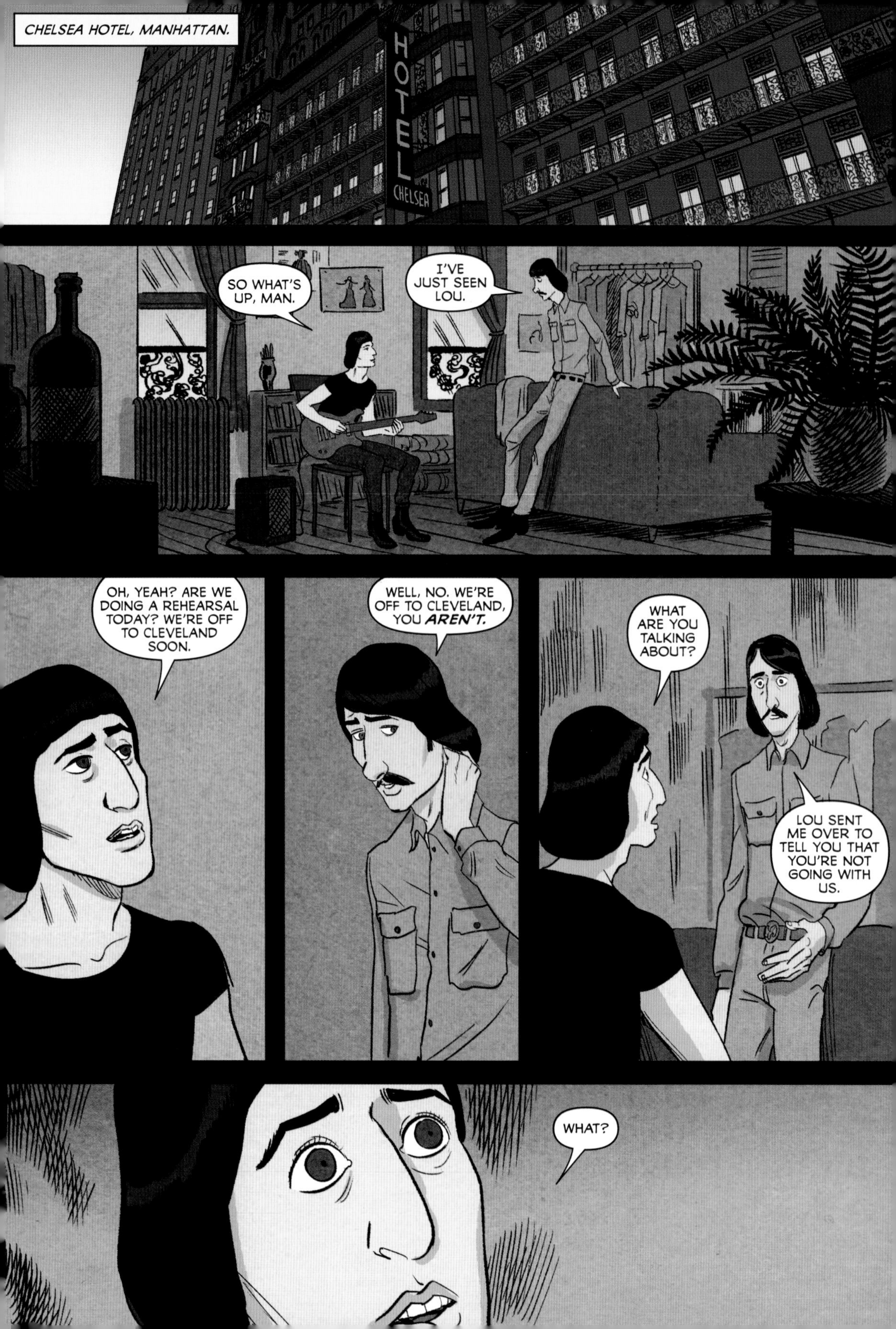
CHELSEA HOTEL, MANHATTAN.
HOTEL
CHELSEA
SO WHAT'S UP, MAN.
I'VE JUST SEEN LOU.
OH, YEAH? ARE WE DOING A REHEARSAL TODAY? WE'RE OFF TO CLEVELAND SOON.
WELL, NO. WE'RE OFF TO CLEVELAND, YOU AREN'T.
WHAT ARE YOU TALKING ABOUT?
LOU SENT ME OVER TO TELL YOU THAT YOU'RE NOT GOING WITH US.
WHAT?

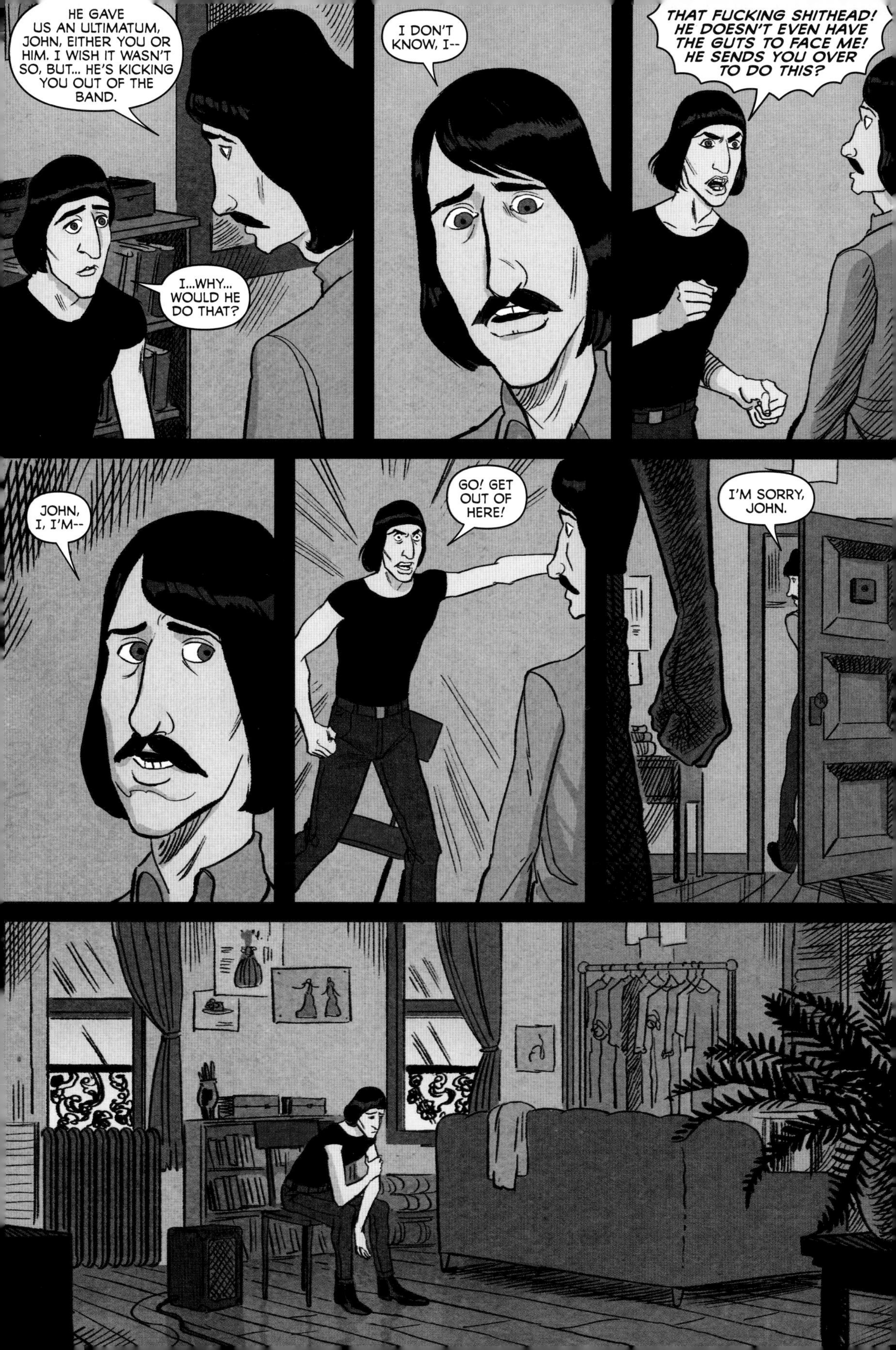
HE GAVE US AN ULTIMATUM, JOHN, EITHER YOU OR HIM. I WISH IT WASN'T SO, BUT... HE'S KICKING YOU OUT OF THE BAND.
I...WHY... WOULD HE DO THAT?
I DON'T KNOW, I--
THAT FUCKING SHITHEAD! HE DOESN'T EVEN HAVE THE GUTS TO FACE ME! HE SENDS YOU OVER TO DO THIS?
JOHN, I, I'M--
GO! GET OUT OF HERE!
I'M SORRY, JOHN.

NEW YORK
1970

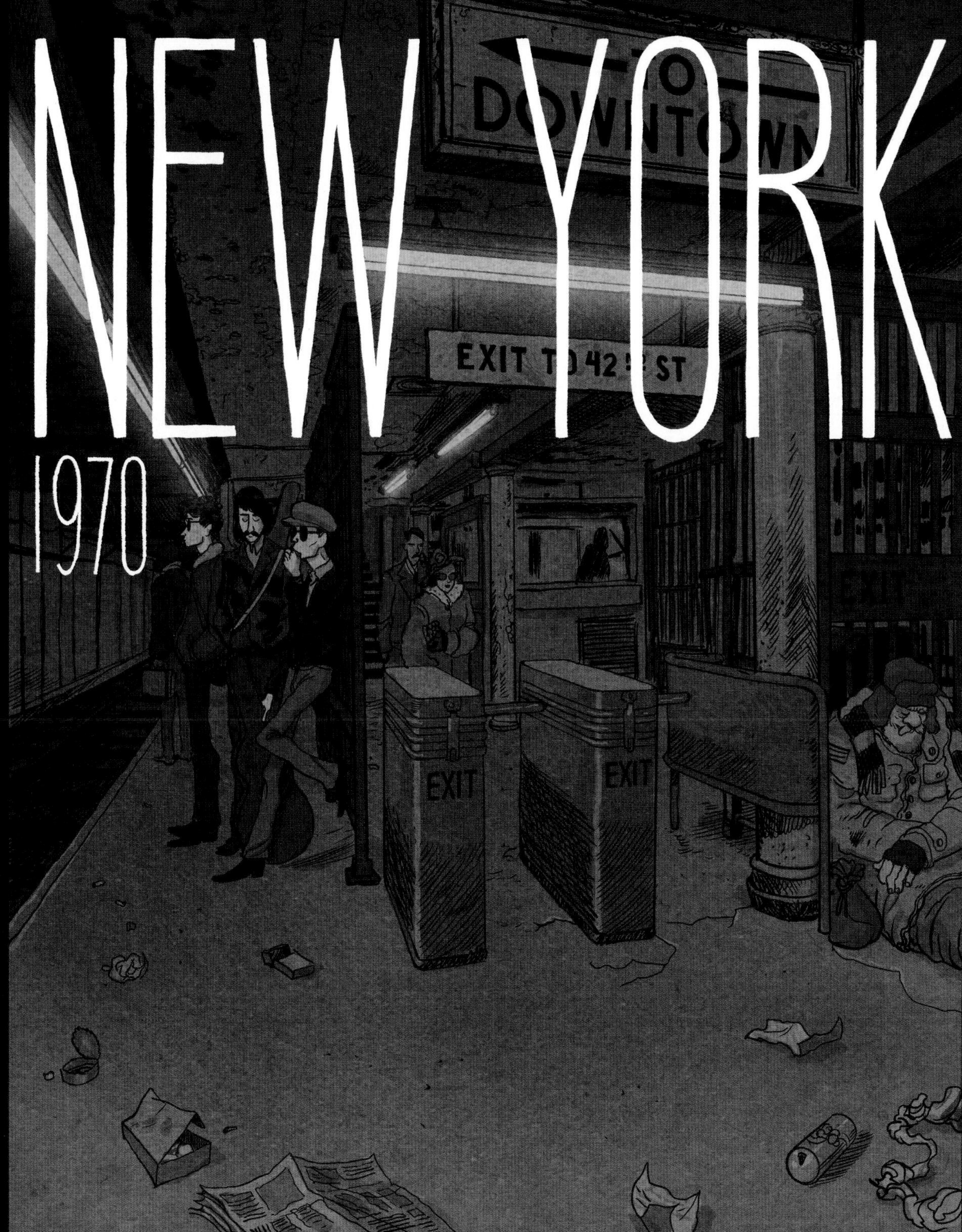
TO DOWNTOWN
EXIT TO 42ND ST
EXIT
EXIT

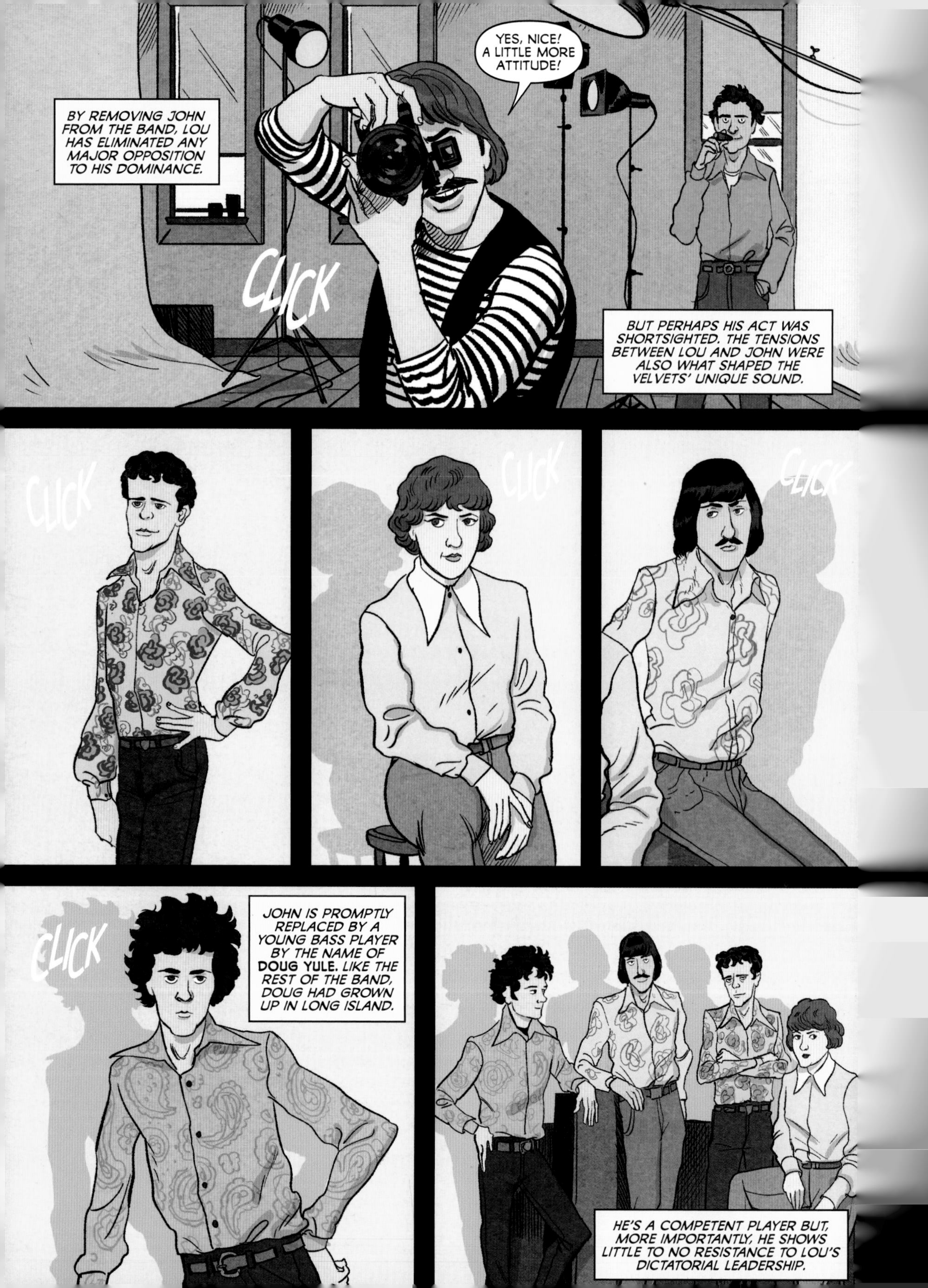
BY REMOVING JOHN FROM THE BAND, LOU HAS ELIMINATED ANY MAJOR OPPOSITION TO HIS DOMINANCE.
YES, NICE! A LITTLE MORE ATTITUDE!
CLICK
BUT PERHAPS HIS ACT WAS SHORTSIGHTED. THE TENSIONS BETWEEN LOU AND JOHN WERE ALSO WHAT SHAPED THE VELVETS' UNIQUE SOUND.
CLICK
CLICK
CLICK
CLICK
JOHN IS PROMPTLY REPLACED BY A YOUNG BASS PLAYER BY THE NAME OF DOUG YULE. LIKE THE REST OF THE BAND, DOUG HAD GROWN UP IN LONG ISLAND.
HE'S A COMPETENT PLAYER BUT, MORE IMPORTANTLY, HE SHOWS LITTLE TO NO RESISTANCE TO LOU'S DICTATORIAL LEADERSHIP.

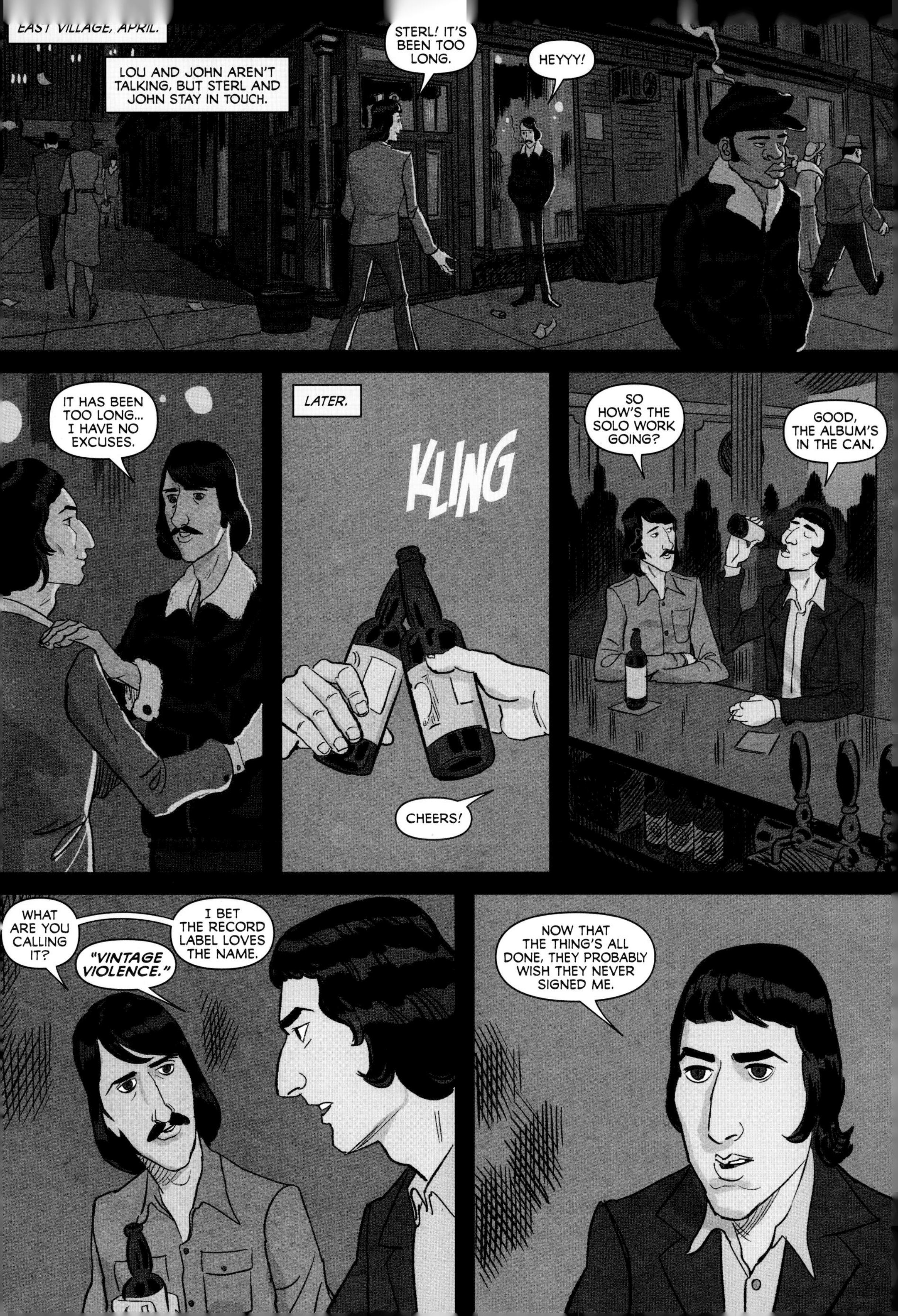
EAST VILLAGE, APRIL.
LOU AND JOHN AREN'T TALKING, BUT STERL AND JOHN STAY IN TOUCH.
STERL! IT'S BEEN TOO LONG.
HEYYY!
IT HAS BEEN TOO LONG... I HAVE NO EXCUSES.
LATER.
KLING
CHEERS!
SO HOW'S THE SOLO WORK GOING?
GOOD, THE ALBUM'S IN THE CAN.
WHAT ARE YOU CALLING IT?
"VINTAGE VIOLENCE."
I BET THE RECORD LABEL LOVES THE NAME.
NOW THAT THE THING'S ALL DONE, THEY PROBABLY WISH THEY NEVER SIGNED ME.

HOW'S THINGS WITH THE BAND?

SHIT... I DUNNO. MOE HAD TO TAKE SOME TIME OFF BEING *PREGNANT* AND ALL.

HER BELLY'S SO BIG SHE CAN'T EVEN REACH THE DRUMS.

WE'VE STARTED RECORDING THE NEXT ALBUM.

GOOD STUFF?

IT'S GOOD... YEAH, BUT IT ALMOST DOESN'T SOUND LIKE US.

IT'S LIKE THE LOU AND DOUG SHOW. I'VE KIND OF CHECKED MYSELF OUT, YOU KNOW? I JUST SHOW UP WHEN I FEEL LIKE IT.

IF I CAN'T HAVE A SAY, THEN...WELL, FUCK IT.

IT'S LIKE THEY'RE CONSPIRING TO TURN US INTO *THE CARPENTERS* OR SOMETHING.

I HEAR YA.

MAYBE SOME *LIGHTER* MATERIAL ISN'T ALL BAD?

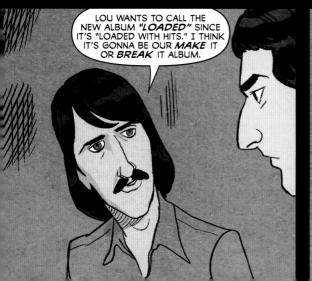

LOU WANTS TO CALL THE NEW ALBUM *"LOADED"* SINCE IT'S "LOADED WITH HITS." I THINK IT'S GONNA BE OUR *MAKE* IT OR *BREAK* IT ALBUM.

THEN AGAIN, LOU'S ALREADY *BROKEN* EVERYTHING, HASN'T HE? NOTHING LEFT BUT TO "MAKE IT."

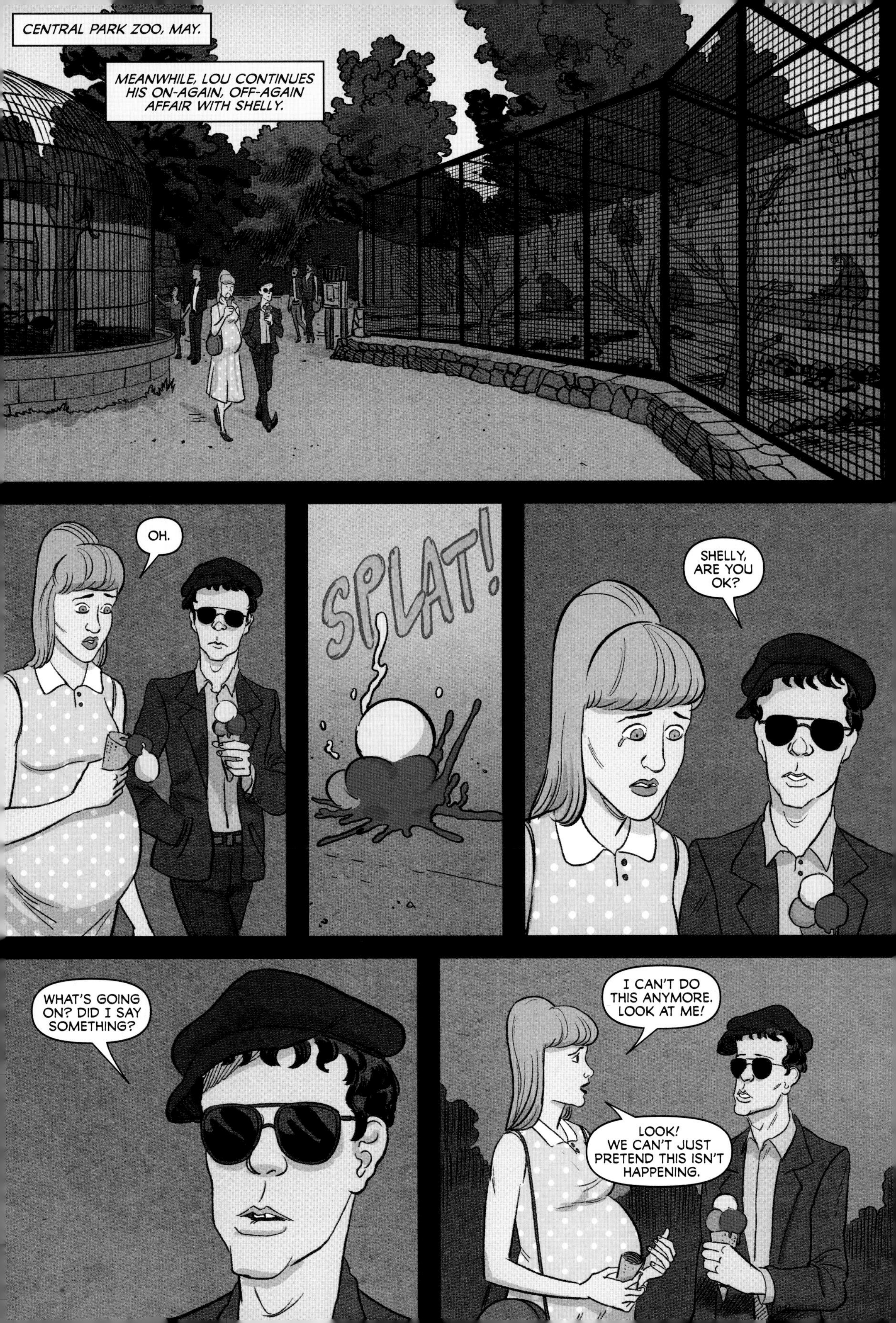
CENTRAL PARK ZOO, MAY.
MEANWHILE, LOU CONTINUES HIS ON-AGAIN, OFF-AGAIN AFFAIR WITH SHELLY.
OH.
SPLAT!
SHELLY, ARE YOU OK?
WHAT'S GOING ON? DID I SAY SOMETHING?
I CAN'T DO THIS ANYMORE. LOOK AT ME!
LOOK! WE CAN'T JUST PRETEND THIS ISN'T HAPPENING.

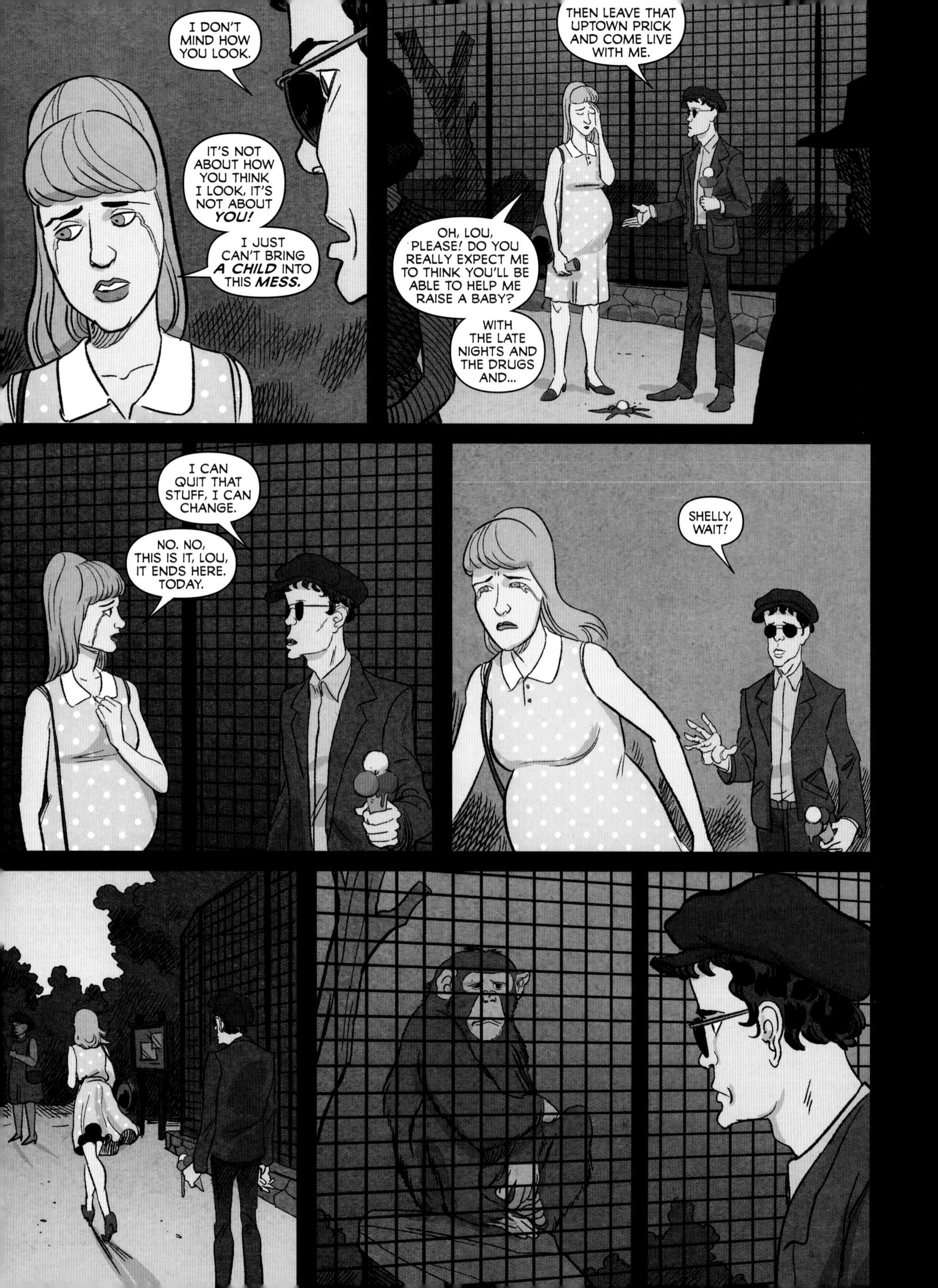
I DON'T MIND HOW YOU LOOK.
IT'S NOT ABOUT HOW YOU THINK I LOOK, IT'S NOT ABOUT *YOU!*
I JUST CAN'T BRING *A CHILD* INTO THIS *MESS.*
THEN LEAVE THAT UPTOWN PRICK AND COME LIVE WITH ME.
OH, LOU, PLEASE! DO YOU REALLY EXPECT ME TO THINK YOU'LL BE ABLE TO HELP ME RAISE A BABY?
WITH THE LATE NIGHTS AND THE DRUGS AND...
I CAN QUIT THAT STUFF, I CAN CHANGE.
NO. NO, THIS IS IT, LOU, IT ENDS HERE. TODAY.
SHELLY, WAIT!

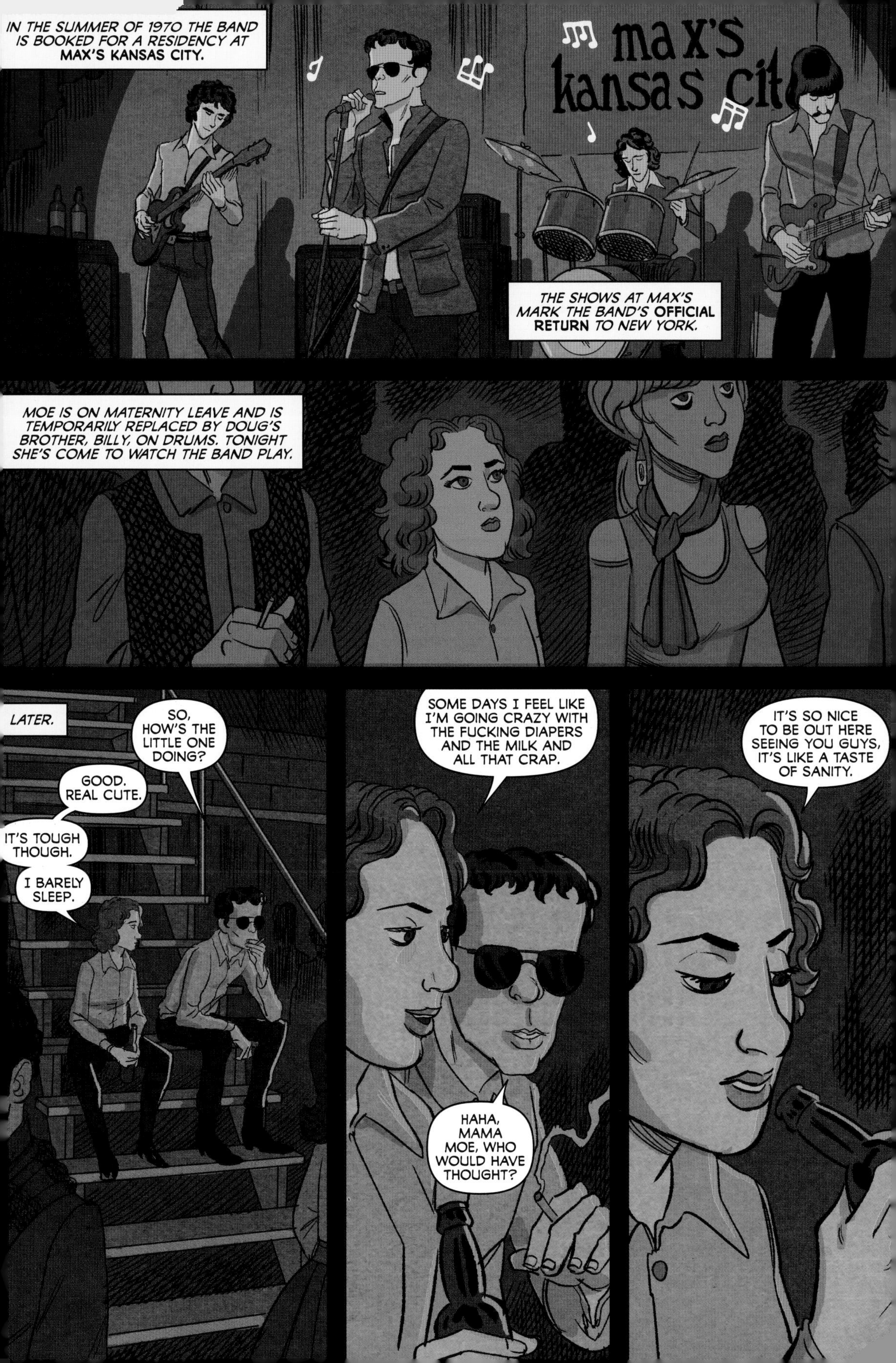
IN THE SUMMER OF 1970 THE BAND IS BOOKED FOR A RESIDENCY AT MAX'S KANSAS CITY.
max's kansas cit
THE SHOWS AT MAX'S MARK THE BAND'S OFFICIAL RETURN TO NEW YORK.
MOE IS ON MATERNITY LEAVE AND IS TEMPORARILY REPLACED BY DOUG'S BROTHER, BILLY, ON DRUMS. TONIGHT SHE'S COME TO WATCH THE BAND PLAY.
LATER.
SO, HOW'S THE LITTLE ONE DOING?
GOOD. REAL CUTE.
IT'S TOUGH THOUGH.
I BARELY SLEEP.
SOME DAYS I FEEL LIKE I'M GOING CRAZY WITH THE FUCKING DIAPERS AND THE MILK AND ALL THAT CRAP.
HAHA, MAMA MOE, WHO WOULD HAVE THOUGHT?
IT'S SO NICE TO BE OUT HERE SEEING YOU GUYS, IT'S LIKE A TASTE OF SANITY.

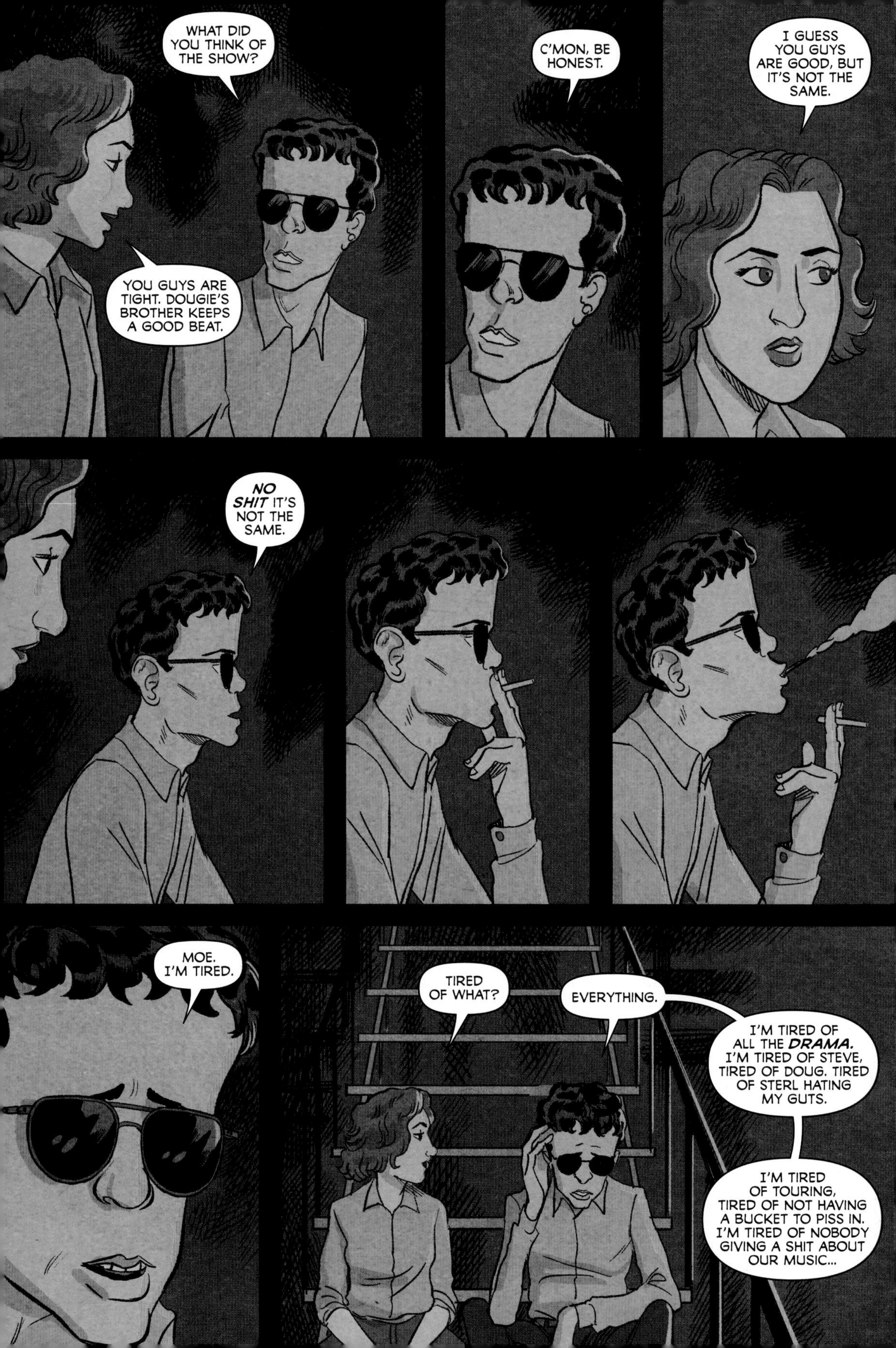
WHAT DID YOU THINK OF THE SHOW?
YOU GUYS ARE TIGHT. DOUGIE'S BROTHER KEEPS A GOOD BEAT.
C'MON, BE HONEST.
I GUESS YOU GUYS ARE GOOD, BUT IT'S NOT THE SAME.
NO SHIT IT'S NOT THE SAME.
MOE. I'M TIRED.
TIRED OF WHAT?
EVERYTHING.
I'M TIRED OF ALL THE ***DRAMA.*** I'M TIRED OF STEVE, TIRED OF DOUG. TIRED OF STERL HATING MY GUTS.
I'M TIRED OF TOURING, TIRED OF NOT HAVING A BUCKET TO PISS IN. I'M TIRED OF NOBODY GIVING A SHIT ABOUT OUR MUSIC...

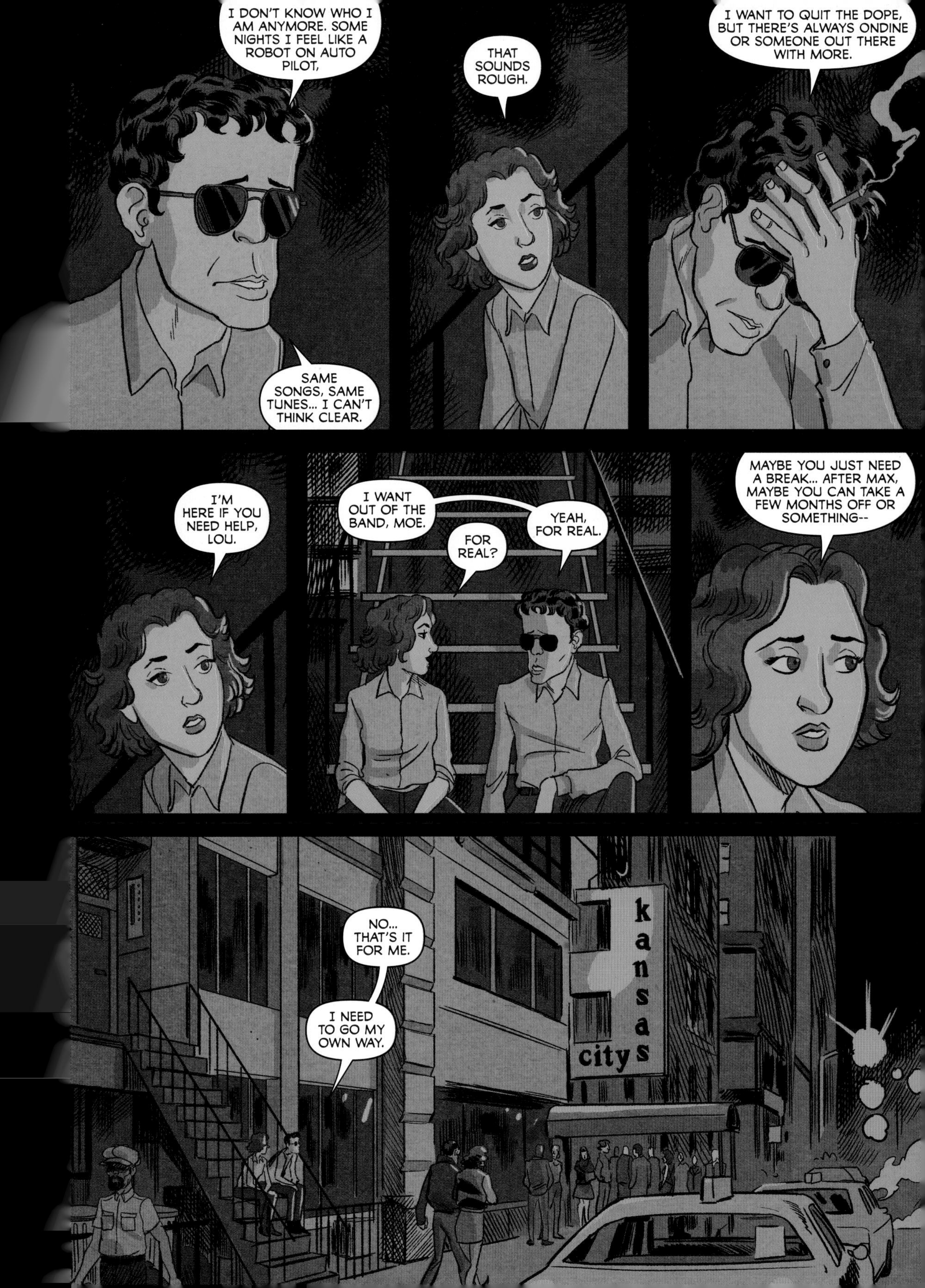
I DON'T KNOW WHO I AM ANYMORE. SOME NIGHTS I FEEL LIKE A ROBOT ON AUTO PILOT,
SAME SONGS, SAME TUNES... I CAN'T THINK CLEAR.
THAT SOUNDS ROUGH.
I WANT TO QUIT THE DOPE, BUT THERE'S ALWAYS ONDINE OR SOMEONE OUT THERE WITH MORE.
I'M HERE IF YOU NEED HELP, LOU.
I WANT OUT OF THE BAND, MOE.
FOR REAL?
YEAH, FOR REAL.
MAYBE YOU JUST NEED A BREAK... AFTER MAX, MAYBE YOU CAN TAKE A FEW MONTHS OFF OR SOMETHING--
NO... THAT'S IT FOR ME.
I NEED TO GO MY OWN WAY.
kansas
city

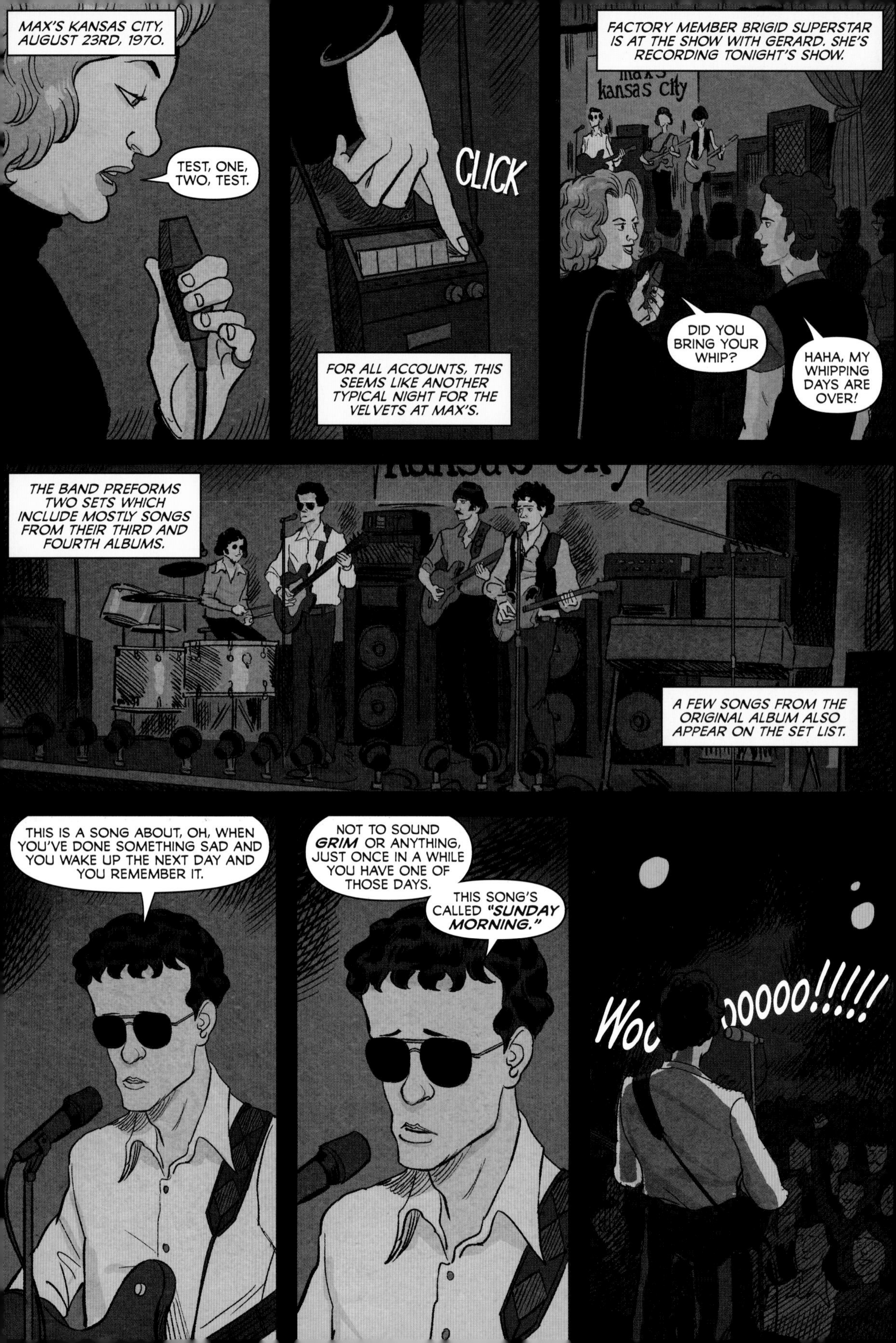
MAX'S KANSAS CITY, AUGUST 23RD, 1970.
TEST, ONE, TWO, TEST.
CLICK
FOR ALL ACCOUNTS, THIS SEEMS LIKE ANOTHER TYPICAL NIGHT FOR THE VELVETS AT MAX'S.
FACTORY MEMBER BRIGID SUPERSTAR IS AT THE SHOW WITH GERARD. SHE'S RECORDING TONIGHT'S SHOW.
max's kansas city
DID YOU BRING YOUR WHIP?
HAHA, MY WHIPPING DAYS ARE OVER!
THE BAND PREFORMS TWO SETS WHICH INCLUDE MOSTLY SONGS FROM THEIR THIRD AND FOURTH ALBUMS.
A FEW SONGS FROM THE ORIGINAL ALBUM ALSO APPEAR ON THE SET LIST.
THIS IS A SONG ABOUT, OH, WHEN YOU'VE DONE SOMETHING SAD AND YOU WAKE UP THE NEXT DAY AND YOU REMEMBER IT.
NOT TO SOUND GRIM OR ANYTHING, JUST ONCE IN A WHILE YOU HAVE ONE OF THOSE DAYS.
THIS SONG'S CALLED "SUNDAY MORNING."
WOO OOOOO!!!!!

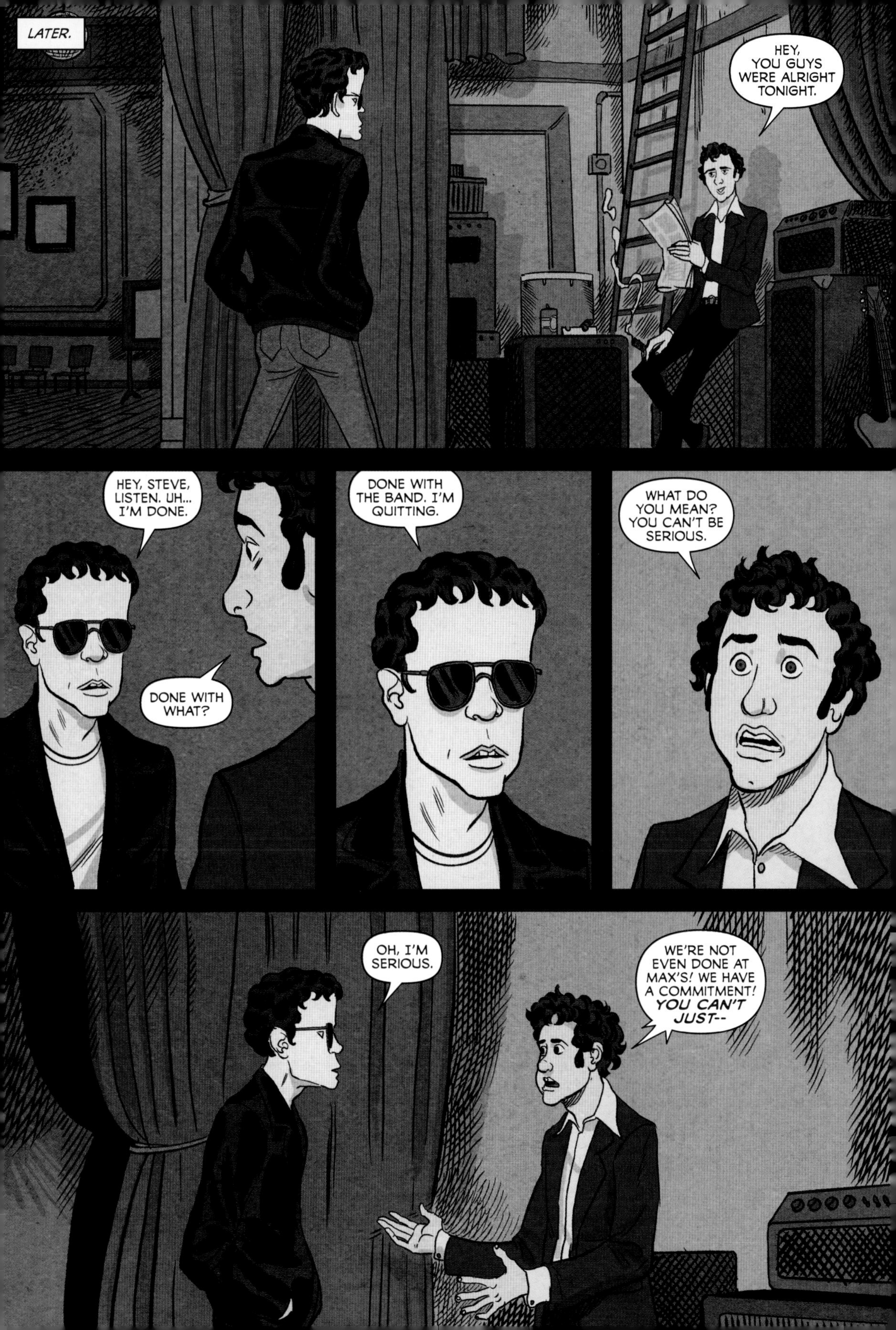
LATER.
HEY, YOU GUYS WERE ALRIGHT TONIGHT.
HEY, STEVE, LISTEN. UH... I'M DONE.
DONE WITH WHAT?
DONE WITH THE BAND. I'M QUITTING.
WHAT DO YOU MEAN? YOU CAN'T BE SERIOUS.
OH, I'M SERIOUS.
WE'RE NOT EVEN DONE AT MAX'S! WE HAVE A COMMITMENT! *YOU CAN'T JUST--*

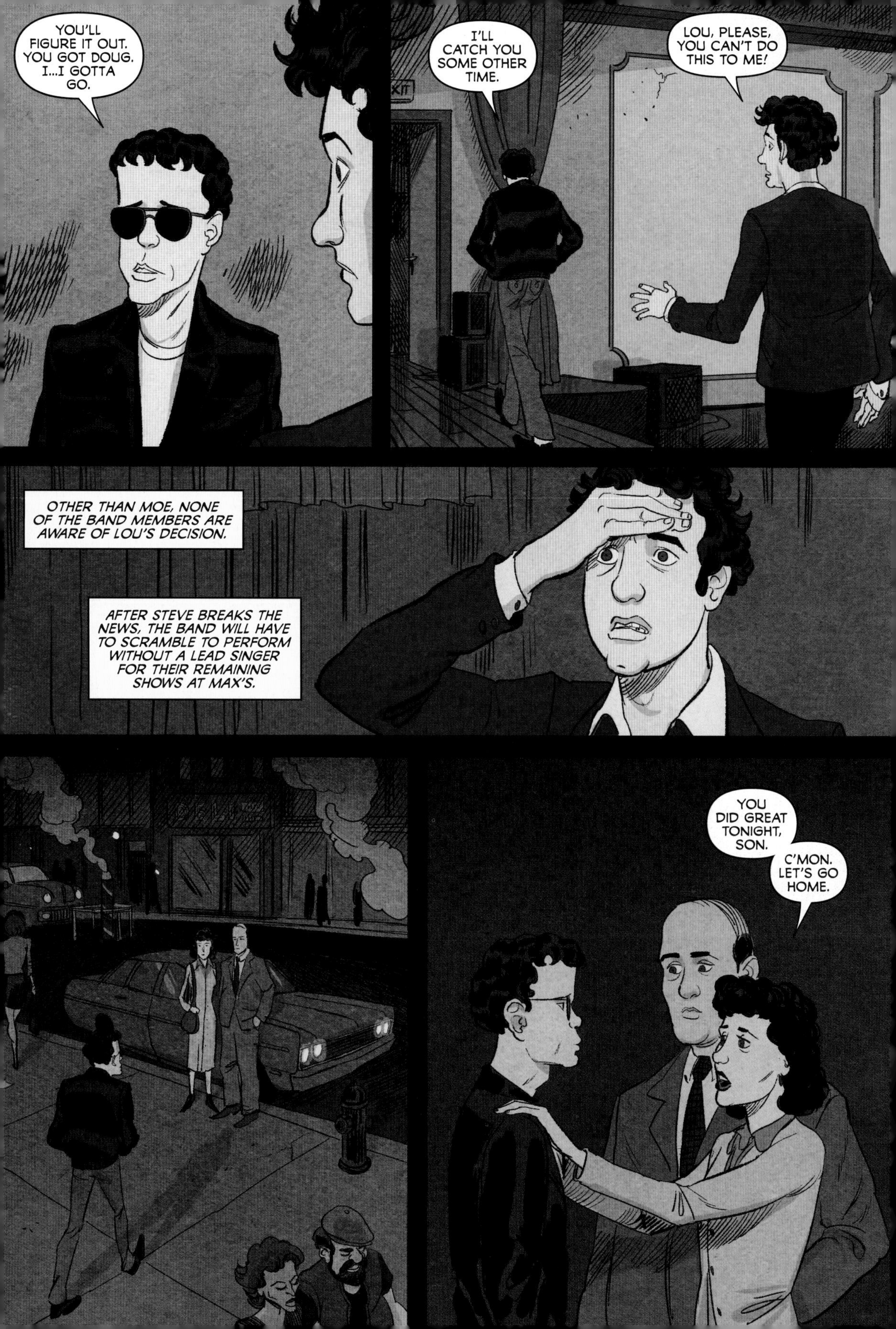
YOU'LL FIGURE IT OUT. YOU GOT DOUG. I...I GOTTA GO.
I'LL CATCH YOU SOME OTHER TIME.
LOU, PLEASE, YOU CAN'T DO THIS TO ME!
EXIT
OTHER THAN MOE, NONE OF THE BAND MEMBERS ARE AWARE OF LOU'S DECISION.
AFTER STEVE BREAKS THE NEWS, THE BAND WILL HAVE TO SCRAMBLE TO PERFORM WITHOUT A LEAD SINGER FOR THEIR REMAINING SHOWS AT MAX'S.
YOU DID GREAT TONIGHT, SON.
C'MON. LET'S GO HOME.

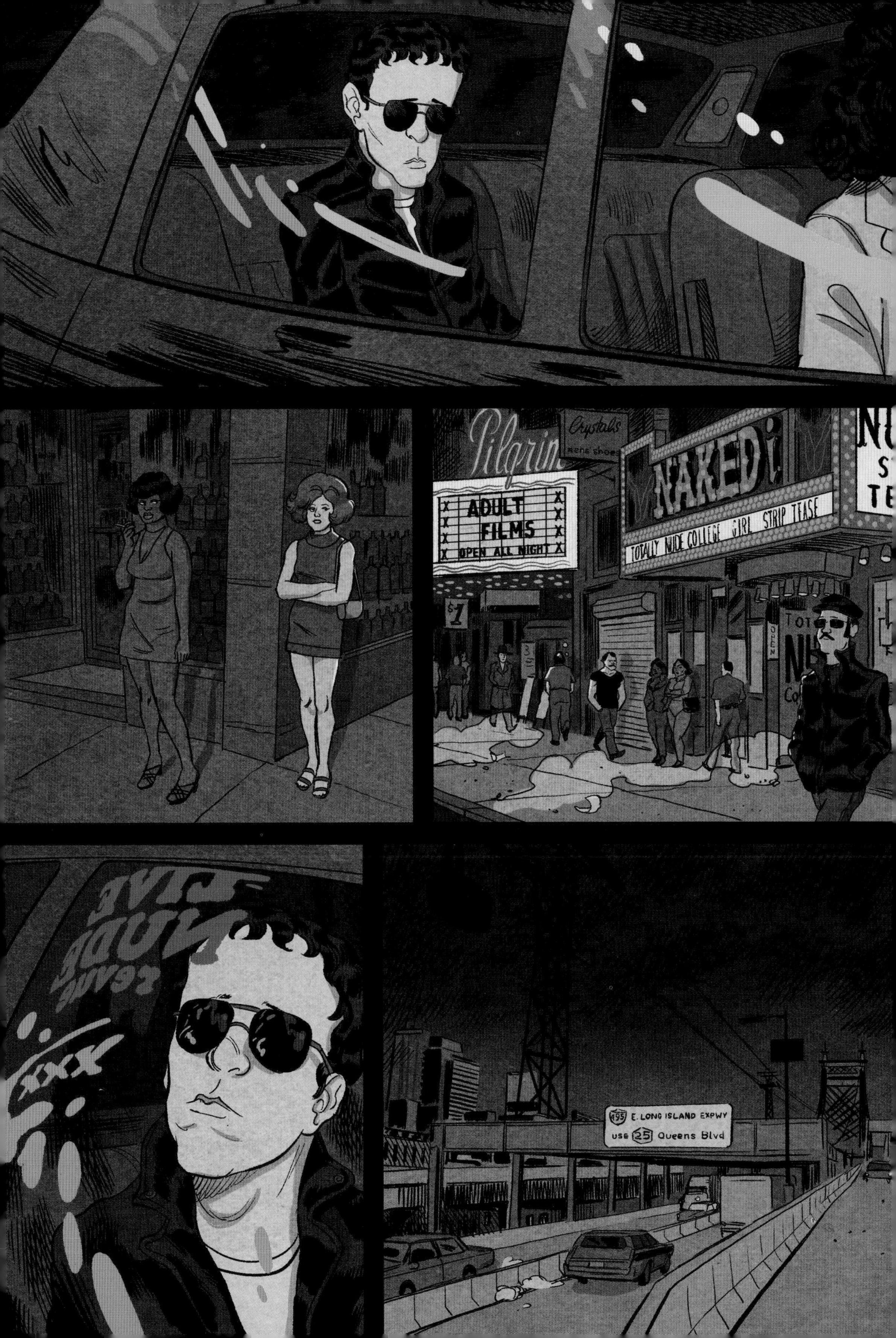
Pilgrim
Crystal's
mens shoes
ADULT FILMS
OPEN ALL NIGHT
$1
NAKED!
TOTALLY NUDE COLLEGE GIRL STRIP TEASE
OPEN
495 E. LONG ISLAND EXPWY
USE 25 Queens Blvd

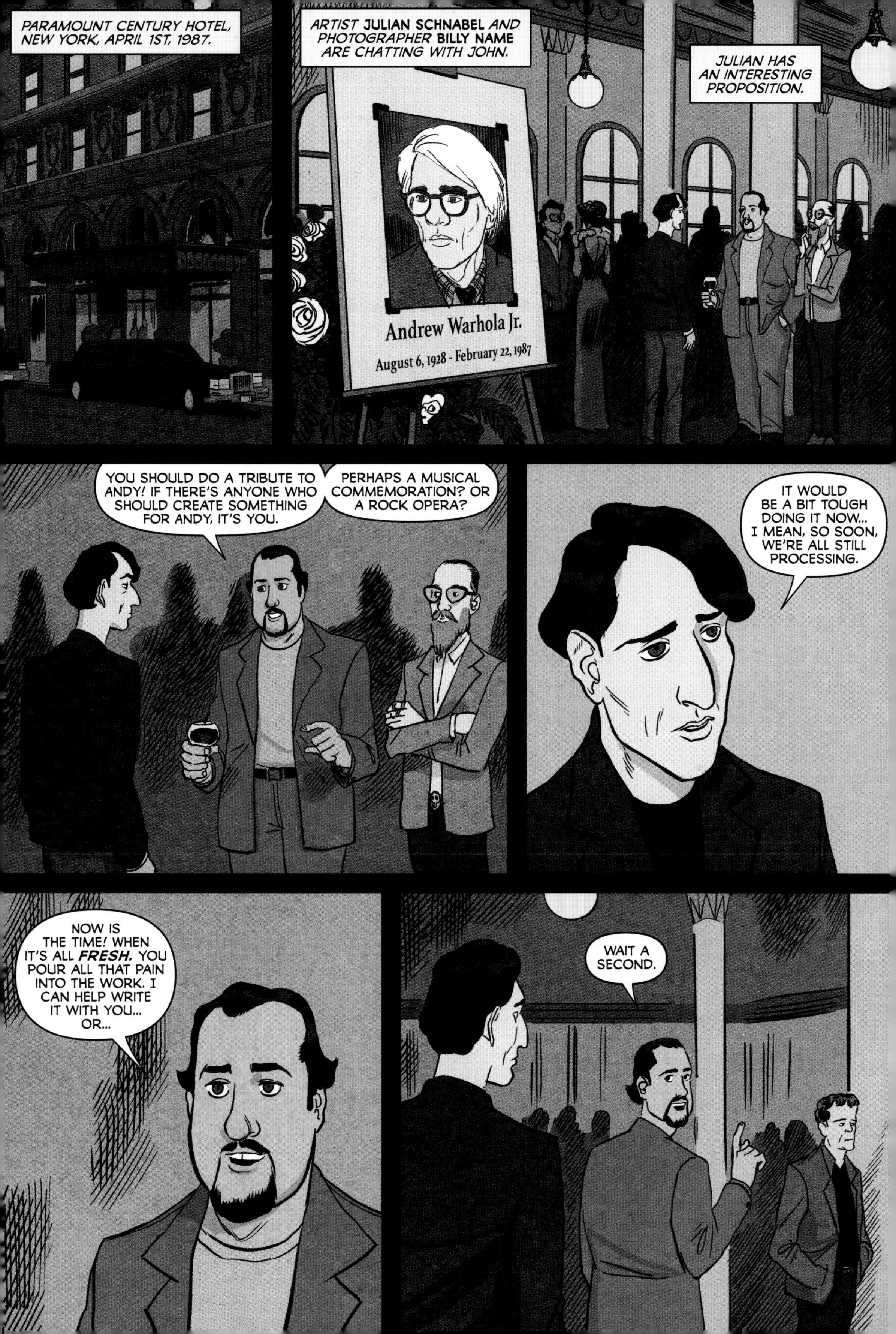
PARAMOUNT CENTURY HOTEL, NEW YORK, APRIL 1ST, 1987.
ARTIST **JULIAN SCHNABEL** AND PHOTOGRAPHER **BILLY NAME** ARE CHATTING WITH JOHN.
Andrew Warhola Jr.
August 6, 1928 - February 22, 1987
JULIAN HAS AN INTERESTING PROPOSITION.
YOU SHOULD DO A TRIBUTE TO ANDY! IF THERE'S ANYONE WHO SHOULD CREATE SOMETHING FOR ANDY, IT'S YOU.
PERHAPS A MUSICAL COMMEMORATION? OR A ROCK OPERA?
IT WOULD BE A BIT TOUGH DOING IT NOW... I MEAN, SO SOON, WE'RE ALL STILL PROCESSING.
NOW IS THE TIME! WHEN IT'S ALL ***FRESH.*** YOU POUR ALL THAT PAIN INTO THE WORK. I CAN HELP WRITE IT WITH YOU... OR...
WAIT A SECOND.

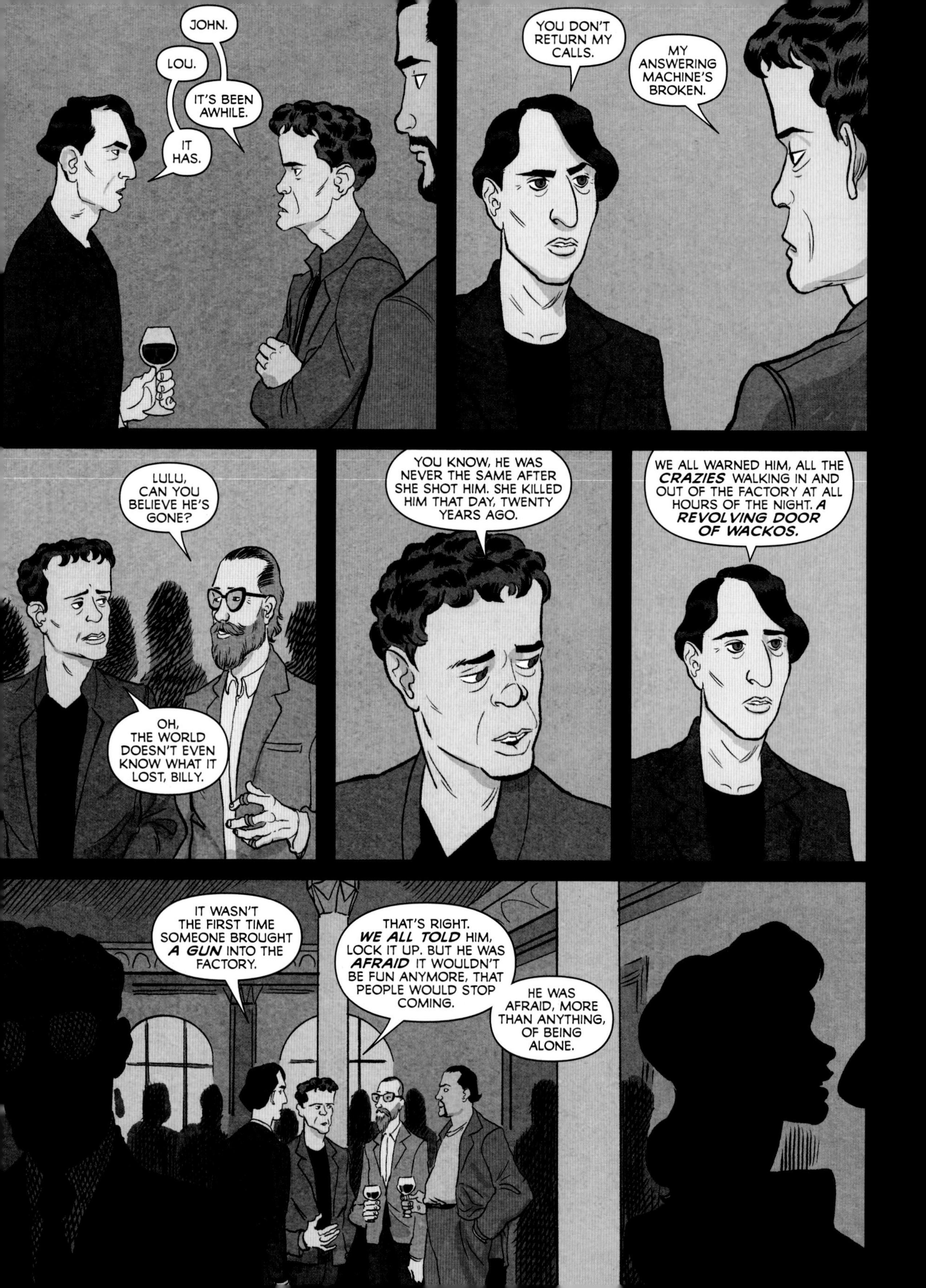
JOHN.
LOU.
IT'S BEEN AWHILE.
IT HAS.
YOU DON'T RETURN MY CALLS.
MY ANSWERING MACHINE'S BROKEN.
LULU, CAN YOU BELIEVE HE'S GONE?
OH, THE WORLD DOESN'T EVEN KNOW WHAT IT LOST, BILLY.
YOU KNOW, HE WAS NEVER THE SAME AFTER SHE SHOT HIM. SHE KILLED HIM THAT DAY, TWENTY YEARS AGO.
WE ALL WARNED HIM, ALL THE ***CRAZIES*** WALKING IN AND OUT OF THE FACTORY AT ALL HOURS OF THE NIGHT. ***A REVOLVING DOOR OF WACKOS.***
IT WASN'T THE FIRST TIME SOMEONE BROUGHT ***A GUN*** INTO THE FACTORY.
THAT'S RIGHT. ***WE ALL TOLD*** HIM, LOCK IT UP. BUT HE WAS ***AFRAID*** IT WOULDN'T BE FUN ANYMORE, THAT PEOPLE WOULD STOP COMING.
HE WAS AFRAID, MORE THAN ANYTHING, OF BEING ALONE.

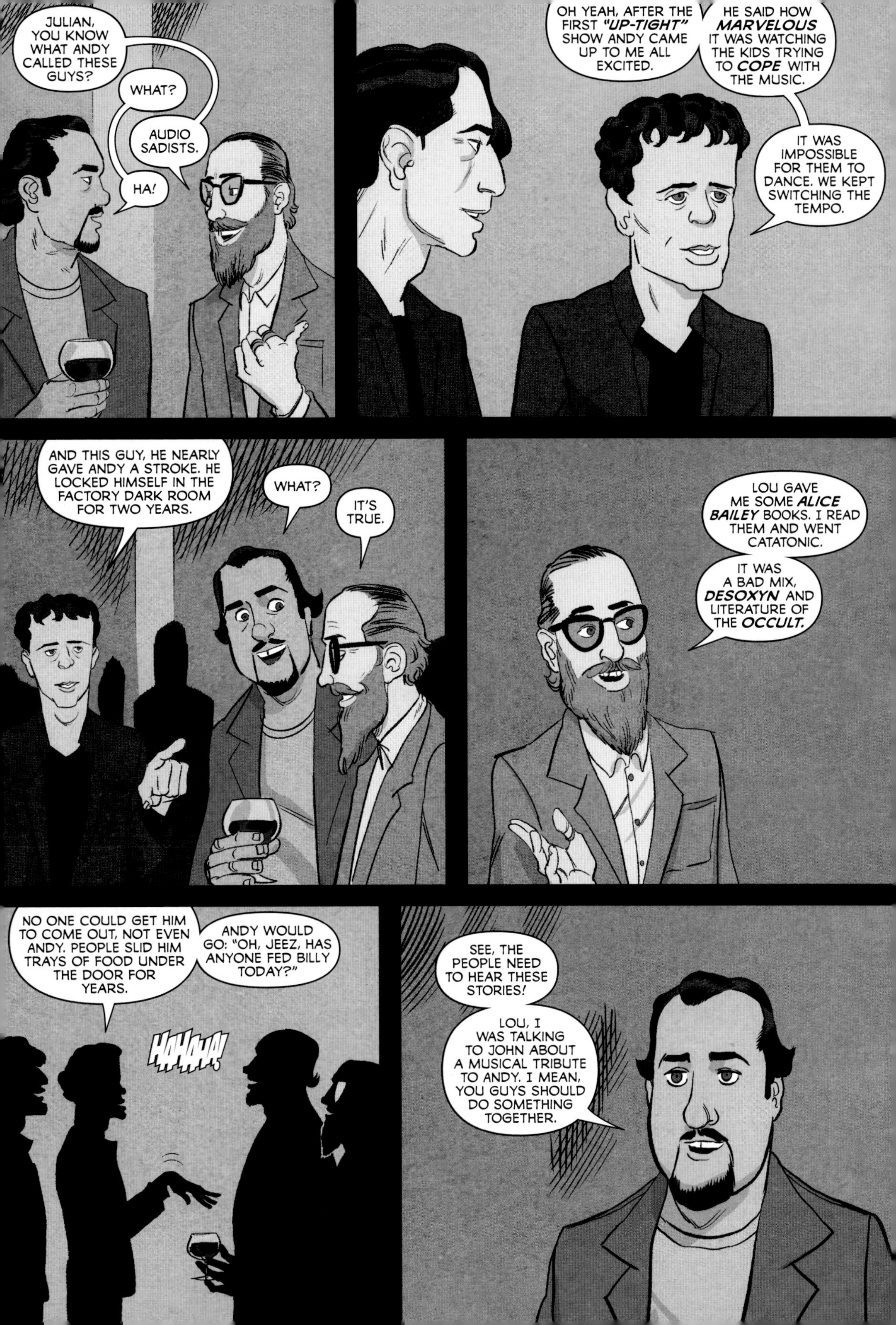
JULIAN, YOU KNOW WHAT ANDY CALLED THESE GUYS?
WHAT?
AUDIO SADISTS.
HA!
OH YEAH, AFTER THE FIRST "UP-TIGHT" SHOW ANDY CAME UP TO ME ALL EXCITED.
HE SAID HOW MARVELOUS IT WAS WATCHING THE KIDS TRYING TO COPE WITH THE MUSIC.
IT WAS IMPOSSIBLE FOR THEM TO DANCE. WE KEPT SWITCHING THE TEMPO.
AND THIS GUY, HE NEARLY GAVE ANDY A STROKE. HE LOCKED HIMSELF IN THE FACTORY DARK ROOM FOR TWO YEARS.
WHAT?
IT'S TRUE.
LOU GAVE ME SOME ALICE BAILEY BOOKS. I READ THEM AND WENT CATATONIC.
IT WAS A BAD MIX, DESOXYN AND LITERATURE OF THE OCCULT.
NO ONE COULD GET HIM TO COME OUT, NOT EVEN ANDY. PEOPLE SLID HIM TRAYS OF FOOD UNDER THE DOOR FOR YEARS.
ANDY WOULD GO: "OH, JEEZ, HAS ANYONE FED BILLY TODAY?"
HAHAHA!
SEE, THE PEOPLE NEED TO HEAR THESE STORIES!
LOU, I WAS TALKING TO JOHN ABOUT A MUSICAL TRIBUTE TO ANDY. I MEAN, YOU GUYS SHOULD DO SOMETHING TOGETHER.

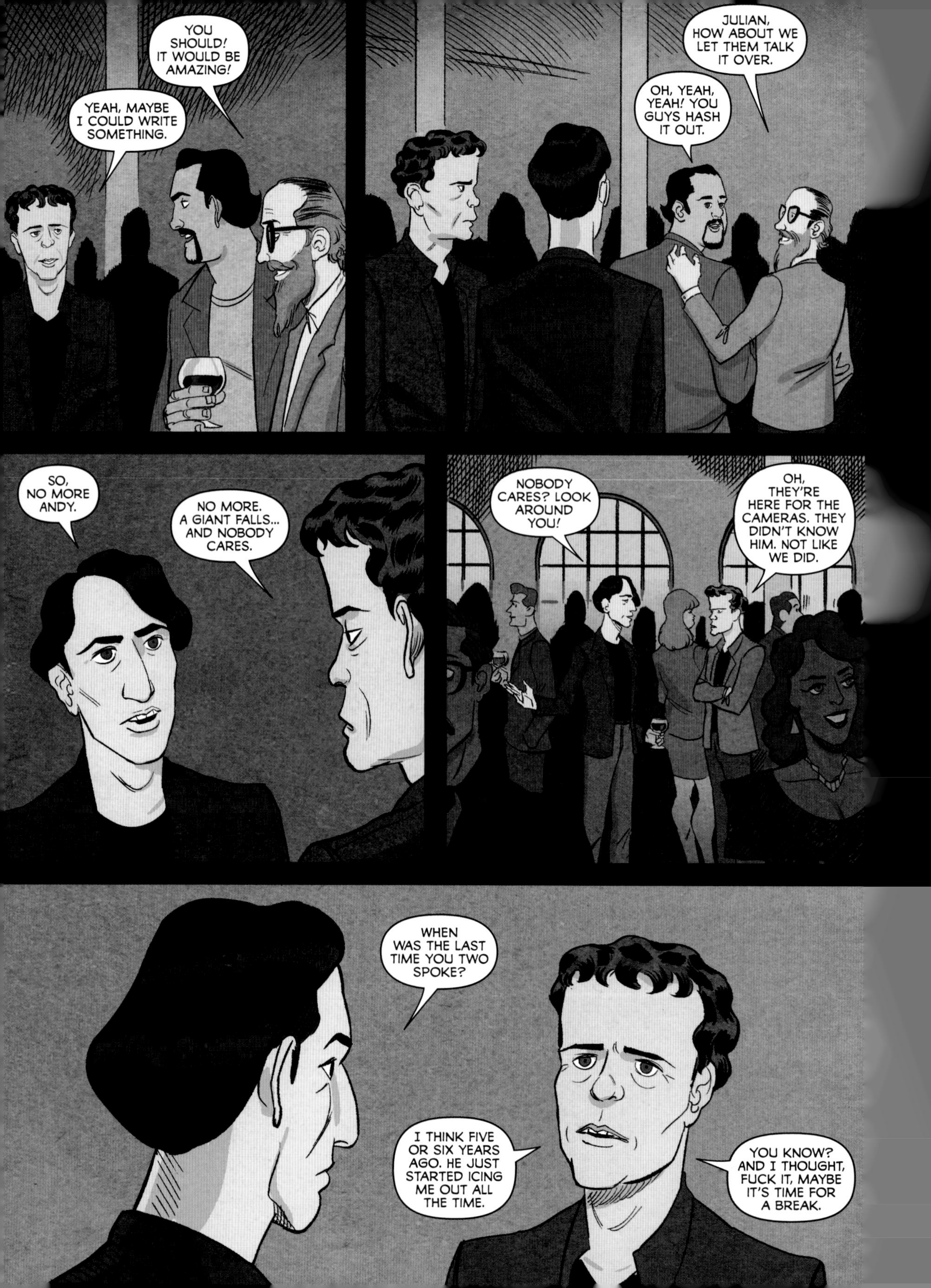
YOU SHOULD! IT WOULD BE AMAZING!
YEAH, MAYBE I COULD WRITE SOMETHING.
JULIAN, HOW ABOUT WE LET THEM TALK IT OVER.
OH, YEAH, YEAH! YOU GUYS HASH IT OUT.
SO, NO MORE ANDY.
NO MORE. A GIANT FALLS... AND NOBODY CARES.
NOBODY CARES? LOOK AROUND YOU!
OH, THEY'RE HERE FOR THE CAMERAS. THEY DIDN'T KNOW HIM. NOT LIKE WE DID.
WHEN WAS THE LAST TIME YOU TWO SPOKE?
I THINK FIVE OR SIX YEARS AGO. HE JUST STARTED ICING ME OUT ALL THE TIME.
YOU KNOW? AND I THOUGHT, FUCK IT, MAYBE IT'S TIME FOR A BREAK.

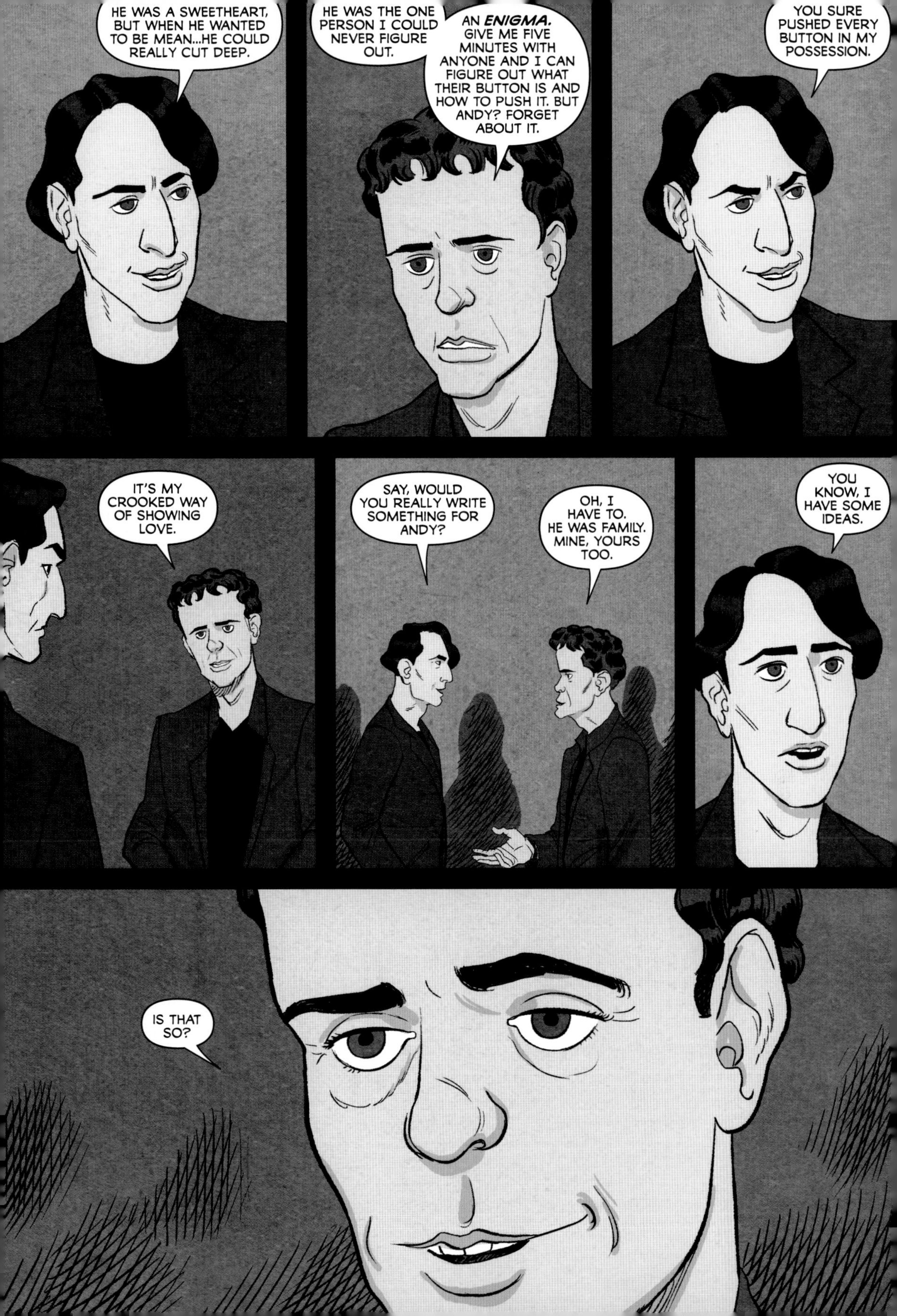
HE WAS A SWEETHEART, BUT WHEN HE WANTED TO BE MEAN...HE COULD REALLY CUT DEEP.
HE WAS THE ONE PERSON I COULD NEVER FIGURE OUT.
AN ENIGMA. GIVE ME FIVE MINUTES WITH ANYONE AND I CAN FIGURE OUT WHAT THEIR BUTTON IS AND HOW TO PUSH IT. BUT ANDY? FORGET ABOUT IT.
YOU SURE PUSHED EVERY BUTTON IN MY POSSESSION.
IT'S MY CROOKED WAY OF SHOWING LOVE.
SAY, WOULD YOU REALLY WRITE SOMETHING FOR ANDY?
OH, I HAVE TO. HE WAS FAMILY. MINE, YOURS TOO.
YOU KNOW, I HAVE SOME IDEAS.
IS THAT SO?

LOU REED / JOHN CALE
SONGS FOR DRELLA

ON JANUARY 7 AND 8, 1989, CALE AND REED PERFORMED "SONGS FOR DRELLA" AT THE CHURCH OF ST. ANNE'S IN BROOKLYN. A STUDIO ALBUM WAS RELEASED IN 1990. IT WAS THE PAIR'S FIRST STUDIO COLLABORATION SINCE 1968'S *WHITE LIGHT/WHITE HEAT*. BY THE END OF RECORDING CALE VOWED NEVER TO WORK WITH REED AGAIN DUE TO PERSONAL DIFFERENCES; PLANS TO SUPPORT THE ALBUM WITH A TOUR WERE SHELVED. STILL, THE ALBUM ANTICIPATED THE BAND'S ULTIMATE REUNION. AND INDEED, IN 1993 THE VELVET UNDERGROUND LINEUP--INCLUDING REED, CALE, MORRISON, AND TUCKER--WOULD GO ON TOUR IN EUROPE.

FOLLOWING THE SUCCESSFUL EUROPEAN REUNION TOUR, A SERIES OF U.S. TOUR DATES WERE SET, INCLUDING AN MTV UNPLUGGED PERFORMANCE, AND POSSIBLY EVEN NEW STUDIO COLLABORATION. BEFORE ANY OF THIS COULD COME TO FRUITION, CALE AND REED FELL OUT AGAIN, BREAKING UP THE BAND ONCE MORE.

Afterword
By Koren Shadmi

So why, of all bands, did I pick The Velvet Underground?

Rewind to the year 2000. I was 19, roughly midway through serving my mandatory three years in the Israeli Defense Force. I was lucky enough to land a cushy job as a Graphic Designer for the "Educational Force." The daily assignments were boring and I was often mistreated by my commanding officer, but it could have been a lot worse. As a "Jobnik" (office soldier) I was at the lowest level of the military totem pole, a laughingstock to "real" soldiers who were out on the frontlines. But I was happy to stay away from where the action was. I got to go home every day, I worked on projects that were vaguely in my field of interest, and best of all, I got to serve with likeminded "wimps." One of these "wimps" was Rotem, a wacky guy who joined my department about a year after I had. He was a talented graphic designer and artist. We shared an affinity for underground comics, art films, and offbeat music. To combat the boredom of the dull days we would each bring CDs to listen to. The musical taste at the office varied wildly, but Rotem would always bring excellent stuff. He introduced me to Roxy Music, Robert Wyatt, The Yardbirds and many others. One day he popped in a CD that I never heard before. The music was haunting, it alternated from being harsh and bitter to sweet and melodic. Sometimes a female singer would emerge and croon in

the most bizarre voice I'd ever heard. The sound was fresh, glittering, but there was also something old about it, the rough recording perhaps, I couldn't tell. All I knew was that I'd never heard anything like it. "What is this?" I asked Rotem. It was The Velvet Underground & Nico.

I remember seeing the iconic banana album in the various record stores I would frequent. I was vaguely aware of the existence of the band and the importance of the record. But somehow till that day I had never heard the actual music. That evening I went into my brother's room. "What do you want?" he grunted (he was weary of my coming in and giving him a hard time when he played the keyboard). "Can I borrow this?" I asked, pointing at the banana album, which my brother had bought at some point. "You can have it," he said. "I really don't like their stuff." I took the CD into my room, popped it in the sound system, and played it again. There was something hypnotic about the music. Something primal. It's as if I got a glimpse into the source code of all the music I loved. I didn't realize it at the time, but almost every band I admired was greatly influenced by the Velvets. Sonic Youth, The Smashing Pumpkins, Nirvana, R.E.M, they had all covered VU songs at one time or another. I would later find out that nearly every musical act I would come to like was indebted to the Velvets: Bauhaus, Bowie, Eno, Iggy and The Stooges, to name a few.

During my army years, I felt increasingly trapped in my surroundings. In my teens I had already begun building a cartooning career for myself. This career was now cut short, as I was not allowed to do any work outside the army. Instead, I spent my time drawing morbid existential comics that reflected my poor mental state. Much like young John and Lou, I often found myself dreaming about escaping my provincial home. I knew that sticking around Israel would likely be a dead end. One day a friend from the military film department stopped by our office with a catalog for The School of Visual Arts in New York. I browsed the catalog and was impressed. Up to that point I was only aware of the Joe Kubert School for Cartooning. But SVA looked better. I applied. A few months later I was accepted with a scholarship. And so, in the summer of 2002, only a couple of weeks after being discharged from the IDF, I was up in the sky headed to New York City to study illustration. The New York that I arrived in was a far cry from the one that Lou Reed had written so many love songs to. The city had already been cleaned up by Giuliani and turned into an expensive theme park for tourists. Still, there was lots of culture to be had, and pockets of the old New York prevailed. I loved the raw energy of the town and the sense of infinite possibility. It was time for me to start a new chapter.

———

In their book *Please Kill Me* Legs McNeil and Gillian McCain cleverly trace back the origins of punk music to the Velvet Underground. Although there were other musical precursors to punk in the '60s–such as The Sonics, The Spades, and The Electric Prunes–none of those bands embodied the spirit of punk quite like the Velvets.

Musically, the Velvets' mission was to aggravate, confuse, and alienate their audience. Their sound was abrasive, yet laced with notes of pop. Their look, inspired in part by the Factory crowd, included leather jackets, sunglasses, and accessories borrowed from the S&M world. Cale had long hair and wore jewelry. Moe dressed like a boy. Reed pranced on the stage like a dandy. Later, in his early solo performances, Reed would sport a dog leash, black nail polish, and white makeup. The inventive sound and visuals of the Velvet Underground would all be reincarnated in the Punk movement.

John and Lou were born one week apart in 1942. They both experienced traumas as young men. They shared a burning anger against the reality to which they were born, against circumstances that were not under their control. For those reasons they found themselves most comfortable on the fringes of society, pushing against norms. But as the true outsiders that they were, they were never truly at ease with people or with themselves. The brilliance of Lou Reed's lyrics is that they dared to deal with subject matter that no one else would touch; the lives of misfits and outcasts, drug use, fluid sexuality and fetishism. Things that, at the time, any musician with a desire to succeed would not dare touch. Influenced by the works of Hubert Selby Jr. and John Fante, Reed was interested in the parts of America that most law-abiding citizens would rather not acknowledge. In Reed we also see the true contradictory nature of the band, on the one hand a voice that is defiant, rebellious, and antagonistic, yet also one with a deep need for acceptance and love. When listening to the Velvets one is constantly being pushed away, then sweetly lured back in. The abusive nature

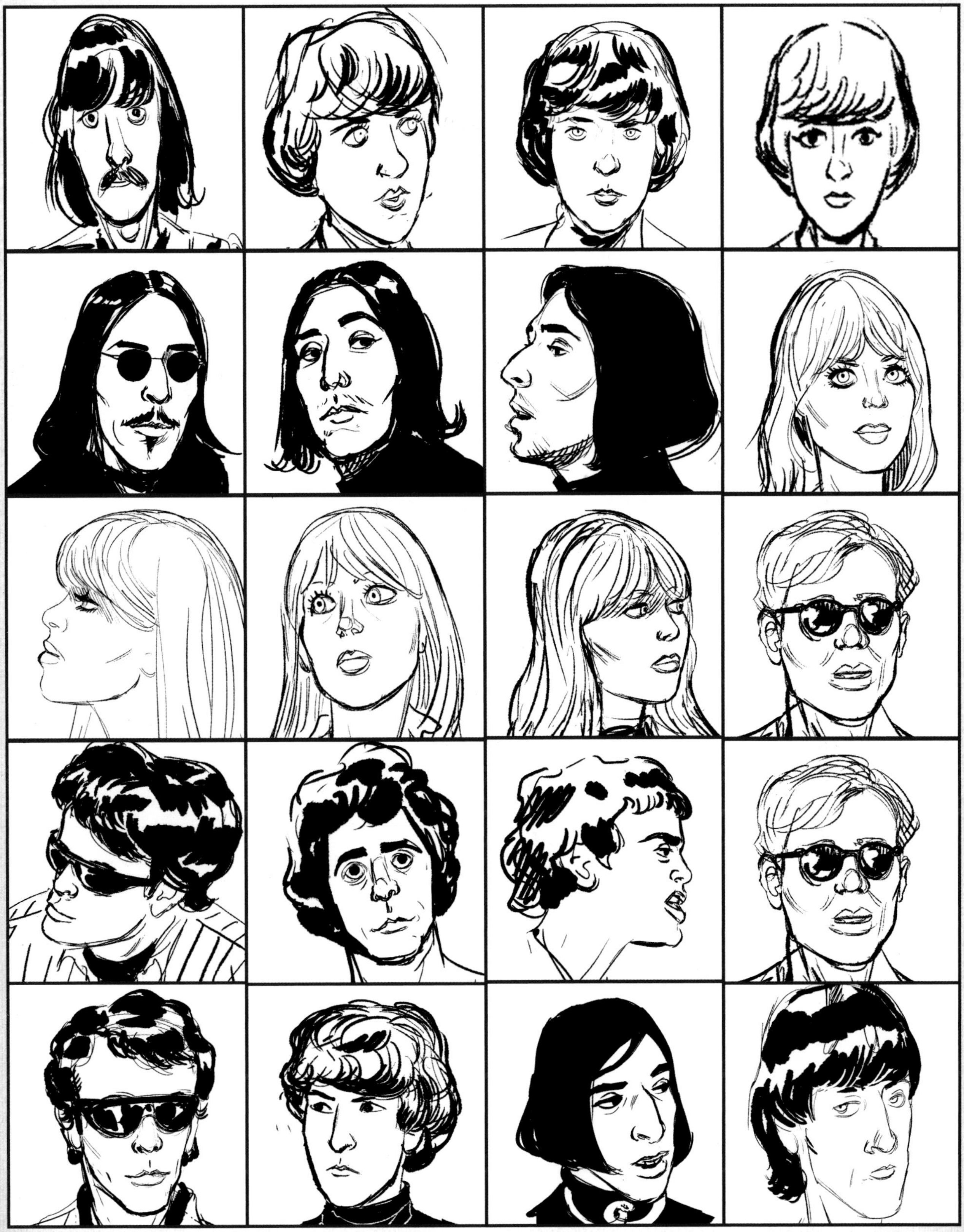

of the music is also reflective of Reed's own persona, his cutthroat narratives more honest than anything else being recorded at the time.

The other shining star of this book, John Cale, has unfortunately often been overshadowed by Reed's flamboyance, but he's just as talented and enigmatic. Cale is responsible for the incredible orchestral depth of the Velvet Underground's music, his drones shift the listener into another world, a place where baroque ornamentation meets Zen Buddhism. It's no accident that Cale later became one of the most seminal punk rock producers of all time. With his classical training he was able to give Reed credibility. It was Cale that challenged Reed to stop imitating the rock stars of the era and instead blaze his own trail. Even after Cale and Reed parted ways one can still see Reed swinging wildly from commercial records to experimental ones (i.e., *Sally Can't Dance* followed by the nearly unlistenable *Metal Machine Music*). It's almost as if a ghost of Cale forever haunted Reed, preventing him from becoming a sellout.

When I first began thinking about the narrative of this book, I thought one of the driving forces of the plot could be the question: Could the Velvets have made it without Warhol? Yet the more I read, the more the story became about John and Lou. When Warhol enters the plot, he becomes the "new girlfriend," briefly stealing Lou away from John. The deeper I dove into research, the less of an antagonist Warhol became. Before working on this book, I had viewed Warhol with a level of contempt—his elimination of drawing skill and reliance on reproductive means was another step in the complete deconstruction of art. But my low opinion of Warhol was mostly due to my ignorance about his life and work. Cartoonists often view fine artists with a combination of scorn and envy. Roy Lichtenstein, a compatriot

of Warhol, was a terrible draftsman who became rich and famous by thieving the work of cartoonists. How was Warhol different? Well, for starters, Warhol could draw, and he began his career as an illustrator. He had a strong work ethic and produced an impressive body of work before he began delegating most of his process to his assistants. The more I read about Warhol, the more I appreciated the enigma of his personality as well as his unique sense of humor. Much like Reed, Warhol had an ambivalent relationship to his audience. He had a very strong sense of defiance and need to push against conventions, but also a deep-rooted need to be accepted and included. In Warhol we also see the origins of punk. The need to shock, to call out for attention by pissing people off. The leather and S&M.

Warhol liked mocking and pranking New York City's high society, clearly seen in how he used the Velvets to shock and terrorize his audience at the Psychiatrist Ball. Warhol stoked the band's creative fires by letting them incubate in his studio. He acted as a passive mentor, just by bringing them into his fold.

———

Everyone I know who lives in New York has their Lou Reed story, either they had a brush with him or knew someone who did. I won't go into these here, since I can't confirm any of these encounters. But I did see him once myself. It was 2010, I had gone to see a French New Wave film at The Film Forum in the West Village. Miscalculating my commute, I had gotten to the theater way too early. There was only one guy in front of me in line to get tickets. He looked like a hobo—frizzy white hair, tattered clothes, and a pair of dirty Uggs. After getting my tickets I told one of the ushers that the man looked a lot like Lou Reed. They told me it was indeed Reed, and he was there all the time. "He likes to get here early so no one bothers him," they added. I stood there, digesting the information, but naturally didn't attempt an interaction. Everything about Reed, at least on that day, screamed STAY AWAY!

A few years later, while visiting my family in Israel, I was shopping in a record store in Tel Aviv. I was debating if I should buy a live recording of Cale, Nico, Brian Eno, and Kevin Ayers. While holding the CD in my hand, I noticed that John Cale's solo album was playing on the store speakers. Strange coincidence, I thought. Then I suddenly noticed that Cale was actually at the store, signing records. He had come to Israel for a show. I walked up, shook his hand, and told him I saw him perform years ago in New York.

He was kind and friendly. He signed my CD, which I still own.

———

So here I am, over twenty years since listening to *The Velvet Underground and Nico* for the first time, and the album still holds a unique magic for me. It reminds me of a time when music made me feel less alone. The Velvets, and the multitude of bands that they inspired, have shown me that my struggles in life are not entirely unique. I never thought that one day I would make a whole book about the band, but I'm glad I did. The more I dug in, the more I discovered there's a great story to be told, worth sharing in graphic novel form. I've spent nearly two years with Lou, John, Sterl, Moe, Nico, and Andy. I've gotten to know them better, or at least I think I have, but now it's time to say goodbye. If you love the Velvets music, I hope this book will help shed light onto this important period in the band's life. If you've never listened to their music, please, put on an album right now, close your eyes, and start listening.

In the Studio

For Pencils-

1. This page is supposed to showcase an end of an era for the band. They are turning their back on New York. In reality no one turns their back on New York, the city couldn't care less! It's just that they had had enough rejection and Lou had burned the bridge with Andy.

(frame 2) Steve Sesnick doesn't appear that much in the book, so I made his character design on the fly in this frame, as opposed to other recurring figures who I did many character sketches for.

(frame 3) The Boston Tea Party, it operated from 67 to 70, and was housed in a building that was formerly a Synagogue. The structure has since been demolished and is now a House of Blues.

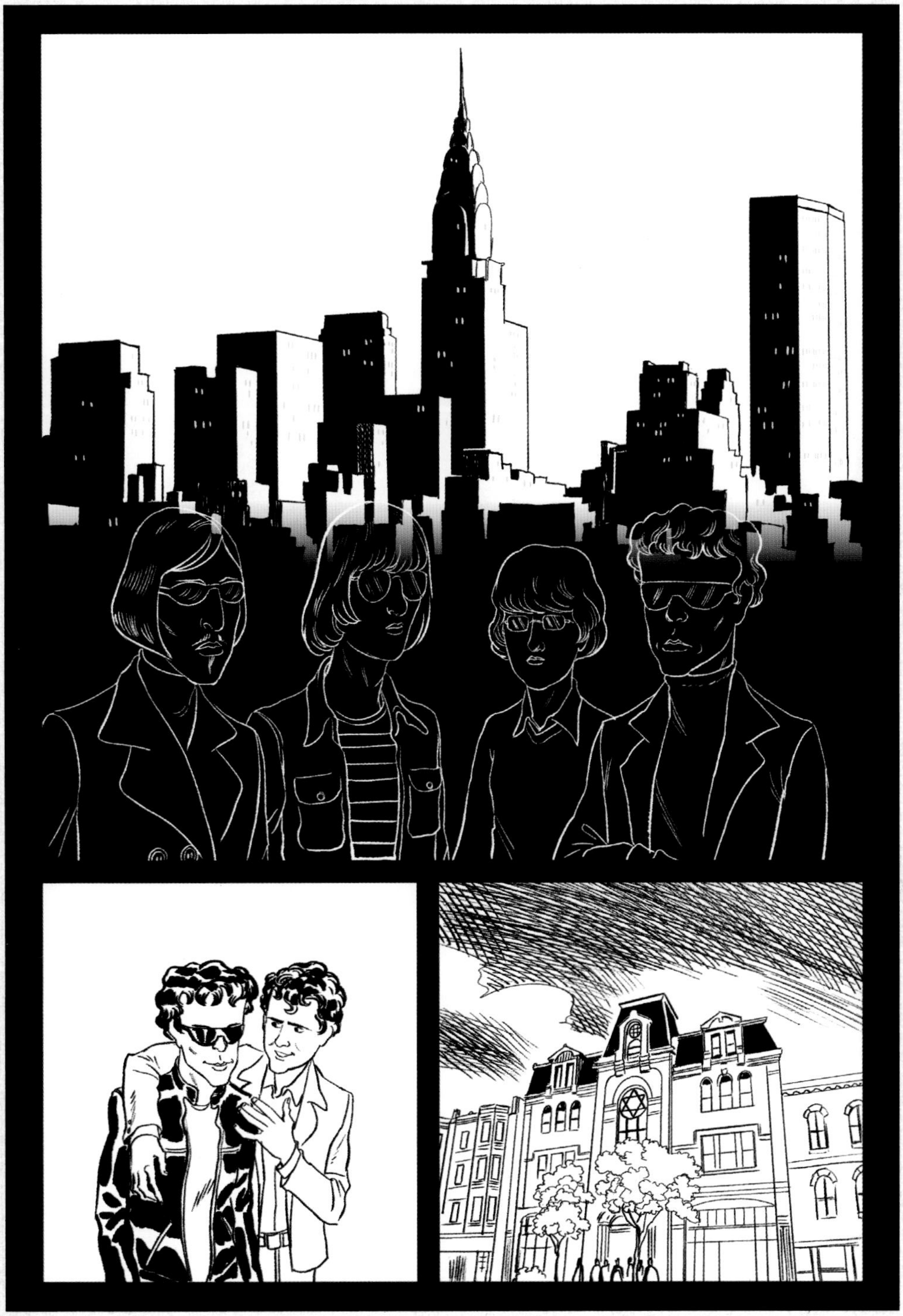

For Inks-

2. After the editor's first pass, we decided to move the band so they are under the NYC skyline, that way they look less triumphant. This is one of the only places I used white outline in the book. Luckily my files are digital and the change was easy to make.

For Colors-

3. I tried to restrict my color palettes in the book, this purple/blue color scheme worked best for the night sky and the somber atmosphere of the page. It is the same color scheme as in the first few pages of the book.

Bibliography

Up-Tight, The Velvet Underground Story - Bockris, Victor & Malanga, Gerard, Music Sales Corp (1983)

The Andy Warhol Diaries - Warhol, Andy & Hackett, Pat, Twelve (1989)

Transformer, The Complete Lou Reed Story - Bockris, Victor, Harper (1994)

Please Kill Me: The Uncensored Oral History of Punk, McCain, Gillain, / McNeil, Legs, Grove Press (1996)

What's Welsh for Zen: The Autobiography of John Cale - Cale, John & Bockris, Victor, Bloomsbury (2000)

Popism, The Warhol Sixties - Warhol, Andy & Hackett, Pat, Mariner Books (2006)

All Yesterdays' Parties: The Velvet Underground in Print, 1966-1971 – Heyline, Clinton, Da Capo Press (2006)

The Velvet Underground (Icons of Pop Music) – Witts, Richard, Indiana University Press (2006)

Lou Reed, A Life - DeCurtis, Anthony – Little, Brown & Co (2017)

White Light/White Heat: The Velvet Underground Day-By-Day - Unterberger, Richie (2017)

The Velvet Underground Experience – Monograph – Gable, J.C, Hat & Beard Press (2019)

You Are Beautiful and You Are Alone: The Biography of Nico - Otter Bickerdike, Jennifer, Hachette (2021)

Film

The Making Of An Underground Film - CBS News (1965)

The Velvet Underground And Nico – Warhol, Andy (1966)

Arsenal: Sterling Morrison, Huerga, Manuel (1986)

Velvet Underground - South Bank Show (1986)

Arsenal : The Velvet Underground: Feed Back (1986)

Songs For Drella: Interview with John Cale and Lou Reed, A&E (1990)

Nico: Icon - Ofteringer, Susanne (1995)

Lou Reed: Rock & Roll Heart - Greenfield-Sanders, Timothy (1998)

John Cale, BBC - Marsh, James (1998)

Laurie Anderson & Lou Reed Interviewed by Charlie Rose (2003)

Andy Warhol: A Documentary Film – Burns, Ric (2006)

Velvet Underground: Under Review – Barbor – Might, Tom (2006)

The Velvet Underground - Haynes, Todd (2021)

Koren Shadmi is an American-Israeli, Award-winning illustrator and cartoonist. He studied illustration at The School of Visual Arts in New York where he now teaches. His books have been published internationally and include *In The Flesh*, *The Abaddon*, *Highwayman*, *Rise of The Dungeon Master*, *The Twilight Man: Rod Serling and the Birth of Television*, and most recently *Lugosi: The Rise and Fall of Hollywood's Dracula*. Koren has contributed illustrations and comics to: *The New York Times*, *The New Yorker*, *The Wall Street Journal*, *Newsweek*, *Business Week*, *Playboy*, *Mother Jones*, *The Washington Post*, *The Boston Globe*, *Wired*, and others. His illustration work has won several awards at the Society of Illustrators.

The
TWILIGHT MAN
KOREN SHADMI
Rod Serling and the Birth of Television
E=mc²
Life Drawn

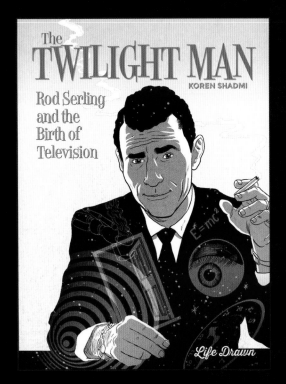

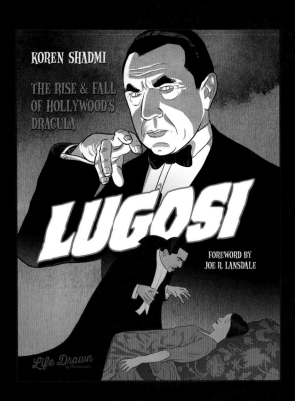

The Twilight Man: Rod Serling and the Birth of Television

A biographical tale that follows Hollywood revolutionary Rod Serling's rise to fame in the Golden Age of Television, and his descent into his own personal Twilight Zone.

KOREN SHADMI
THE RISE & FALL OF HOLLYWOOD'S DRACULA
LUGOSI
FOREWORD BY
JOE R. LANSDALE
Life Drawn

Lugosi: The Rise and Fall of Hollywood's Dracula

A biography chronicling the tumultuous personal and professional life of horror icon and Hungarian activist Bela Lugosi.